CALLIGRAPHY AND PALAEOGRAPHY

ALFRED FAIRBANK, C.B.E.

CALLIGRAPHY AND PALAEOGRAPHY

Essays presented to

on his 70th birthday

Edited by A. S. Osley

OCTOBER HOUSE INC.
NEW YORK

First Published in the United States of America 1966
by October House Inc.
134 East 22nd Street
New York 10, New York
LIBRARY OF CONGRESS CATALOG
CARD NO. 66–15273

© 1965 by Faber & Faber Ltd

MANUFACTURED IN GREAT BRITAIN

ALFREDO FAIRBANK

Excellentissimi Ordinis Imperi Britannici Commendatori, A.D. IV
Idus Iulias A.S. MCMLXV, lustris quattuordecim peractis.

FELIX QUI SEPTEM DECIES NUNC RESPICIS ANNOS

    ARTIFICE ET CALAMO TANTA PERACTA TUO.

LITTERA LANGUERAT PRISCA SPECIEQUE CAREBAT,

    SCRIBARUM TURBAE CURA NEQUE ULLA FUIT;

EXEMPLO ET PIETATE TUA SUNT DAMNA REDEMPTA,

    DAEDALEAQUE TUA EST FORMA RENATA MANU.

APTA QUIDEM TIBI SUNT CELEBERRIMA VERBA PROPERTI:

    'NONNE PUTAS MIRAS HUNC HABUISSE MANUS?'

ACCIPE QUAS DABIMUS MERITAS CUM MUNERE LAUDES

    FAUTORUM COETUS DISCIPULIQUE TUI!

SCRIPSIT W. J. MOLONEY

INTRODUCTION

I would not have ventured to write a Foreword to this book were it not that both my father and my mother were deeply interested in handwriting and calligraphy and were happily associated with Alfred Fairbank in more than one enterprise. They would surely have wished to be associated with this tribute also.

The book contains a varied fare. If the reader's special delight is in medieval manuscripts and palaeography, he will find fine scholarship on these subjects. There is much, too, of more general interest. Where excellence abounds, it is perhaps invidious to single out individual items, and each reader will have his preference. But I myself was particularly attracted by the accounts of the great writing masters. The many plates and illustrations in the text are of high quality. All in all, this is a splendid volume, which deals with lettering and handwriting in a fuller and more exciting way than any that I remember.

But it is more than that. Every aspect covered in the volume is germane to what Alfred Fairbank has himself done. His great achievement is, of course, his own exquisite script. As a former civil servant, I have been led to speculate whether, in his long service with the Admiralty, the naval traditions of individual vigour, panache and movement within a framework of clear regulations and discipline can have contributed at all to Fairbank's fluent, lucid and controlled hand: certainly in his pages all is ship-shape and Bristol fashion.

Moreover, he has not been content to be simply a supreme artist in his own field. Looking backward, he has carried out scholarly research on the historic models which are the foundation of his own script: looking forward, he has developed means by which others can base their writing on a model which fully meets contemporary needs. He has given unstintedly from his harvest of knowledge and experience to societies and organizations of those who believe in the value of good handwriting, not only for themselves but as an essential accomplishment in any sensible system of education. No man of our time has done more for good handwriting, whether for the individual or the community, than Alfred Fairbank.

BRIDGES

PREFACE

Although I have known Alfred Fairbank as friend and Admiralty colleague for a quarter of a century, I underestimated his age by a year. So this tribute for his 70th birthday had to be prepared at a less leisurely pace than I had originally contemplated, and I was compelled to be more exigent with my contributors than is, perhaps, customary.

It is a proof of the extraordinary respect and affection in which Mr Fairbank is held by his friends, both here and overseas, that they responded helpfully and uncomplainingly to the demands made upon them, with the result that the time-table was met without difficulty. I am very grateful for their co-operation.

I am responsible for the organization of the book, including the arrangement of the essays, the selection and deployment of the illustrations and plates, and the index. Any shortcomings here have accordingly to be charged to my account. I have tried throughout to make all the necessary acknowledgements. If errors or omissions have occurred, they are unintentional. It is inevitable in a book of this kind that some duplication in the material submitted will be found. I have aimed to eliminate redundancy as far as possible: but small overlaps were unavoidable.

I wish to thank particularly Berthold Wolpe (of Messrs Faber & Faber) for constant advice and encouragement; John Dreyfus (of the Cambridge University Press) for the interest which he has taken in the book; D. T. Worthy (of the British Museum) for a variety of assistance; and Sheila Osley not only for much typing and re-typing, but also for accepting the dislocation of domestic routine attendant on having an editor about the house.

A. S. OSLEY

CONTENTS

Contents

ARRIGHI AND HIS CONTEMPORARIES

SOME WRITING MASTERS

Contents

Contents

PEN TO PAPER

AN ANTHOLOGY OF ARTICLES REPRINTED FROM
The Bulletin and Journal of the Society for Italic Handwriting

Contents

The following designs have been contributed to this book:

The monogram on the binding
CHRIS BRAND

The wood-engraving on the title page
REYNOLDS STONE, C.B.E., R.D.I.

The wood-cut *Winter Grasses* on page 278
MARGARET DARRELL

LIST OF PLATES

List of Plates

LIST OF LINE ILLUSTRATIONS IN TEXT

Line Illustrations in Text

Line Illustrations in Text

THE SCHOLAR PENMAN

J. A. COLE

A Scholar Penman

When Alfred John Fairbank was 12 years old, his mother took him to a phrenologist at Cleethorpes. At that time they were staying with relatives in Grimsby, where the boy had been born on 12 July 1895, six weeks before his father, an engine fitter, moved to Gillingham in Kent to become a chargeman in Chatham dockyard. This consultation was not undertaken in a holiday spirit but was a serious attempt to obtain careers guidance (the elder Fairbank had, in fact, successfully changed his occupation on a phrenologist's advice). The phrenologist, whose north-country clients, even in their most optimistic seaside mood, had no grand ideas of what they were likely to become, interpreted the bumps in practical and prosaic terms. He told Mrs Fairbank that her son would do well in any of four occupations: as a civil servant, a shorthand writer, a wood carver or a sign-writer. Distrusting what seemed to him a form of divination, Alfred listened sceptically, but he accepted as sensible the analysis of his talents. Already he was aware of government service as a desirable goal.

One of the aims of the Wesleyan Higher Grade School, Gillingham, which he had been attending since 1903, was to secure places for its boys, either as apprentices or civil servants, in Chatham Royal Dockyard. Preparation for the two-day entrance examinations in ten subjects required strenuous and unremitting drill in English, handwriting and mathematics. The classes consisted of over fifty boys; but the discipline was Victorian, and the only sounds in a classroom during a lesson were the master's voice and what novelists used to call the scratching of pens. Alfred was good at most subjects, including handwriting; he excelled in mathematics—the phrenologist does not appear to have given due weight to this gift. No amount of ability would have availed, however, without good handwriting; it had a paper to itself and so rated a decisive number of marks. A candidate who could not write a fast and legible hand reduced his chances. The headmaster, H. R. Redman, was merely doing

3   I-2

his duty to his pupils when he made handwriting seem of considerable importance. On one occasion, as a gesture of encouragement, he established a prize fund of 5s. and from this provided ten prizes of 1d. for each of six weeks. The incentive was highly effective. To the boys of the Wesleyan Higher Grade School these awards were not negligible; at that time, in the more fortunate working-class households, a penny was often a child's pocket money for a week and would buy four ounces of sweets.

On 23 March 1911, at the age of 15, Alfred Fairbank triumphantly entered Chatham Royal Dockyard to start—not as an apprentice but as a 'boy writer' at a salary of 9s. a week—a civil service career. Soon he was engaged for part of his time in the second occupation selected for him by the phrenologist, taking letters in shorthand.

One of the clerks in the Constructive Manager's Department of the dockyard was William C. K. Primmer, who although twelve years older and senior in grade, formed a friendship with Fairbank which has lasted to this day. He introduced him to calligraphy and the work of William Morris. The inspiration which Fairbank drew from Morris has led him to a unique achievement: he has restored a style of handwriting which gives pleasure to those who write and read it. Who would have supposed that, in a century of typewriters and telephones, this neglected craft could have been so vigorously revived and given such a beautiful form? Few of us, within the context of our own chosen activities, can hope for any comparable attainment.

At 70, Alfred Fairbank, C.B.E. (he received the honour in 1951 for services to calligraphy), lives with his wife, Elsie, in Hove, where he settled after retiring from the Admiralty on pension. He is a tall, lean, scholarly looking man, with a thoughtful face, thick spectacles, youthful hair and, as you would expect, sensitive hands. To me, he seems to have altered little in the thirty years since I met him on a Sunday morning when, although welcoming, he was slightly distracted because he was encountering trouble with an *a* for an exemplar. Excusing himself for not having appeared promptly, he laid before me a sheet covered with specimens of this letter. I thought them all perfect but, when he explained what was bothering him, I got worried too. In a curious, self-effacing way, he can convey the importance of calligraphy to a non-calligrapher. 'I think I can perhaps show you what I mean,' he says diffidently, as he reaches for a book. I look at the page he indicates and wish quite sincerely that I could see it with his eyes. This quality of arousing respect for an art and communicating his own satisfaction enables him to be an outstanding teachers' teacher. His multitudes of teacher-students have spread his influence through the world; at the time of writing, he is holding a course for teachers from Malaysia, Cyprus, Malta, Buganda, Kenya, Antigua, Barbados and Jamaica.

4

Less well known is his work as a palaeographer, to which subject I shall return later. He has also designed a type known as Condensed Bembo Italic (although it is referred to in at least one house as Fairbank Italic). It has been used very little but has, nevertheless, a reputation among typographers. His work as a type-designer has been to him, however, the least satisfactory aspect of his career.

The Cleethorpes phrenologist's diagnosis had, understandably, omitted the palaeography and type-designing, but it is due to that practitioner to record that he scored on all his four points. In a modest way Fairbank has shown his skill as a wood-carver and sign-writer. While living at Box in Wiltshire and working long hours in an Admiralty office in Bath, he cut garden gate-signs in oak—unusual specimens of Fairbank's art which can still be found in the neighbourhood.

The interests of this 'compulsive abecedarian' (his expression) are not confined to manuscripts and printed works. Although no collector, he appreciates Greek figurines, Chinese pottery and bronzes, Japanese swords, Roman coins, strange ink-pots, Wedgwood and Tassie seals, and New Hall Pottery. He does not play an instrument, but he has a musical sense and he especially enjoys chamber music. In the small garden behind his house he tends (with only slight success, he protests) roses, pinks and violas. On country walks he searches for wild flowers, his particular favourite being the English orchis. In any weather he can be seen striding along the Brighton promenade, his long legs giving him a turn of speed which soon has his shorter companions out of breath. Never robust—he was medically rejected by the Army in the First World War and he all but succumbed to 'Spanish 'flu' in 1918—he looks as if the south coast suits him. He confesses to wasting time reading thrillers, of which he is, he says, 'much too fond', but there can be few 'retired' men who waste less time than he does.

Fairbank's 70th birthday affords an occasion to put on record an outline of his career as a calligrapher. The background to his individual achievements is a story of committees, societies, exhibitions and, above all, of personalities in the arts and crafts movement whose inspiration, support or other contribution he is anxious to acknowledge. Let us return, then, to his friendship with William Primmer and go on from there to relate this history very much as Fairbank told it to me in a series of conversations.

Primmer's move to the Admiralty during the First World War enabled him to recommend Fairbank's transfer to London in 1917. Together they visited museums and art galleries; Fairbank recollects looking at books and designs by William Morris in the Victoria and Albert Museum and the manuscript books of Graily Hewitt at an exhibition.

Graily Hewitt became Fairbank's teacher in 1920 at the Central School of Arts and Crafts evening classes in writing and illuminating. Both Hewitt and another instructor, Lawrence Christie, noticed Fairbank's enthusiasm and gave him special attention. He remembers his teachers as contrasting personalities, Hewitt definite and clear in his instructions, impressive in his blackboard demonstrations, formal and dogmatic, but at times charming; Christie kindly, tolerant and very shy. He and Fairbank soon became close friends.

Fairbank also encountered W. R. Lethaby. 'I recall that great scholar and architect appealing to us students at the Central School of Arts and Crafts to improve our handwriting, and saying, as he took off his glasses with a very shaky hand: "If you will try, I will try too." I remember thinking that I would, though it was too late for him to do so. He liked my work enough to write me a testimonial when I was applying (but without success) for a post to teach calligraphy at an evening class. Lethaby seemed to me the wisest of men. Alfred Powell had printed a small book about Lethaby and his sayings called *Scrip's and Scraps* [sic], in which the following "syllabus of his accumulated experience" by the late Lord Esher was quoted: *Life is best thought of as service; service is common productive work; labour may be turned to joy by thinking of it as art; art, thought of as fine and sound ordinary work, is the widest and best form of culture; culture is a tempered human spirit.* I have often regretted that when he suggested to me that I should make drawings of Roman inscriptions in London I did not do so.'

In 1921 Christie, Louisa Puller and Dorothy Hutton worked to establish the Society of Scribes and Illuminators.[1] The other founder members, of whom Fairbank was one, were or had recently been students of Hewitt and Christie. 'If most of us were then half-baked', Fairbank comments on this period, 'we had the examples of Edward Johnston and Hewitt to set a standard. Hewitt was remarkably able at gilding, itself a difficult craft, which few have quite mastered. What we were concerned to do in the Society of Scribes and Illuminators was to make unique works of art by calligraphy and illuminating. Gradually, by discussions, limitation of membership, and exhibitions, we began to be accepted as a serious society, and our exhibitions attracted royal visitors. The society gave me many friends. I served for a short time as treasurer, then as secretary, and for twelve years I was president.'

It was Edward Johnston's book *Writing & Illuminating & Lettering* which, in 1920, aroused Fairbank's interest in Renaissance handwriting, and started him on those researches and experiments which led him to discover the fascination of sixteenth-century writing manuals. In 1922 he exhibited and sold his first manuscript book. Fairbank talks feelingly of Johnston.

'I was not taught by Edward Johnston, though I was very much a disciple of his. I regarded him as a genius and one of the finest products of the Arts and Crafts Movement. I often quote from *Ecclesiasticus*: "Let reason go before every enterprise", which certainly relates to alphabetical design, and I think this is what I learnt from Johnston. He once said: "When a thing is different, it is not the same!" and this obvious statement is illuminating and clarifying so often when arguments seem founded on the opposite. The simple question to a student: "What is it?" shook her into a contemplation of her intention which was not clear. When I said to him: "I don't believe in perfection," he promptly replied: "I believe in the Book of Kells." He certainly did, and felt he had to confess his shortcomings in his inscriptions. On an inscription which he wrote in 1934 for presentation by the Society of Scribes and Illuminators to me he wrote: "...it has serious faults—too rough Vell. (tried too late) led to mending many edges (largely spoiling the MS.)...", and yet he later remarked of this very work and its faults: "But in many ways the manuscript is yet my best." The scribe sees his failures clearly, for every stroke of the pen may depart from his intention.

'Johnston was an eccentric. Once when Lawrence Christie and I were in his house, his alarm-clock rang at 10.20 p.m. and he remarked in a matter-of-fact way: "That is to remind me to go to bed." At a meeting of the Council of the Arts and Crafts Exhibition Society when he was president, there was a discussion as to the time to be fixed for a meeting, which called for clear thinking. Johnston observed: "I think clearly when I am about to have a bath. Something occurs to me and I huddle myself about and make notes." Whereupon he actually brought out of a pocket a notebook with a title *Ante-bath Notes* written on it. One did not talk with him but just listened. Once when I wanted to discuss lettering, he talked to me about sin.'

Johnston reciprocated Fairbank's feelings, and he paid him the most valued compliment he ever had on his calligraphy. In 1935 when invited to select scribes' works for an exhibition, he replied that if he did he would have 'to reject everything but some of Fairbank's and mine (and, then, on second thoughts, by strict conscientiousness, would have to reject them also)'. As president of the Arts and Crafts Exhibition Society, he asked Fairbank to become an honorary secretary.

As another major influence in his career, Fairbank names Mrs Louise Powell, *née* Lessore. A small, shy but practical designer with an indomitable will, she had worked with Graily Hewitt when young and had added illuminating to manuscript books begun by Morris. She had an unusual ability of seeing in imagination the designs for her pages without resort to sketching. She scarcely knew Fairbank (who was some years younger than herself) when, in 1925, she invited him to co-operate with her; she illuminated manuscript books which Fairbank had written out and gilded. In taking this partner she was following her instinct, and she merely said: 'I know who I can work with.' Their association, though formal, was a very easy one; for she accepted his work as he did hers, and they were to collaborate in complete trust for thirteen years—this, he gratefully acknowledges, gave him status and clients.

The exhibition and sale of *Comus*, a joint work of Louise Powell and Fairbank, in 1926, when he was still a junior civil servant and a 'Sunday calligrapher', helped to establish him. It occurred at one of the infrequent displays of the Arts and Crafts Exhibition Society formed in 1888, of which William Morris and Walter Crane had been presidents, and now succeeded by the Society of Designer Craftsmen. Fairbank had been elected a member in 1925, when W. R. Lethaby was president, St John Hornby was treasurer, and Noel Rooke and Schultz Weir were the honorary secretaries, while among the members of the Council were May Morris and Emery Walker. The distinguished names in the catalogue reveal the standard of the 1926 exhibition. On view were furniture by Edward Barnsley, Peter Waals, Gordon Russell and Ambrose Heal; bindings by Douglas Cockerell, Katharine Adams and Sybil Pye; pottery by W. Staite Murray, Bernard Leach, Shoji Hamada and Alfred and Louise Powell; other works by Eric Gill, William Simmonds, George Friend, J. H. Mason, Stephen Gooden, John Farleigh and Reco Capey; and manuscripts by Edward Johnston, Graily Hewitt, Madelyn Walker and Dorothy Hutton.

The production of *Comus* attracted the attention of C. H. St John Hornby, who had already given commissions to Louise Powell. Fairbank describes St John Hornby as 'a Florentine Prince of a man'. He was an Oxford Blue, a barrister, a scholar, a collector of manuscripts, the famous printer of the private Ashendene Press and (through Lord Hambledon) he had become a partner in W. H. Smith and Sons. He persuaded A. D. Power, a biblical scholar and a partner in W. H. Smith, to commission Louise Powell and Fairbank to write an *Ecclesiasticus* of his editing, now in the Fitzwilliam Museum (Plate 1). He later commissioned Fairbank to write both a *Horace* and a *Virgil*, the latter a seven-year task. Fairbank speaks with great respect of St John Hornby's judgement. 'As a client he was incomparable, for he understood about book design and the making of manuscript books. He was encouraging and patient. When I took sheets of writing for him to see, he never asked me when the book would be completed, but he used to say: "Would you like a refresher?" It was a splendid challenge to work for a man whose taste was so exact that, on one occasion, he suggested a difference of one-sixteenth of an inch in the margin of one of the books I was to make for him.'

A Scholar Penman

By 1926 Fairbank had designed a model of what was to become the script associated with his name. For scribes interested he offered to write copy-books, and he sold twenty-four of these at 6*d.* each to members of the Society of Scribes and Illuminators.

His interest in handwriting had become known to Sir Sydney Cockerell and Professor E. A. Lowe (whom he taught to cut a quill). Cockerell, who had helped Edward Johnston at the beginning of his career, was an authority on illuminated manuscripts. Lady Cockerell had been an illuminator of distinction. Cockerell at that time seemed to expect little of Fairbank but, despite a cold and formal manner, he was sympathetic to scribes.

It was Cockerell and Lowe who drew Robert Bridges' attention to Fairbank's work. Bridges, whose interest in the italic hand went back to 1879, wanted a special edition of *A Testament of Beauty* to be printed wholly in Fairbank's italic type. 'About a fortnight before he died I went to Oxford to see him about phonetic symbols, which he wished me to design. On my departure he said to me: "Do you understand what I want? For you will not be here again. Don't grieve for me; I shall be glad to go." By the way, his wife had published a book on italic handwriting in 1898 and in the following year sent a book on palaeography to Edward Johnston, which I possess. One of her ancestors, John Hodgkin, who was born in 1766 and died in 1845, was a writing master.[2] With Bridges' death the project of making another alphabet collapsed, and so did the hopes of a "distinguished career as a designer of symbols" which he had promised me.'

Here I depart from the rough chronological order in which this account is written to record the fate of another set of symbols which Fairbank devised for a different purpose. In the year 1953 he was invited by James Pitman, M.P. (later Sir James Pitman), to make a 42-letter alphabet for use in teaching infants to read. Fairbank based the forms on a simplified italic alphabet, but, when eventually the system designed by Pitman was presented in a Roman style alphabet (i.t.a.), he lost interest, as it seemed to him that whilst the teaching of reading might thus be made easier, the teaching of handwriting would be more difficult.

The problem of italic pens was solved in the 1930's with the help of H. Roderick Hughes, who owns St Paul's Pen Works in Birmingham and whose trade name is Geo. W. Hughes. 'Without his support it might well have proved impossible for me to publish a manual and writing cards', Fairbank acknowledges. 'The support he gave me was in making a dip-pen which is called "The Flight Commander", and this was the first italic pen to appear on the market. I had written to him in 1931 asking him to produce a metal stub with a straight edge. At that time he had not studied the old scripts, but liked to design pens for various handwritings and had even designed one for a Tibetan. He recalled that a colleague in the First World War wrote a half-uncial hand which he had admired and he thought that might be the script I had in mind. So he called on me. With great care and enthusiasm he made five proto-types before he and I were satisfied. All makers of italic pens owe him a debt.'[3]

From 1931 to 1933 Fairbank was honorary secretary of the Society of Scribes and Illuminators—a busy period during which he published *A Handwriting Manual* and *Woodside Writing Cards*; started the current handwriting reform in schools by reading a paper on the teaching of handwriting to a crowded meeting of educationalists at the Royal Society of Arts; and was awarded the Diploma of Fellowship of the Central School of Arts and Crafts.

Outside the Society there were occasional gatherings of what he terms 'The Ascham Society' consisting of James Wardrop, Professor Geoffrey Tillotson, Professor John Butt, Rev. C. M. Lamb and Fairbank. They met for a meal and discussed such matters as Italic, Italian writing masters, and pens.

Harry Peach, of Dryad Handicrafts, and Joseph Compton, Director of Education at Barking and Ealing, supported him in his aim to revive italic handwriting.

'Harry Peach was a "character"—direct, frank, enthusiastic and generous. He was a supporter of many causes in Leicester and believed strongly in the crafts and in handwriting reform. He worked, too, for the Design and Industries Association and the Council for the Preservation of Rural England. His passion for quality in design led him to put on in London an exhibition of photographs he had taken of ugly advertising, which caused one very large firm to mend its ways. One day he came to see me at the Admiralty when I was in a very junior grade and he said casually, without seeming to make social contrasts: "I've had lunch with the Prime Minister and, whilst I was this way, I thought I would call on you." He had spent a few minutes whilst waiting for me to come into the office in trying to interest a colleague in italic handwriting.

'Joseph Compton persuaded some head teachers in Barking in 1936 to try out italic handwriting in their schools and got the Dryad Press to produce the *Barking Writing Cards* (now called the *Dryad Writing Cards*). I was given the opportunity to teach teachers at weekly evening classes. Compton sat in a class and developed in time a superb version of the hand. The experiment at Barking became known and was influential, but was broken by the evacuation of schools in 1939. When the institution of the Society for Italic Handwriting was under consideration by the Society of Scribes and Illuminators, it was felt that Joseph Compton was the inevitable chairman. He was well known for his interest in the reading of poetry and was a member of the Arts Council.

'A head teacher who attended several of my courses but who has now retired is Miss Winifred Hooper, the author of two *Beacon Writing Books*. Her teaching in her primary school has not been equalled elsewhere, but remarkable results have been obtained in many schools and the italic hand usually runs away with prizes when competitions on a national scale are held.'

In 1934, Fairbank became joint honorary secretary of the Arts and Crafts Exhibition Society with J. H. Mason and later with F. H. Spear, a stained-glass painter. 'We were responsible for the organization of the exhibition held in 1935 at Dorland House,' he recalls, 'at a time when it had become fashionable to praise industrial art and to look sideways at the craftsman's works. To run an exhibition, which had sixteen selection committees, on top of my office job was an ordeal such as I have not had before or since, but I was determined to do what I could to make it a success—which I think it was—if it killed me. At this exhibition I met Berthold Wolpe and a long and fruitful friendship began.'

Fairbank's manual went out of print in 1939 after being reduced from 3s. 6d. to 2s. 6d. He regarded the book as a failure, but, as the affairs of the workmen in the royal dockyards during the war generally occupied him for over seventy hours a week, he could not make another attempt. When the war was over interest revived.

'To my astonishment several publishers sought to reissue my manual and there arose quickly, from causes unknown, an interest in handwriting. My King Penguin, *A Book of Scripts*, had a colossal sale and in 1949 was the Penguin book of the year. The pressure of this new interest on the Society of Scribes and Illuminators was an embarrassment; for the Society's concern was illuminated manuscripts and professional calligraphy. Accordingly, Miss Heather Child, then honorary secretary and now chairman, at my instigation put to the committee a proposal to found a Society for Italic Handwriting. At the inaugural meeting in November 1952 Sir Francis Meynell spoke in favour, and so did Gerald Hayes, a cartographer and musicologist, who is remembered for his books on musical instruments and his anthology, *Kings' Music*. He was the first of my friends at the Admiralty to perceive what I was trying to do and to reform his scribble into a fine italic hand. So the Society for Italic Handwriting came into being and thrives today.'[4]

Fairbank's last manuscript book, which he made in 1949, has a kind of historic interest. It was a gift from Earl Attlee to Mrs Eleanor Roosevelt, and contained speeches made by Attlee as Prime Minister, Sir Winston Churchill and the Dean, when a memorial to F. D. Roosevelt was unveiled in Westminster Abbey (Plate 2).

At the age of 60 Fairbank, then a senior executive officer, retired from the

Admiralty. One of the tributes which he treasures is a letter from Sir John Lang, the Secretary of the Admiralty at that time, who wrote as follows:

4th November, 1955

Sir,

On your retirement from the public service I am commanded by My Lords Commissioners of the Admiralty to express to you Their appreciation of the valuable services which you have rendered during a long career in the Department and Their good wishes for your future welfare.

It has been a privilege for the Admiralty to have had as a member of its staff a person who has reached so eminent a position in calligraphy and it was a source of pleasure to Their Lordships when his late Majesty King George VI honoured you, in recognition of the service which you have given to this art, by appointing you as Commander of the Most Excellent Order of the British Empire.

I am, Sir,
Your obedient Servant,

J. G. LANG

A. J. Fairbank, Esq., C.B.E.

Among the numerous projects he has carried out since then, the one best known to the public is the design and production, with a team of a dozen scribes, of the Books of Remembrance now to be seen in St Clement Danes' Church in the Strand. He and his wife checked the 150,000 names[5].

The extent to which a calligrapher can make contributions to palaeography has been shown by the significant work Fairbank has done in this field. In 1952 Sir Hilary Jenkinson arranged for him to study the Domesday Book when it was being rebound in the Public Record Office. Fairbank was invited to give his views on two questions: how many scribes had been engaged in writing the book and how long had it taken them? Eccentricities in the writing throughout the book led him to conclude that only one scribe had worked on it—an opinion in conflict with the accepted one then. As he could write in the Domesday style, an estimate of the probable time taken could be formed.

His studies took him to Rome for a month, where he looked at Roman inscriptions

A Scholar Penman

and manuscripts. In his searches in the British Museum and elsewhere for Renaissance handwriting, supported by Leverhulme Research Awards, he has brought to light many examples which have created interest. Over a hundred photostats of the hands of sixteenth-century Cambridge scholars which he made were shown a few years ago at the University Library, Cambridge. With Professor Bruce Dickins he produced *The Italic Hand in Tudor Cambridge* (a monograph with forty-one illustrations of the Cambridge Bibliographical Society). The Library has over 200 photostats of Cambridge penmen from his collection of negatives. *Renaissance Handwriting: An Anthology of Italic Scripts*, a joint production with Berthold Wolpe, shows many of his and Wolpe's discoveries. Since then Fairbank has made numerous other finds, the most important perhaps being the manuscript by Pomponio Leto, understood to be the only one in the United Kingdom. This was, he says, 'a great stroke of luck'; it shows a script very like the first italic type, the Aldine italic. He has also attributed manuscripts to Bartolomeo San Vito, A. Tophio, Antonio Sinibaldi and Ludovico degli Arrighi.[6]

What Fairbank likes to ponder are the characteristics and influences that have gone to make alphabetical excellence in the past and what circumstances may produce excellence now or in the future. He holds that there is a large field for both practice and investigation by the calligrapher, who, by the instant construction of vast numbers of words when writing and an understanding of letter design, is in a special position. 'There are the established inscriptions that have won appreciation over the centuries and the ephemeral works that fit purposes, occasions and the fashions of the day.' Though the letters of the alphabet, he remarks, are symbols of sound, they lend themselves at times to geometrical considerations through features that are perpendicular, horizontal, oblique, round, oval, angular. 'Alphabets may be static or dynamic, and they may display strength in construction or weakness.' Fairbank thinks that there is yet much to learn about legibility. 'In establishing shape and proportion, taste combines with reason. The letterer's reasonable questions are not only what are the ideal forms, but why they are. Is an alphabet suitable for its purpose of attracting attention or of being unobtrusive; and is its purpose known and understood?'

What is needed now is a film of Fairbank writing his script; for he often remarks that handwriting is a system of movements involving touch[7] and that the static models of the copy-books are less impressive than a teacher's blackboard demonstrations. Fairbank had hoped, through the support of the West Sussex Education Authority, to make such a film, and sufficient was produced, including a loop-film, to show the possibilities, but circumstances prevented its completion.

13

To conclude I put two questions to Fairbank. The first was: why the italic hand? Fairbank said that a break in the Victorian tradition of handwriting had been obviously desirable and he quoted Robert Bridges' condemnation of 'the soulless models of the school copybooks' which had suffered 'ultimate degradation in Lawyers' offices from vulgar clerks, who scrupulously perfected the very most purely ugly thing that a conscientious civilisation has ever perpetrated'. So much for copperplate. To explain his choice of italic Fairbank remarked that handwriting reached a peak of excellence in the Italian Renaissance and he cited Arrighi who, writing in 1523, held that the 'littera cancellaresca' (italic hand) took first place, although he also wrote a fine version of the Roman script. Fairbank then said: 'I have written in both styles extensively and though, of course, I acknowledge the greater clarity of Roman, I think the italic hand is more of a designer's script, and a greater challenge to the calligrapher. The challenge is in the fact that it can be written in a set form by precise and slow strokes, but also in free form at great speed. Both set and free italic scripts can have distinction that pleases. Obviously it requires more skill to write well at a great pace than when speed is unimportant and gives way to precision.'

As my last question, I wanted to know what belief had inspired all that activity of committees, societies and exhibitions, and what it is to which so many people now respond. His answer was simple.

'I believe in the importance of the unique work, of things made for particular purposes. I claim the superiority of actual script over reproduced copies, on the same grounds as one believes in the painting more than in its reproduction, or the playing of an orchestra rather than the gramophone record. The reproduced work is an expedient, although valuable for its service and essential to commerce. Handwriting is not done for reproduction, unless it is expedient, and it is not often that. For such as myself, it involves the play of taste and reason. Some think it must be an automatic activity and fully express personality or individuality, even if this means illegibility and unattractiveness, but all those who have visual taste must surely have some degree of writing-consciousness and half an eye on the graphic pattern, and must therefore wed discipline and freedom. Such persons, I think, generally wish they could write better. The person of graphic taste who finds little opportunity to create has an outlet, however modest, in his handwriting, and this is why so many adults take to the italic hand.'

NOTES BY EDITOR

1 The Rev. C. M. Lamb writes in greater detail about the S.S.I. on pp. 245 *et seq.* below.

2 The reader will learn more about John Hodgkin from Mr S. Godman's article below on pp. 149 *et seq.*

3 Mr Hughes's own account, which first appeared in the *Journal of the Society for Italic Handwriting*, No. 32 (autumn 1962), is reprinted below on pp. 265 *et seq.*

4 See also Miss Anna Hornby's article on pp. 251 *et seq.* below.

5 This project is more fully described below (pp. 29 *et seq.*) by Air Chief Marshal Sir Theodore McEvoy who was closely associated with the project.

6 See the various articles reprinted in the section of the book which deals with the Society for Italic Handwriting. (pp. 255 *et seq.*).

7 Professor Lloyd Reynolds develops this theme in his article below (pp. 197 *et seq.*).

RUARI McLEAN

Alfred Fairbank's Opus

Poets should write in Italic. Since we cannot, like the Chinese, write and draw simultaneously, it is our best way to write. Walter de la Mare almost wrote an italic hand;[1] Robert Bridges did, and so did his wife Monica, who also, as far back as 1898, wrote *A New Handwriting for Teachers*, a little book entirely set in Fell Italic, with a facsimile of a sonnet of Michael Angelo's in his own exquisite hand, as well as of the version of Italic which she was trying to publicise. William Morris also practised Italic: as Mr Fairbank has recently pointed out, he owned Arrighi's two writing manuals, and may be said to have started the modern movement to reform handwriting as well as printing.

In 1926, Robert Bridges published the first of his two Society for Pure English Tracts on English Handwriting: the thirty or so examples of contemporary hands include only one that is a true Italic, a letter in Stanley Morison's hand which is closely allied to Michael Angelo's. In the pages headed 'Artistic Comment' which follow, by Roger Fry, it is odd that this fact is not noticed, and Morison's hand (I would have thought, by far the most elegant and legible of all shown) receives no comment.

Robert Bridges' second Tract on English Handwriting appeared the following year. It contains Alfred Fairbank's first published article, entitled 'Penmanship', and it is printed in his own handwriting from line blocks (Fig. 2). There is also a collotype facsimile of a letter written by Fairbank, showing the neatness, precision and mastery of his hand fully developed. The differences between his writing and Stanley Morison's, or for that matter Michael Angelo's, are considerable: Fairbank's is smaller, sharper, more rounded, with less vertical emphasis (partly due to the curving finishes to his *d*'s, *q*'s, and *y*'s), yet brilliantly controlled.

His manuscripts are written either in roman or italic script of exceptional purity. He strove for perfection in the two basic western renaissance hands: few would question that he has achieved it. His initial letters are also perfectly executed: but where they are the most important feature of a page, they are usually illuminated, nearly always by another hand. It is therefore essentially on his writing of text that Fairbank's fame will rest. Plate 1 shows a page from his *Ecclesiasticus*.

Fairbank's contribution to book design consists mainly of the lettering he designed for the Gregynog Press between 1936 and 1938. This included an alphabet of roman capitals, chapter headings, various initials and lettering on maps drawn by Berthold Wolpe. His letters were all engraved on wood by R. J. Beedham and appeared in *The History of St Louis* (1937) and *The Lovers of Teruel* (1938). They are most handsome, comparable with the work of Johnston, Gill and Reynolds Stone.

His only contribution to type design has been the so-called Narrow Bembo Italic, designed in 1928 and cut by the Monotype Corporation. It was conceived as an italic type to be used entirely in its own right, and not in any way related to 'Monotype' Bembo, which Fairbank had not then seen. Interesting notes on its design were published by Fairbank in *The Journal of the Society for Italic Handwriting*, No. 33. For the sake of clarity, the lower-case letters were given a slope of only 5°. To design an Italic for continuous reading is very difficult. Frederic Warde was as near success as anyone with Vicenza, the Italic first used in the Officina Bodoni's *Crito* (1926), and later with his Arrighi (or Centaur Italic) of 1929. Goudy's Deepdene Italic (1928) and Van Krimpen's Romanée Italic (1959) are also in the running. Narrow Bembo appears to be extremely readable, although it is for specialized use. It has been cut only in 10, 12, 13 and 16 point sizes. Of these, the 10 point is particularly attractive, and seems to cry out for use in a small, elegant book of poetry or romance. It has been insufficiently used: the principal public appearances seem to have been in *Typography* 4 in 1937, in Walter de la Mare's long poem *The Traveller* (Faber and Faber, 1946) (where it was also used, blown up, on the jacket) and in Fairbank's own *A Roman Script for Schools* (Ginn, 1961), where it is excitingly contrasted with bold black roman pen letters in a wide line. It was also used by Grant Dahlstrom for the Book of Genesis, in his contribution to *Liber Librorum*, 1955. Like many other faces, it is the better for leading, to set off the vertical pattern of its ascenders and descenders. It is certainly a most beautiful design, and deserves more attention than it has had from typographers and printers.

Fairbank's italic calligraphy has been pressed into service for letter-headings, book plates, monograms, certificates, advertisements (e.g. for Gordon Russell Ltd., and Heal's, two leading producers of well-designed furniture) and even for London Underground posters. Two of the most successful examples of his calligraphy put to a working use are the cheque forms he designed for the British Council and Penguin Books. Here, calligraphy is at home and eminently suitable.

Alfred Fairbank's Opus

Fairbank's *A Handwriting Manual* was first published, in pink paper boards, in 1932, by the Dryad Press, Leicester, in the same year as the first of his *Dryad Writing Cards*. This edition is now a collector's piece: it was in the blue cloth edition of 1947 that it began to attain the world-wide circulation it now enjoys (the 4th, 5th and 6th editions have been published by Faber & Faber, who have now reissued it as a paperback). It was an entirely modest little book, illustrated with diagrams, sketches and examples of Fairbank's methods, and an excellent selection of half-tone reproductions of fine italic hands, written by experts, ranging from the Duke of Urbino (1559) to a school-girl (*c.* 1947). It remains a classic: unpretentious and satisfying, the keystone of modern enjoyment of italic handwriting.

The King Penguin *Book of Scripts* (1949, and at least four times reprinted) was an anthology chosen and edited by Fairbank, which brought fine writing to millions of people. Fairbank's methods for teaching Italic in schools were fully and finally expounded in the six *Beacon Writing Books* (Ginn, from 1957), which are still being constantly reprinted. The *Beacon Writing Books* are themselves most pleasant to handle and peruse (Fig. 2).

England is fortunate to have produced, in a comparatively few years, first Edward Johnston, to be followed by such masters of writing as Graily Hewitt, Eric Gill, Stanley Morison, James Wardrop, Reynolds Stone and Fairbank. Of these, Fairbank is the teacher who has introduced the beauty of italic writing to the public, not only in England, but all over the world. If English handwriting as a whole has really improved (and there was room), it is largely due to the labours and perseverance of Alfred Fairbank. In terms simply of pleasure, both in writing and looking, it is a very great achievement indeed.

NOTE

1 See *A Tribute to Walter de la Mare on his Seventy-Fifth Birthday* (Faber and Faber, 1948) with a reproduction of de la Mare's handwriting and a critique of it by Alfred Fairbank.

Ruari McLean

CATALOGUE OF ALFRED FAIRBANK'S WORKS

Manuscript books

1921–2 17 Rolls of Honour of L.C.C. Schools, made under the direction of Lawrence Christie.

1922 *The Bull*, by Ralph Hodgson. Paper. Bought by Edwin J. Evans.

1922 *Winter Nightfall*, by J. C. Squire. Parchment.

1922 Marriage Service. Parchment. Illuminated by Mary H. Robinson.

1923 *Eve & Other Poems*, by Ralph Hodgson. Paper.

1923 *Poems*, by W. H. Davies. Paper.

1923 Eight Poems by R. L. Stevenson. Parchment.

1923 Biggleswade Book of Remembrance. Parchment. Illuminated by Lawrence Christie.

1924 *The XII Months*. Parchment. Drawings by Lawrence Christie. (Two copies, one purchased by Ambrose Heal.)

1924 *Thoughts in a Garden*, by Andrew Marvell. Parchment. Illuminated by Marta Bowerley. Bought by Ambrose Heal.

1925 Three Poems. Parchment. Commissioned by G. B. Clothier.

1925 *Sirena*, by Michael Drayton. Parchment.

1926 *Comus*, by John Milton. Paper. Illuminated by Louise Powell. In the possession of Leonard Schlosser, New York.

1926 Deed of Gift of Bronze Bust of Wm. Archer. Written for the British Drama League.

1926–9 *Ecclesiasticus*. Parchment. Illuminated by Louise Powell. Commissioned by A. D. Power, who edited it. Fitzwilliam Museum, Cambridge (Plate 1).

1926 The Book of Ruth. Paper. In the possession of Miss Catherine Powell.

1926 25 Sonnets of Shakespeare. Paper. Illuminated by Louise Powell. Commissioned by Edwin J. Evans.

1926–7 24 Manuscript Copy-books of the Italic Hand. One in the Pierpont Morgan Library.

1927–32 The *Odes* and *Epodes* of Horace. Vellum. Illuminated by Louise Powell. Commissioned by St John Hornby.

1931 *Aesop & Rhodope*, by Savage Landor. Paper. Presented to Ambrose Heal.

1931 *Lines on the Euganean Hills*, by P. B. Shelley. Parchment. Illuminated by Louise Powell. In the possession of Philip Hofer.

1932 Sampler Book of Sonnets, written in five italic hands. Paper. Commissioned by the Dryad Press, Leicester.

1932 Twelve Poems. Vellum. Commissioned by H. H. Peach.

1932–8 The *Eclogues* and *Georgics* of Virgil. Vellum. Illuminated by Louise Powell. Commissioned by St John Hornby.

1939 Book of Names, for presentation to Tom Jones, C.H. Decorated by Berthold L. Wolpe.

1949 Speeches on unveiling of memorial to President F. D. Roosevelt, in Westminster Abbey. Vellum. Presented by the Prime Minister to Mrs Roosevelt (Plate 2).

Published works

1932   *A Handwriting Manual.* Dryad Press, Leicester: first edition, 1932; revised editions, 1947, 1948. Faber and Faber Ltd.: new and enlarged edition, 1954; 5th edition, 1956; revised and enlarged edition, 1961; paperback edition, 1965.

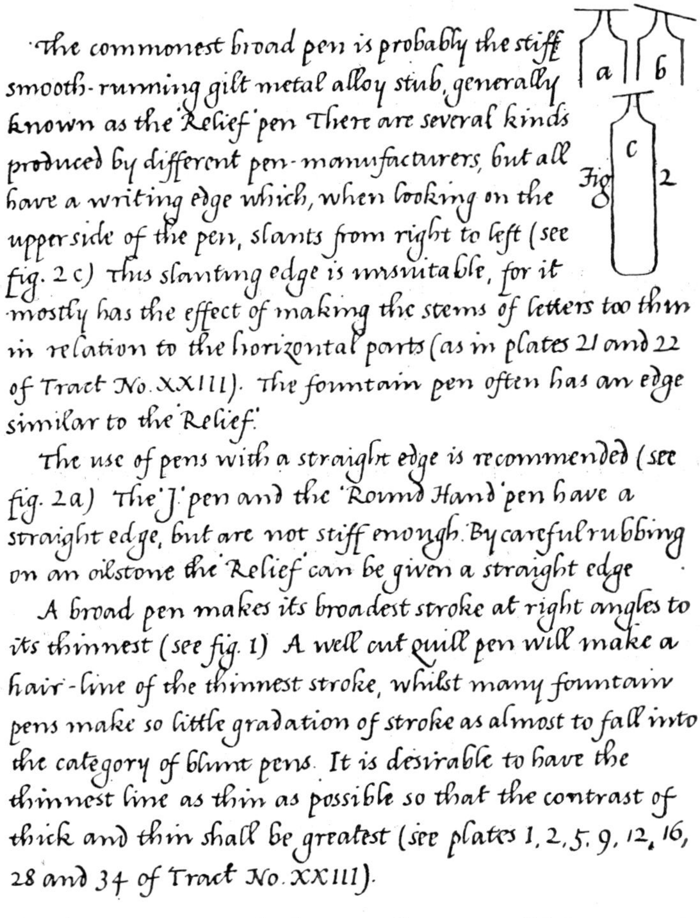

The commonest broad pen is probably the stiff smooth-running gilt metal alloy stub, generally known as the 'Relief' pen There are several kinds produced by different pen-manufacturers, but all have a writing edge which, when looking on the upper side of the pen, slants from right to left (see fig. 2 c) This slanting edge is unsuitable, for it mostly has the effect of making the stems of letters too thin in relation to the horizontal parts (as in plates 21 and 22 of Tract No. XXIII). The fountain pen often has an edge similar to the 'Relief'.

The use of pens with a straight edge is recommended (see fig. 2 a) The 'J' pen and the 'Round Hand' pen have a straight edge, but are not stiff enough. By careful rubbing on an oilstone the Relief can be given a straight edge

A broad pen makes its broadest stroke at right angles to its thinnest (see fig. 1) A well cut quill pen will make a hair-line of the thinnest stroke, whilst many fountain pens make so little gradation of stroke as almost to fall into the category of blunt pens. It is desirable to have the thinnest line as thin as possible so that the contrast of thick and thin shall be greatest (see plates 1, 2, 5, 9, 12, 16, 28 and 34 of Tract No. XXIII).

Fig. 1. From 'Notes on Penmanship', Society for Pure English Tract no. XXVIII, 1927.

1932   *Woodside Writing Cards.* Dryad Press, Leicester (out of print).

1932   *Dryad Lettering Card No. 2.* Dryad Press, Leicester (out of print).

1935   *Barking Writing Cards,* later renamed *Dryad Writing Cards.* Dryad Press, Leicester. Numerous reprints.

1949   *A Book of Scripts.* Penguin Books. Revised editions, 1950, 1952, 1955, 1960. French edition, 1952.

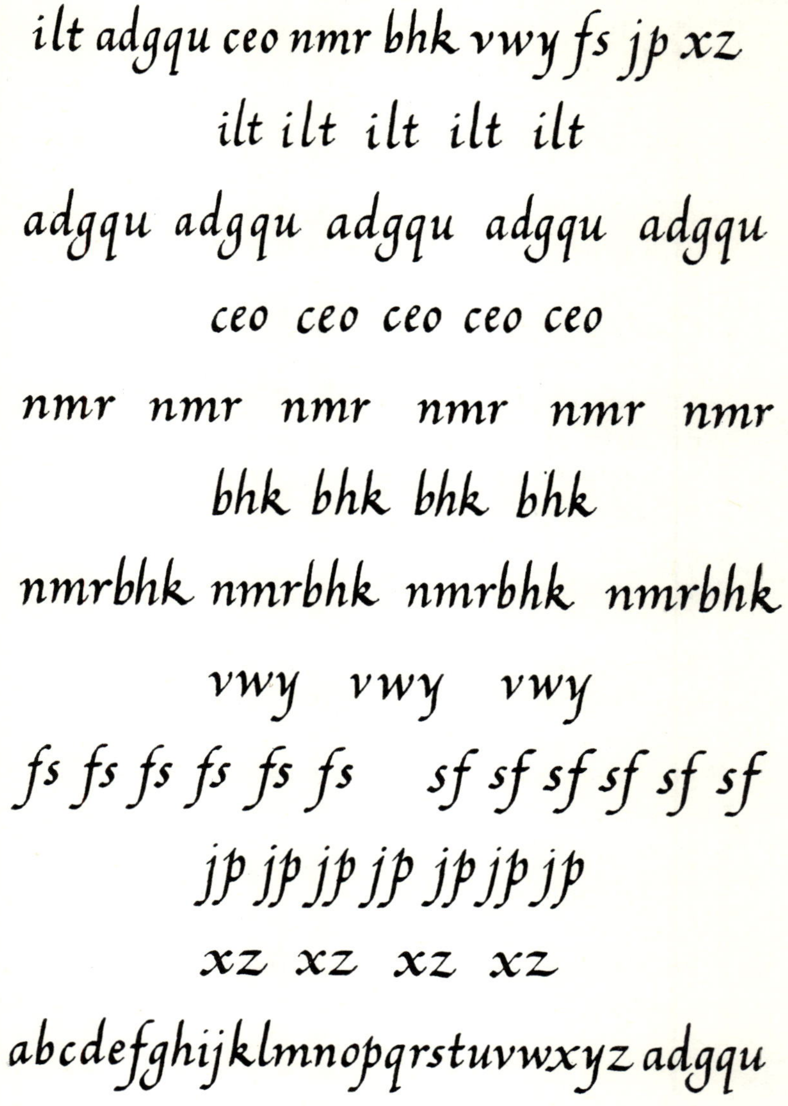

ilt adgqu ceo nmr bhk vwy fs jp xz

ilt ilt ilt ilt ilt

adgqu adgqu adgqu adgqu adgqu

ceo ceo ceo ceo ceo

nmr nmr nmr nmr nmr nmr

bhk bhk bhk bhk

nmrbhk nmrbhk nmrbhk nmrbhk

vwy vwy vwy

fs fs fs fs fs fs   sf sf sf sf sf sf

jp jp jp jp jp jp jp

xz xz xz xz

abcdefghijklmnopqrstuvwxyz adgqu

Fig. 2. From *Beacon Writing Books* (Book Five), 1957–63.

To The Worshipful Company of Goldsmiths of London this Record is Most Gratefully Dedicated

Fig. 3. From Frontispiece to *The London Goldsmiths*, by Ambrose Heal, 1935.

1957–63 *Beacon Writing Books.* (Editor and calligrapher.) Ginn and Co. (Fig. 2).
    Books One and Two, and Supplements One and Two. With Charlotte Stone.
      Book One, 1957, 1957, 1960, 1963; Book Two, 1957, 1957, 1960.
      Supplement One, 1961; Supplement Two, 1961.
    Books Three and Four. By Winifred Hooper, with examples by A.J.F.
      Book Three, 1958, 1959, 1961; Book Four, 1958, 1959, 1962.
    Books Five and Six. By A.J.F.
      Book Five, 1958, 1959, 1961, 1963; Book Six, 1959, 1959, 1961.
    How to Teach the Italic Hand through the Beacon Writing Books, 1963.

1960 *Renaissance Handwriting: An Anthology of Italic Scripts.* With Berthold L. Wolpe. Faber and Faber, 1960. World Publishing Co., U.S.A., 1960.

1960 *Humanistic Scripts of the Fifteenth and Sixteenth Centuries.* With R. W. Hunt. Bodleian Library, Oxford.

1961 *A Roman Script for Schools.* Ginn and Co.

1962 *The Italic Hand in Tudor Cambridge.* With Bruce Dickins. Cambridge Bibliographical Society Monograph no. 5. Bowes and Bowes.

23

Film strip

1958   How to Write the Italic Hand. With Thomas Barnard. Descriptive instruction to 30 frames. Hulton Press.

Articles

'Notes on Penmanship' (reproduced in facsimile). Society for Pure English Tract no. XXVIII: *English Handwriting*. Edited by Robert Bridges. 1927 (Fig. 1).

'Calligraphy and the Manuscript Book.' *London Mercury*. May 1930.

'Edward Johnston und die englische Kalligraphie.' *Schrift und Schreiben*. December 1931.

'Italic Handwriting.' *The Dryad Quarterly*. April 1932.

'The Teaching of Handwriting: A Suggested Reform.' *Journal of the Royal Society of Arts*. 16 December 1932.

'Writing Reform.' *The Teacher's World*. 11 January 1933.

'English Calligraphy and Illuminating.' *Die Zeitgemasse Schrift*, no. 32. January 1935.

'Calligraphy.' *Lettering of Today*. Studio Ltd. 1937, 1941, 1945, 1949. Edited by C. G. Holme.

'Handwriting Reform.' *Typography*, 4. Autumn 1937. Repeated in *P.M. Journal*, U.S.A., December–January 1938–9.

'On writing "fair".' *Tribute to Walter de la Mare on his Seventy-fifth Birthday*. Faber and Faber Ltd. 1948.

'Tribute IV.' *Tributes to Edward Johnston Calligrapher*. Maidstone School of Art, 1948.

'Handwriting Reform in England.' *Schweizer Graphische Mitteilungen*. August 1948. Repeated in *Printing Review*. Spring 1950.

'Italic Handwriting.' *Journal of the Royal Society of Arts*. 19 October 1951.

'With Pen in Hand.' *Children's Newspaper*. 26 January 1952.

'Handwriting.' *Manchester Evening Chronicle*. 26 November 1952.

'This is Everyman's Handicraft.' *Christian Science Monitor*. 9 March 1953.

'Take Pen and Write.' *Venture: Journal of the Civil Service Council for Further Education*. September 1953.

'A Graceful Cure for the Common Scrawl: A Fair Italic Hand.' *London Illustrated News*. 12 March 1955.

'Cursive Handwriting.' *The Calligrapher's Handbook*. Faber and Faber Ltd. 1956. Edited by C. M. Lamb.

'Die Cancellaresca in Handschrift und Drucktype: Die Schreibbücher von Arrighi, Tagliente und Palatino.' *Imprimatur*, 1956/7. Edited by Siegfried Buchenau und Dr Georg Kurt Schauer.

'Italic Handwriting.' *The Schoolmaster*. October/November 1960.

'Morris and Calligraphy.' *The Journal of the William Morris Society*. Winter 1961.

'Bartholomew Dodington: Elizabethan Scholar and Penman.' *Motif* 9. Summer 1962. Edited by Ruari McLean.

'Looking at Letters and Words.' *Studies in Honor of Berthold Louis Ullman*. Volume II. *Edizioni di Storia e Letteratura*. 1964. Edited by Charles Henderson, Jr.

'Italic in its Own Right.' *Alphabet 1964*. Edited by R. S. Hutchings.

Better is a poor man, being sound and strong of
   constitution,
Than a rich man that is plagued in his body.
Health & a good constitution are above all gold;
And a strong body above wealth without measure.
There is no riches above a sound body;
And no joy above the joy of the heart.
Death is better than a bitter life,
And eternal rest than a continual sickness.
Delicacies poured out upon a mouth that is closed
Are as messes of meat laid upon a grave.
What doth an offering profit an idol?
For neither shall it eat nor smell:
So is he that is afflicted of the Lord,
He seeth with his eyes and groaneth,
As an eunuch embraceth a virgin and sigheth.
Give not over thy soul to sorrow;
And afflict not thyself in thine own counsel.
Gladness of heart is the life of a man;
And the joyfulness of a man prolongeth his days.
Love thine own soul, and comfort thy heart:
And remove sorrow far from thee;
For sorrow hath destroyed many,
And there is no profit therein.

1.   From *Ecclesiasticus*: written by Alfred Fairbank (1926–9): see p. 8. (Reduced)
Fitzwilliam Museum, Cambridge (MS. 2-1959, D. 50)

THE LEADER OF THE OPPOSITION
THE RIGHT HON. WINSTON S. CHURCHILL
O.M., C.H., F.R.S., M.P.

I JOIN with the Prime Minister in paying our tribute to the great Statesman with whom we worked in comradeship, trust and goodwill during the years of fearful ordeal through which we have so lately passed.

Macaulay wrote of Westminster Abbey as "that temple of silence & reconcilation where the enmities of twenty generations lie buried." But now to-day it is not the ending of enmities that we celebrate. This tablet to the memory of Franklin Roosevelt proclaims the growth of enduring friendship & the rebirth of brotherhood between the two great nations upon whose wisdom, valour and virtue the future of humanity in no small degree depends. Long may it testify upon these ancient walls.

2. Speech by Sir Winston Churchill on unveiling of Roosevelt Memorial in Westminster Abbey. From a collection of speeches for the occasion, presented by Lord Attlee to Mrs Roosevelt and written on vellum by Alfred Fairbank (1949): see p. 11.

Arts & Crafts
Exhibition Society

Exhibition of
Arts & Crafts

at Dorland House
Lower Regent Street
November 4 to 30

Admission 1s.6d.   Season Ticket 3s.

Hours 10 to 7, except   Book to Piccadilly
Wednesdays 10 to 9
& Saturdays 10 to 5

ALFRED FAIRBANK & FRANCIS H. SPEAR

3.   Poster for London Underground by Alfred Fairbank & Francis H. Spear:
one of number executed 1933–35: see p. 25. (Reduced)

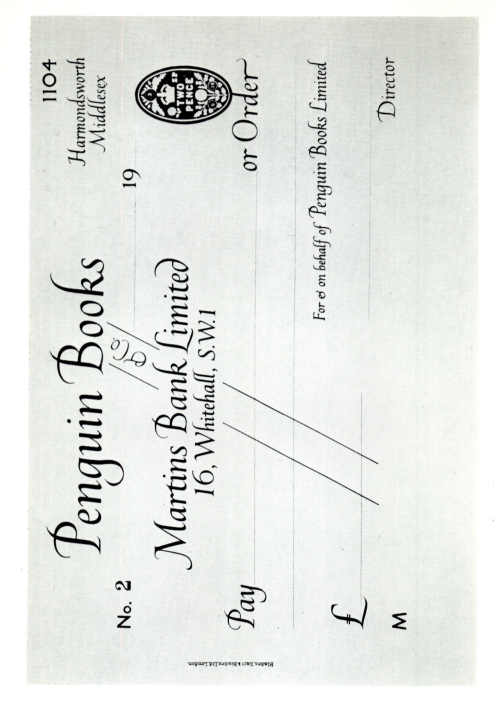

4. Cheque designed for Penguin Books Ltd. by Alfred Fairbank (1938): see p. 25.
    Reproduced with the permission of Sir Allen Lane

[*To face p. 2*

Alfred Fairbank's Opus

Short articles in the Bulletin and Journal of the Society for Italic Handwriting

'A Note on Speed.' *Bulletin* 3, summer 1955.
'The Recent History of Italic Handwriting.' *Bulletin* 6, spring 1956.
'A System of Movements.' *Bulletin* 13, winter 1957–8.
'Some Renaissance Manuscripts.' *Bulletin* 15, summer 1958.
'Ascenders in Writing Models.' *Bulletin* 17, winter 1958–9.
'Nomenclature.' *Bulletin* 18, spring 1959.
'Bartholomew Dodington.' *Bulletin* 19, summer 1959 (reprinted p. 258 below).
'Let Reason Go before Enterprise.' *Bulletin* 21, winter 1959–60.
'The Mystic Art.' *Bulletin* 21, winter 1959–60.
'A Writing Lesson.' *Bulletin* 24, autumn 1960.
'More about Arrighi.' *Bulletin* 26, spring 1961.
'Bartolomeo San Vito.' *Bulletin* 28, autumn 1961 (reprinted p. 264 below).
'Three Renaissance Scripts.' *Journal* 32, autumn 1962.
'The Script of Pietro Cennini.' *Journal* 33, winter 1962.
'Condensed Bembo Italic.' *Journal* 33, winter 1962.
'The Arrighi Style of Book Hand.' *Journal* 35, summer 1963 (reprinted p. 271 below).
'Scripts from Papal Briefs.' *Journal* 36, autumn 1963.
'Italic at Brighton.' *Journal* 39, summer 1964.
'What makes a Good style?' *Journal* 42, spring 1965.
'More of San Vito.' *Journal* 42, spring 1965.
'A Ten-hour Manuscript.' *Journal* 43, summer 1965.
'Simple Geometric Aspects of Italic.' *Journal* 44, autumn 1965.

Also illustrated notes on letters written by or from Sir John Cheke, Roger Ascham, Edward Raven, Bartholomew Dodington, John Still, Cardinal Medici, Antonius Laudus, Pasqual Spinula, Johannes Mallard, and Titian.

Calligraphy and lettering for reproduction

1933–5 Lettering for posters for display on Underground Stations (Plate 3).
1935 Frontispiece inscription to *The London Goldsmiths*, by Ambrose Heal (Fig. 3).
1936–8 Chapter headings, alphabet of roman capitals, various initials, engraved on wood by R. John Beedham. Also lettering on maps drawn by Berthold L. Wolpe. Gregynog Press.
1936/8 Design of cheques for British Council and Penguin Books Ltd. (Plate 4).
1936 The Six Maxims of George V. Engravings by John Farleigh and R. John Beedham.
1946 'Welcome Home' letter. Corsham Parish Council.
1947 Chapter heading and initial for 'The Last Room at the Inn', by John Connell. *Strand Magazine*.
1922–62 Advertisements, letter-headings, certificates, invitations to weddings, Christmas cards, book plates, monograms, devices, phonetic alphabet, and menu.
  (Items also included under 'Published works' and 'Exemplars'.)

Type designs

1928–9 Condensed Bembo Italic (made originally as an italic in its own right). Monotype Corporation (see example on p. 12 of this book).

1938 Alphabet of roman capitals and several other initials. Gregynog Press. (See above.)

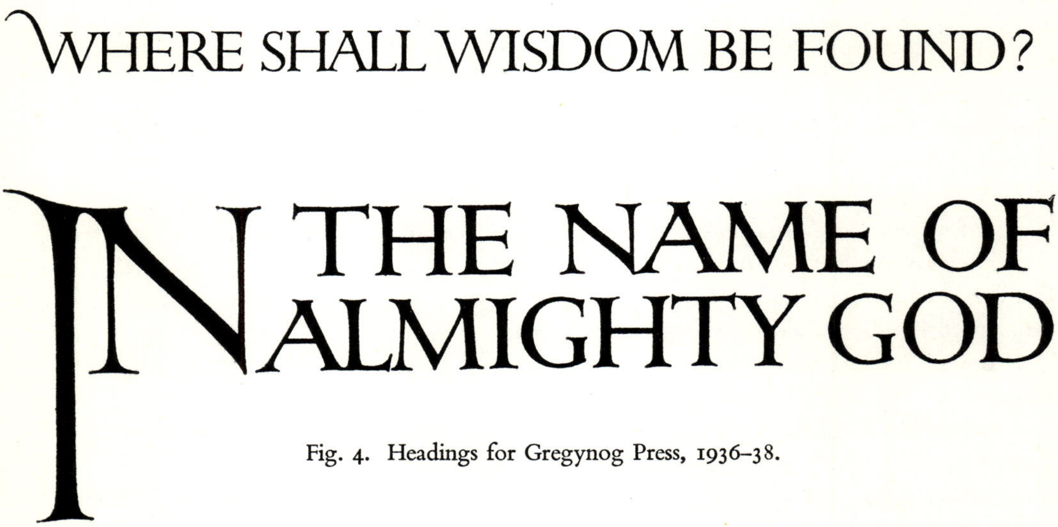

WHERE SHALL WISDOM BE FOUND?

IN THE NAME OF ALMIGHTY GOD

Fig. 4. Headings for Gregynog Press, 1936–38.

Exemplars

1929–34 Book opening of two sonnets, made on two occasions for the Victoria and Albert Museum (Plate 5).

1935 Model church notice made for the Church Building Society as a guide for their calligraphers.

1936 Two broadsides showing a roman and an italic script, for the Leicester School of Art, and reproduced for students.

1956 Model page of names for the Royal Air Force Books of Remembrance, St Clement Danes Church, for the guidance of scribes.

Other models scripts are included in separate lists:

24 copy-books. 1926–7.

Illustrations to *A Handwriting Manual*. 1932.

Woodside Writing Cards. 1932.

Lettering Card for Dryad Press. 1932.

Dryad Writing Cards. 1935.

Beacon Writing Books. 1957/61.

Exemplar Sheet for Society for Italic Handwriting. 1960 (Fig. 5).

A Roman Script for Schools.

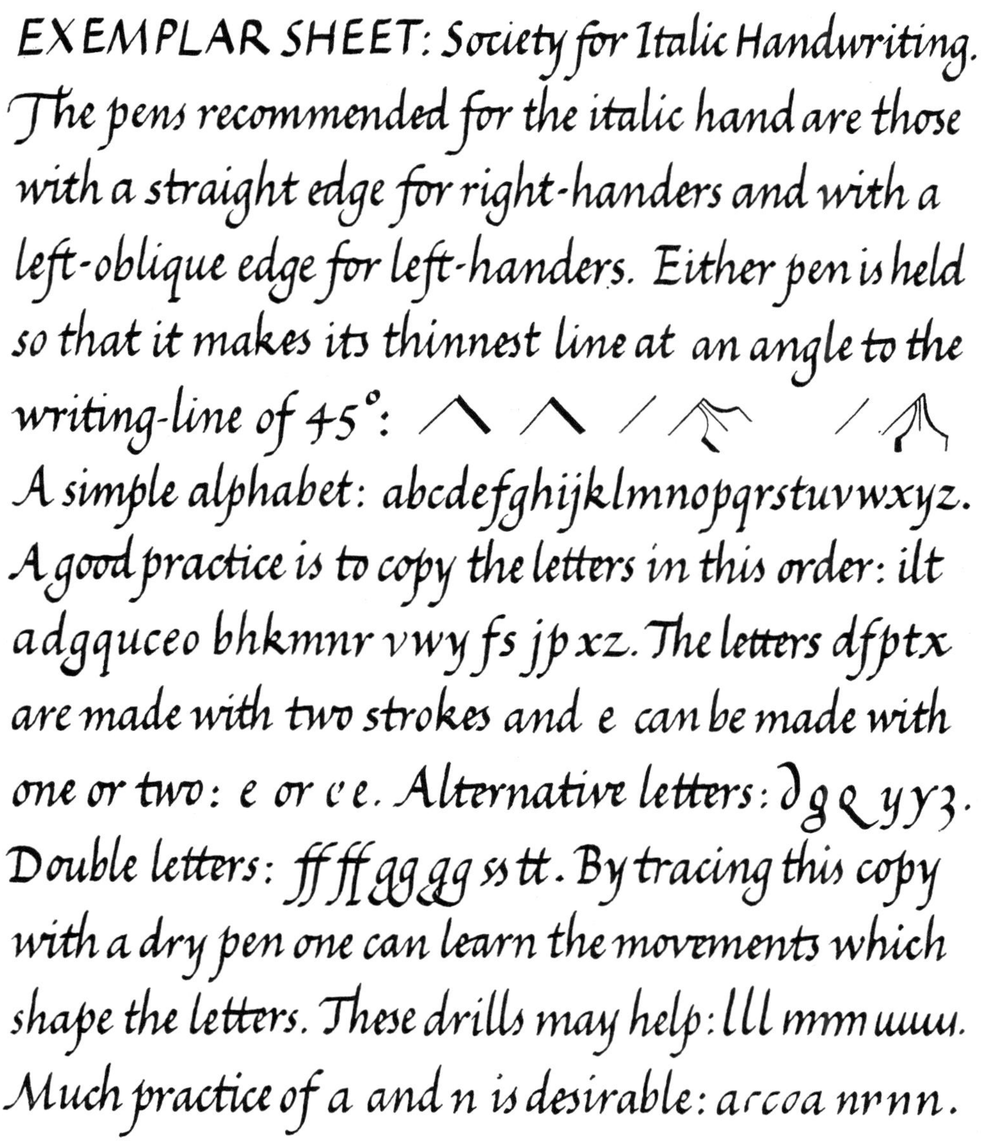

EXEMPLAR SHEET: Society for Italic Handwriting.
The pens recommended for the italic hand are those
with a straight edge for right-handers and with a
left-oblique edge for left-handers. Either pen is held
so that it makes its thinnest line at an angle to the
writing-line of 45°: ∧ ∧ / ⌐ / ⌐
A simple alphabet: abcdefghijklmnopqrstuvwxyz.
A good practice is to copy the letters in this order: ilt
adgquceo bhkmnr vwy fs jp xz. The letters dfptx
are made with two strokes and e can be made with
one or two: e or c e. Alternative letters: ∂ g ℓ y γ ʒ.
Double letters: ff ff gg gg ss tt. By tracing this copy
with a dry pen one can learn the movements which
shape the letters. These drills may help: lll mmm uuuu.
Much practice of a and n is desirable: arcoa nrnn.

Fig. 5. Left-hand sheet of exemplar for the Society for
Italic Handwriting, 1960.

Ruari McLean

Calligraphy and lettering not included in other lists

1921–57 Numerous inscriptions as broadsides for wall decoration, etc.

1923–49 24 presentation addresses, testimonials, lists of names.

1933   Pedigree of a family named Reynolds, with heraldry by Louise Powell.

1943–63 11 gate signs cut in wood.

1949   Inscriptions on vellum for War Memorial, King's School, Canterbury.

Book reviews

Lettering, by Graily Hewitt. *Book Collector's Quarterly*. March–May 1931.

Schatzkammer der Schreibkunst, by Jan Tschichold, and *Les Ecritures Financière et Italienne Bastade par Louis Barbedor* (facsimile). *Signature*, New Series, no. 2. 1946.

Handwriting Sheets, by Dom Patrick Barry, O.S.B. *Time and Tide*. 22 May 1954.

Edward Johnston, by Priscilla Johnston. *Bulletin of Society for Italic Handwriting*, 20, autumn 1959.

Arte Subtilissima, by Juan de Yciar, and *Formulary for Divers Fair Hands*, by Wolffgang Fugger (facsimiles). *The Book Collector*. Winter 1960.

A Newe Booke of Copies 1574 (facsimile), edited by Berthold L. Wolpe. *The Book Collector*. Summer 1962.

New Horizons for Research in Handwriting, edited by Virgil E. Herrick. *Journal of Educational Studies*. November 1963.

The Count and the Calligrapher, by Alan Fern in *Apollo*. *Journal of the Society for Italic Handwriting*, no. 39. Summer 1964.

THAT time of year thou mayst in me behold

When yellow leaves, or none, or few, do hang

Upon those boughs which shake against the cold,

Bare ruin'd choirs, where late the sweet birds sang.

In me thou see'st the twylight of such day

As after sunset fadeth in the west;

Which by and by black night doth take away,

Death's second self, that seals up all in rest.

In me thou see'st the glowing of such fire,

That on the ashes of his youth doth lie,

As the death-bed whereon it must expire,

Consumed with that which it was nourish'd by.

This thou perceivest, which makes thy love more strong,

To love that well which thou must leave ere long.

5. One of two sonnets written by Alfred Fairbank for the Victoria and
Albert Museum (1929–34): see p. 26.

[To face p. 28]

M

Ian Cameron MacDonnell

Stanislaus McDonnell

Baldwin Childenose MacDougall

John Joseph McDougall

Archibald McDowall

Hugh Stewart McDowall

Alfred Mace

Neil McEachran

Arthur Mark McElhinney

George Edward Henry McElroy
M.C. D.F.C.

Victor Henry McElroy D.F.C.

Edward McEvoy

Francis McEvoy

George Clapperton McEwan

Charles William Macey

Alexander McFall

Archibald McFarlan

Foster Murray MacFarland

John McFarland D.S.M.

Donald McIntyre McFarlane

Harold Embleton MacFarlane

James McFarlane

James Lennox MacFarlane

Peter MacFarlane

William McFarlane

William Smith MacFarlane M.C.

Leonard Lawrence McFaul

Thomas Malcolm McFerran

James McGarry

Peter Liddell McGavin

Eustace Joseph McGee

Wilfred Raworth McGee

David Hegler McGibbon

John McGibbon

Douglas McGill

James Andrew McGill

Alexander George McGillivray

Charles Allister McGillivray

Wilfrid Joseph McGinn

Alexander McGregor

Donald Argyle Douglas Ian
MacGregor

Donald Mallock McGregor

Thomas Charles Stuart MacGregor

Joseph Alexander McGuckin

Albert McGuinness

Peter McGuire

Thomas Francis McGuire

John MacHaffie

Alexander William McHardy

Lorne Hunter McHarg

James William McHattie

John Egbert Machin

Roland Frank Charles Machin

Thomas Shanks MacIlroy

Julian M. MacIlwaine

Edward Phillips McIndoe

Alexander McBain McIntosh

Edward James McIntosh

100

6. From the Royal Air Force Book of Remembrance: see p. 29. (Reduced)
St Clement Danes, London

[To face p. 29]

SIR THEODORE McEVOY

The Book of Remembrance, St Clement Danes

Among Alfred Fairbank's many enterprises, one in particular lies close to the heart of the Royal Air Force—the direction of the task which resulted in the completion of ten volumes of the Book of Remembrance at St Clement Danes (Plate 6).

The idea that the Royal Air Force should have its own church and that a Roll of Honour should be kept there came in 1945 from Sir John Slessor, who was then Air Member for Personnel in the Air Council. When it was eventually suggested that the blitzed shell of St Clement Danes should be rebuilt to this end, the Diocese of London was quick to acquiesce, and a magnificent response to a world-wide appeal brought in £150,000 (including £30,000 from the United States Air Force, whose dead are also honoured there). In October 1958, the restored church was reconsecrated by the Bishop of London in the presence of Her Majesty the Queen and other members of the Royal Family.

But much work lay behind this fulfilment and what was yet to follow. At the first meeting of the 'St Clement Danes Executive Committee', held in November 1955, one of the items on the agenda was 'Roll of Honour'. The note to be considered under this heading stated that Mr A. J. Fairbank, C.B.E., a senior executive officer in the Department of the Engineer-in-Chief, Admiralty, had been approached and had expressed his willingness to select the craftsmen, divide the work, and undertake all supervision and direction required in the actual execution of the project. This offer the Committee gladly accepted.

Once the policy had been settled, years of devoted work began, culminating in the successive dedication of the finished volumes between May 1962 and April 1964.

From the first, a high standard of calligraphy was insisted on. The scribes were supplied with a model script to ensure a degree of uniformity. They were not, however, expected to follow this slavishly but to maintain a harmonious relationship with it. The principal object, to which they were asked to direct attention, was the achievement of a 'clear and graceful script rather than a decorative one'. Mr Fairbank's operational orders for organizing his mission are a model of brevity and effectiveness, which would do credit to a staff college. As they also have a strong historical interest, I think it is of value to reproduce them here.

Specification for Scribes

1. The writing to be of a high standard of formal calligraphy.
2. The capital letters to be Roman and it is suggested they should be less in height than the minuscules with ascenders.
3. The minuscules to be an upright compressed Roman (Foundational) hand, such as that indicated in the photostat. A relationship to this script is intended but not a direct copy, and the choice of serifs is left to the scribe.
4. The aim in writing to be to achieve a clear and graceful script rather than a decorative one.
5. Whilst the scribes are not required to copy the script of the photostat they should conform to style and sizes so as to achieve as much unity as possible in the books as a set. Each book will be of the scribe's making, and the name of the scribe will appear, of course, in the colophon: that is, the books will each be individual but related to the design indicated in the photostat.
6. The sheets to be Band's manuscript vellum and to be written on both sides.
7. Vellum sheets will be obtained from Messrs H. Band & Co. and distributed by Mr A. J. Fairbank, who will have all dealings with the vellum makers.
8. The skins to be folded with the flesh side inwards. Two skins to form a section for binding.
9. The size of skins will be $17'' \times 24\frac{1}{2}''$, which slightly exceeds twice the size of the intended page ($12'' \times 16\frac{1}{2}''$). Mr Sydney Cockerell, the binder, will cut the leaves to a size and square if desired, to make ruling up simpler, but in doing so the leaves need not be cut to the exact finished size, and a final trimming can be given before binding.
10. Ruling of lines should not be obtrusive and it is suggested a 6H pencil or ruling stylus can be used.
11. The ink for names to be a carbon ink of the best quality and as black as possible.
12. The ink for decorations to be vermilion, except where the decoration is V.C. or G.C., when raised burnished gold is to be used. The vermilion used is the choice of the scribe. Where the decoration has a bar, it is to be shown in colour ampersand bar.
13. Typed lists of names will be provided by the Air Ministry. In copying them, Christian names are to precede surnames, as indicated in the photostat. Where two names are the same, the Service number is to be shown, for identification. The decorations and Service numbers are to be the height of the minuscule 'o' of the names.
14. The pages are to be numbered, but the numbering must await a decision as to whether 'Notes' are to precede the lists of names.
15. Where the name (or name plus decoration) is long it may be continued on the next line, but with an indentation of $\frac{1}{2}''$.
16. The dimensions of the page to be: $12'' \times 16\frac{1}{2}''$. Top margin to first line $2\frac{1}{4}''$. Inner margin $1\frac{3}{4}''$.

Margin between the two columns $\frac{1}{2}$". Spacing of lines $\frac{3}{8}$". Length of lines $3\frac{1}{2}$". 30 lines to a column.

17. The arrangement for payment will be that on completion of a certain number of pages (normally 16) the scribe will submit his work to Mr Fairbank by hand or by registered post in a parcel securely packed and protected. Subject to a certificate by Mr Fairbank that the work is of the high standard required, payment will be made direct to the scribe from the Air Ministry. A specimen form (not to be used) is attached for information.

18. The rate of pay, namely 1s. 3d. per name, has been fixed as appropriate to the best craftsmanship, quality of work, and materials. Corrected errors in copying will be accepted only when erasures do not impair the appearance of the finished pages. Missing words cannot be inserted afterwards.

19. Any question of doubt should be settled with Mr Fairbank. Normally, at the end of the names of each letter of the alphabet a break of 3 blank lines should be left, but Mr Fairbank should be informed as to where on the page these would occur. Mr Fairbank should be shown the first 4 pages of writing so as to confirm that the work is proceeding correctly.

20. At the beginning of the names of each letter of the alphabet the initial is to be in raised burnished gold, placed as indicated in the photostat. It may be decided also to have the initial letter in red in the margin of each verso page. If so, instructions will be issued by Mr Fairbank.

21. If an error is made that allows half the skin to be used, an overlap for binding must be allowed. Moreover, another half-skin with overlap will be necessary to preserve the sequence of sides: hair to hair and flesh to flesh.

22. The titles pages will be the subject of a separate specification.

Since few may read the colophons that show who wrote what amount to nearly 160,000 entries in these volumes, let attribution be made here:

VOLUME	NO. OF NAMES	SCRIBES
I	13,322	Mrs Sheila Waters and Miss Joan Pilsbury
II	14,227	Mrs Sheila Waters and Miss Irene Base
III	13,730	Mrs Dorothy Mahoney
IV	11,369	Miss Ann Camp and Miss Joan Pilsbury
V	15,622	Miss Rosemary Ratcliffe
VI	15,123	Miss Ida Henstock
VII	14,582	Mr Derek Benney
VIII	13,980	Mr John Woodcock
IX	9,956	Miss Irene Base
X	9,938*	Miss Irene Base and Miss Ida Henstock
Total	131,849	
U.S.A.F. Roll	19,105	Mrs Sheila Waters, Mrs Pat Russell, Miss Heather Child, Mr David Howells
Grand total	150,954	

* Up to 30 June 1963. (The work continues, for lives are given in peace as well as in war.)

Sir Theodore McEvoy

The volumes were bound by Mr Sydney Cockerell, who, since their delivery, has conducted a lively campaign for their preservation. It has not been easy to exclude dust and corrosive London fumes from books that have to be easily accessible, and this inevitable difficulty has been aggravated by heat from the lighting of the books, by heating ducts that until recently ran directly beneath the shrines and by unsuitable angling of the platforms on which the volumes lay. However, with advice from British Museum experts, some 11,000 readings of temperature and other data relating to the shrines have been correlated and used to devise modifications which will halt the damage already being done to leaves and bindings.

It would be difficult to over-estimate Mr Fairbank's share in the burden of the whole project. Mr Cockerell has given some measure of it by citing the mass of correspondence in which he himself was involved, between December 1955 and January 1965, including 79 letters and 33 postcards from Mr Fairbank. When we remember that these communications dealt only with the binding of the books, we may form some idea of what the sum of Mr Fairbank's correspondence must have been with all those concerned in the project.

We owe him a great debt of gratitude. He may be as touched, as I was, to know that, when my daughter was to be married at St Clement Danes, she asked that on the day the Book of Remembrance should lie open at the name of her godfather, who gave his life for us and is honoured there.

MAINLY PALAEOGRAPHICAL

A. E. & J. S. GORDON

Three Latin Inscriptions
of 52 B.C.

We present three Latin inscriptions of 52 B.C. for a description and comparison of their lettering. Two of them are on stone (one on marble, the other on local limestone), the third on bone or ivory. The one on marble and the last-named are from Rome; the one on limestone from Osimo in the Italian Marche (ancient Auximum, in Picenum). A description of their lettering, accompanied by photographs, will, we hope, be a useful addition to the rather scanty corpus of Republican inscriptions described in detail and illustrated.[1]

(1) The handsomest (Plate 7a) is one found 12 March 1955 in Rome in Via Alberto Mario on Monte Verde Vecchio[2] and now placed (according to A. Degrassi, 1963) 'in Tabulario', i.e. in the Tabularium built in 78 B.C. on the south-east slope of the Capitoline, above which Boniface IX built the Palazzo Senatorio. The stone measures as follows: overall width 90 cm maximum; height 59·2 cm maximum; thickness 10·9–13 cm; the writing field has a width of 67·8 cm at the top, 68·1 cm below, and a height of 43·1 cm at left, 43·2 cm at right. The inscription was apparently first published by Bernard Andreae in *Archäologischer Anzeiger, Beiblatt zum Jahrbuch des deutschen archäologischen Instituts* (Rome), vol. LXXII, 1957 (Berlin, 1958), col. 235, no. 19; then by M. Alfred Merlin in *L'Année épigraphique* for 1959 (Paris, 1960), p. 39, no. 146 (from Andreae, but with the incorrect addition of an interpunct between *Non.* and *Quinct.*, line 5); then by Attilio Degrassi in his *Inscriptiones Latinae liberae rei publicae*, fasc. 2 (Florence, 1963), pp. 188 f., no. 786 a, who says that the stone is of Luna marble and its dimensions are 0·59 × 0·90 × 0·13 m. In none of these publications is the inscription illustrated by photograph or drawing.

The text reads:

> SEX·AEMILIVS·SEX·L
>
> BARO
>
> FRVMENTAR
>
> INIGNEM·INLATVS·EST
>
> PRID·NONQVINCT
>
> CN·POMPEIO·COS·TERT

Sex(tus) Aemilius Sex(ti) l(ibertus) Baro, frumentar(ius), in ignem inlatus est prid(ie) Non(as) Quinctil(es), Cn(aeo) Pompeio co(n)s(ule) tert(ium). That is, Sextus Aemilius Baro, a freedman of Sextus (Aemilius), a corn-dealer (or victualler), was cremated the day before the Nones of Quinctilis, while Gn. Pompeius was consul for the third time (i.e. 6 July 52 B.C.).

The letter heights are: for line 1, 5·9–6·4 cm; line 2, 6·1–6·3 cm; line 3, 5·7–6·2 cm (M, A, respectively); line 4, 5·3–5·7 cm; line 5, 4·6–5·3 cm; line 6, 3·8–4·2 cm. (These measurements are from a squeeze.) All the lines show a tendency to have slightly shorter letters at the end. The letters of lines 1–3 seem intended to be of the same height; then lines 4–6 decrease. The surface of the stone is not polished; it shows tool marks. The cutting of the letters is sharp and crisp, but not very broad or deep. The arrangement of text is one of centring; it is not perfect, but fairly good, with a rather good balance except for the last line, which is not, as one would expect, centred, but simply indented. The punctuation consists of large triangles, all but one approximately equilateral; a point is always at the top. It is omitted after 'Non' in line 5, as well as after the preposition in line 4 (such omission after a preposition we have noted for a long time).[3] The triangles are not perfectly placed, several being lower than mid-height. There seem to be no guide-lines visible.

Shading: there is no noticeable contrast between thick and thin strokes, the variation in breadth of cutting being very slight. Perhaps the diagonals down from left to right are broader than those in the opposite direction (see A, M, V, X), but the difference is not more than a millimetre and not consistently maintained. Verticals for the most part are slightly wider than horizontals, but again not more than 1 mm. This slight variation occurs in the curved strokes also, but the location of broader and narrower parts is not consistent: see the O's.

Serifs: there are modest ones, not always clearly defined and not entirely consistent. They are absent from the tail of Q and from the pointed joins at the tops of A, M, N; those on the lowest horizontal of most E's, on the horizontal of L, and on most of the R diagonals soften into a curve. C has a heavy serif on both lower and upper curve, though of the lower ones only that of the C of 'Cn' in line 6 splays out in both

SEX·AEMILIVS·SEX·L
BARO
FRVMENTAR
INIGNEM·INLATVS·EST
PRID·NON·QVINCT
CN·POMPEIO·COS·TERT

7*a*. Latin inscription of 52 B.C. from Rome, recording cremation of Sextus Aemilius Baro: see p. 35. Photograph by Joyce S. Gordon. (Reduced)

7*b*. Latin inscription of 52 B.C. from Osimo: an official dedication to Gnaeus Pompeius Magnus, perhaps of bust or statue: see p. 37. Photograph by Joyce S. Gordon. (Reduced)

To face p. 36]

8. *Tessera nummularia* of bone or ivory, 52 B.C.: see p. 38. (Enlarged)
Cabinet des Médailles, Bibliothèque Nationale, Paris

directions, down as well as up; at least one S also (the first in line 4) has such a lower serif.

Individual letters: A is noticeably broad and has a high bar. B, E, L, and S are moderate in size and of about the same width, B being the narrowest. T and X are of about the same width, somewhat broader than E and S. P is rather like the lower part of B, so is one of the narrower letters. D suggests two strokes only and is about two-thirds of a circle. Like it, G is not especially broad. Note that the top arm of G finishes on a line with the left side of the last stroke, the upright. The C's are rather broad and less regular. O is circular, though never quite perfectly so. M is symmetrical, with angles equal or nearly so. The middle bar of E and the lower bar of F are shorter. N and R are relatively narrow, though the bow of R is not narrow (but comparatively short, like the upper bow of B and the bow of P)—rather, the diagonal, which begins from the bow not far from the vertical stroke, does not extend very far right.

(2) The other inscription on stone (Plate 7 *b*) is cut on a thick slab which must be the (somewhat damaged) front of what was described as a large base when found in 1657 at Osimo (according to testimony quoted by *CIL*, I² and 9) and, when seen by us on 9 May 1956, this slab was still in the *atrio* of the Palazzo Comunale there, where it had been long before Mommsen copied it sometime before 1863. We were assured by Mons. Carlo Grillantini of Osimo that the stone is a local limestone, probably from Monte Cónero. (None of the publications listed below mentions the kind of stone.) We found the slab attached to the right-hand wall of the Palazzo as one enters. In its present condition, it measures: maximum width *c.* 65 cm; width of writing field 60 cm; overall height 59 cm; maximum height of writing field 54 cm; maximum thickness 19·5 cm. The writing field seems complete at the lower right corner: one can see the curve of the molding as it starts round the corner. Chief publications: Ritschl, *op. cit.* plate LXXXVI C (only a facsimile, without transcription or restoration of text); Th. Mommsen, *CIL*, vol. I, ed. I (Berlin, 1863), p. 180, no. 615; *idem*, *CIL*, vol. IX (1883), p. 564, no. 5837; H. Dessau, *Inscriptiones Latinae selectae*, vol. I (Berlin, 1892), p. 196, no. 877; E. Lommatzsch, *CIL*, vol. I, ed. 2, pars posterior, fasc. I (Berlin, 1918), p. 544, no. 769; Degrassi, *ILLRP*, fasc. I (1957), p. 221, no. 382.

The text reads:

]OMPEIO·CN·F̣[
]GNO·IMP·COS·TER[
]TRONO·PVBLICE·

[*Cn(aeo) P*]*ompeio Cn(aei) f(ilio)*[4] [*Ma*]*gno imp(eratori), co(n)s(uli) ter[t(ium)]* (or

37

ter(tium)?),[5] [*pa*]*trono, publice*. That is, To Gnaeus Pompeius the Great, son of Gnaeus, *imperator*, consul for the third time, patron (of Auximum), at public expense (i.e. an official dedication, perhaps of a bust or statue that surmounted the base).

The surface shows the ravages of time. The letter heights, as measured on a squeeze, are: line 1, 7–7·5 cm; line 2, 5·6–6 cm; line 3, *c.* 5 cm.

Punctuation: apparently planned as an equilateral triangle with base parallel to the line of writing and a point at the top, but none is well cut and all now are more nearly punched holes without clean edges or crisp definition; between all words and at the end of at least the last line. No letters are improperly made, but many are now damaged.

Arrangement: apparently progressive indentation, since the length of line 2 precludes centring. There are traces of guide-lines.

Lettering: the cutting was probably never quite clean or crisp, though weathering makes it hard to be certain (see, for example, the B in line 3). The verticals tend to slant right, many of them very much so. There seems to be no shading. Serifs are present, but they vary from large, definite ones (see, for example, the letter I, or the P and C in line 1) to very small, ill-defined finishing strokes (E horizontals, top of right vertical of N). Note the B in line 3, with a small serif at the top, and a large one at the bottom, of the vertical (the photograph does not do justice to the bottom one). Nor do the letters maintain a constant module (proportion of width to height); the O's, for example, range from one broader than tall to quite definite ovals. The angles of M are probably meant to be equal, but this plan failed in the first one. Note that the points of M are unserifed (so also of N, as to be expected); we have no A's to compare. C is serifed at top and bottom, E is narrow in lines 2 and 3, with equal bars; in line 1 the lowest bar seems to have been lengthened for some reason. R is squat and its bow takes up more than half the height; its diagonal appears to end in a serif on the right side only, but this serif was not cleanly cut. The T bar gave trouble: at the end of line 2 T and E run into each other, and the serifs of the single bar are not clear; in line 3 note the rounded join of the T vertical and bar, the left side now not being clear.

(3) Our third piece (Plate 8)[6] is a *tessera nummularia* of bone or ivory,[7] which was found in Rome in 1892 (so Babelon, no doubt from Froehner) and is now in the Cabinet des Médailles of the Bibliothèque Nationale, Paris. Publications: *CIL* I²: 2: 1, p. 568, no. 931; Babelon, *op. cit.* in footnote 7, p. 16, no. 17 (with life-size photograph of the first side—our line 1—only, Pl. II, fig. 19); Degrassi, *ILLRP*, fasc. 2, p. 275, no. 1049. Dimensions: 4·9 × 0·9 × 0·75 cm; writing fields (minus the knob) 4·2 × 0·9 cm (lines 1, 3) and 4·2 × 0·75 cm (lines 2, 4); slight varia-

tion according to place of measurement; writing fields are marked off by a single incised line at left and right; the knobs are flat on sides 1 and 3, cut back or shaped on sides 2 and 4, and are pierced from side 2 to side 4 for string or whatever was used to attach them to the bags of money that they served to verify. Material: we have been unable to ascertain whether bone or ivory.

The text:

PHILARGVRVS

ACONI

SP·PR · K·MAI

CN·POM·COS·TER

Philargurus Aconi (*servus*) *sp*(*ectavit*) *pr*(*idie*) *K*(*alendas*) *M*(*aias*) *Cn*(*aeo*) *Pom*(*peio*) *co*(*n*)*s*(*ule*) *ter*(*tium*). That is, Philargurus, slave of Aconius, verified (the bag to which this tag was attached) on the day before the Kalends of May (29 April), when Gnaeus Pompeius was consul for the third time.

There seems no planned shading, but we think that the verticals are mostly broader than the horizontals, and many of the lines a little wedge-shaped, being thicker towards the bottom. There are quite well-developed serifs. Apparently the curves gave trouble: witness the tops of C, G, P, R, the top and bottom of S; see also O. There is a fairly obvious irregularity in letter heights (2·5–3·5 mm), quite apart from K, which is intended to be tall[8] (it goes up to *c.* 4·5 mm), and O, which manages to be somewhat less tall than the letters on either side of it; it is also clearly meant to be a circle. The horizontals of E are of equal length, fairly long. Other notably broad letters are C, G, and L; H is rather markedly narrow. Also noteworthy (and characteristic of the period) are the unserifed points of A, M, N (the upper points of M and N), and V. The left vertical of N tends to be shorter than the right. The punctuation (sides 3 and 4) consists of a triangle, fairly equilateral, relatively large, and always with a flat side down and a point at the top. (Some imperfections and marks in the photograph are doubtless due to its being a photograph of a replica, not of the original.)

Comparison of the three pieces. Points in common: no careful contrast of thicks and thins, i.e. no true shading, though the *tessera* in particular and the marble from Rome to some extent have the verticals consistently a little broader than the horizontals. All have serifs, those of the *tessera* being the largest in proportion to the size of the writing; all lack serifs on the tops of the A, M, and N points (at least this seems to be the intention); all have serifs on the bottom curves of C and S, but not all of them of the same character. All have orthodox classical capital letter-shapes. Moreover, M has equal angles (or seems intended to have), O is circular, P has its second stroke open but curving back towards the vertical. The interpuncts in all are of the same type and orientation; they are all comparatively large and prominent. Differences: the Roman stone's broad, high-barred A, R with bow less than half letter-height, E with slightly shorter middle bar; the *tessera*'s N with second vertical a little taller and with what almost seems a serif at bottom right (cf. the central V of M also), its comparatively thicker and deeper strokes, short-looking O, flattening of curves: note how C looks like a 3-stroke letter. (The obviousness of some of this is no doubt due to our using an enlarged photograph of the replica.) Note also the heavier serifs of the E and T horizontals and the splayed serif at the bottom of the S's in lines 3 and 4 of the *tessera*.

The two stones show how satisfactory marble is as a material for letter cutting, how clean and uncluttered lettering with small serifs and practically no contrast in width of cutting may look, and how effective it can be if well arranged and of good proportions. The *tessera* seems to be more of a harbinger of things to come in stone, in the matter of heavier lettering with shadow and shading and prominent serifs. It may be the tiny size of the letters, the material used, and the engraving instruments that are responsible for all this, and only an accident that stone lettering progressed in that direction. This is not meant to suggest that such *tesserae* influenced stone cutting, but only that perhaps they were earlier in reflecting the influences that writing with a flexible instrument (a brush, for example) or a broad-nibbed pen would exert on lettering in other materials.

NOTES

1 Fr. Ritschl's *Priscae Latinitatis monumenta epigraphica*...(Berlin, 1862) contains no text or descriptions, but only facsimiles—lithographs—of Republican inscriptions; the *Corpus inscriptionum Latinarum*, vol. 1, ed. 2, contains a few, not very good, photographs; O. Gradenwitz's *Simulacra* (Tübingen, 1912), accompanying Bruns's *Fontes iuris Romani antiqui*, has fourteen good photographs, mostly of legal bronzes; we have detailed descriptions and photographs of a half dozen in the *Album of Dated Latin Inscriptions*, part 1 (Berkeley and Los Angeles, 1958); and the handbooks of Latin epigraphy have a few.

2 So we were informed by Sig. Perazzini at the Antiquario Comunale on the Celian, where we studied the stone on 13 March 1956 with the kind permission of Dr Carlo Pietrangeli, Inspector of the Musei Comunali, Rome.

3 See our *Contributions to the Palaeography of Latin Inscriptions* (Berkeley and Los Angeles, 1957, *Univ. Calif. Publ. Class. Archaeol.* III, 3), p. 184.

4 Previous editors do not record the interpunct after CN. or any trace of the following F, of which the bottom serif and about 1 cm of the upright became clear after the removal of some extraneous material (our photograph was taken before this, so still shows the material in the cuttings).

5 The question is whether TERT or only TER was cut. There is no concrete evidence extant of a second T, though there seems to be just room enough for it (with its bar short or perhaps running over—but note how the first T here and the T in line 3 join the following letter at the top). *Tert.* is much the commoner abbreviation of *tertium* and was read here by Mommsen in *CIL*, 1, ed. 1. But it may have been only TER, as in our third inscription, line 4, where space is very limited. That in either case it is an abbreviation with the meaning 'for the third time' (rather than the unabbreviated TER, 'three times') we are confident, but this is not the place to argue it

fully. In brief, we believe that the very brevity of the inscription—its omission of Pompey's other offices (propraetor, proconsul, etc.—see T. Robert S. Broughton, *The Magistrates of the Roman Republic*, vol. II [New York, 1952, *Philological Monographs publ. by the Amer. Philol. Ass. no.* xv, vol. II], p. 703, *s.v. Cn. Pompeius Cn. f. Sex. n. Magnus*)—clearly indicates that it is not a summary of his career, but a statement of his position in one particular year, 52. This must have been the view also of Ritschl and Mommsen (in *CIL*, 1, ed. 1), since they date the inscription in 52 (and Mommsen reads *TER*[*T* at the end of line 2); but Mommsen in *CIL*, 9 reads only *TER* (though on p. 759 of the indices he dates the inscr. in a single year, a.u.c. Varr. 701/a.C. 53, which must be a slip for 702/52, and 5836 a slip for 5837); so also Dessau and Lommatzsch; Degrassi too reads *TER*, but in his indices varies between 52 only and 70, 55, 52 for the year(s) (cf. pp. 420 and 466).

6 A photograph of the four inscribed sides of a plaster-of-Paris replica, kindly furnished by the Bibliothèque Nationale, Paris. Our photograph is enlarged to twice the size of the original *tessera*.

7 On these see R. Herzog, *Paulys Real-Encycl. der class. Altertumsw.*, Neue Bearb., vol. xvII, 2 (Stuttgart, 1937), col. 1415–56, *s.v. Nummularius*; for a succinct statement in English, M. Cary

The Journal of Roman Studies, xIII (London, 1923), pp. 110–13; for the latest ed. of those of Republican date, Degrassi, *ILLRP*, fasc. 2, pp. 255–78, nos. 987–1063; for four newly acquired ones of Imperial date, C. Pietrangeli, *Bull. della Commissione Archeol. del Governatorato di Roma*, vol. LXVIII, 1940 (Rome, 1941), pp. 200–2, nos. 3–6 (with drawings); for photographs of twenty-four in the Cabinet des Médailles in the Bibliothèque Nationale, Paris, see Plate 2 of *Aréthuse*, vol. v, 1, fasc. 18 (Paris, 1928), with the accompanying article by Jean Babelon, pp. 6–18. From a study of the photographs on this plate in particular, of a half dozen replicas in our possession, of the drawings in Pietrangeli's report, and of the earlier ones included in a study by Ritschl cited by Herzog and others, it is clear that the *tesserae*, most of which come from Rome, fall into groups not only according to the pattern of the text and the order of its presentation (see Herzog for this), but also according to the shape of the knobs and the character of the lettering, and that these attributes reflect the date of the *tesserae*. Tentatively, it seems allowable to conclude that probably there was in Rome a single supplier who used the same engraver for the bulk of the *tesserae* over a period of years, and then another engraver, and so on.

8 Cf. our *Contributions* (*op. cit.* above, note 3) p. 202.

F. WORMALD

A Fragment of a Tenth-Century English Gospel Lectionary

By now it is fully recognized that the second half of the tenth century was one of the outstanding periods in the history of English script and illumination. It was a period which influenced and was much admired by the late Edward Johnston and is, therefore, a fitting subject with which to honour Alfred Fairbank. The subject of this short contribution relates to a fragment of a manuscript which illustrates very clearly at least one of the Carolingian influences on the so-called Winchester School of illumination so closely associated with the monastic reforms in the second half of the tenth century. These Carolingian elements may be seen in the introduction of the Caroline minuscule not only in the more formal bookhands but in the documents as well. Illumination itself was changed by influences from a number of the Carolingian Schools. In the figure styles derivations from the Court School, the 'Metz' and later the 'Rheims' Schools are clear. For their initials the English artists drew inspiration from the native Anglo-Saxon ornament of the ninth century and from the continental manuscripts of the 'Metz' and the North French Carolingian Franco-Saxon Schools.[1] This Franco-Saxon influence is to be seen most clearly in some of the large initials ornamenting Gospel Books.[2] They are marked by a use of interlace finials with animal heads ultimately deriving from insular models, but which are more nearly Carolingian in type than properly insular.

College of Arms, Arundel MS. XXII, fols. 84–85ᵛ, is a fragment of a lectionary of the Gospels for use at the Mass.[3] Unlike the usual Gospel Books these lectionaries contain the portions of the Gospels divided up into their liturgical order. Though a number of them are found on the continent, they are extremely rare in English manuscripts and another example has not been found for the period under discussion. The contents of the fragments are as follows: fols. 84, 84ᵛ Lections for the Vigil of

Christmas, and for the midnight Mass; fols. 85, 85ᵛ, Lections for the Wednesday and Friday after the Epiphany.⁴ It will be at once evident from this that, although the leaves are conjoint they are not consecutive, a number of important masses intervening between the Christmas Vigil and the days after the Epiphany. It is possible, therefore, that they originally formed the outside pair of a gathering.

The fine initial which opens the fragment will be discussed later. The text, which occupies twenty-one lines, is written in a single column. The headings of each lection are written in golden uncials and at the opening letter of the lection is a large golden capital (Plate 9). From the plate reproduced it will be seen at once that the hand is a stately Caroline minuscule which closely resembles the type found in three English books of the second half of the tenth century: the Benedictional of St Æthelwold, now British Museum Add. MS. 49598; a Benedictional in Paris, Bibliothèque Nationale fonds latin 987, fols. 1–84; and the magnificent Psalter, probably written at Winchester, now British Museum, Harley MS. 2904.⁵ The charter of King Edgar to the New Minster, Winchester, British Museum, Cotton MS. Vespasian A. VIII, is also written in a Caroline minuscule which bears a certain resemblance to these hands. On the whole, the script of the College of Arms fragment seems to be nearest to the hand of the Paris Benedictional, though some letters are closer to the other manuscripts. None of these manuscripts is precisely dated, though the Benedictional of St Æthelwold must have been written before the saint's death in 984, and the New Minster Charter is probably not later than Edgar's death in 975. The date of the fragment is, therefore, probably early in the last quarter of the tenth century.

By far its most splendid feature is the large initial page with which the lection for the Mass *in vigilia* opens (Plate 10). It consists of a large initial I with the opening words of the passage written in golden capitals and uncials. The whole is surrounded by a border of typical 'Winchester' acanthus framed in gold with corner bosses of acanthus leaves. In the middle of each side is an ornament composed of interlace ending with beasts' heads in the insular manner. The large initial is constructed in a rather similar way with interlace, beasts' heads and acanthus. In colour the composition is richer than the Benedictional of St Æthelwold. What is most striking is the way in which the acanthus ornament is strictly confined within the golden framework which surrounds it. This is very unlike other English illuminated manuscripts of the period, where this element usually breaks loose from its frame and climbs about and over it, using it much as a climbing plant uses a trellis. The interlace with beasts' heads in the middle of each border is also not found in other contemporary English illuminations. The effect of the whole is in fact a good deal more restrained than is usual.⁶

et spm tanquam columbam descen
dente & manente sup eum · Et uox
facta est de caelis · tu es filius meus di
lectus · in te complacui · FER · UI ·
Seq̄ sc̄a euc̄ sc̄o IOHANNE ᵢ.₁₉.
In illo tempr̄ · Uidit iohannes ih̄m
ueniente ad se · & ait · Ecce agnus di ·
qui tollit peccati mundi · Hic est
de quo dixi · Post me uenit uir qui
ante me factus est quia prior me erat ·
& ego nesciebam eu · Sed ut manifeste
tur in irl̄ael · propterea ueni ego in
aqua baptizans · Et testimonium
perhibuit iohannes dicens · Quia
uidi spm descendentem quasi columbā
de caelo & mansit sup eum · & ego
nesciebam eu · Sed qui misit me bap
tizare in aqua · ille mihi dixit · Sup
quem uideris spm descendente & ma
nentem sup eu · hic est qui baptizat
in spū sc̄o · Et ego uidi & testimoniū

caꝑ · x

9. From a fragment of tenth-century English Gospel Lectionary: see p. 44. (Reduced)
College of Arms, London (Arundel MSS. XXII, fol. 85ᵛ)

10. Initial page from same Lectionary (fol. 84): see p. 44. (Reduced)

It is clear that the most influential style in this decoration is that of the Northern French group of illuminations, which go under the name of the Franco-Saxon school. All of the decorative elements in the College of Arms fragment are to be found in manuscripts with this style of illumination, though no single book contains all of them together. The border composed of conventional leaves is to be seen in such manuscripts as the Sacramentary from Corbie, called the Missal of St Eloi now in the Bibliothèque Nationale in Paris,[7] though the English version is rather freer and has conventional frames, resembling borders of other Carolingian Schools.[8] The practice of placing roundels at the corners of the rectangular frame is found in a number of Franco-Saxon books, such as the Gospel Book in Leiden and a Gospel Book in the Chester Beatty Collection,[9] and the interlaces ending in creatures' heads recall ornaments found in the Second Bible of Charles the Bald.[10] This Franco-Saxon influence is fairly frequently found in English initials of this period, but our fragment is one of the closest followers of its Carolingian model. An even closer English copy of a Carolingian original is to be found in a later tenth-century Psalter from St Augustine's, Canterbury, now MS. 411 in the library of Corpus Christi College, Cambridge.[11] Here the artist has copied his original most faithfully, so closely in fact as to lead Dr M. R. James to give the book a continental origin. Both the script and certain of the contents preclude this.[12]

It is not possible or prudent to suggest where this fragment was made. The script has been shown to be related to manuscripts which may come from either Winchester or Canterbury, and it is known from Corpus Christi 411 that the copying of Franco-Saxon models was practised at Canterbury. The situation is not made any easier by the close relationship established between the various ecclesiastical centres at this time. The very existence of such a document as the *Regularis Concordia* with its application to all the English abbeys makes any attempt to attribute certain manuscripts to certain localities a dangerous business. It is perhaps wisest to say South England and leave it at that. On the other hand, this is a fragment of a noble book which displays most clearly the debt that the late Anglo-Saxons owed to the Carolingian scribes and illuminators.

I wish to express my warmest thanks to Garter Principal King of Arms and the Chapter of the College of Arms for their kind permission to publish this fragment.

NOTES

1 See F. Wormald, 'Decorated Initials in English MSS. from A.D. 900–1100', *Archaeologia*, XCI (1945), 107–111.

2 E.g. British Museum, Add. MS. 34890, fol. 11, see T. D. Kendrick, *Late Saxon and Viking Art* (1949), pl. VI.

3 College of Arms, London, *Heralds Commemorative Exhibition, 1484–1934, Enlarged and Illustrated Catalogue* (1936), no. 32, pp. 48, 49. For further information on the MS., see *The Seege or Batayle of Troye*, ed. Mary E. Barnicle, E.E.T.S. 172 (1927), pp. xvii, xviii.

4 Matth. I, 18–21; in vigilia media nocte, Luc. II, 1–4, the lection is incomplete; Feria IV post Theophaniam, Marc. I, 4–11; Feria VI post Theophaniam, John I, 29–34.

5 For British Museum, Add. MS. 49598 (Benedictional of St Æthelwold), see Palaeographical Society, *Facsimiles of Ancient MSS., etc.*, First Series, pl. 142; for Paris lat. 987, see New Palaeographical Society, *Facsimiles of Ancient MSS., etc.*, pl. 83. A small piece of the script of British Museum, Harley MS. 2904 is reproduced by Charles Niver in *Mediaeval Studies in Memory of A. Kingsley Porter*, p. 673, fig. 2.

6 Cf. the New Minster Charter, British Museum, Cotton MS. Vespasian A. VIII, fol. 2b and British Museum, Royal MS. ID.IX, fol. 70, both reproduced in British Museum, *Reproductions from Illuminated Manuscripts*, series I (1910), pls. IV, VI.

7 Bibliothèque Nationale, lat. 12051, see A. Boinet *La Miniature Carolingienne* (1913), pl. CXI.

8 Cf. Bible of St Paul without the Walls, Boinet, *op. cit.* pl. CXXVII A.

9 Leiden University MS. 48, see Boinet, *op. cit.* pl. CVIII A, B; E. G. Millar, *The Library of A. Chester Beatty, A Descriptive Catalogue of the Western Manuscripts*, I, pls. XXIII, XXV.

10 Bibliothèque Nationale, lat. 2, see Bibliothèque Nationale, *Peintures et Initiales de la Seconde Bible de Charles le Chauve*, pl. 36.

11 See F. Wormald, 'Late Anglo-Saxon Art: some Questions and Suggestions', in *Studies in Western Art, Acts of the Twentieth International Congress of the History of Art* (New York, 1961), I, 20, fig. I.

12 The piece of evidence which clearly confirms the English origin of Corpus Christi MS. 411 is the prayer *ad omnes confessores* on fol. 138b where both Saints Gregory and Augustine (of Canterbury) are mentioned together; see M. R. James, *A Descriptive Catalogue of the Manuscripts in the Library of Corpus Christi College Cambridge* (1912), II, 298.

B. L. ULLMAN

More Humanistic Manuscripts

Alfred Fairbank's great interest and expertness in humanistic handwriting of the fifteenth century leads me to make some additions to the list of manuscripts written by notable scribes of that century.[1] Some of these additions, indeed, have been identified by Mr Fairbank, who was so kind as to pass his discoveries on to me. The scribes are:

POGGIO

In a revision of my *Studies in the Italian Renaissance*, which is now in press, I very tentatively add four manuscripts to the Poggio list:

Florence, Laur. S. Marc. 230 (Plautus, first eight plays); 262 (Cicero, *De oratore*); 643 (Augustine, *De libero arbitrio, Soliloquia, De immortalitate animae, De vera religione*); 665 (Augustine, *Contra academicos, De ordine, De trinitate*).

The last three came from the library of Niccolò Niccoli, and the first may have come from the same source. Niccoli died in 1437. All are unsigned. Only script and orthography can determine whether Poggio wrote them. I am far from claiming that these are Poggio's, as I have not had the time to study them.

In a forthcoming number of *Scriptorium*, Professor A. S. Dunston will challenge my attribution to Poggio of Vat. lat. 1843, 1849, 1852, and Laur. 49, 24. Professor Dunston's great courtesy in sending me a copy of his article in manuscript form has made it possible for me to defend my position in the same issue.

Dr Helmut Boese has suggested to me that Deutsche Staatsbibliothek, East Berlin, Ham. 125 may have been copied by Poggio. This manuscript contains Caesar's *Gallic War* and the *Civil War*, as well as the *Alexandrine*, *African*, and *Spanish* wars attributed to Caesar. I am inclined to think that Poggio copied this manuscript, perhaps early in his career, but I reserve detailed discussion for another occasion (Plate 11).

Florence, Ricc. 551; *Scriptores Historiae Augustae*. E. Hohl, in *Klio*, XIII (1913), 279, n. 2, says that this manuscript was copied by Poggio. It certainly looks like it. But it may have been done by the French scribe whom, as Poggio says in 1426, he had taught to write 'litteris antiquis' and was then at work on Spartianus, i.e. *Historia Augusta* (*Humanistic Script*, p. 87).

British Museum, Add. 21520 contains an autograph letter of Poggio's dated 14 June 1455.

Among the books once owned by Poggio is Vat. Ross. 81, Priscian, *c.* 1100. On fol. 212ᵛ: 'Liber...Borromei, quem Dominicus Brasichillensis...emit a Poggio Florentino secretario XII ducatis MCCCCLIIII.'²

EARLY FIFTEENTH CENTURY

After my book was published, I stumbled upon some notes I had made about 1933 and entirely forgotten. They showed that I had become interested in the origin of humanistic script much earlier than I thought. These notes deal with a manuscript of Giovanni Dominici's *Lucula noctis*, now in the University of Chicago Library.³ The work was composed and copied in Florence in 1405. The text is written in Gothic, but the technical corrector, or proof reader, regularly used the straight *d* and the long final *s* of humanistic script. This shows that Poggio's new script took root immediately in Florence, no doubt through Coluccio's influence and encouragement, and explains why it flourished there even after Poggio left for Rome in 1403. The work was dedicated to Coluccio, and this is the dedication copy. Coluccio started to answer Dominici's points in a very long letter but died on 4 May 1406 before he could finish it.

Another early manuscript with humanistic traits is Laur. 36, 3; Ovid, *Met.*, copied 2 August 1406. It has tall interior *s*, round final *s*, 'dumbbell' *g* (two rings connected by a vertical line), straight *d*, the spellings *mihi*, *coelum*, etc.

GIOVANNI ARETINO

Oxford, D'Orville 78 (S.C. 16956); Cicero, eight orations. They are the speeches discovered by Poggio in France and Germany. The manuscript is not signed or dated, but the scribe was identified by Dr R. W. Hunt, with whom I am in complete agreement, as is Mr Fairbank.⁴ A. C. Clark had selected four manuscripts as closest to the then-missing copy made by Poggio.⁵ This missing archetype has now been discovered by A. Campana; it is Vat. lat. 11458. One of Clark's four manuscripts is Laur. Conv. Soppr. 13. I called attention to the similarity of the colophons in this manuscript to those in the newly discovered Poggio manuscript and suggested that the former was a copy of the latter (*Humanistic Script*, p. 49, n. 48). Clark's view was thus confirmed. Another of Clark's four is the Oxford codex. A comparison should be made of the text of the Vatican manuscript with that of the four manuscripts listed by Clark. The close relation between the Oxford and Vatican manuscripts furnishes a welcome indication of a connection between Giovanni and Poggio. As Poggio sent his manuscript to Niccoli, it was probably the latter who had Giovanni copy it.

The Oxford manuscript once belonged to Cosimo de' Medici, as did several other of Giovanni's productions. My guess is that Niccoli arranged to have Giovanni copy it for Cosimo, just as he hired Antonio di Mario for the same purpose (*Humanistic Script*, p. 106).

GIACOMO CURLO

The known output of this master is so small that additions are particularly welcome. Thanks to Professor P. O. Kristeller another can be added.[6]

Toledo, Biblioteca Provincial 222; Lactantius, *Divinae Institutiones*. The colophon reads (fol. 185^v): 'Ex omnibus Cambi Zambeccarie, vir optime atque clarissime,[7] voluminibus quos[8] umquam me transcripsisse meminerim, hic tuus codex satis tuae nature tuisque sanctissimis moribus conferens, ut opinor, septimus est quem feliciter absolvi XV kl. Iunii MCCCCXXVIII, circiter horam praeconizatae[9] et celebratae pacis Italicae inter Insubrum ducem et dominium Venetorum. Ita felix faustumque sit. Tuus Iacobus Curulus Ianuensis.' This colophon is of great interest from several points of view. It adds one more to the list of five existing manuscripts of Curlo. He lived in the formative period of humanistic script and was a contemporary of Giovanni Aretino. This manuscript is specified by Curlo as the seventh that he copied. Dated in 1428, it would be third in my list, which means that four manuscripts copied earlier have been lost and suggests that Curlo copied a fair number. The manuscript passed to, and perhaps was written for, Antonio Panormita; for below the colophon is the entry (in a different hand): 'Antonii Panhormitae est.' Who is the person addressed in the colophon if not Panormita? But there are other connections between Curlo and Panormita. It is perhaps just a coincidence that one of Curlo's lost manuscripts contained a work of Panormita (*Humanistic Script*, p. 97). A letter written to Panormita by Curlo indicates that Curlo, though very busy, has not interrupted the copying of Panormita's work, and hopes to finish it that week; this was in 1455.[10] In 1445 Facio writes to Curlo about Panormita's postponement of a trip to Palermo, and in 1449 Aurispa sends regards to Curlo by Panormita.[11]

The colophon of the Toledo manuscript says that it was copied from an old codex belonging to Cambio Zambeccari. This man was a collector of manuscripts who

B. L. Ullman

lived in Milan from 1426 on.[12] A letter of Domenico Feruffino, written to Panormita in 1430, says: 'maximus Cambius (Zambeccari) noster, qui pro eius ferventissimo in te amore vult sibi omnia Panhormitana negotia vendicare'.[13] The two men exchanged letters.[14]

The Toledo manuscript fills a gap in Curlo's life. The last known volume copied in Florence was made in 1425. Soon after he must have gone to Milan, where he produced the Toledo codex in 1428. In that same year he planned to go to Cyprus to live.[15] Then we hear no more until 1441, when Curlo went to the Queen of Jerusalem and Sicily as ambassador of the Doge of Venice. In 1445 he was *scriptor* of the King of Naples, in 1446 he was legate of Genoa to Florence, in 1448 and 1450 he was in Milan, in 1451 in Naples, then back to Genoa. He transcribed manuscripts in Naples from 1455 to 1459. In 1461 he wrote a poem commemorating a Genoese victory over the French. That is the last we hear of him; he must have died soon after.

Still another Curlo manuscript was unearthed by Ruysschaert:[16] Vat. lat. 11463; Livy 21–30, parchment, fol. 429: 'Manu Iacobi Curli ut mos gereretur clarissimo et litterarum studiosissimo Antoniotto Grillo summa et singulari amicicia coniuncto.' This Grillo was a correspondent of Panormita.[17]

The Syracuse manuscript copied by Curlo is now in the Biblioteca Alagoniana (No. 7), according to Kristeller.

On the Liverpool manuscript of Curlo's epitome of Donatus' commentary on Terence (one of six known to Kristeller), the latter said that a photostat of the first page 'seems to suggest that this manuscript might very well have been written by Curlo himself'. On examining the photostat, which Professor Kristeller kindly lent me, I concluded that it definitely was not copied by Curlo. He perhaps transcribed the dedication copy of his book, now lost, of which we have a good description (De Marinis, *La biblioteca napoletana dei re d'Aragona*, II, 57).

Ruysschaert quotes Ross as saying that Vat. lat. 5268 was copied by Curlo.[18] But Ross says nothing about the handwriting, merely noting that Curlo assisted Facio in revising Vergerio's translation of Arrian (not Appian). The book belonged to King Matthias Corvinus of Hungary. We have a letter of Taddeo Ugoleto, who bought manuscripts for Corvinus in Italy, saying that he was sending the Arrian (which he had arranged to be copied) to Budapest. Ross says that Ugoleto went to Italy in 1487. The manuscript must have been written between that date and 1490, when Corvinus died. Curlo died about 1461, over twenty-five years before the Arrian was copied.

GHERARDO DEL CIRIAGIO

The Virgil manuscript belonging to Lady Christian Martin (my number 9, p. 113),

50

which I was unable to see, was sold at auction by Christie in 1962. Later in that year it was offered for sale in catalogue 11 of Alan G. Thomas of Bournemouth, who, as he kindly informed me, sold it to the Bibliothèque Royale, Brussels. 'Scriptus autem fuit per me Gherardum Iohannis del Ciriagio civem et notarium Florentinum de anno domini millesimo quadringentesimo quinquagesimo quinto de mense Iunii in magnifica civitate Florentina tempore sanctissimi in Christo patris et domini domini Kalisti divina providentia papae tertii pontificatus sui anno primo.'

Vat. Reg. Lat. 1404; *Terence*, is added to the Gherardo manuscripts by Ruysschaert but he supplies no details.

ANTONIO DI MARIO

Oxford, New College 249. Albinia de la Mare says that fols. 1–91 of this manuscript were 'almost certainly copied by Antonio'. She mentions a monogram A. M. on fol. 66.[19]

ANTONIO SINIBALDI

Florence, Naz. Panc. 126, fols. 1–9, parchment; Piero de' Medici, translation from the Greek of Leonardo Bruni, *De Florentinorum republica*. Dedication copy to Piero's father Lorenzo, 1484. 'Medici Laurentii ac ornatissimi et doctissimi Petri perpetuus servitor Antonius Sinibaldus scripsit.' G. Pesenti, in *Atene e Roma*, New Series, XII (1931), 92–3. This is the only manuscript in which Sinibaldi mentions the Medici, for whom he seems to have made at least eight manuscripts (*Humanistic Script*, p. 119).

Dr Helmut Boese kindly called my attention to a manuscript of Sinibaldi in the Deutsche Staatsbibliothek, East Berlin, Ham. 482. A microfilm shows that it contains Francesco Patrizi, *Poematum libri IV*, addressed to Pius II. At the end (fol. 92ᵛ): 'A.S. scripsit anno Domini MCCCCLXI XI kal. Octobris.' This could be the earliest Sinibaldi in existence, as the other one written in 1461 does not give the month.

Mr Fairbank discovered from a plate in De Marinis[20] that an unsigned *Valerius Maximus* in the New York Public Library was copied by Sinibaldi, except that the chapter headings were done by Bartolomeo San Vito. I can confirm the identification after examining the manuscript. Fairbank has found other manuscripts in which San Vito wrote only the headings [see e.g. *Journal of the Society for Italic Handwriting*, 42 (1965): EDITOR].

Florence, Naz. Magl. XXX, 239; Dante, *De monarchia*. This is mentioned by Kristeller, but, as he has neither seen it nor given further details, this manuscript must remain doubtful until it is studied.

An eighteenth-century owner of Laur. Acq. e Doni 152; Petrarch's *Trionfi* and *Canzoniere*, asserted on the title page that Sinibaldi copied it in 1406. The manuscript is not dated or signed by Sinibaldi nor was it copied by him. He was born in 1443.

Ruysschaert refers to De Marinis, II, 157, for a *Tertullian* in Leiden (B.P.L. 2) sometimes attributed to Sinibaldi, but De Marinis does not mention that scribe here. Keil and others attributed the writing to Antonio di Mario.

PIETRO CENNINI

Cennini was not one of the great scribes, but I included some examples of his hand to illustrate the cursive script on its way to becoming Italic. The seventeen volumes I listed seemed sufficient to give a fair idea of his script. Perhaps, however, I should have furnished more than two illustrations of his writing, for it varies a great deal and is hard to pin down.

A number of additional manuscripts have turned up. José Ruysschaert in particular has listed several.[21] His earliest is the Cesena *Martial* (1463), which I placed second to the Paris *Servius* (1462), unknown to him.

New manuscripts are:

(*a*) Florence, Naz. Magl. II, IX, 14; Miscellany. 6 January 1466 (Florentine dating, i.e. 1467); 30 August 1473; 11 May 1474; 1 March 1475. For full description, see G. Mazzatinti and A. Sorbelli, *Inventari dei Manoscritti delle Biblioteche d'Italia*, XI (Forlì, 1901), 258.

(*b*) Ruysschaert also identified my No. 7 (p. 124), which I was unable to locate in the Vatican, as Vat. Pal. lat. 1587; Sidonius, *Paneg.*; Serenus, *Liber medicinalis*; Benedictus Crispus. The date is 20 October 1468 (not 1469). Ruysschaert has a plate of fol. 101ᵛ.

(*c*) Laur. 34, 34; *Juvenal, Persius, Lactantius*. No date. Parchment.

(*d*) My No. 6, *Suetonius*, is now in the Archivio di Stato, Milan, Papadopoli collection.

In his review of *Humanistic Script* Ruysschaert adds:

(*e*) Florence, Naz. Magl. 28, 51. Miscellany. 1464.

(*f*) Florence, Ricc. N. II, n. XXIX. *Scholia in Vergilium*. 1468.

Klara Csapodi-Gárdonyi adds the following:[22]

(*g*) Györ, Bibliothèque du séminaire épiscopal, 1, 1; Flavio Biondo, *Roma instaurata*, 'Excriptus Florentiae VI. Idus Iulias MCCCCLXVII.' Fig. 7 in Berkovits.[23]

(*h*) Budapest, National Library, Cod. lat. 13; *Suetonius*. Before 1470. Unsigned; therefore doubtful.

(*i*) Vienna, lat. 133; *Appian*, translated by P. Candido. 1460–70. Unsigned; therefore doubtful.

(*j*) Budapest, National Museum, 427; *Asconius*. 1460–90. Unsigned; therefore doubtful, but pl. XIV in Berkovits (see n. 23) seems to support the identification.

(*k*) Budapest, National Museum, 426; Basil, *Homiliae*. Before 1472. Unsigned; therefore doubtful. Fig. 29 in Berkovits[23] definitely opposes the identification.

Ilona Berkovits adds:[23]

(*l*) Budapest, National Széchényi Library Clmae 415; Basil, *De divinitate filii et spiritus sancti*. Parchment. Pl. XIII seems to indicate that the identification is correct.

I add:

(*m*) London, British Museum, Harl. 4868; *Vita* of Pliny the Elder; *De duobus Pliniis*; *De viris illustribus*; Pliny, *Epistulae*. Parchment. 15 May 1467.

A manuscript of 1464 that has disappeared contained Benedetto Accolti, *De bello a Christianis contra barbaros gesto*. It was in the Libreria Rosselli-Del Turco in 1759.[24]

L. F. Casson thinks that a manuscript of Landino's *Xandra* in the South African Library, Cape Town (MS. Grey 3 c 12) was copied by Cennini.[25] The first of two plates (fol. 1ʳ) seems to me to show a script quite unlike Cennini's. The second (fol. 35ᵛ) comes closer to his script, but I do not think it is his.

NOTES

1 I.e. additions to the lists I gave in my *Origin and Development of Humanistic Script* (Rome, 1960).
2 H. Tietze, *Die illuminierte Handschriften der Rossiana* (Leipzig, 1911), p. 56 (from Ruysschaert's review of my book in *Scriptorium*, xv, 1961, 213). Through a misprint he gives the date as MCCCLIIII.
3 See B. L. Ullman, *Studies in the Italian Renaissance* (Rome, 1955), p. 257.
4 R. W. Hunt, in *The Journal of the Society for Italic Handwriting*, xxxvii (1963), 6, with a photograph (reprinted in present volume, pp. 272 et seq.).
5 *Inventa Italorum* in *Anecdota Oxoniensia*, xi (1909), 10.
6 In his review of my book in *Manuscripta*, v (1961), 35.
7 I expand thus Kristeller's *v. optime atque cl.*
8 If this is the scribe's error for *quae*, it suggests that the colophon is not Curlo's but was copied from his. Thus the attribution to Curlo is doubtful.
9 'proclaimed.'
10 T. De Marinis, *La biblioteca napoletana dei Re d'Aragona*, i (Milan, 1952), 14; G. Resta, *L'Epistolario del Panormita* (Messina, 1954), p. 176.
11 R. Sabbadini, *Carteggio di Giovanni Aurispa* (Rome, 1931), pp. 108, 120.
12 R. Sabbadini, *Carteggio*, p. 61, n. 1.
13 R. Sabbadini, *Epistolario di Guarino Veronese*, iii (Venice, 1919), 277.
14 L. Barozzi and R. Sabbadini, *Studi sul Panormita e sul Valla* (Florence, 1891), pp. 4, 36. A large number of letters by Panormita to Zambeccari are printed in R. Sabbadini, *Ottanta lettere inedite del Panormita* (Catania, 1910). A long letter of Lamola to Guarino praises Cambio and mentions his devotion to Lactantius (R. Sabbadini, *Epistolario di Guarino*, i, 636), when the Toledo manuscript was copied.
15 T. De Marinis, *op. cit.* i, 13.
16 Described by him in his catalogue of *Codices Vaticani Latini 11414–11709* (1959), p. 100. This was not available to me when I wrote my book.
17 Resta, *op. cit.* p. 197.
18 J. Ruysschaert, *op. cit.* p. 213; D. J. A. Ross in *Scriptorium*, xi (1957), 104.
19 See too Hunt, *op. cit.* p. 274 and n. 5.
20 *Op. cit.* ii, 166 and pl. 248.
21 'Dix-huit manuscrits copiés par le florentin Pietro Cennini', *La Bibliofilia*, lix (1957; appeared in 1959), 108. This had not arrived when I was writing my book. Only the first items come from his article; the next are taken from his review of my book.
22 'Les Scripteurs de la Bibliothèque du Roi Mathias', in *Scriptorium*, xvii (1963), 25. This is apparently a translation of a Hungarian article in *Magyar Könyv-Szemle* (1958), p. 328.
23 Ilona Berkovits, *Illuminated Manuscripts from the Library of Matthias Corvinus* (Budapest, 1964).
24 Carlo Frati in a review of C. Marchesi, *Bibliofilia*, xiii (1912), 271.
25 *Studies in the Renaissance*, x (1963), 44.

multitudine: uno tempore pgressus hauddita longe a cesaris castris con
stitit in campo. Quib. reb. cognitis cesar ubr milites q extra munitione
minitarum modeste pcellerant. qq pabulandi lignandiq aut etia mu
nrendi gratia uallem peterant. qq ad eius rei opus erant omnes intra
munitiones minitarum modesteq sine tumultu ac timore se recipere
atq in ope consistere · Equitib. autem q in statione fuerant precipit ut
usq eo locum obtinerent in quo paulo ante constitissent · donec ab ho
ste telum missum ad se puenirat · quod si ppius accederet q honestissie
se intra munitiones reciperet · Alii qq equitatu edicit uti suo quisq loco
paratus armatusq presto essa · Ad hec non ipse pse coram eu de uallo
pspeculauret sed mirabili pritus scientia bellandi in pretorio sedens p
speculatores et nuntios imperabat qd fieri uolebat. Animaduertebat eni
qq magnis essent copiis aduersariu freti tam sepe a se fugatis pulsisq
territisq et concessam uitam et ignota peccata: quib. reb. nunq tanta
suppeteret ex ipsou mentis conscientiaq animi uictorie fiducia ut ea
tra sua aderiri auderent · pterea ipsius nom auctoritasq magna ex
parte eou exercitus minuebat iudicia · tu egregie munitiones castro
ru atq ualli fossiaq altitudo et extra uallu stili cecis mirabilem in mo
dum consita · que sine defensorib. aditum aduersariu phibebant · scor
pionum catapultau coeterou q telou que ad defendendum solent para
ri magnam copiam habebat · atq hec ppter exercitus sui presentis pau
citatem et tyrocinium preparauerat: non hostium ui et metu comotus.
sapienter se timiduq hostium opinioni prebebat · Neq idcirco copias qq
erant pauce tyrouniq non educebat in aciem quia uictorie sue diffi
deret: sed referre arbitrabat cuiusmodi uictoria essa futura · Turpe eni

11. From a MS. of Caesar's Gallic etc. Wars: written probably by Poggio: see p. 47.
Deutsche Staatsbibliotek, East Berlin (Hamilton 125)

[To face p. 54]

seruilia erunt cum de sabbato dicatur. Omne opus seruile non facietis.
Propter quod & per ezechielem prophetam dicitur. Et sabbatum mea de
di eis in signum inter me & eos ut sciant quia ego dominus qui sanctifi
co eos. Hoc perfecte tunc sciemus quando perfecte uacabimus & perfecte
uidebimus quia ipse est deus. Ipse etiam numerus etatum uelut dierum
si secundum eos articulos temporis computetur qui in scripturis uidentur
expressi. iste sabbatismus euidentius apparebit. qm septimus inuenitur. ut
prima etas tanq primus dies sit ab adam usq ad diluuium secunda inde usq
ad abraham. non equalitate temporum. sed numero generationum. Denas
quippe habere reperiuntur. Hinc etiam sicut matheus euangelista deter
minat tres etates usq ad xpi subsecuntur aduentum. que singule denis &
quaternis generationibus explicantur. Ab abraham usq ad dauid una. al
tera inde usq ad transmigrationem in babiloniam. tertia inde usq ad xpi
carnalem natiuitatem. fiunt itaq omnes quinq. Sexta nunc agitur nul
lo generationum numero metienda. propter id quod dictum est. Non e
uestrum scire tempora. que pater posuit in sua potestate. Post hanc tanq
in die septimo requiescet deus. cum eundem diem septimum quod nos
erimus in se ipso deo faciet requiescere. De istis porro etatibus singulis nunc
diligenter longum est disputare. hec tamen septima erit sabbatum nostru
cuius finis non erit uespera. sed dominicus dies uelut octauus eternus q
xpi resurrectione sacratus est. eternam non solum spiritus uerum etia
corporis requiem prefigurans. Ibi uacabimus & uidebimus. uidebimus &
amabimus. amabimus & laudabimus. Ecce quod erit in fine sine fine.
Nam quis alius noster est finis nisi peruenire ad regnum. cuius nullus e
finis? Videor michi debitum ingentis huius operis adiuuante domino
reddidisse. Quibus parum uel quibus nimium est michi ignoscant. qui
bus aut satis est non michi sed deo mecum gratias congratulantes
agant.

EXPLICIT LIBER VIGESIMVS SECVNDVS ET VLTIMVS BEA
TI AVGVSTINI DE CIVITATE DEI. DEO GRATIAS.

PETRVS STROZA ABSOLVIT FLORENTIE DIE SEPTIMO MEN
SIS DECEMBRIS. MCCCCXLIIJ.

12. From a MS. of St Augustine, *De Civitate Dei*, written by Piero Strozzi (1443): see p. 59. (Reduced)
Vatican Library (MS. Vat. Ottob. Lat. 113, fol. 332)

[To face p. 55]

ALBINIA DE LA MARE

Messer Piero Strozzi, a Florentine Priest and Scribe

Students of the development of humanistic script in the fifteenth century[1] have up till now largely concentrated their attention on scribes who were in the habit of signing and dating their manuscripts. This is an understandable and desirable way in which to provide a chronological framework for studying the development of the script, but other important scribes may be overlooked because of it. Even scribes who have been studied in detail did not sign all the manuscripts that they copied, and others who were equally skilled preferred to remain anonymous, or signed only a minute proportion of the manuscripts that they wrote. One such is the Florentine, Piero Strozzi. In an unpublished life of Piero's father Benedetto di Pieraccione Strozzi, Vespasiano da Bisticci, the fifteenth-century Florentine bookseller, called Piero 'il più bello scriptore abbi avuto questa età et il più emendato' ('the most beautiful scribe of the day and the most accurate').[2] Vespasiano had employed some of the best scribes of his day, and if his opinion had been known, Piero, who has received some attention, notably from Tammaro de Marinis,[3] would surely have attracted a fuller study before now.

I became interested in Piero when I discovered that he was the 'Messer Piero' who, in 1458, was copying the last volume of the *Livy* that Vespasiano was producing for Piero de' Medici.[4] It turned out in the end that Piero's relations with Vespasiano were better documented than those of any other scribe, and, when I had become familiar with his hand, I found that he had copied many manuscripts which probably came from Vespasiano's shop. In my view he is quite as skilled and consistent a scribe as his much-admired contemporary, Gherardo del Ciriagio, who also had links with Vespasiano. Piero's style of writing, in the tradition of Giovanni Aretino, probably influenced later Florentine scribes such as Antonio Sinibaldi, as well as Giovanmarco

Cinico ('Velox') of Parma, who claimed Piero as his master. In the colophons of several of the manuscripts that he copied, Giovanmarco calls himself 'Petri Strozae Florentini discipulus'.[5]

Piero was born in about 1416[6] and grew up in surroundings propitious for his career as a scribe. His father Benedetto di Pieraccione Strozzi (1387–1457),[7] a distant relative of Palla Strozzi, was a close friend of some of the most famous Florentine humanists and book collectors, especially of Leonardo Bruni and Giannozzo Manetti, but also of Fra Ambrogio Traversari and Niccolò Niccoli. He copied a great many books for himself 'to spend his time profitably'. They included not only works by sacred and classical authors (especially Cicero, and historians and oratorical writers) and many by his humanist contemporaries (Bruni, Traversari, Leonardo Giustiniani and Francesco Barbaro), but also works on music (he was a skilled musician), arithmetic and geometry. Benedetto was a very careful copyist, and Leonardo Bruni always wanted him to make the first copy of any of his works. He was also very scrupulous in his choice of exemplars, with the result that his copies were themselves much in demand as exemplars among the discerning.[8] Benedetto, Vespasiano says, suffered from very heavy taxes (this was probably punitive taxation imposed after his relative Palla Strozzi had been exiled in 1434) and thus, to supplement his income, he occasionally copied for payment, for his friends, 'so as not to be a burden on anyone'.[9] Palla Strozzi owned several books copied by Benedetto, which are listed in his will (1462).[10] It is unfortunate that none of the manuscripts which he copied has so far been identified. However, we do know of two manuscripts copied for him in Florence in the early days of humanistic script. One is a *Suetonius*, whose present whereabouts is unknown to me, transcribed for him in 1419 by a Milanese notary, who had settled in Florence, Ambrosius Jacopi de Marudis.[11] In the previous year the same scribe had copied a *Cicero* for Matteo di Simone Strozzi.[12] The second is MS. Florence Laur. 49, 6, Cicero's *Epistolae ad Familiares* copied in 1420 by the famous scribe Antonio di Mario, who ended: 'Tibi Benedicto Strozo salutes plurimas. Lege feliciter, meique sis memor.'[13] This manuscript later came into the possession of Cosimo de' Medici.[14]

Piero, like his father and most or all of the best scribes of his day in Florence, although he copied for payment, did not become a scribe by profession. In 1445 he was studying at Bologna[15] when a friend urged him to take holy orders. He was willing to do so, if he could find a benefice, and wrote on 18 April to Giovanni di Cosimo de' Medici, who was then in Rome, asking to be recommended if a suitable benefice fell vacant.[16] Vespasiano claims that it was he who at last secured a benefice for Piero: he says that he recommended Piero for a living when he visited the newly

13. From a MS. of Livy, *Decades IV*, written by Piero Strozzi (1458): see p. 57. (Reduced)
Biblioteca Laurenziana, Florence (Laur. 63, 12, fol. 1)

To face p. 56]

filiuſ coniuratione aduerſuſ ceſarem facta bellum moliens oppreſſuſ ⁊
occiſuſ eſt. Liber Quartuſ xiiijᵘˢ decadoſ

CESAR rebuſ compoſitiſ ⁊ omnibᵘˢ prouinciiſ in certam formã
redactiſ auguſtuſ quoq cognominatuſ eſt. ⁊ menſiſ ſextiliſ in
honorem eiuſ appellatuſ eſt. Cum ille conuentum narbone
eguiſſet: cenſuſ a tribuſ galliiſ quaſ pater uicerat actuſ. bellum aduerſuſ
baſternaſ ⁊ moſſoſ ⁊ aliaſ genteſ a.m. craſſo refertur.

Liber Quintuſ
BELLVM a.m. craſſo aduerſuſ tracaſ ⁊ a ceſare aduerſuſ hiſpa
noſ geſtum refertur. ⁊ ſalaſſi gens alpina perdomiti.

Liber Sextuſ.
RECIA a tiberio nerone ⁊ druſo ceſariſ priuigno domita.
Agrippa ceſariſ gener mortuuſ. ⁊ a druſo cenſuſ actuſ eſt.

Liber Septimuſ.
IVITATES germanie ciſrhenum ⁊ tranſrhenu poſite oppu
gnantur a druſo. Et tumultuſ qui ob cenſum exortuſ in gal
lia erat comprimitur. Aram ceſariſ ad confluentem mariſ ⁊ rhodani de
dicat ſacerdote creato.c.iulio uerecunda dubrio eduo. Liber Octauuſ.

RACES domiti a cepione. Item conſei centhrei chauci alieq
germanorum tranſrhenum genteſ ſubacte a druſo referuntur.
Octauia ſoror auguſti defuncta ante amiſſo filio marcello: cu
iuſ monumenta ſiũt theatru ⁊ porticuſ nomini eiuſ dicata.

Liber Nonuſ.
ELLVM aduerſuſ traſrhenanaſ genteſ a druſo geſtum refer
tur. in quo inter primoreſ pugnauerunt conſtituſ ſenectiuſ
⁊ auectiuſ tribuni ex ciuitate neruiorũ. Dalmataſ ⁊ pannonioſ nero
frater druſi ſubegit. Pax cum priſthiſ facta eſt. ſigniſ a rege eorũ que
ſub craſſo ⁊ poſtea ſub antonio capta erat redditiſ. Liber Decimuſ.

ELLVM aduerſuſ germanorum tranſrhenu ciuitateſ geſtum
a druſo refertur. Ipſe ex fractura equo ſuper cruſ eiuſ elapſo tri
geſimo die. q̃ id acciderat mortuuſ. Corpuſ a nerone fratre qui
nuntiuſ ualitudiniſ euocatuſ raptim accurrerat romam peruectum ⁊ in
tumulo.c.iulii conditum. Laudatuſ eſt a ceſare auguſto uictrico ⁊ ſup
miſ eiuſ multoſ honoreſ dedit.

EXPLICIT EPYTOMA SEXTI RVFFI.
LIBER PETRI DE MEDICIS COS FIL

14.   The end of the *Epitomes*: MS. written by Piero Strozzi (1458): see p. 59. (Reduced)
Biblioteca Laurenziana, Florence (Laur. 63, 12, fol. 233ᵛ)

etiam si intercidat commodum iuris quiddam autem temporis ad anticipationem congruit. Nihilominus id tempus iustum erat his qui non inanibus uocibus semet confidunt sed res plurimas cernunt Vti non cum uariae fuerint circustantes res non congruere ad anticipationem uisa sunt quae putabantur iusta in ipsis rebus ea iusta non erat. Vbi uero uanescentibus circustantibus rebus uisa sunt non congruere ad anticipationem quae existimata sunt iusta. Vbi uero uanescentibus rebus iam non utilia erant ea clam posita iura: Hic autem tum quidem iusta fuere quando erant utilia societati mutuae simul conuersantiū. Postea uero non iam fuerunt iusta quando neq utilia erant. Quibus rebus externis minime confidere preclare constituit. Hic ea quidem quae sunt possibilia propinqua & familiaria efficit. Quae uero huiusmodi nō sunt non aliena sane. Quae autem non poterat eis se studuit non immiscere exclusitq omnia quae agere non conducebat. Quicumq uim exceperunt ut se ex eis maxime ad confidendum pararent que sunt propinqua & finitima. Hi etiam ad inuicem uixere iucundissimam uitam firmissimam habentes fidem ac probationem certissimamq propinquitatem assi assumentes lamentis prosecuti non sunt defuncti celeriorem obitum a475.

FINIT LAERTIVS DIOGENES DE VITA ET MO
RIBVS PHILOSOPHORVM FOELICITER.

PETRVS STROZA SEPTVAGENARIVS.

15. From Diogenes Laertius, *De vita et moribus philosophorum*: MS. written by Piero Strozzi
(*c.* 1486?): see p. 59. There is a crease in the vellum. (Reduced)
Biblioteca Laurenziana, Florence (Laur. 65, 23, fol. 167)

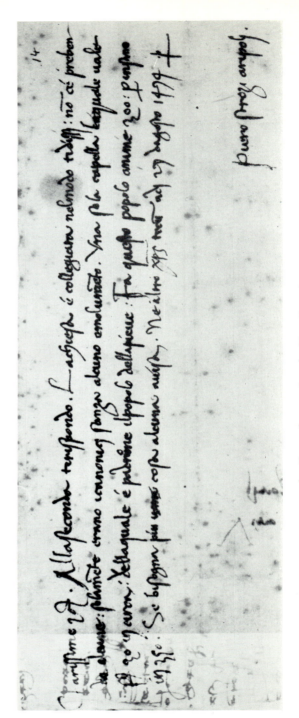

16a. From a letter written by Piero Strozzi: see p. 59.
Archivio di Stato, Florence (Arch. Medico avanti il Principato, Filz. XX, 274)

16b. From a letter written by Piero Strozzi: see p. 59.
Archivio di Stato, Florence (Carte Strozziane, Ser. III, Filz. 180, fol. 14)

elected Pope Nicholas V (late in March 1447) and that he was given the 'Pieve di Ripoli' very soon afterwards.[17] Piero was granted this benefice by a Bull of 13 April 1447[18] and apparently remained rector of San Pietro di Ripoli, a decayed collegiate church on the outskirts of Florence,[19] until 1491, when he renounced the benefice, presumably in favour of his nephew, who became rector in 1492.[20] I have not been able to discover when Piero died, though he may still have been alive in 1492.[21] Vespasiano called him 'the ornament of the priests of his time; he always lived most devoutly, in great fear of God and in continence and wanted, like his father, to live by his own labours. Having been given Ripoli by Pope Nicholas, he never wanted another benefice.... He made up his income from the Pieve by copying for payment, to salve his conscience, for he did not wish to live on charity' (see Appendix I, Document I). That Piero really needed the money is borne out by the letter that he wrote to the young Lorenzo de' Medici in March 1463/4, begging a third time for payment for some *Lives* that he had copied for Lorenzo through the agency of Vespasiano: 'I beg you to make the payment soon, for I am in the greatest need' (see Document II).

I know of only four manuscripts signed by Piero, and only two of these are precisely dated—in 1443[22] and 1483; oddly enough, both are copies of St Augustine's *City of God* (nos. 1–2 in Appendix II). The third, in which he signed himself 'septuagenarius', is probably to be dated *c.* 1486 (Appendix II, no. 3) and the fourth, to judge from its decoration and script, was also copied late in his life (Appendix II, no. 4). Piero seems to have remained remarkably active: in December 1482 he was named as one of six scribes in Florence who were working for the Cardinal of Aragon[23] and, according to Litta, he copied one MS., a *Libro di Laudi*, as late as 1492.[24] We can definitely attribute two further manuscripts to Piero on documentary evidence. The manuscript of the fourth *Decade* of Livy, which Vespasiano was preparing for Piero de' Medici in 1458, is mentioned in two of Vespasiano's letters to him. On 19 May he said: 'Messer Piero seguita l'agiunta della quarta Decha del chontinovo'[25] and on 23 June he said more precisely: 'Messer Piero Strozi a finite l'abreviationi e olle date a Pipo le mini' (Appendix II, Document III). Both 'l'agiunta' and 'l'abreviationi' are probably to be identified as the Epitomes added at the end of the fourth *Decade* of Livy (MS. Laur. 63, 12: no. 8 below).[26] 'Pipo' must be the illuminator Filippo Torelli, whose unmistakable square, muscular *putti*, strange black and white birds and very fine vinestem borders[27] are found throughout the manuscript (Plate 13). The second document which refers to a manuscript written by Piero Strozzi is in a register of books lent from the Medici private library: 'A Girolamo de' Rossi da Pistoia...si prestò a dì 24 di gennaio [1481/2], de' libri di Lorenzo, Apitio, Cornelio

Tacito de Sito Germanie e l'Epistole di Diogene insieme, di mano di messer Piero Strozzi, coperto verde.'[28] This is identifiable by contents and script as MS. Laur. 73, 20 (Appendix II, no. 5). I cannot identify with any certainty the *Lives* that Piero had copied for Lorenzo de' Medici in 1463/4: the title is too vague. Could they however be one or both of the famous pair of manuscripts of Plutarch's *Lives* (Laur. 65, 26 and 27, nos. 15–16 below), one of which has a miniature signed by Francesco di Antonio? They both have the ex-libris of Lorenzo's father Piero. These superb manuscripts are certainly in Piero Strozzi's hand and cannot, as has generally been assumed, be the set of Plutarch's *Lives* which Vespasiano was preparing for Piero de' Medici in 1458.[29] That copy was being made by 'Messer Marco'.[30]

It seems that, at this time in Florence, skilled scribes normally worked independently, making their own agreements (often with a bookseller as intermediary), and were not tied to the shop of any one bookseller or 'cartolaio'. Yet Vespasiano has already figured prominently in this account of Piero's career, and, in addition to the documents already mentioned linking him with Piero, two payments to him from King Ferrante of Naples, in connection with a *Seneca*[31] and a *Livy*,[32] may both refer to surviving manuscripts copied by Piero (Appendix II, nos. 4 and 24). So theirs may have been an unusually close collaboration. Almost all Piero's known manuscripts were copied for collectors who were, or probably were, Vespasiano's clients and, since they were also amongst the richest of his clients, the books are all beautifully produced and often richly decorated. Identifiable clients include two, possibly three, generations of Cosimo de' Medici's family, the Aragonese kings of Naples and members of their family[33] and court;[34] Federigo da Montefeltro, Duke of Urbino; the Englishman William Gray, who later became Bishop of Ely;[35] and the Hungarian Archbishop Janos Vitez.[36]

When we come to study Piero's script we are easily able to follow his development because we have dated or datable examples from the beginning, middle and end of his career. Using the style of illumination and what knowledge we have of early provenance as further aids to dating, it is possible tentatively to place all the manuscripts listed below in one of three approximate periods:

(1) *Early. Up to mid-1450's:* nos. 1 (1443); 21 (? may belong in period 2) and 22 (between 1445–54); 36 (c. 1452); 10–12; 27.

(2) *Middle. Mid-1450's to early 1470's:* nos. 6–8 (1458); 9 (1461?); 17 (1464?); 23 and 30 (1464 or earlier?); 13, 15–16, 18 (all 1469 or earlier); 33 (1471?); 20 and 29 (1472 or earlier); 5; 19; 26.

(3) *Late. After early 1470's:* nos. 24 (1479?); 35 (between 1474–82); 2 (1483); 3 (1486?); 4, 28 (1480's?); 14; 25; 31; 32; 34.

17. From a letter written by Piero Strozzi: see p. 59.
Archivio di Stato, Florence (Arch. Mediceo avanti il Principato, Filz. V, 589)

face p. 58]

Messer Piero Strozzi

Piero's beautiful, regular bookhand changes remarkably little in basic form over a working period of at least forty years: his hand is equally unmistakable in the dated manuscripts of 1443 (Plate 12) and 1483.[37] I have said already that it is in the tradition of Giovanni Aretino.[38] Piero forms his minuscule *g* in the same way as Giovanni, with the lower bowl joined to the upper by a stroke bending to the left; like him, too, he makes strong serifs on both ascenders (the top of which often have a forked appearance) and descenders (which are always slightly bent), and capitals, e.g. A and M. Again like Giovanni, he generally marks his *y* with a stroke and dot, and often puts a stroke over an *i*, for clarity. Piero's early capital Q, when used in the body of the text is also rather similar to Giovanni's: it has a rather small bowl, and a long tail undulating to the right. In his later manuscripts the tail becomes straighter. Indeed, the most noticeable development in Piero's script is in his capitals, which become increasingly formal. In his early manuscripts he generally uses an *F* with a top stroke ending in a hook; a round *h*; a long-tailed *y* and *g* (sometimes even a round *g*); also, but rarely, a round *e*; *R*, *P* and *B* sometimes have a stroke extending to the left at the top.[39] Some of these features (the *F*, *h* and *y*) still occur occasionally in the middle period but are quite given up by the last period. A feature found only in the early period is the long-tailed minuscule *x*. Piero's use of the æ diphthong may also be useful for dating his manuscripts. It appears rarely or not at all in his early work, up to *c.* 1460: e.g. in the middle group it is not used in nos. 5, 6–8 (1458), 10–12, 18, but does appear quite often in nos. 9 (1461?), 18, 23 and seems to be regularly used in nos. 15–16, 20, 26, 29. Later, it is a normal feature, though not used with complete consistency. Piero's ampersand is a characteristic feature; it normally sits upright on its tail, with the rounded bottom of the tail resting on the line, but it is less upright in the earliest MSS. and sometimes, especially at the beginning of no. 1 (1443) the body actually rests on the line (Plates 12–15). Piero's earlier manuscripts, as one might expect, have a greater solidity and firmness than his late ones; the ascenders in particular are shorter and thicker. The script of the late manuscripts has a thin effect, even in comparison with those of the middle period. No. 1 (1443) may be a very early effort of Piero's, for it shows some uncertainty; more indeed than no. 2, copied in 1483, which Piero said that he had written 'manu tremula'.

As an interesting comparison I have included plates of three letters written by Piero, dated April 1445, March 1463/4 and August 1474 (Plates 16*a*, 16*b* & 17). They are written in a quite ordinary cursive which gives no inkling of the skill of his book-hand. Another feature of Piero's copying which should be mentioned is his quire numbering. He almost invariably numbers each quire in Roman numerals at the end, at the bottom of the page and near the inside margin, below the catchword when there is one. The only exceptions that I have seen are nos. 5 and 9, both of which are comparatively short manuscripts with catchwords only. He does not always add catchwords, but when he does they are horizontal.

I hope that the plates found here, of documented manuscripts representing Piero's script at the beginning, middle and end of his career, together with the many reproductions of his hand to be found elsewhere (generally made because of the illumination in the manuscripts concerned) may justify Vespasiano's claim that he was the most beautiful scribe of his day. I cannot vouch for the second part of the claim, that he was the most accurate as well, but he certainly seems generally to have checked his copies with care. The MS. in the Bodleian Library, Digby 231 (no. 23), is a good example of the kind of corrections that he made. The list of identified manuscripts printed below shows that Piero was a prolific, as well as a careful, scribe. But it is a list that makes no claim to completeness: for I have not made a systematic search for manuscripts copied by Piero. I came across most of the items which have not been reproduced in photographs, only by chance, when I was looking for manuscripts produced by Vespasiano. I feel sure that further manuscripts wait to be identified.

NOTES

1 See especially B. L. Ullman, *The Origin and Development of Humanistic Script* (Rome, 1960), henceforth referred to as *Ullman*.

2 Paris, B.N., MS. Rothschild IV. 2. 68, fol. 48. See Document 1. I hope to print this life in full in the study of Vespasiano which I am preparing.

3 T. de Marinis, *La Biblioteca Napoletana dei re d'Aragona* (henceforth referred to as *De Marinis*) (Milan, 1947, 1952), I, 87. He knew the life of Benedetto by Lorenzo di Filippo Strozzi (d. 1549), which is in fact little more than a précis of Vespasiano's life; (it is pr. P. Stromboli, *Le Vite degli Uomini Illustri della Casa Strozzi, comentario di Lorenzo di Filippo Strozzi*, Florence, 1892, pp. 47–8). Vespasiano's collection of Strozzi lives, in the Rothschild MS., was dedicated to Lorenzo's father Filippo. Of Piero's script Lorenzo merely says: 'non era inferiore lo scritto suo di bellezza e corretione a quel del padre'. Piero is also mentioned by *Ullman*, p. 126.

4 See p. 57. It was fortunate that there was a MS. in the Biblioteca Laurenziana signed by Piero (no. 3) which could be directly compared with Piero's *Livy* (nos. 6–8), but it was disconcerting when I first opened it to find that the first quire was utterly different! In fact it had been added much later.

5 *De Marinis*, I, 46–7, 50, nos. 2, 3, 4, 6, 7, 9, 10, 11, 16, 22 (dated between 1465–70), 59, 60. Cinico's earliest reference to Piero is in a manuscript dated 30 July 1465, where he called Piero 'distinguished in virtue and nobility'. In an undated MS. (no. 59), he also called Piero 'clarissimus simul atque callidissimus scriptor'. Cinico's known work was done in Naples. His earliest dated MS. is of September 1463.

6 *De Marinis*, I, 94 n. 18.

7 On Benedetto, in addition to the lives cit. in notes 2–3, see C. Guasti (ed.), *Alessandra Macinghi negli Strozzi, lettere di una Gentildonna Florentina del secolo XV*...(Florence, 1877), pp. 141–2; C. Carnesecchi, 'Un Potestà di Castelfiorentino del secolo XV', *Misc. Stor. di Valdelsa III*, II (1895), 113–21; A. Della Torre, *Storia dell'Accademia Platonica di Firenze* (Florence, 1902), pp. 233, 286–7, 304.

8 Vespasiano, in Rothschild MS. cit., fol. 46–7. For an example of one of his contemporaries specifically asking for a MS. copied by Benedetto, see Della Torre, *op. cit.* p. 304.

9 Vespasiano, *loc. cit.* fol. 47.

10 Ed. G. Fiocco, 'La bibl. di P.S', *Studi di Bibliog. e Stor. in Onor e T. de Marinis*, 1964, II, p. 298.

11 Lot 302 in Sotheby sale, 21 June 1860. Colophon:

'...Anno domini ab ipsius salutifera incarnatione MCCCCXVIIII die tertia mensis Julii feliciter explicit in domo Nobilis egregii generosique Viri Simonis Filippi domini Leonardi de Strozzi de Florentia pro Nobili Facundoque bonorum morum ac virtutum perito Juveni Benedicto Pieri de Strozzis Inclitissimae ac Serenissimae civitatis eiusdem cive. Per me Ambroxium olim ser Jacopi de Marudis olim de Mediolano ac nunc districtuale prelibate civitatis notarium scriptus....'

12 Florence, Bibl. Naz., MS. Magl. VI, 185, Cicero, *De Oratore*. Dated 3 August 1418. See Galante, 'Index Codd. Class. Lat. Flor. in Bybl. Magl.', I, *Studi Ital. di Filol. Class*. X (1900), no. 21, pp. 335–6. The MS. is written in a humanistic hand similar to that in *Ullman*, pl. 44.

13 *Ullman*, p. 99, no. 4.

14 Cosimo's ex-libris: 'liber cosme de medicis de florentia', written in a space between books on fol. 83, has apparently passed unnoticed. For other examples of his writing it in the middle of books, see MSS. Laur. 16, 31; 30, 21; 34, 6; 48, 27; and R. W. Hunt, 'Humanistic Script in Florence in the early fifteenth century', *Journal of the Society for Italic Handwriting*, 37 (1963), 7 (reproduced below, pp. 272 *et seq*.).

15 He was probably studying law, for apparently only knights and jurists could be called 'Messer' (L. Martines, *The Social World of the Florentine Humanists*, London, 1963, p. 169).

16 Florence, Arch. di Stato, Arch. Med. av. il Principato, Filz. V, 589. See Plate 17. Other extant letters of Piero are *ibid*. Filz. XX, 274 (Doc II and Plate 16 *a* below); XXIX, 37, January 1473, recommending his brother Francesco to Lorenzo de' Medici; Arch. cit., Carte Strozziane, Ser. 3, Filz. 180, fols. 14 (Plate 16 *b*), 16, both written in August 1474 to Filippo Strozzi.

17 Vespasiano, *Vite di Uomini Illustri*, ed. Frati (henceforth referred to as *Frati*), I, p. 46. Vespasiano says that his visit to the Pope was the day before the Florentine envoys were officially received. We learn from a letter of Alessandro Sforza dated 1 April 1447 that they had been received shortly before then (L. Osio, *Docc. Diplom. tratti dagli Arch. Milanesi*, III, Milan, 1872, Doc. CCCCVIII, p. 508).

18 *De Marinis*, I, 87.

19 For the church, see E. Repetti, *Dizionario geografico-fisico storico della Toscana*, IV (Florence, 1841), 777. For the state of the church, see the letter in Plate 16 *b*, and Piero's second letter to Filippo Strozzi, cit. above, note 16: 'Questa chiesa quando io l'ebbi era collegiata: sono morti

i canonici (in his other letter he says that they were unpaid): non ne vive se non uno....'

20 P. Litta, *Celebri Famiglie Italiane*. *Strozzi di Firenze* (Milan, 1839), tav. XI.

21 See note 24.

22 The date of this MS. (see Plate 12) was misread by Mercati (see Appendix II, no. 1 below) as 1453, and subsequent writers have followed him.

23 *De Marinis*, I, 86.

24 Litta, *loc. cit*. He said that it was in the Magliabecchiana. I have not identified this manuscript.

25 Letter pr. *Frati*, III, 334–5. First pr. V. Rossi, *Tre lettere di Vespasiano da Bisticci* (Nozze Cipolla–Vittone) (Venice, 1890), pp. 16–17; but this work is very rare. Rossi also first printed Vespasiano's letter to Piero dated 19 April 1458 and his letter to Cosimo.

26 There is no separate MS. of Florus with Piero's ex-libris, which he seems normally to have put in his books. His other *Decades* of Livy, mentioned in Vespasiano's letters of 19 April 1458 (*Frati*, III, 333–4) and 19 May, are also in Piero Strozzi's hand. The Epitomes at the end of *Dec*. IV may have been written a little later than the main body of the text, as Vespasiano's letter suggests; though they continue on the page on which *Dec*. IV finished, their production is slightly different: they are rubricated (by Piero, as usual in red capitals) while the main body of the manuscript is not, and there are catchwords only, instead of the usual quire numbering in Roman numerals.

27 Cf., for example, P. D'Ancona, *La Miniatura Fiorentina* (Florence, 1914), tav. LXVI.

28 Pr. most recently by M. del Piazzo, *Protocolli del carteggio di Lorenzo il Magnifico* (Florence, 1956), pp. 227–8.

29 See for example A. Campana, 'Una lettera inedita di Guarino Veronese e il Plutarco mediceo della bottegha di Vespasiano', *Italia Medioevale e Umanistica*, V (1962), 174–7. V. Rossi, *op. cit*. p. 13, was the first to suggest this identification.

30 See Vespasiano's letter of 19 May 1458 cit. above and note 25. I have not succeeded in identifying Messer Marco or the manuscript he was copying. Perhaps the MS. was never finished; the assembling of texts was clearly causing much difficulty. Could Messer Marco have been Piero's pupil Giovanmarco Cinico, whose earliest MS. dated from Naples is of 1463 (see above, note 5)?

31 On 24 May 1488 Vespasiano was sent fl. 9...d. 8 'per certi quarterny de carta per la opera de Seneca' (G. Percopo, 'Nuovi Docc. sugli scrittori e gli artisti dei tempi aragonesi', *Arch. Stor. Prov. Nap*. XX, 1895, 328). The payment may have been delayed, for Giuliano Gondi was paid in

April 1487 for a volume of the works of Seneca which he had had transcribed in Florence for the Duke of Calabria (*De Marinis*, II, Doc. 676 B).

32 *De Marinis*, II, Doc. 531: payment to Vespasiano, through Giuliano Gondi, for the third *Decade* of Livy, 1 August 1479.

33 Alfonso, Duke of Calabria, who was then heir to King Ferrante and later became King Alfonso II.

34 Count Iñigo d'Avalos, Ferrante's court chamberlain (d. 1484), owned no. 19 and Narciso Verduno, cr. bishop of Mileto in 1473 (d. 1477), owned no. 27. On Iñigo as a collector, see Vespasiano's Life, pr. *Frati*, I, 331–4, which suggests that Vespasiano had personal knowledge of him. De Marinis says that his collection was absorbed into Ferrante's after his death (*op. cit.* I, 41). Another Florentine MS. with Iñigo's arms was copied by Antonio di Mario in 1445/6 (Laur. 65, 25; *Ullman*, p. 103, no. 31, does not mention the arms). On Narciso, the 'lecenceato', whose

manuscripts were also added to the Royal collection, see *De Marinis*, I, p. 175; Vespasiano in his life of Narciso, pr. *Frati*, I, pp. 258–61, claims to have known him personally.

35 See R. A. B. Mynors, *Cat. MSS. Balliol College* (Oxford, 1963), pp. xxiv–xliv. Vespasiano wrote Gray's life (pr. *Frati*, I, pp. 230–2) and implied that he had had him as a client.

36 See also Vespasiano's life, pr. *Frati*, I, pp. 238–44. For Vitez's collection, see G. Fraknoi in *Magyar Könyv-Szemle* (1878), 79–91, 190–201; (1880), 9–15. See also A. de Hevesy, 'Les miniaturistes de Matthias Corvin', *Revue de l'Art Chrétien*, LXI (1911), 2.

37 *De Marinis*, IV, tav. 309 B.

38 Cf. *Ullman*, pls. 46, 49.

39 Almost all these features (except the round **G**) are also found in MSS. copied by Giovanni which I have seen.

APPENDIX I

Documents

I. *Extract from Vespasiano's Life of Benedetto di Pieraccione Strozzi* (Paris, Bibliothèque Nationale, MS. Rothschild IV. 2. 68, fol. 47ᵛ–48): . . . In casa sua [i.e. of Benedetto] si viveva con grandissima honestà et allevo molto bene la sua famiglia, alieni da ogni vitio et con grandissimo timore di dio. Enne ancora hoggi messer Piero che è suo figliuolo che è l'ornamento de' sacerdoti della sua età: essendo vivuto sempre religiosissimamente, et con grandissimo timore di dio, et d'una continentissima vita et ha imitato le vestigie paterne di voler vivere della sua fatica. Avendo avuto la pieve a Ripoli da papa Nicola non ha voluto altro beneficio! È stato il più bello scriptore abbi avuto questa età et il più emendato et quello gli è mancato oltre alla pieve ha supplito con lo scrivere a prezo per salvare la sua conscientia et non volere di quel di persona. . . .

II. *Vespasiano's Letter to Piero de' Medici, 23 June 1458* (Forlì, Biblioteca Comunale, Autografi Piancastelli. I owe knowledge of this letter to Dr Cecil Clough).

Address on back: [Clariss]imo atque elo[quenti]ssimo Viro Piero [di Cos]imo de Medicis [maiori su]o honorando.

Clarissime atque eloquentissime vir post recomandatione premissa. Il Prinio e lla Decha sono di tutto finiti in buona forma in modo credo vi piaceranno sommamente. aregli arechato chostassu ma alla porta nommi arebbono lasciato venire. Mandate uno con qualche panno da involgerli che non si guastino. Messer Piero Stroczi a finite l'abreviationi e olle date a Pipo le mini e subito si legeranno le manderò. Ad voi mi rachomando. In Firenze adi 23 di gugnio 1458.　　　Vespasiano di Filippo

III. *Piero Strozzi's letter to Lorenzo de' Medici, 2 March 1463/4* (Florence, Archivio di Stato, Archivio Mediceo avanti il Principato, Filz. XX, 274).

Address on back: Docto Juveni Laurentio [P]etri de Medices tanquam fratri: Pisis.

Petrus Stroza Laurentio s.d. Iam bis scripsi: significans vitas illas iam diu fuisse absolutas: et nullas ad me de hoc litteras dedisti. Scripsisti ad Vespasianum: et ipse ostendit mihi litteras tuas: in quibus dicis: velle te mihi de reliquo satisfactum iri: et tamen adhuc non commisisti alicui: ut hoc expediatur. Rogo ergo te maiorem in modum: ut id quamprimum efficere velis: nam sum in maxima necessitate constitutus: ut alias ad te scripsi. Vale. Ex Florentia vj°.non. martii. 1463. See Plate 16a.

APPENDIX II

*List of identified manuscripts**

Signed manuscripts

1. *Rome, Vatican Library, Ottob. Lat. 113*; St Augustine, *De Civitate Dei* (G. Mercati, *Codd. Latini Pico Grimani Pio* (Studi e Testi 75), 1938, p. 291, n. 3. He misreads the date as 1453). Parch. 332 fols. Fol. 332, caps.: Petrus Stroza absolvit Florentie die septimo mensis decembris MCCCCXLIII. Vinestem border on fol. 2 with *putti*, birds, butterflies, erased coat of arms; miniature of St Augustine in initial. Seen by me only in photographs. See Plate 12.

2. *Vat. Reg. Lat. 128*; St Augustine, *De Civitate Dei* (A. Wilmart, *Codd. Reg. Lat.* I, 1927, 304. Colophon reprod. *De Marinis*, IV, tav. 309B). Parch. 1+432 fols. 395 × 272 mm. 34 lines. Fol. 431, caps.: Petrus Stroza sexaginta et septem annos agens scripsit manu tremula: anno domini millesimo quadringentesimo octogesimo tertio VII idus Novembris finitum est. Painted initials with decorated coloured backgrounds. Seen by me only in photographs.

3. *Florence, Bibl. Laurenziana 65, 23*; Diogenes Laertius (Bandini, *Cat. Lat. Laur.* II, 1775, col. 737). Parch. 167 fols. 342 × 226 mm. Spaces left for initials not filled in. Corrections by scribe. Gaps left for Greek. Piero's first quire has been lost, and replaced by 13 leaves in a much later hand imitating his. Fol. 167, red caps.: Petrus Stroza septuagenarius. On the last line of text before the explicit, '1475' has been written in a cramped hand which may be Piero's, but, if it is, he has made a curious mistake about either the date or his own age. See Plate 15.

4. *Valencia Univ. 894 (formerly 827)*; Seneca, *Op. Var.* (*De Marinis*, II, 150; III, tav. 223–5; M. Gutierrez del Caño, *Cat. MSS. Bibl. Univ. Valencia*, 1914, III, no. 2150). Parch. 256 written fols., paginated. 390 × 275 mm. 35 lines. Written in three separate sections; the later ones beginning on p. 122 (*De Ira*) and p. 338

* These have been seen by me unless I have made a statement to the contrary.

(*Tragedies*). Many corrections by scribe. P. 512, red caps.: Petrus Stroza absolvit. Title page illuminated in style of Attavante. Later borders in style of Francesco di Antonio. Arms of Alfonso, Duke of Calabria. Original red velvet binding.

Possibly the MS. of Seneca prepared in Florence in the 1480's for which Vespasiano had provided 'carta' (see note 31).

Documented manuscripts

5. *Laur. 73, 20*; Apicius; Tacitus, *De Orig. et Situ Germaniae*; Diogenes, *Epist.*, trans. F. Aretino with dedication to Pope Pius II (Bandini, *op. cit.* III, 1776, cols. 44–5; E. Chatelain, *Paléog. Class. Lat.* II, pl. CXLVII, 2). Parch. 84 fols. 221 × 155 mm. 26 lines. The vinestem border on fol. 1, with the Medici arms, *putti*, birds and a 'portrait' in the initial is by an illuminator who decorated a number of MSS. which can be definitely associated with Vespasiano, e.g. MS. Budapest Univ. 1 (reprod. in L. Mezey, *Codd. Lat. Med. Aevi* (Bibl. Univ. Bud. Cat. MSS. I), Budapest, 1961, pl. 44; I. Berkovits, *Illuminated MSS. from the library of Mat. Corvinus*, Budapest, 1964, pl. 1). Mrs Alison Brown first kindly drew my attention to Chatelain's reproduction of this MS. It belonged to Lorenzo de' Medici in 1482. See above, p. 58.

6–8. *Laur. 63, 10–12*; Livy, *Dec.* I, III, IV (Bandini, *op. cit.* II, cols. 689–90; P. D'Ancona, *Min. Fior.* II, nos. 399–401). Parch. 213; 210; 233 fols. *c.* 370 × 250 mm. *Dec.* IV has 36 lines. Many corrections by scribe. Title pages with square gold frames panelled in colours; borders vinestem, very fine quality. *Dec.* IV is documented as being illuminated by Filippo Torelli. Medici arms. Ex-libris of Piero di Cosimo de' Medici. The *Epitome* of Florus begins on fol. 164ᵛ in Laur. 63, 12.

The set of Livy produced for Piero by Vespasiano in 1458. See above, p. 57 and Plates 13 & 14.

Unsigned manuscripts which I believe to be in Piero Strozzi's hand

9. *Cambridge, Fitzwilliam Museum 180*; Donato Acciaiuoli, *Vita Caroli Magni* (M. R. James, *Cat. MSS. Fitzwilliam*, 1895, p. 386). Parch. 4 + 47 + 6 fols. *c.* 248 × 160 mm. 26 lines. Corrections by scribe. Circular-framed title page and fine vinestem decoration in two hands. Royal arms of France. Probably the dedication copy of this work, which Donato Acciaiuoli presented to King Louis XI of France on 2 January 1462 (see diary of the Florentine envoys sent to congratulate Louis upon his accession, ed. Milanesi in *Arch. Stor. Ital.* ser. III, 1, part 1 (1865), p. 25; see also Vespasiano, *Vite*, ed. Frati, II, 256, 285; III, 188).

10–12. *Florence, Bibl. Naz., Banco Rari 34–6*; Livy, *Dec.* I, III, IV (*De Marinis*, I, 139, n. 4; II, 94–5; III, tav. 135–40). Parch. 263; 250; 279 fols. *c.* 310 × 210 mm.

34 lines. Corrections by scribe. Title pages in *Dec.* I and III, with square frames. Vinestem borders with *putti*, birds, etc., probably by the same bottega as no. 9. Arms of King Alfonso I of Naples.

13. *Florence, Laur. 16, 22*; St Cyprian, *Op. var.* (Bandini, *op. cit.* I, cols. 267–9; D'Ancona, II, no. 766). Parch. 259 fols. *c.* 330 × 220 mm. 30 lines. Corrections by scribe. Illuminated by Francesco di Antonio. Ex-libris of Piero de' Medici.

14. *Laur. 30, 1*; Ptolemy, *Cosmographia*, in Latin (Bandini, II, cols. 67–8). Parch. 64 fols. of text. 595 × 430 mm. 2 cols. of 45 lines. Another scribe, possibly identifiable with the Frenchman Ugo de Comminellis, who seems to have specialized in copying MSS. of Ptolemy (he copied MSS. Vat. Lat. 5699; Vat. Urb. Lat. 277; Paris, B.N., Lat. 4802), began the MS., and copied fols. 1–10, 13–14, which should run continuously, but have been misplaced in binding. Piero completed the text (fols. 11–12ᵛ, which should come after 63ᵛ, 14ᵛ–64) and wrote all the headings. The illumination, very elaborate on fol. 1, which is left unfinished with blank spaces for arms and emblems, is in the style of Gherardo and Monte di Giovanni (cf. e.g. D'Ancona. *Min. Fior.* tav. LXXXIX).

15. *Laur. 65, 26*; Collection of Plutarch's *Lives*, in Latin (Bandini, II, cols. 740–5; D'Ancona, II, no. 792 and tav. LXVIII; G. Biagi, *50 tavole da codici della R. Bibl. Med. Laur.* 1914, tav. XXXIV). Parch. 337 fols. 360 × 252 mm. Probably 35 lines. Corrections by scribe. The famous MS. signed by the illuminator Francesco di Antonio. No title page, but list of contents in red caps. on verso of flyleaf. Ex-libris of Piero de' Medici.

16. *Laur. 65, 27*; More *Lives* of Plutarch in Latin (Bandini, II, cols. 745–8; D'Ancona, II, no. 793). Parch. 358 fols. *c.* 360 × 250 mm. 35 lines. Illuminated by Francesco di Antonio. Ex-libris of Piero de' Medici.

17. *Laur. 79, 4*; Aristotle, *Nicomachean Ethics*, trans. Argyropoulos, with dedication to Cosimo de' Medici (Bandini, III, col. 171; D'Ancona, II, no. 460). Parch. 158 fols. 270 × 175 mm. 27 lines. Many corrections by scribe and some spaces left (for diagrams?). Blank leaf after end of Book IV (fol. 63ᵛ) and Book V starts new quire. Simple vinestem border on fol. 1, with laurel wreath and Medici arms. The dedicatory preface forms a separate gathering. This may be the *Ethics* of which Vespasiano wrote to Cosimo (probably early in 1464) saying that it was ready (letter pr. *Frati*, III, 332. Rossi suggested the date). Cosimo rarely wrote his ex-libris in his books. It is the only MS. that fits Vespasiano's letter.

18. *Laur. 82, 4*; Pliny, *Nat. Hist.* (Bandini, III, cols. 188–9; D'Ancona, II, no. 469). Parch. 485 fols. 393 × 278 mm. Title page with square frame. Elaborate, fine vinestem borders possibly by Torelli. Ex-libris of Piero de' Medici, but may have

been written for his brother Giovanni, for Piero's ex-libris is also in MS. Laur. 82, 3, which is probably the Pliny that was being copied for him by 'Benedetto' in 1458 (*Frati*, III, 333). Piero put his ex-libris in other MSS. known to have been written originally for Giovanni, e.g. MSS. Laur. 48, 31 and 66, 9.

19. *London, B.M. Add. 15246*; St Augustine, *De Civitate Dei* (G. F. Warner, *Illum. MSS. in B.M.* London, 1903, no. 57 and plate; *B.M. Reproductions from Illum. MSS.* ser. III, 1925, pls. 39–40; D'Ancona, II, no. 1365). Parch. 354 fols. *c.* 405 × 285 mm. 37 lines. Many corrections by scribe. Magnificent title page in roundel (fol. 28ᵛ) possibly by same illuminator as no. 23 below and first fol. of text with flower border, filled with tiny *putti*, animals, birds, medallions with virtues and scenes from life of St Augustine, by the same illuminator as no. 20 below. Arms of Count Iñigo d'Avalos of Naples (see note 34).

20. *Munich, Staatsbibl., Clm. 15731*; Livy, *Dec.* I (D'Ancona, II, no. 738; de Hevesy, *Les miniaturistes de Mat. Corv.* cit. p. 9 (plate)). Parch. 218 fols. 377 × 246 mm. 36 lines. Many corrections by scribe and some in another humanistic hand (Vitez?). Magnificent architectural title page, and elaborate vinestem border, with medallions, etc., by same illuminator as no. 19. Arms of Archbishop Janos Vitez (d. 1472) (see note 36). Clm. 15732–3, *Dec.* III and IV, not seen by me, are listed by Fraknoi as also belonging to Vitez.

21. *Oxford, Balliol College 140*; Virgil, *Opera* (Mynors, *Cat.* pp. 120, 121). Parch. 215 fols. *c.* 365 × 220 mm. 30 lines. Corrections by scribe. Simple vinestem initials (some cut out). Given to Balliol by William Gray (see note 35). This and the following MS. were probably copied for Gray when he was in Italy, *c.* 1444–53. Other, dated, MSS. were copied for him in Florence in 1445–8.

22. *Balliol Coll. 249*; Pliny, *Nat. Hist.* (Mynors, *Cat.* p. 273). Parch. 451 fols. *c.* 390 × 265 mm. 40 lines. Many corrections by scribe. Good vinestem initials, many cut out. Also given to Balliol by Gray.

23. *Bodleian Library, Digby 231*; Cicero, *Orationes* (O. Pächt, *Italian Illum. MSS. 1400–1550* (Cat. of Exhib. in Bodleian Library), 1948, pl. III (no. 80), reprod. part of fol. 1). Parch. 340 fols. *c.* 390 × 265 mm. 34 lines. Many corrections by scribe. Some lacunae, with explanatory notes, e.g. 'Deficit hic multum' (fol. 16). On fol. 1 magnificent vinestem border with animals, *putti* playing, etc. Original arms erased. Note by Digby that he bought the MS. from the Piccolomini library at Siena, so it may have been written for Pope Pius II.

24. *Valencia University 385 (formerly 762) and 384 (formerly 763)*; Livy, *Dec.* I and III (*De Marinis*, II, 96, 98; III, tav. 142, 149–50; Gutierrez del Caño, *op. cit.* II, nos. 1313–14 and Lam. xv). Parch. 255 and 243 written fols. 370 × 255 mm. and 360 × 250 mm.

Both 32 lines. Corrections by scribe. Elaborate title pages and first borders, attributed to Gherardo and Monte di Giovanni. Arms of Aragonese kings of Naples. This may be the Livy of which Vespasiano had produced *Dec.* III for King Ferrante in 1479 (see note 32).

25. *Valencia Univ. 482 (formerly 608)*; Florus, *Epitome* (*De Marinis*, II, 95; III, tav. 102; Gutierrez del Caño, II, no. 984). Parch. 272 written fols. *c.* 370 × 255 mm. 32 lines. Corrections by scribe. First fol. of text lost, later borders of flower type, with Neapolitan emblems. Rubrication not completed.

26. *Valencia Univ. 731 (formerly 741)*; Xenophon, *Cyropaedia*, trans. Poggio for King Alfonso I (*De Marinis*, II, 178–9; IV, tav. 292, title page and binding only); Gutierrez del Caño, II, no. 1189; Dominguez Bordona, *MSS. con pinturas*, 1933, II, figs. 670–1). Parch. 166 written fols. *c.* 255 × 180 mm. 24 lines. Corrections by scribe. Fine architectural title page on fol. 3ᵛ, vinestem borders of very fine quality, on fol. 1 with *putti*, animals, birds, profiles, apparently by same illuminator as no. 23. Arms of Aragonese kings of Naples. Original Florentine binding of green stamped leather with tiny inlet studs.

27. *Valencia Univ. 770 (formerly 779)*; St Augustine, *Retractationes* (*De Marinis*, II, 22; Gutierrez del Caño, I, no. 38). Parch. 91 fols. *c.* 228 × 160 mm. 27 lines. Many corrections by scribe. Simple, good quality vinestem decoration, with *putti*, birds, etc. The note 'lecenceato' on the front pastedown means that the MS. originally belonged to Narciso Verduno, Bishop of Mileto, and came into the royal library at Naples after his death in 1477 (see note 34). The Aragonese arms have been added on fol. 1.

28. *Vienna, Nationalbibl. 6*; Seneca, *De Beneficiis, etc.* (*De Marinis*, II, 149; IV, tav. 219–221; H. J. Hermann, *Illum. Hss. der Nat. Bibl. Wien* (Beschr. Verzeichnis Illum. Hss. in Oesterreich VIII), VI, 3, no. 72 and tav. 22–3). Parch. 2 + 263 + 1 fols. 395 × 277 mm. 33 lines. Many corrections by scribe. Fine title page (roundel with flowers, *putti*, etc., surmounted by interlacing coloured branches) and first border of flower type in style of Francesco di Antonio. Arms of Duke Alfonso of Calabria.

29. *Vienna, Nationalbibl. 11 (old Salzburg 1 A)*; Cicero, *Orationes* (Hermann, *op. cit.* no. 59 and pl. XIII). Parch. 3 + 317 + 3 fols. 380 × 265 mm. 35 lines. Many corrections by scribe. Spaces left for lacunae which were found in 'antiquissimo' or 'vetustissimo exemplari' (fols. 14ᵛ, 47, 49, etc.). Fine title page (scrolled circular frame with flowers) and first border with *putti*, birds, etc., probably by the second illuminator of no. 9 above. Arms of Archbishop Vitez (see also no. 20). Original Florentine binding of red stamped leather, clasps with Vitez's arms.

30. *In Palazzo Piccolomini, Pienza*; 'Leonardus Dathus ad sanctissimum patrem

Pium II Pontificem in Gesta Porsenne Regis et Clusinorum per G. Vibemnam conscripta nuperrime reperta sermone thusco' (red caps.). Florentine vinestem initial. 26 lines. Seen on exhibition but not examined by me. On this 'Etruscan fake', see F. Flamini, 'Leonardo di Piero Dati', *Giorn. Stor. Lett. Ital.* XVI (1890), 25. Flamini only knew of one MS.: Vat. Urb. Lat. 411. The provenance of our MS. suggests that it is the dedicatory copy.

Manuscripts not seen by me which appear from published photographs to be in Piero's hand

31. *Florence, Bibl. Riccard. 838*; Ugolino Verino, Carliados (M. L. Scuricini Greco, *Miniature Riccardiane*, Florence, 1958, pp. 174–5, no. 148 with plate). 176 fols. 277 × 180 mm. Illuminated by Gherardo and Monte. Appears to have royal arms of France.

32. *Paris, Bibl. Nat., Lat. 6310*; Aristotle, *Nicom. Ethics*, trans. Argyropoulos, *Economics and Politics*, trans. Bruni (*De Marinis*, II, 16; III, tav. 16; D'Ancona, II, no. 1384). 222 fols. 332 × 227 mm. Copied for King Ferrante of Naples. Flower border with *putti*, birds, etc., in style of Francesco di Antonio.

33. *Paris, Bibl. Nat., Lat. 8533*; Cicero, *Ep. Fam.* (*De Marinis*, II, 45, says that it is in 2 vols.; III, tav. 57, from 2nd vol. N.B. the first vol. need not be in Piero's hand). 178 and 228 fols. 373 × 260 mm. Miniatures of flower type with *putti, imprese,* vignettes. Possibly bought in Florence, 1471, by Marino Tomacelli for King Ferrante.

34. *Vat. Ottob. Lat. 1449*; Cicero, *Rhetorical works* (*De Marinis*, II, 46–7, 327 and tav. 2). II + 289 fols. 385 × 270 mm. Original first fol. gone. Aragonese arms and *imprese* in other borders, which are of the flower type.

35. *Vat. Urb. Lat. 273*; Francesco Berlinghieri, *Geographia* (C. Stornajolo, *Codd. Urb. Lat. I*, 1902, 251; idem, *Ritratti e gesta dei Duchi d'Urbino nelle min. delle Cod. Vat. Urb.* (Collez. Paléog. Vat. II), 1913, tav. III). 204 fols. 458 × 312 mm. Arms of Federigo da Montefeltro as Duke (i.e. 1474 or later).

36. *Now in collection of Major J. R. Abbey*; Giannozzo Manetti, *De dignitate et excellentia hominis* (*Vendita Hoepli. MSS. e libri figurati*, 3–4 May 1928, no. 182 and tav. LXXVII; G. Zonta, *Storia della letteratura ital.* II (Il Rinascimento), part I, Turin, 1930, tav. VII, facing p. 400. Said to have been in coll. of T. de Marinis in 1913; *De Marinis*, II, 105, as in collection of Prince Ginori Conti, Florence). 120 fols. 267 × 238 mm. Vinestem border with simple type of Aragonese arms. Probably the dedication copy to King Alfonso I and therefore datable to *c.* 1452. I owe knowledge of the present whereabouts of this MS. to Mrs E. Leonard.

BERTHOLD WOLPE

Florilegium Alphabeticum: Alphabets in Medieval Manuscripts

P alaeographers and others interested in the physical appearance of medieval manuscripts have studied and considered for many years the shapes of innumerable scripts. Needless to say, their main material for study was, and is, made up of actual books, letters and documents. In assessing the characteristics of letter forms, and in fitting them into a system of nomenclature, certain contemporary scribal treatises, specimen- and advertisement-sheets have been invaluable. They were carefully described and listed by S. H. Steinberg in *The Library*.[1] In addition to this, articles by Professor Carl Wehmer in *Miscellanea Giovanni Mercati*[2] and by S. J. P. van Dijk in *Scriptorium*[3] enlarge our knowledge of writing masters' specimen-sheets of the late Middle Ages. Professor B. L. Ullman has thrown his net wider by including in his consideration of Abecedaria[4] Etruscan, early Greek, Roman and medieval alphabets: all this as an introduction to a rare Renaissance alphabet page by Panigallius.

Having listed existing articles in this field, I find that other material has survived which may be worth describing. Apart from the treatises on the art of writing, with their purposeful display of letter forms, many specimen-sheets of the writing masters do not show alphabets. They usually confine themselves to passages, very often short ones, in different hands of various sizes which the master was willing to teach or ready to use in manuscripts to be commissioned by the prospective customer.

The aim of this article is mainly to show alphabets which happen to appear in books as an essential ingredient of their make-up. It is of course exciting to find complete alphabets casually inscribed on flyleaves or margins. A ninth- or tenth-century manuscript mainly of the letters of Alcuin comes to mind, where an early eleventh-century hand has added in the upper margins of two pages an alphabet including the

Anglo-Saxon letters, significantly followed by the opening words of the Lord's Prayer (B.M. Harley, 208, fols. 87ᵛ and 88).[5] The linking of ABC and prayer is not without importance, as it marks an early stage of teaching: first the letters were to be learnt one by one and then the knowledge was to be applied to the reading of words and sentences.

The prayer-book, known also as the primer, sometimes opens with the alphabet followed by the Lord's Prayer. As we all know, the scanning of catalogues takes time but is often rewarding. For instance, I recently came across a catalogue reference to a Middle English prayer-book in the Hunterian Museum of the University of Glasgow.[6] The manuscript, written in fluent text hand soon after 1382, belonged in 1682 to Samuel Woodford,[7] poet and divine. The alphabet of textura minuscules (Plate 18) does not include the Anglo-Saxon letters later used in the prayers; thus following in the black letter abc the earlier Latin tradition, and not taking into account the Wycliffian innovation of employing the vernacular. In a marginal note an early owner of this book wrote in a sixteenth-century hand: 'John morys is Boke of Blake water.... | Thys boke ys gud and profytte | byl for a man þat can not | vnderstond Latyn or for one thayt....'[8]

A very similar prayer-book also from the Woodford library and at the Hunterian Museum,[9] but in Latin and English, is without the alphabet on the Lord's Prayer page. I should like to venture the assumption that this indicates that the book mentioned previously was written for a young person who had first to learn his abc from this same book; whereas the second was for someone who already could read.

A fine manuscript at the Bodleian,[10] apparently written for the young Marguerite de Ste Maure, the wife of Guillaume d'Ogremont, can be roughly dated as having been written soon after 1386, the year of their marriage. Like the other two manuscripts, it contains calendar, prayers and hymns for private use. The illuminated initial letter P (Plate 19) displays the arms of Ogremont quartered with Ste Maure with overall Amboise. Guillaume d'Ogremont was the third son of Pierre d'Ogremont, and his wife was a daughter of Pierre de Ste Maure and Marguerite d'Amboise. The prominence of the Amboise heraldic bearings points to the wife's ownership of the manuscript. The mention of 'Clemens Papa VII' in a rubric is probably a reference to the Anti-Pope, 1378–94. The composition of the calendar shows evidence of Parisian origin. The decorative cross which precedes the abc is common to most of the pages here under review; it indicates that these manuscript books are also the forerunners of all the printed primers and reading books. Their more primitive cousins are the hornbooks, which also start with the 'criss-cross-row', which means Christ's Cross followed by the alphabet.

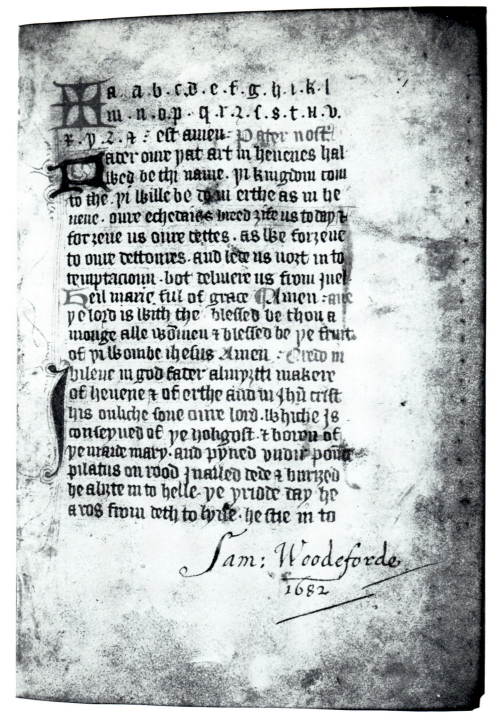

18.   From a Primer (*c.* 1382): see p. 70.
Hunterian Library, Glasgow (MS. V. 6. 22)

19.   From a Prayer-book (*c.* 1386): see p. 70.
Bodleian Library, Oxford (MS. Rawl. liturg. e40, 15829)

20.   From the Primer of Maximilian I (*c.* 1467): see p. 71.   (Reduced)
Austrian National Library, Vienna (Cod. 2368)

21. From the Primer of Maximilian I (*c.* 1467): see p. 71. (Reduced)
Austrian National Library, Vienna (Cod. 2368)

22. From fragments of MSS. 2981, Pepys Calligraphic Collection (*c.* 1400): see p. 72.
Magdalene College, Cambridge

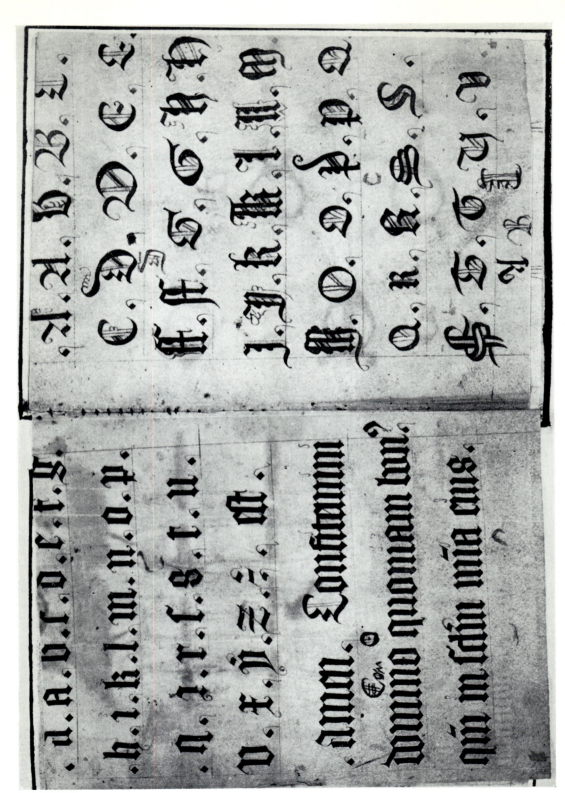

23. From fragments of MSS. 2981, Pepys Calligraphic Collection (c. 1400): see p. 72.

Magdalene College, Cambridge

In this connection it is fascinating to find in Dominique Martin Meon's *Nouveau Recueil de Fabliaux et Contes...des poètes français des XI, XII, XIII et XV siècles* (Paris, 1823) the chanson of a clerk-trouvère who laments the loss at dice of all his belongings. In this song the prodigal waste of his treasured books is bemoaned in full detail. What is particularly interesting to us here is that the catalogue of his miseries is headed by the loss of his ABC-cum-Pater Noster; in fact the lines I now quote more or less make up the primer here under consideration:

> Quar je cuit que il n'ait chastel
> En France que je n'i alaisse,
> Et de mes livres n'i lessaisse.
> A Gandelus lez La Ferté
> La lessai-je mon *A.B.C.*,
> Et ma *patrenostre* à Soisson,
> Et mon *credo* à Monleon,
> Et mes *set siaumes* à Tornai,
> Mes *quinze siaumes* à Cambrai,
> Et mon *sautier* à Besençon,
> Et mon *kalendier* à Dijon...etc.[11]

Now that we have looked at both a homely, unadorned English manuscript and a noble, illuminated French one, each with alphabets as preludes to further learning, we continue our survey by examining a princely codex of a similar but more pronouncedly educational kind. The school books of Emperor Maximilian I[12] are of great importance in the history of teaching methods in the late Middle Ages. The one which is most relevant to the present theme is Cod. 2368 of the Austrian National Library in Vienna. This book was written before 1467. The first page (Plate 20) opens with the identical arrangement which the two previously discussed works have made familiar to us, but with a difference of scale and splendour. The stately text alphabet is surmounted by the Imperial arms which are placed between those of Austria and Portugal. The initial letter to the Latin text shows the young Maximilian being taught by his tutor the first elements of reading. Actually the prince is pointing to a minute ABC on the left-hand page of the open book, which is rather touchingly supported by his teacher. Later on in the same codex the Lord's Prayer in German, and this time in a current black letter hand, is preceded by a one-line alphabet (Plate 21).

The whole group of manuscripts is written in a variety of styles in order to make the prince familiar with the full range of letter forms. In addition to this, the leaves

20 to 27 in the first book of this series are covered with a variety of initial letters in alphabetical order and with a textura alphabet in scroll work. The first page in this section carries the monogram yhs and the last three the initials of Maximilian's father. The presence of decorative material of this kind in a school book is very interesting to us as it helps us to identify, and to place in their proper position, two fragments of vellum manuscripts in English collections, and to reconstruct the missing parts.

The Pepysian Library at Magdalene College, Cambridge, possesses a fragment of five leaves dating from about 1400, probably of English provenance, here reproduced for the first time (Plates 22–25). The leaves are closely cropped and this destroys, among other evidence, that of possible folio numbers.

The presence of the ihc monogram and of a variety of decorative alphabets, as in the Vienna manuscript (see above), and of the decorative cross as in the Bodleian and Glasgow prayer-books (preceding the abc), enables us to assume that the Pepys manuscript is either the remainder of, or a scribe's copy-book for, such a primer.

Professor Francis Wormald has discovered and now owns a fascicule of three vellum leaves which he has kindly allowed me to mention in my survey (Plate 26). This fragment displays on five pages initial letters of the alphabet drawn by the scribe with the pen in ink outline according to the style of the thirteenth century. Careful examination reveals that some of the curves were drawn with the help of dividers. The initials are decoratively arranged, not always in strict alphabetical order. The sixth page shows two initials which have been painted in colour, possibly at a later date, over similar outline drawings. As the leaves are folioed 2ʌ, 28 and 29, and as thirty-three prick marks are preserved on the extreme edge of the outer margins, we can assume with a fair degree of confidence that the lost leaves 1–26 were covered by a text of thirty-two lines to the page. Was this text that of a prayer-book like the one which belonged to the young Archduke Maximilian?

To recapitulate: in that first prayer-book of his the series of decorative initial letter alphabets did cover the folios 20–27. This can help us, if conjecture is permissible at all, to reconstruct a text which may have been destroyed at the time of the Reformation.

We may well wonder whether other examples exist which could be added to this account of alphabets in medieval manuscripts. Our material has so far been drawn only from English, French and German sources. I was therefore pleased to find a beautifully illuminated Boethius: *De Consolatione Philosophiae*, cum Commento,[13] written in 1385. It belongs to the Hunterian Museum at Glasgow and is, needless to say, on vellum, as are all the other manuscripts under discussion here. The first two facing pages are framed in elaborate borders of gold, blue and red. Folio 1ᵛ displays gilt letters A, the scribe's initial, in the four corners of the border which encloses a minuscule alphabet in blue, most of the letters written twice with exuberantly exaggerated descenders and ascenders (Plate 27). Folio 2ʳ shows a splendid double alphabet panel of capital letters in red and blue surmounted by the *Nunc Dimittis* and followed below by four lines of the *Credo* in two sizes and the *Magnificat* in further reduced scale (Plate 28). The first line of this page and the four lines of the *Credo* are in black, but the others are in red and blue. The last line carries the scribe's autograph: 'Ego enim sum minimus omnium scriptorum frater Amadeus subscriptus', and this line is repeated in an abbreviated form at the end of the Introduction on fol. 3ʳ. Within the lower border can be found in raised gilt letters: 'Istud opus est Gregorij de Janua. MCCCLXXXV'.

These two handsome pages at the beginning of the manuscript show the different sizes of Rotunda employed in the bulk of the codex, together with the scribe Amadeus's colophon and the ex-libris of his patron Gregorius of Genoa who commissioned the book—a remarkable combination the value of which is heightened by the presence of the specimen alphabets. As with the primers, they act as a key to the text and we observe that they were penned with joy and a certain pride by Amadeus, who by contrast modestly describes himself as the least of all scribes.

In a way, this investigation of alphabets appearing in certain manuscripts of the Middle Ages is an exploration of a new field, and I hope it will be of interest to palaeographers and to others engaged in studies of educational methods. It is well known, of course, that different kinds of alphabet are found in other types of medieval manuscript. Grammatical and other treatises also show ABC's; Hrabanus Maurus, for example, comes to mind. The material in Pontificals, which we intend to treat at a later date, also should reward careful consideration. May I conclude with the hope that this survey may cause other manuscripts of the kind here treated to be brought to light.

NOTES

1 S. H. Steinberg, 'The *Forma Scribendi* of Hugo Spechtshart', *The Library*, new series, XXI (1941); 'Medieval Writing Masters', *The Library*, 4th series, XXII (1941); 'A Hand-list of Specimens of Medieval Writing Masters', *The Library*, new series, XXIII (1943); also a letter p. 203, *The Library*, 5th series, II (1948).

2 C. Wehmer, 'Die Schreibmeisterblätter des späten Mittelalters', *Miscellanea Giovanni Mercati*, vol. VI, *Studi e testi*, CXXVI (Vatican City, 1946), 147–61.

3 S. J. P. van Dijk, 'An Advertisement Sheet of an early Fourteenth-century Writing Master at Oxford', *Scriptorium*, tome X (Amsterdam, 1956).

4 B. L. Ullman, 'Abecedaria and their Purpose', *Transactions of the Cambridge Bibliographical Society*, III (1961), no. 3.

5 See E. Maude Thompson, *Catalogue of Ancient Manuscripts in the British Museum*, part 2 Latin. (London 1884), for a reproduction of fol. 88.

6 John Young and P. Henderson Aitken, *A Catalogue of Manuscripts in the Library of the Hunterian Museum* in the University of Glasgow (Glasgow, 1908).

Berthold Wolpe

7 Samuel Woodford (1636–1700), see *DNB*, LXII, p. 396.

8 Primer, Hunterian MS, V. 6. 22. Size $7\frac{1}{2}'' \times 5\frac{1}{4}''$, fols. 90.

9 Prayer-book, Hunterian MS. V. 8. 15. Size $6\frac{3}{4}'' \times 4\frac{3}{8}''$, fols. 226.

10 Bodleian MS. Rawl. liturg. e 40 (15829); size $8\frac{3}{4}'' \times 6\frac{1}{4}''$, fols. ii+174.

11 See Helen Waddell, *The Wandering Scholars* (London, 1944), Appendix, for a free translation.

12 Heinrich Fichtenau, *Die Lehrbücher Maximilians I und die Anfänge der Frakturschrift*, Maximilian Gesellschaft, issued by Dr Ernst Hauswedell and Co. (Hamburg, 1961). Reviewed by B. L. Wolpe in *The Book Collector*, autumn 1962.

13 Hunterian MS. V. 1. 11. Size: $13\frac{3}{8}'' \times 10''$, fols. 110.

ACKNOWLEDGEMENTS

I am extremely grateful to Dr R. O. MacKenna, librarian and keeper of the Hunterian Books and Manuscripts, Glasgow University, who made three MSS. available to me, and to Dr J. H. P. Pafford and Miss Joan Gibbs of London University Library who enabled me to study them. I also acknowledge with gratitude permission to reproduce extracts from two of these MSS.

Thanks for assistance and similar permission are due to Dr R. W. Ladborough, Pepysian Librarian, and to the Master and Fellows of Magdalene College Cambridge; to Dr R. W. Hunt and Mr J. J. G. Alexander of the Bodleian Library; to Professor Heinrich Fichtenau, Dr Ernst Hauswedell and the Maximilian Gesellschaft.

Fig. 6. Teaching the alphabet (woodcut from Geiler von Keiserberg, *Ein heylsame lere und predig*, 1490).

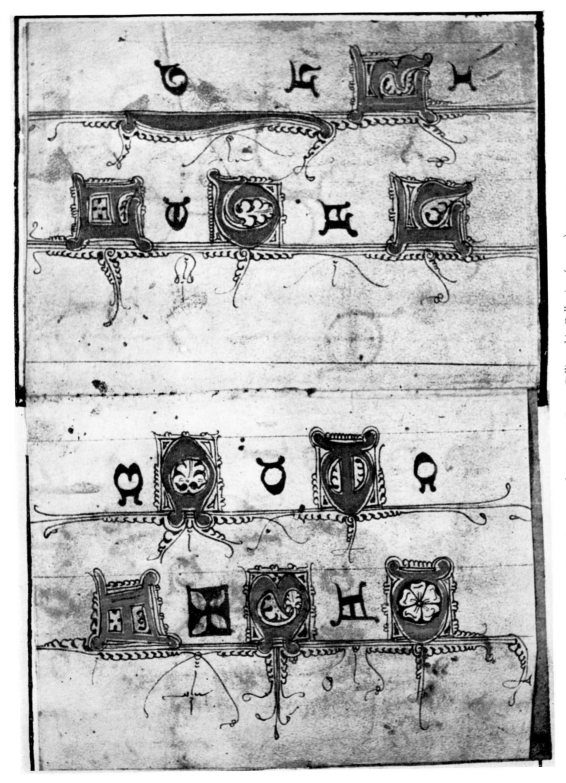

24. From fragments of MSS. 2981, Pepys Calligraphic Collection (*c.* 1400): see p. 72.
Magdalene College, Cambridge

[*To face p. 74*]

25. From fragments of MSS. 2981, Pepys Calligraphic Collection (*c.* 1400): see p. 72.
Magdalene College, Cambridge

26. From a fragment of a thirteenth(?)-century MS.: see p. 72. (Reduced)
In possession of Professor Francis Wormald

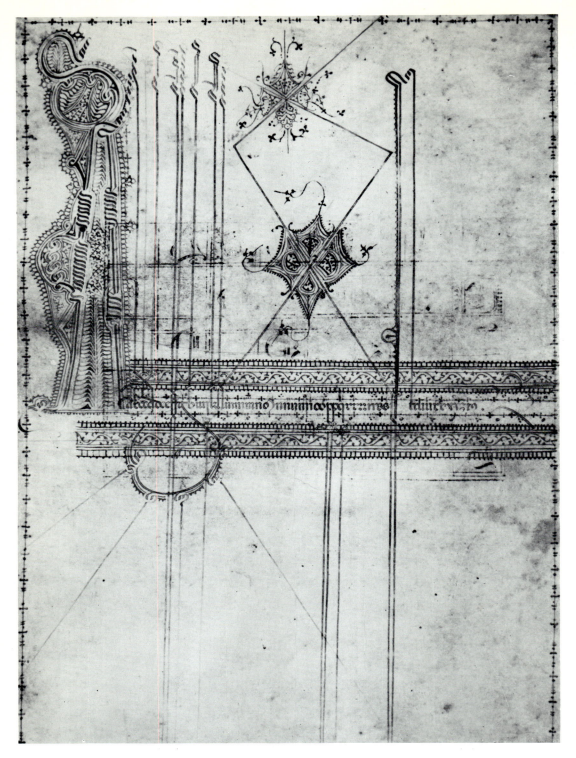

27. From Boethius, *De Consolatione Philosophiae* (1385): see p. 73. (Reduced)
Hunterian Museum, Glasgow (MS. V. 1. 11)

28. From Boethius, *De Consolatione Philosophiae* (1385): see p. 73. (Reduced)
Hunterian Museum, Glasgow (MS. V. 1. 11)

Ingentia exempla contra uarronis sententiam de car
tis reppiuntur. Namq; cassius hemina uetustissim[us]
auctor annalium. quarto eorum libro prodidit cū
uertentium scribam agrū suū in ianiculo repastinan
dū effodisse archam in qua numa qui romae regnauit
situs fuisset. in eadem libros eius reptos. P. cornelio
us. L. filio cethego. M. bebio. q. filio pamphilocos. ad
quos a regno nume colligunt[ur] anni quingenti tri
ginta quinq; Hos fuisse carta maiore etiam nunc
miraculo quod tot infossi durauerint annis.
Quapropter hic recenta ipsius heminae uerba ponā.
Mirabantur alii quorū illi libri durare potuissent.
Ille ita rationē reddebat lapidem fuisse quadratū
circiter in medio arce uinctum candelis quaqua
uersum in eo lapide insup libros impositos fuisse
propterea arbitrari eum ñ potuisse libros ceratos
tineas tangere. In his libris scripte erant phyloso
phiae. Hoc idem tradit ipse censorius primo com
mentariorum. s; libros septem iuris pontificiy totidem
pythagoricos fuisse. Syluanus uero decimo nume
decretorum fuisse. Ipse uarro humanarum antiquatū
vii antiquis socios libros fuisse ex his pontificales lati
nos. totidem grecos p̄cepta phylosophiae continentes.
Idem ĩ eos ponit quo comburi placuerit eos. Inter
omnes uero conuenit sybillam tres libros attulisse. ad tarquiniū suprbū
ex quibus in his duo cremati ab ipsa. ĩ cius cū capitoli
o sullanis temporib; Preterea mutianus ter consul

marginal notes:
mandante tabula nili
aqua ubidus lign un gla
tinis pbrin te cū pmo
supina tabula sceda alia
nte longitudine papyri
q potuit ēe rei ignitatub;
amputatis utrinq; ūfa
transuersa
Numa r libar̄ cō
.p. cōneli?
.l. filio cethec?
.m. ebi.
heminal r̄ uba ex
ei hystoria.
pythagorice eosq; combusto
a petilio ptore. quia philo
sophice scripti sent.
udita[n]
yarro.
Anti[?] fo.
Sibylla Tarqn?
Mutian?

29.   From a MS. of Pliny, *Historia Naturalis*, Book XIII (27), which once belonged to Coluccio Salutati: see p. 77.
Bodleian Library, Oxford (MS. Auct. T. I. 27, fol. 59ʳ)

[To face p.

R. W. HUNT

A Manuscript from the Library of
Coluccio Salutati

There are many manuscripts in our libraries which, through the accidents of time, have lost their earlier notes of provenance, but have an air of distinction either in their text or annotation. The rediscovery of the history of such volumes is bound to be a matter of luck or chance, but, with the increasing facilities for photographic reproduction, it becomes easier to make comparisons and to check possibilities. A volume in the Bodleian Library containing Pliny's *Natural History*, books VI–XV, is a fair example. Its only note of provenance is the inscription written along the outer margin of what is now the second leaf of the text: 'Paraphé au desir de l'arrest du 5. juillet 1763 Mesnil.' This is the inscription, which is found in the manuscripts from the Jesuit Collège de Clermont (or Louis le Grand, as it should properly be called at this time) in Paris.[1]

When the Jesuit order in France was suppressed in 1763, the College was handed over to the University of Paris. Funds were needed for its maintenance, and it was decided that its library should be sold. Application was made to the Parlement de Paris for permission to proceed with the sale. The court in its decree laid down that all the manuscripts should be 'paraphés sur la première page de chacun desdits volumes ou cahiers, avec indication du nombre de feuillets contenus dans ledit volume ou cahier', and that they should be packed in boxes or hampers and sent to the Abbey of St Germain des Prés for appraisal and cataloguing.[2] A number of the learned Benedictines there set to work and in a remarkably short time a very good catalogue was produced. It was chiefly the work of Dom Clément, who is remembered as the author of the *Art de vérifier les dates*. Under the number DCCXII he described our manuscript in the following terms:[3] 'Codex membranaceus in-fol. eleganti charactere saeculi XII[i] ineuntis exaratus, at prae mucore et situ ita corruptus

75

ab initio ad medium et ultra, ut omnino legi non possit. Ibi continetur *Plinii secundi Historia naturalis.* (Folia 71. complectitur.)'

The manuscript in its present state is not damaged by mould and decay as far as the middle and beyond, but a seventeenth-century foliation from 45 to 116 shows that a number of leaves were lost at some time. The directions laid down in the order of the court already quoted may supply a clue. The official of the court was directed to put his *paraphé* on the *front* page of each volume with an indication of the number of leaves contained in it. This he did, and the number 71 is written at the top of the second leaf. Dom Clément, as his custom was, reproduced this figure in his description. It is a correct reckoning if we count the leaf bearing the *paraphé* mark as the first. But, as the volume stands now, there is a leaf preceding it, somewhat rubbed, with damage repaired, and a piece of parchment pasted over the first eleven lines of the first column of text, which contained the end of book v. It may be suggested that the official disregarded in his reckoning the part of the book *prae mucore et situ corruptus*, and that when the book was put in order the 'illegible' leaves were found to be beyond repair, and so were discarded, except for that which is now fol. 1. The motive for patching it up and saving it is plain. It contained the beginning of a new book.

The Catalogue contained a notice at the beginning (p. viii) that the manuscripts would be sold individually at a date to be fixed, provided that the Administrators of the Collège de Louis le Grand did not receive an offer for the whole collection before 1 September following. Such an offer was made by the bookseller De Bure le jeune on behalf of the Dutch collector, Gerard Meerman, the author of *Origines typographicae.* After the failure of a half-hearted approach to the Royal Library, the offer was accepted, and the manuscripts were sent to Holland, with the exception of thirty-nine volumes which were stopped on the way on the King's behalf. For these the King invested Meerman with the Order of St Michael. The collection was incorporated in Meerman's library. The bindings were put in order. Our volume was repaired and given its present plain vellum cover.[4]

On the death of Gerard Meerman's son, John, his collection of books and manuscripts was sold at auction at The Hague in 1824. The chief bidder was Sir Thomas Phillipps, but, for the classical manuscripts, he had a competitor in Thomas Gaisford, Regius Professor of Greek in the University of Oxford, and a very active curator of the Bodleian Library.[5] Gaisford secured fifty-eight volumes for the Bodleian, among them the present manuscript, which was lot 637. In the Bodleian Library it was referenced MS. Auct. T. I. 27.[6]

So much for the later history of the manuscript. The clue to its earlier provenance lies in the extensive marginal annotations. They are chiefly in two Italian hands of the late fourteenth and mid-fifteenth centuries. Those in the earlier hand consist almost entirely of words in the text written out in the margin to form a kind of index. The second hand chiefly made corrections in the text, evidently with the aid of another copy of the work. Thanks to the appearance of Professor B. L. Ullman's book on *The Humanism of Coluccio Salutati*,[7] it is now easy to see that the earlier annotator was Coluccio Salutati. The script, which is of the type known as *fere humanistica*, and the method of annotation are those described and figured by Ullman. But we are not dependent for the identification on the evidence of script alone. In his list of the books which survive from the library of Coluccio, Ullman describes a volume now in the Bibliothèque Nationale at Paris, MS. lat. 6798, which contains books XVI–XXXVII of Pliny's *Natural History*.[8] Like our manuscript, it was written in the twelfth century. It has the same measurements (400 × 295 mm), but more significant, in both manuscripts each quire is numbered at the end in a hand of the twelfth century. The Paris volume, which has kept its fifteenth-century Italian binding, begins with the last leaf of quire XVIII. The Bodleian volume begins with the last leaf of quire IX and continues to quire XVII, followed by seven leaves of quire XVIII, of which the eighth leaf begins the Paris part. There can be no doubt that the two volumes were originally one book. Its script and decoration suggest that it was executed in the Mosan region about the middle of the twelfth century. We do not know where or how Coluccio got it. From a reference in one of his letters written in 1378, we know that he could not find a copy of the work in Florence. It is clear from his book *De fato*, written about 1398, that he had by that time come into possession of one copy. From then on he made much use of it. Ullman in describing the Paris part says that it contains 'thousands of Coluccio notes, mostly names, with some content words'.[9] The same is true of the Bodleian part. Specimens can be seen in Plate 29.

At the end of the Paris part is not only the ex-libris of Coluccio, but a well-known subscription which records the names of the next two owners.[10] From the sons of Coluccio it was bought by another Florentine humanist and chancellor, Leonardo Bruni; and from his sons it was bought by Antonio Panormita, the secretary of King Alfonso I of Aragon and of his son Ferrante. Panormita corrected the text extensively in his careful humanist hand, using another manuscript. Here the subscription ends, but we know that both parts of the manuscript passed into the possession of Ferdinand III, King of Naples. After his time the two parts were separated. Volume II, the Paris part, was among the books bought from King Ferdinand by Cardinal Georges I d'Amboise, Archbishop of Rouen. In the list of his manuscripts drawn up in 1508, no. 77 is 'Secunda pars Plinii'.[11] No first part is found in the list. The second part came eventually into the Royal Library at Paris. The first part was less fortunate, and for a century and more we lose sight of it. We do not even know when it reached the Jesuit College, but it was certainly there before 1685, when that very eccentric scholar Père Jean Hardouin, who was a scriptor and later professor at the College, published his monumental edition of Pliny's *Natural History*.[12] He called the manuscript 'codex optimae notae' and gave it the *siglum* 'Par' but only made occasional use of it.

This is not quite the end of the story. To go back to the time when the two parts were still together in the library of King Ferdinand, they were partly collated by Politian on the edition of Pliny printed at Rome in 1473 by Sweynheym and Pannartz. An almost contemporary transcript of these notes is entered in the margins of a copy of this edition of Pliny, which is one of the treasures of the Bodleian (Auct. Q. I. 2). Politian in a note at the end, dated 1490, says[13] that he collated the text with two manuscripts in the Library of San Marco at Florence, which he denoted by the letters 'a' and 'b', and with a third which belonged to King Ferdinand 'quod et Leonardi quondam Arretini fuerat'—'and which also belonged to Leonardo Bruni'. This, which can be no other than the manuscript now divided between Paris and Oxford, he denoted by the letter 'c'. From XIII. 14 to XXI, it was his main authority because of lacunae in his other manuscripts: 'Hic intercisus erat vetustior codex usque ad principium xxi libri: sed et hinc emendavi cum regio .c.' Politian's note goes on to say that he gave private classes for the space of seven months to certain young Portuguese and Englishmen who had come to Florence to study. The Englishmen were Thomas Linacre and William Grocyn. It is perhaps not too fanciful to suggest that our volume of Pliny was sometimes on the desk of Politian when he gave these classes.

It is the descent among the Italian humanists of the fifteenth century that gives our manuscript its interest.[14] Its value for the text of Pliny is not likely to be great. The Paris volume was occasionally cited by editors up to the time of Sillig (1851), but when Detlefsen made the first serious attempt to sort out the manuscripts of Pliny, he dismissed it as of no consequence,[15] and it has not been used since. The Bodleian volume was reported on briefly by a Scottish scholar, D. J. Campbell,[16] but he was not aware of its connection with Paris lat. 6798. From an examination of a small part of the text, he concluded that it was closely related to the manuscript known to editors of Pliny as E^2, that is the correcting hand of another Paris Pliny, MS. latin 6795. This is not the place to pursue the inquiry into the position of our manuscript in the tradition. Despite the remarkable progress made by the editors of Pliny in the nineteenth century, it remains true that no scholar armed with modern palaeographical knowledge and technique has examined the text of Pliny.[17] The length of the *Natural History* makes it a daunting task, but it would surely now be possible to date and place the manuscripts more accurately and so to make better sense of the relationship between them.

NOTES

1 For its history, see G. Dupont-Ferrier, *Du Collège de Clermont au Lycée Louis-le-Grand 1563–1920* (Paris, 1921–5). The library is treated at I. 122–6, 456–7.

2 H. Omont, 'Documents sur la vente des manuscrits du Collège de Clermont à Paris (1764)' *Bulletin de la soc. de l'hist. de Paris et de l'Ile de France*, XVIII (1891), 8.

3 *Catalogue codicum manuscriptorum collegii Claromontani* (Paris, 1764), p. 274.

4 At the top of the spine is PLINII/Historia/Naturalis/Manuscript. This is the type of binding and lettering described by V. Rose, *Die lat. Meerman-Handschriften des Sir Thomas Phillipps in der königl. Bibliothek zu Berlin* (1892), p. iv.

5 A. N. L. Munby, *Phillipps Studies* (London, 1954), III, 35–6.

6 F. Madan, *Summary cat. of western manuscripts in the Bodleian Library at Oxford* (Oxford, 1897), IV, 436, no. 20621. It was briefly mentioned in H. Schenkl, *Bibl. patrum latinorum Britannica* (Vienna, 1891), p. 23.

7 Medioevo e umanesimo 4 (Padua, 1963).

8 *Ibid.* pp. 195–6, no. 100. For details, see F. Lehoux, 'Un manuscrit des rois aragonais de Naples et des archevêques de Rouen', *Bibl. de l'école des chartes*, CI (1940), 229–33.

9 Ullman, *op. cit.* p. 246.

10 Facsimile in T. de Marinis, *La Biblioteca Napoletana dei re d'Aragona*, I (Milan, 1952), p. 214.

11 L. Delisle, *Le cabinet des manuscrits de la Bibliothèque impériale* (Paris, 1868), I, 236.

12 Vol. I, praef., sign. o ii[v]: 'Usi praeterea et altero optimae notae codice quem Parisiensem nuncupamus, quod sit is in ea urbe in qua sumus, et in Bibliothecae, quam curamus, scriniis reconditus.' See also the *conspectus codicum*, sign. b. iii. On Hardouin, see Owen Chadwick, *From Bossuet to Newman* (Cambridge, 1957), pp. 49 f.

13 J. M. S. Cotton, *Mod. Lang. Rev.* XXXII (1937), 394–6, where further references will be found. It has hitherto been assumed that the annotations in this book are in the autograph of Politian, but A. Perosa in a lecture, delivered in Oxford in 1962 but not yet published, demonstrated that the main body of the annotations was a transcript of Politian's notes.

14 There are annotations in at least one other humanist hand.

15 *Philologus*, XXVIII (1869), 300.

16 *American Journal of Philology*, LVII (1936), 120–3.

17 Cf. W. Kroll, 'Die Kosmologie des Plinius' (*Abh. der Schles. Gesellschaft für vaterländische Cultur*, Hft. 3, 1930), p. 79.

NOTE ON THE PLATE

The hand of Coluccio is seen in the indexing notes 'Numa et libris eius, P. Cornelius', etc.; the hand of Panormita adds a piece omitted from the text, beginning 'pythagorice' and makes corrections in the text, e.g. line 11 'in re tanta'. The hand of an unidentified humanist is seen in the variant 'recensa' in the margin at line 11, and in the DE LIBRIS NUMAE in the top margin.

JOAN GIBBS

Seymour de Ricci's
'Bibliotheca Britannica Manuscripta'

For many years Alfred Fairbank has been a regular and welcome user of the University of London Library and, in particular, of the Palaeography Room. Yet it is doubtful if even he has ever made use there of the *Bibliotheca Britannica Manuscripta*.[1] In this respect he is like most other students, and so it may be of interest to draw attention here to this material—transferred to its present surroundings in 1953 so that it might be made 'more accessible to scholars'[2]—indicating both its uses and its limitations, but trying first of all to sketch the scope and history of the project.

The story begins and ends with Seymour Montefiore Robert Rosso de Ricci, a French bibliographer of immense industry and wide-ranging interests.[3] In 1934, after ten years' labour, he had just seen to press the first volume of his *Census of Medieval and Renaissance Manuscripts in the United States and Canada*.[4] Work on this project had shown him the desirability of a similar survey of manuscript sources in the British Isles, but he was aware, none better, of the bibliographical spade-work necessary before such an undertaking could usefully be begun. However, his expansive ideas outran even his great energies, and these very energies could not be satisfied with mere bibliographical routines. This dichotomy of approach de Ricci never fully resolved: had he done so there would now be no story to tell.

When de Ricci first wrote to the Institute of Historical Research in September 1934, he enclosed a memorandum on his projected 'Survey of Manuscripts in the British Isles',[5] suggesting that the Institute Committee might undertake responsibility for compiling and publishing the work, already conceived on far more ambitious lines than those of the American *Census*. Not only was it to extend to 1837, but it was to include in its coverage archives as well as literary manuscripts. Guy

Parsloe, then Secretary of the Institute, opened his side of a long correspondence on 27 September saying that 'there will be general agreement as to the usefulness of such a survey' and he promised that the memorandum would receive 'very careful and sympathetic consideration'. The problem would be one of finance. The matter was referred by the Committee in the following month to the Migrations of MSS. Sub-Committee[6] for examination and report, and it was suggested that de Ricci might come to London (his home was in Paris) to expound his ideas.

He agreed with alacrity, replying to the invitation on the very day of its receipt (16 October) with a nine-page letter setting out some of the 'numerous points which would have to be settled, the most essential to my mind being the actual amount of detail advisable in a work of that description, since each chapter of the Survey could, without real difficulty, either be condensed in ten lines or padded out to a hundred pages...the main points to keep in view seem first to ascertain exactly what scholars need and secondly exactly what they can or cannot easily obtain from available printed sources'. But in the next paragraph he threatens to depart from these excellent principles: 'personally I would be tempted to go as far as to print skeleton lists in numerical order, even of well-known series of manuscripts.' It is proposed, for example, that the printed catalogues of M. R. James should be digested to half a page of the survey. 'With archives and muniment rooms it is even easier to give in a few words a fairly satisfactory analysis of an extensive collection'. The arrangement would be geographical—England, Wales, Scotland and Ireland, then by counties, towns and parishes. He suggested that the chapters on Phillipps and Ashburnham in his work on *English Collectors of Books and Manuscripts*[7] would give members of the Sub-Committee 'a foretaste of my Survey'. To de Ricci, finance presented no problem: 'I do not believe that the expense involved by this project would be heavy...I fancy that the actual printing could be paid for out of the sale of the book. If my plan of treating each county separately be found feasible, we might expect some local help and even some local subsidies.'

De Ricci met the Sub-Committee (including Charles Johnson and A. G. Little) in London at the end of November 1934, and exhibited 'some thousands of bibliographical cards which he had already collected, as well as a few sections drafted in full to illustrate the suggested treatment of individual libraries'. The Sub-Committee's report continues: 'Mr de Ricci urged that the scheme might go so far as to list in brief form all manuscript volumes in public and private collections in the British Isles. It was felt that such an undertaking, far more extensive than that outlined in Mr de Ricci's memorandum, could scarcely be contemplated at the present time, but that the first step should be a compilation of a list of all printed catalogues of collections of manuscripts in Great Britain, both in public and private hands, arranged under place of deposit, with references to works bearing directly upon their history and arrangement. This would be a valuable and practicable undertaking, laying the foundation for fuller treatment at a later date, if desired.' De Ricci was agreeable; he was promised some secretarial assistance; and the Institute's financial responsibility was to be limited to the costs of publication. The Institute Committee approved the report at its meeting of 13 February 1935.

In June 1936, Parsloe wrote asking for a progress report. De Ricci replied on 12 June that 'I now feel it possible to outline the projected work far more definitely than two years ago.... Up to the present moment the following portions of the work have been dealt with. I have brought together in Paris a large specialized library, containing several thousand catalogues and other books relating to the proposed survey. From French and English libraries and from a number of miscellaneous sources I have already collected over twenty thousand detailed cards covering a large portion of the field. My present assistant, Miss Grace Vogel, of Winnipeg, has drafted under my directions an alphabetical list, on eleven thousand cards, of all the early manuscripts which have passed through English salerooms in the last forty-five years.' He anticipated much further research, the checking of periodicals and visiting repositories. 'All this, I can not do single-handed and I can not afford to continue the expenditure involved by the full-time employment of my secretary Miss Vogel. I believe that it would be necessary to obtain assistance for at least three years, at a salary which I value at two hundred pounds per annum.'

At this same period de Ricci prepared a 25-page memorandum on the sources of information for a *Bibliotheca Britannica Manuscripta*, and sent it to Parsloe, who replied on 14 August, obviously perplexed, even after due reflection. 'Your memorandum, I imagine, was written while you intended to substitute a comprehensive *Bibliotheca Britannica Manuscripta* for the limited *List of Catalogues of Manuscripts*. Now that you have decided to publish the *List* as a preliminary measure, I am puzzled as to its relationship with the *Bibliotheca*. Do you intend the latter to incorporate all the entries in the former? If not, of what will the *Bibliotheca* consist? To reprint the *List* in the *Bibliotheca* seems extravagant, but it would be irritating to have to consult two books instead of one. Perhaps because I do not fully understand your plan, I feel at present that it would be better to get the Committee to consider the merits of the *Bibliotheca* as a substitute for, rather than a development of, the *List*. I believe they could be convinced.'

De Ricci's prompt reply of 16 August 1936 is of interest in stating his attitude to his work. 'It is a kind of wager for any individual to attempt single-handed to sift three centuries of miscellaneous literature on manuscripts in the British Isles....As far as I could gather, the members of the Sub-Committee—like yourself to a certain degree—were afraid that my efforts would not be equal to the task I had set myself and they not unnaturally suggested that the immediate preparation of a preliminary bibliography of libraries would be an advisable first step towards a fuller survey giving the bibliography, not only of each collection, but of each item....You are too well posted on the subject not to acknowledge that the dividing line between the two works is shadowy to the extreme. You fully realize that the actual differences between a *catalogue* and a *calendar*, between a *calendar* and an *edition* are, to a large extent, a matter of individual appreciation. For me I do not pay any real attention to these differences: all is grist that comes to my mill.' He favoured publication in two parts not least because 'the Survey, as I told you, is distinctly a one man's job; is it wise to postpone all attempts towards publication until the distant moment when I will feel that I have covered the whole of my field? There are too many instances, in the history of research, of first-class men who have delayed publication until they were no longer able to accomplish it. I would like to "make hay while the sun shines" and I am by no means certain that such is not the most sensible course.'

Parsloe undertook to report these matters to the Migrations of MSS. Sub-Committee of the Anglo-American Historical Committee, 'under which your work is nominally being done', after de Ricci had supplied him with the latest information (9 September 1936): 25,000 cards completed ('many thousands...on individual manuscripts in each of the collections described'); an alphabetical index on 11,000 cards of all manuscripts which have appeared in London auction sales from 1893 to 1936; two-thirds of the preliminary research work completed; 'of the more detailed survey of individual items, hardly *one tenth*'. The preliminary bibliography he thought might run to 500 pages, $9'' \times 7''$. De Ricci pointed out with satisfaction that his activities had induced the trustees of the Duke of Newcastle to entrust to him the cataloguing of 'three or four hundred practically unknown manuscripts in the Duke's library'.[8]

In his last letter, Parsloe had enclosed a query from the Rev. Paul Grosjean, S.J., asking about manuscripts thought to be at Holkham Hall[9] and, in his next, Parsloe was thanking de Ricci for 'an authoritative answer'. It was only the first of many occasions when an appeal was made to de Ricci for information, and he was usually able to find something useful in the long-gestating *Bibliotheca*. A year later, Parsloe was writing 'I fear that your fame is spreading so fast here that it is difficult to keep enquirers at bay'.[10] But such demands, if occasionally importunate, could not but be encouraging to de Ricci in his labours. 'You doubtless realize', he wrote to Parsloe on 16 August 1936, 'how anxious I feel to be supported by the sympathy of all fellow-workers.'

And indeed the de Ricci correspondence does include a number of pleasant letters of appreciation from scholars. Robin Flower[11] wrote (12 September 1934) from the Department of Manuscripts, British Museum: 'The more I think of it the more attractive your scheme seems to me to be, and no day passes without an illustration of what a very present help it would be to us here and to all scholars interested in these matters.' Sydney Cockerell[12] wrote from the Fitzwilliam Museum, Cambridge, on 26 September 1934. His very personal style may perhaps sanction quotation *in extenso*.

'What a marvel you are of both industry and courage to be able boldly to embark on so tremendous an enterprise! Here am I with no more done towards sending you particulars of my books, while you can gobble the manuscript contents of the New World in almost no time—& print the detailed list. It is quite a mistake to suppose that I know more than other people about manuscripts in England, or for that matter in Cambridge, or even in the Museum! I have looked at very few manuscripts besides my own since I came here 26 years ago. I have read the prospectus that I return & all I can say is that the project would be more manageable if it came to a full-stop at 1500—leaving everything later than that for a later work—or at any rate if all 'documents' were ruled out. But you know best as to what is desirable as well as possible—also you know how very few people, when it is done, will realise how stupendous a task you have accomplished, or will so much as say thank you.

'I suppose that nearly all such labours are undertaken for one's own personal satisfaction. I feel how very little I have myself done & that it is now too late for me to set to work. The years and months fly past and soon will come the final day.'[13]

M. R. James[14] wrote from the Provost's Lodge at Eton (16 November 1934) to welcome 'your progress with U.S.A. MSS. and applaud your courageous scheme for a Bibl. Brit.... what you can tell me about Phillipps MSS. will be extraordinarily welcome'. Dr G. H. Fowler,[15] convener of the MSS. Sub-Committee, wrote (20 February 1935) of the Committee's preparation of a '*Repertory of British cartularies*',[16] and soon afterwards was encouraging him to visit the Bedfordshire County Record Office 'so that you can see...the kind of collection which is springing up in so many counties'. Arundell Esdaile[17] suggested (14 January 1937) an approach to the Leverhulme Trust for funds. C. R. Cheney[18] wrote in April 1938 to 'acquaint you with a project which I have in hand, together with several other medievalists. It is the making of a census of existing manuscripts and printed books from medieval

English monastic and collegiate and parochial libraries...at present we have about three thousand cards....I need hardly say that we have found invaluable your various bibliographical writings.'[19]

In October 1936 Dr Fowler, convener of the Sub-Committee, had written to de Ricci suggesting that he should attend a meeting to be held in mid-November, later altered to mid-December. Before this confrontation took place, however, Parsloe was writing (on 26 November) to say that the Institute Committee had agreed to make a grant of £50 'toward the salary of your assistant in the compilation of the list of catalogues of manuscripts'.[20]

From de Ricci's letter of 2 December, it is clear that he had just returned from New York, probably also from Washington, for he writes: 'I have a perfectly open mind as to the future developments of my labors on the British Survey. But I feel it my duty towards the Library of Congress to put the finishing touches to my American work[21] before devoting more than my leisure hours to any other task.'

At the meeting de Ricci gave an account of his latest efforts, and, a little prematurely one feels, it was decided to approach the Bibliographical Society about the possibility of joint publication.[22] The Anglo-American Historical Committee received the report of the Sub-Committee and, during the discussion of de Ricci's original memorandum, the Institute's Director, Dr A. F. Pollard, suggested that it be published in the *Bulletin* and comments invited. This was duly done, and the memorandum was preceded by an editorial aspiration: 'This preliminary bibliography is now nearing completion, and it is hoped to publish it as a Special Supplement to the *Bulletin* in 1938.'[23]

But now the trail begins to run cold. Although de Ricci could write to Parsloe (13 May 1938) thanking him and the Institute for a 'kind and flattering patronage',[24] no such Special Supplement ever appeared, nor was it again alluded to, even in the *Annual Report*.[25] Almost a year later (15 June 1939), the Assistant Secretary of the Institute wrote to de Ricci, inviting him to give a progress report on the Survey to the Sub-Committee on 4 July. A postcard sent on the day after the meeting asks for the loan of his own report to the Sub-Committee—'for the purposes of record'. This 'loan' by de Ricci of his own handwritten report was kept (perhaps at his suggestion), and is now filed with the Minutes of that meeting of the Sub-Committee.

He reported 'very substantial progress': but although he had now 40,000 cards of MSS. in permanent locations, and 20,000 in existing or dispersed private collections, he still saw the task as 'a considerable one, but not beyond the possibilities of a conscientious worker'. He was endeavouring, he claimed, to condense the printed catalogues of British Museum manuscripts 'of varying amplitude and merit into something like a uniform handlist, with details of the provenance of each manuscript, so seldom stated in the older catalogues', together with notes on recent literature. He aimed to include the Public Record Office and 'the other London libraries and archives, also possibly the private collections in London and the suburbs'. 'I have endeavoured with some success to reconstruct on paper a number of great collections of the past and I feel that such attempts at tracing the present location of dispersed libraries are not unlikely to prove useful to the scholar.' But, within weeks, war had been declared and the needs of scholars were necessarily shelved. After de Ricci's death during the war, it became unlikely that such a personal undertaking could ever be successfully resumed by anyone else, much less by a committee.

In March 1945 it was reported[26] that de Ricci had died in Paris in 1942, and had bequeathed to the University of London all his material relating to the Survey.[27] The Director of the Institute, then Professor V. H. Galbraith, inspected the material while on a visit to Paris, and in May 1945 it was resolved[28] to recommend its acceptance by the University, and to ask that it be deposited in the Institute of Historical Research. Senate approval was given on 18 May,[29] and, in due course, the material came to the Institute. Its presence in the University was noted in the *Calendar* for 1949–50[30] under the heading 'benefactions', but it would seem that not much use was made of it in those post-war years. This much was admitted in 1952 when the University Library first became interested in the material. The Library was by then developing in the Palaeography Room a university centre for manuscript studies. In the light of this development, it seemed that de Ricci's material might be exploited more fully in this context and also housed more conveniently, since space was inevitably more of a problem in the Institute. Accordingly the proposition to transfer the material was put to the Institute Committee on 10 June 1953, and, in less than a month, the survey material was taken over by the University Library. In 1955, when the Palaeography Room as we know it today was being furnished to meet its particulars, not forgotten were thirty-four neat wooden boxes, specially made to accommodate Seymour de Ricci's *Bibliotheca Britannica Manuscripta*.

It seems at this point that three questions might be posed: why did the enterprise fail, what did it achieve, and how do we stand, bibliographically speaking, today a generation later, in the field of manuscript studies in Great Britain?

The first question is perhaps the easiest to answer. As early as 1934 de Ricci had owned that he had been working 'since 1902 on a general bibliography of catalogues, but after thirty-one years it is still far from complete!'[31] Here, as on so many other occasions, de Ricci stands convicted *ex ore suo*. He had an insatiable desire to gather and record information (though not in any very systematic way),[32] and he seems to have found it impossible to be selective. This very industry militated against bringing such a compilation to a conclusion. He had, as he himself acknowledged, a useful model in the bibliography of printed catalogues of manuscripts available to readers in the MSS. Department of the Bibliothèque Nationale,[33] if only he had followed that. But, as has been suggested, he found it difficult to distinguish between the *Bibliotheca Britannica Manuscripta*, or catalogue of all manuscripts in the British Isles, the 'Survey' of collections and series rather than of individual manuscripts, and the *List* which the Sub-Committee intended should be a list of the printed (and perhaps typescript and handwritten) catalogues of manuscripts in Great Britain. 'A preliminary skeleton bibliography seems to me to be rather the outcome of the larger work than a preparation for it,' he wrote, 'however I will follow on that point the advice of the Committee, and if required can produce such a bibliography of printed catalogues at a fairly early notice'—and this in 1939.[34] With one then of de Ricci's temperament, working abroad on behalf of a committee that met only infrequently, with no sufficient rein on his activities nor direction of his energies, the outcome was almost bound to be inconclusive.

Just what all this industry achieved, on 60,000-odd slips, can be most simply explained by describing the arrangement of the material. It is broken down under eleven rather eclectic subject heads: bibliographies, literary voyages, general works, periodicals, exhibitions, county topography, visitations, cartularies, facsimiles (all these in four boxes), libraries and archives—alphabetically arranged—and collectors and private owners, similarly arranged. The major part, in eighteen boxes, arranged by town and collection, gives an assortment of bibliographical references, but more about collections of manuscripts than about individual items. (These have proved very occasionally of use to students.) This leaves the eleven boxes[35] devoted to dated sales (arranged chronologically from 1684 to 1909, with a few sales up to 1938)[36] and collectors, where the slips are filed alphabetically under each collector's name. Here there are often valuable clues to be followed up.

This is what might be expected, for one of de Ricci's chief interests, as a result of his experience in preparing the American *Census*, was in provenance and, with this object in view, he acquired a great familiarity with booksellers' and auction sale catalogues. Thus he was able to throw light on great private collections and on items that had formerly constituted such collections. It was one of his great regrets that no one had ever elected to investigate the greatest collection of them all. 'I have followed, since many years,' he wrote in 1934,[37] 'the gradual dispersal of the Phillipps manuscripts and I am much distressed that no British scholar should have thought it worth his while to undertake a special study of that immensely important collection.'[38] It may be worth pointing out that, despite his interest in the Phillipps collection, there is no material relating to Sir Thomas Phillipps, that prince of collectors, in the *Bibliotheca*, but Mr Munby has suggested a plausible reason for this.[39]

By 1962 it was found worthwhile in America to publish a *Supplement* to de Ricci's original *Census*. This has been followed by a union catalogue of manuscripts.[40] In England, after thirty years, we are still without a union catalogue of manuscripts. This, if a hindrance to scholarship, is not altogether surprising. But, more shamefully, we are still without any comprehensive bibliography of the printed catalogues of manuscripts in this country—and there are now many of these, particularly if the field is widened to include archives. However, the situation has shown some improvement. For bibliographical information on catalogues of Latin manuscripts before 1600 we are glad to make use of Kristeller's admirable work,[41] but its limitations of language and date are obvious. Dr N. R. Ker has described all surviving Anglo-Saxon manuscripts in his *Catalogue of manuscripts containing Anglo-Saxon* (1957), and the same author has in hand a work for the Standing Conference of National and University Libraries (*SCONUL*) that promises to be of the greatest interest.[42] Although not national in scope, but confined to its own collections, the amalgamated index to manuscripts in the British Museum will be a most valuable working tool when it finally achieves publication.[43]

Long ago, in 1934, de Ricci had considered that 'the most crying necessity of the present moment is an index or catalogue of the collections already described in the reports of the Commission on Historical Manuscripts, with some information as to the whereabouts of all collections which may recently have changed hands.[44] I also consider as greatly needed a bibliographical account of the public (and private?) collections of manuscripts existing in the United Kingdom.'[45] It took the hazards of war to create the National Register of Archives, an offshoot of the Historical Manuscripts Commission, and now that lusty youngster has all but overtaken its Victorian parent. Its aim is 'to record the location, content and availability of all collections of documents, both large and small, in England and Wales (other than those of the central government) without limit of date. These include family papers, the archives of local authorities, religious bodies, charitable organizations, business firms, schools, societies, etc.'[46] The indexes at Quality House[47] are used by many, but the Register's annual *List of accessions to repositories* and its occasional *Bulletin* are published and serve a wider circle of enquirers. Its catalogues and lists of individual collections are reproduced photographically from typescripts; they are subject to select distribution and, very regrettably, are not for sale. It is true that under its present terms of reference—as its name implies—the Register is concerned with documentary sources and family papers rather than with manuscripts of a more literary nature. However, if this country were ever to achieve something like a *Bibliotheca Britannica Manuscripta*, here perhaps would be the machinery for doing so.

NOTES

1 The material remains comprise some 60,000 slips 4¼″ × 7″, now housed in thirty-four boxes in the Palaeography Room, University of London Library, Senate House, London, W.C. 1. They were transferred there from the Institute of Historical Research on 7 July 1953, together with a number of folders containing letters (especially from the Secretary of the Institute to de Ricci, September 1934 to May 1938, drafts by de Ricci to late 1936; for other correspondents see below), draft reports, memoranda, specimen entries, etc., now known as the 'De Ricci Correspondence'. All quotations that follow are made from this material unless another source is given. I am grateful to Dr J. H. P. Pafford, Goldsmiths' Librarian, for permission to quote from this material.

2 I. H. R. Committee Min., 10 June 1953. I am grateful to Professor Francis Wormald, Director of the Institute of Historical Research, for permission to quote from this source and from other official records of the Institute, and to Miss M. E. Higgs, Assistant Secretary, for locating the material for me.

3 De Ricci was born in 1881. His earliest published work in the British Museum's *General Catalogue of Printed Books* dates from 1901, and from then almost until his death in 1942 there followed more than fifty works ranging over the fields of bibliography, engraving, typography, binding, painting and drawing, papyrology, catalogues of bronzes, furniture, porcelain and tapestries belonging to great collectors such as J. Pierpont Morgan, and, of course, catalogues of MSS.

4 Published, with W. J. Wilson, in three vols. (1935–37–40); a *Supplement* by C. U. Faye and W. H. Bond was published in 1962, and is to be added to annually through the channels of the Bibliographical Society of America.

5 Printed several years later in the *Bulletin of the Institute of Historical Research*, XV (1937–8), 65–8. See also vols. XIII (1935–6), 40–1, and XIV (1936–7), 187, for earlier notices of the project.

6 The Sub-Committee (of the Continuation Committee of the Anglo-American Conference of Historians) on the Accessibility of Historical Documents and Migrations of MSS. (henceforth

generally referred to simply as the MSS. Sub-Committee). Sub-Committee Mins., I.H.R.

7 *English Collectors of Books and Manuscripts (1530–1930) and their Marks of Ownership* (1930), being the Sandars lectures for 1929–30.

8 De Ricci claimed that the catalogue would be published 'under the supervision of the Department of MSS., British Museum', but, in fact, it was never sent to press. The author's holograph report, typescript inventory and catalogue of the Clumber MSS., 3 vols, in all (1936), are now in the departmental library of the Dept. of MSS., British Museum. I am obliged to Miss Janet Backhouse, an Assistant Keeper in that department, for information on this point.

9 De Ricci's catalogue of the Earl of Leicester's MSS. had been published in the *Transactions of the Bibliographical Society*, Supplement No. 7, 'Handlist of the MSS. in the Library of the Earl of Leicester at Holkham Hall' (1932).

10 I.H.R. Correspondence, 8 October 1937.

11 Deputy Keeper, Dept. of MSS., British Museum, 1929–44.

12 Director of the Fitzwilliam Museum, Cambridge, 1908–37.

13 Sir Sydney Cockerell died on 1 May 1962 in his 95th year.

14 Provost of Eton, 1918–36.

15 Pioneer county archivist of Bedfordshire, who had been in his day an Assistant Professor of Zoology at University College, London, a naval intelligence officer at the Admiralty throughout the First World War, and the author of a standard manual on practical oceanography; his recreations included ski-ing and 'the repair of ancient documents'.

16 This finally took shape in 1958 as *Medieval Cartularies of Great Britain: a short catalogue*, by G. R. C. Davis.

17 Secretary of the British Museum, 1926–40.

18 Now Professor of Medieval History at Cambridge.

19 This took shape ultimately as N. R. Ker's *Medieval Libraries of Great Britain: A List of Surviving Books* (Royal Historical Society Guides and Handbooks, no. 3), republished in 1964 in a second edition. See also Ker's contribution to

The parochial libraries of the Church of England (Report of the Committee appointed by the Central Council for the Care of Churches to investigate the number and condition of parochial libraries belonging to the Church of England, 1959).

20 The cheque was finally paid over on 23 August 1937.

21 Presumably the second volume of the American *Census* which was published in 1937.

22 R. B. McKerrow, then Secretary, in his letter of 7 March 1937 to de Ricci, was not encouraging, and, in fact, nothing came of the approach.

23 See note 5 above.

24 I.H.R. Correspondence.

25 *I.H.R. 18th Annual Report...1938–39*, p. 35. For other references to de Ricci's work, see the following reports: *14th* (1934–35), p. 29; *15th* (1935–36), p. 35; *16th* (1936–37), p. 32; *24th* (1944–45), p. 2; and *32nd* (1952–53), p. 6.

26 I.H.R. Committee Min., 28 March 1945.

27 Also included in the transfer were thirteen drawers of printed Library of Congress catalogue cards on British history and topography; these are now in the bibliography section of the University Library.

28 I.H.R. Committee Min., 2 May 1945.

29 Senate Min. 2405.

30 *University of London Calendar...1949–50*, p. 53.

31 Letter read to the MSS. Sub-Committee on 14 May 1934. Sub-Committee Mins., I.H.R.

32 'Sometimes inconsistent and idiosyncratic' is how the editor of the *Supplement* describes him.

33 Paris, Bibliothèque Nationale, Département des MSS.: *Catalogue alphabétique des livres imprimés mis à la disposition des lecteurs dans la salle de travail suivi de la liste des catalogues usuels du département des MSS.* 4ᵉ éd. (1933).

34 4 July 1939, Sub-Committee Mins., I.H.R.

35 The thirty-fourth box contains merely a 'Miscellaneous Supplement'.

36 Thus going a little beyond H. Mattingley and I. A. K. Burnett in their *List of Catalogues of English Book Sales, 1676–1900, now in the British Museum* (1915).

37 See note 31 above.

38 This *lacuna* at least has been filled in a masterly way by A. N. L. Munby in his *Phillipps studies*, nos. 1–5 (1951–60).

39 Letter of 8 October 1955 to D. F. Cook, formerly of the University of London Library, and now of the University Library, Liverpool. 'I think I can explain why you have no Phillipps slips in your de Ricci index. De Ricci had made a photostat of Phillipps's own privately printed catalogue [*Catalogus librorum manuscriptorum*] which he interleaved and in which he recorded all the information which came his way. This is now Bibl. Nat. Impr. Fol. 169 *bis* F. I 848. I.' A microfilm of this interleaved catalogue is now in the University of London Library, MIC. 89.

40 *National Union Catalog of Manuscript Collections in the United States*; vols. I and II and an index vol. (1962–4) have so far appeared. See also P. M. Hamer, *A guide to archives and manuscripts in the United States* (1961).

41 P. O. Kristeller, *Latin Manuscript Books before 1600: A List of Printed Catalogues and Unpublished Inventories*, new ed. rev. (1960).

42 This is, in Dr Ker's own words (letter of 17 February 1965 to the present writer), 'to catalogue medieval manuscripts in institutional libraries that haven't been catalogued before (or only in a brief sort of way or in antiquated catalogues that aren't easy to come by). Some of the libraries are public, but most of them are society libraries of one sort & another....A first volume on the London libraries ought to be ready and is nearly ready....' SCONUL (Standing Conference of National and University Libraries) has also sponsored a scheme to list all dated medieval manuscripts, the work to be done initially from printed catalogues.

43 See T. C. Skeat's revised ed. (1962) of *The Catalogues of the Manuscript Collections in the British Museum*, p. 40.

44 For useful information on these points, see *22nd* (1946), *23rd* (1961) and *24th* (1962) *Reports of the Royal Commission on Historical Manuscripts*. Almost as de Ricci wrote, the first section of the index of persons figuring in the H.M.C. reports published between 1870 and 1911 had appeared (1935) and the alphabet was completed in 1938. The index of personal names in reports published since 1911 is now (1965) in the press. There seems to be no plan to extend the topographical index, published in 1914, in a similar way. I owe this information to Miss Felicity Ranger, Assistant Registrar of the National Register of Archives.

45 See note 31 above.

46 *National Register of Archives: Facilities Offered to Students* (1963).

47 National Register of Archives, Quality House, Quality Court, Chancery Lane, London, W.C. 2.

ARRIGHI AND
HIS CONTEMPORARIES

PHILIP HOFER

Variant Issues of the First Edition of Ludovico Arrighi Vicentino's 'Operina'

The first, and the best, printed manual on western calligraphy to be published in the interest of non-professional writers[1] has on the title page of its first edition only the following words: 'La Operina di Ludovico Vicentino, da imparare di scrivere littera Cancellarescha'. In the colophon (and several other places) there is the statement that the work was printed at Rome. The date 'MDXXII' is also given, in three places, but not in the colophon! And throughout the thirty-two pages the author, Ludovico Arrighi Vicentino, seems intent on asserting his inspiration, his handwriting, and his sole responsibility for this remarkable small quarto booklet.

The fact that it is also a 'block book', no leaf of which (in this first edition) is printed from movable type, is a point that has hardly been adequately commented upon, despite the scarcity and interest of this type of printing. No doubt a reason is the comparatively late date, well after 'block books' had ceased to be a practical form of printing, because of the difficulty with which mistakes could be corrected. Indeed, the problem of correction arose directly in the case of this very book and caused some difficulty, as the reader will see later in this essay. On the other hand, Arrighi had really no other alternative for the printing of these specimens of his own writing, since they contain many letter forms, with swash capitals, elaborate ascenders and descenders, ligatures, and so forth, that could not have been composed from movable type. So they were cut on wood blocks like pictorial illustrations of the period.

There is no evidence that Arrighi was a trained woodcutter capable of cutting the blocks himself. On the contrary, there is direct evidence that he was not the cutter of these blocks, however otherwise accomplished, as will also appear later on.

Because of a renewed interest in calligraphy that began, for the western world, in

95

England with William Morris and Edward Johnston at the end of the nineteenth century, Arrighi's pioneering treatise has recently attracted a great deal of attention. It has particularly done so in America because of John Howard Benson's last published work, *The First Writing Book; An English Translation & Facsimile Text of Arrighi's Operina* (issued in a limited edition for the Harvard-Newberry Library *Studies in the History of Calligraphy* by the Yale University Press, 1954). Benson's translation of the Italian text and his explanation of Arrighi's technical terms have again made the book entirely practical for popular use. No wonder, therefore, that this limited edition and a large popular one were quickly exhausted and went into a third printing.

Once Benson had seen his book successfully launched, his scholarly instincts drew his attention back to a bibliographical discrepancy that he had noted when he compared his own copy of the first (1522) edition of the *Operina* (formerly belonging to Carl J. Ulmann)[2] with one belonging to the writer that has been deposited in the Department of Graphic Arts in the Harvard Library. Benson, of course had read A. F. Johnson's short *Catalogue of Italian Writing-Books of the Sixteenth Century*[3] and had also observed in other reference works that collations and descriptions of different copies of the *Operina* did not agree. This fact certainly was not surprising where later editions were involved, but he realized that it was significant when copies purported to be of the same printing. He thereupon set himself the task of unravelling this problem. But he was increasingly harassed by ill health, and was still at work upon it when he died early in 1956.

Most unhappily, Benson kept no written record of his findings. So the writer of this essay, already interested in the project, and wishing to complete it as a tribute to his friend, had to start anew. At least he remembered the general train of Benson's thoughts and had noted on the flyleaf of his own copy that one should make a comparison of signature C 1^r (Fig. 8) in each of the copies in question. These proved to be printed from quite different blocks, involving slightly variant text and widely variant layout. The most obvious point of distinction is an ornamental design in the Harvard copy not present in the Benson copy. Special note may be made also of the word 'Cioe' inserted after line 6 of the text in the Benson copy, but not found in the Harvard copy.

A minute comparison of all the other leaves then led to the discovery that on A 2^r, in the Benson copy, there was a small break between the stem and the loop of the first capital (P), and that, just above, there was a break in the horizontal flourish to the left of the dedication to the reader (Fig. 7). In the Harvard copy, what seemed to be a small printed dash parallel to the top of the signature mark on B 1^r was

Pregato piu uolte, anzi constretto da molti amici
benignißimo Lettore, che riguardo hauendo alla publica utilita e comodo non solamente di
questa età, ma delli posteri anchora, voleßi
dar qualche essempio di scriuere, et regulata-
mente formare gli caratteri e note delle lre(
che (ancellaresche hoggi di chiamano) uoletier
pigliai questa fatica: E perche impossibile era
de mia mano porger tanti essempi, che sodisfa-
ceßino a tutti, mi sono ingegnato di ritrouare
questa nuoua inuentione de lre, e metterle in
stampa, le quali tanto se auicinano alle scrit-
te a mano, quanto capeua il mio ingegno, E se
puntualmente in tutto no te rispondono, sup-
plicoti che mi facci iscusato. Conciosia che la
stampa no possa in tutto ripresentarte la vi-
ua mano, Spero nondimeno che imitando tu
il mio ricordo, da te stesso potrai consequire il
tuo desiderio . Uiui, e sta Sano :~

~: Al benigno Lettore :~

Pregato piu uolte, anzi constretto da molti amici
benignißimo Lettore, che riguardo hauendo alla publica utilita e comodo non solamente di
questa età, ma delli posteri anchora, voleßi
dar qualche essempio di scriuere, et regulata-
mente formare gli caratteri e note delle lre(
che (ancellaresche hoggi di chiamano) uoletier
pigliai questa fatica: E perche impossibile era
de mia mano porger tanti essempi, che sodisfa-
ceßino a tutti, mi sono ingegnato di ritrouare
questa nuoua inuentione de lre, e metterle in
stampa, le quali tanto se auicinano alle scrit-
te a mano, quanto capeua il mio ingegno, E se
puntualmente in tutto no te rispondono, sup-
plicoti che mi facci iscusato. Conciosia che la
stampa no possa in tutto ripresentarte la vi-
ua mano, Spero nondimeno che imitando tu
il mio ricordo, da te stesso potrai consequire il
tuo desiderio . Uiui, e sta Sano :~

Fig. 7.
A 2^r of Harvard (left) and
Benson copies of *La Operina*.

Laccio che' nel scriuer tuo. Tu habbi piu facilita, farai che tutti li caratheri, o uogli dire' littere' pen= dano inanzi, ad questo modo, Virtus omnibus rebus anteit profecto .

Non uoglio pero che' caschino tan= to, Ma cosi feci lessempio per dimostrarti meglio la via doue diste littere hanno da stare' pe denti

C

Laccio che' nel scriuer tuo Tu habbi piu facilita, farai che' tutti li caratheri, o uogli dire' littere' pendano inanzi, ad questo modo Cioe'

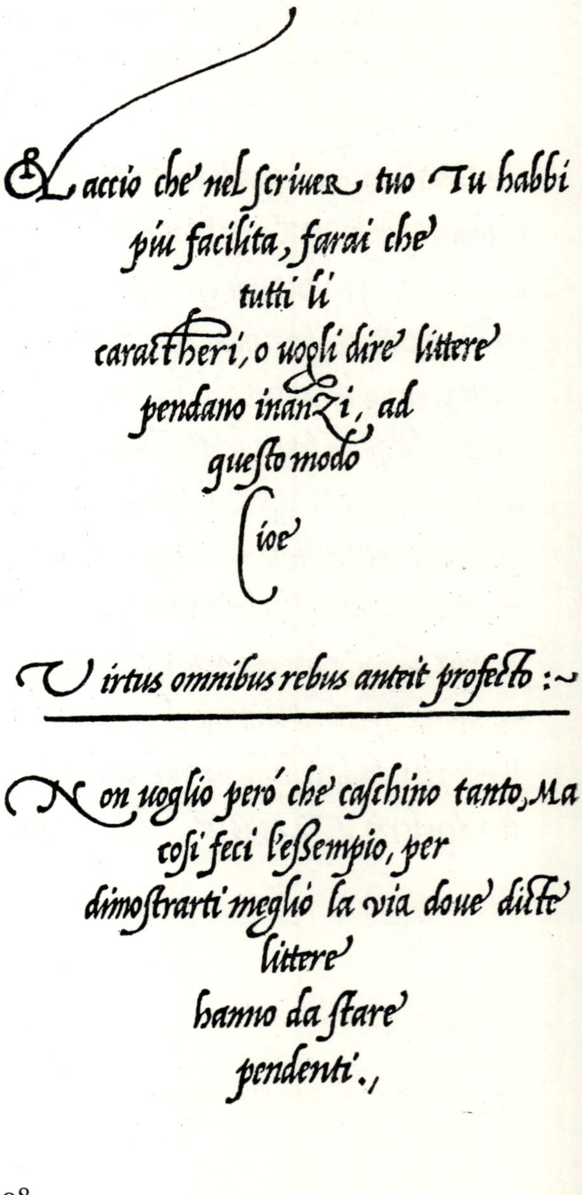

Virtus omnibus rebus anteit profecto :~

Non uoglio pero' che' caschino tanto, Ma cosi feci l'essempio, per dimostrarti' meglio la via doue' diste littere' hanno da stare' pendenti .,

Fig. 8.
C 1ʳ of Harvard (left) and
Benson copies of *La Operina*.

98

probably an accident in inking that page in this copy, which also reveals quite a bit of faint offset printing in the lower margin nearby. The latter can safely be attributed to careless stacking of newly printed sheets when the ink was still wet. Therefore, the differences on this one page could be dismissed as being accidental.[4]

On D 4^v, however, the ornamental woodcut cartouche, in the Harvard copy, did not register at all properly (Fig. 9), whereas in the Benson copy it is parallel to the text, as is fitting. Moreover, the Harvard copy cartouche could be seen to obliterate several words printed beneath it. By holding the book in a strong light at the proper angle, it became possible to read, unmistakably, '& Ugo da Carpi Intagliatore', printed in two lines underneath. In the Benson copy there are no words overprinted by the cartouche. Clearly here was a major correction, and an attempt by Arrighi, the publisher, to suppress the name of the woodcutter simply by cutting off the lower portion of the block. Moreover, the frame of the Benson copy cartouche shows signs of wear, and two breaks in the outer border not present in the Harvard copy (Fig. 9). With these discoveries, which Benson himself also probably made, since he had examined both copies quite a number of times, 'the chase was on!'

The next step was a comparison of watermarks between the two copies, even though only negative evidence—that one copy or the other might not be genuinely of the period—was possible therefrom. The Benson copy showed an anchor in a circle crowned by a six-pointed star. This is nearest to, but not exactly like, Briquet No. 539, which was taken from a book printed at Brescia in 1502. The copy at Harvard had a small crowned eagle, which is a little less close to Briquet No. 93, a book printed at Florence in 1529. No adverse conclusions against either copy, therefore, could be drawn from this evidence. The fact that one Briquet watermark relates to an earlier book than the other carries no weight in this case where neither watermark is exactly like the ones found in the Harvard and Benson copies. It does, however, make the date and locale of printing—Rome, 1522—seem reasonable for both copies. It also suggests that the two copies were not simultaneously printed or they would most likely have been printed from the same batch of paper.

Indeed, all of the principal differences between the two copies point to the *possibility* of more than one issue of the first edition. Was this a fact, or were there merely variant copies, or variant states of one issue? To determine the probabilities on this point, it was necessary to trace as many copies of this first edition as could be found, and to discover how they compared with the two differing copies in question.

Altogether, after a good deal of trouble, nine other copies were located in America and Europe, which were very kindly examined by their owners, custodians, or interested scholar friends. One of the most pristine appeared to be a copy in the New-

Finisce
la
ARTE
di
scriuere littera Corsiua
ouer Cancellares=
cha
Stampata in Roma per inuentione
di Ludouico Vicentino,
scrittore

CVM GRATIA & PRIVILEGIO

Finisce
la
ARTE
di
scriuere littera Corsiua
ouer Cancellares=
cha
Stampata in Roma per inuentione
di Ludouico Vicentino,
scrittore

CVM GRATIA & PRIVILEGIO

Fig. 9. D 4ᵛ of Harvard (left) and
Benson copies of *La Operina.*

berry Library, Chicago, which is in 'a contemporary, or near contemporary, brown leather cameo' binding, as very kindly reported by James M. Wells, its custodian. The fact that it is bound with Arrighi's second work, *Il modo de temperare le Penne*, dated, in several places, both 1523 and 1525, and definitely declared (in the colophon) to have been printed in Venice, *may* suggest that this copy is a late printing of the 1522 edition, which the owner bought and had bound only when the second book had been published. However that may be, in every significant respect enumerated above—the differences on A 2^r, C 1^r, and D 4^v—the Newberry Library copy proved to agree with the Benson one, which, however, had been fairly recently rebound (on the order of Mr Ulmann?) in full plain limp vellum. The Harvard copy is in nineteenth-century full red morocco by Masson-Debonnelle (French), with the ex-libris of a nineteenth-century collector, E. Valdruch. No further conclusions, therefore, are to be gained as to time of printing by a comparison of the Harvard and Benson bindings, since they are both rebound copies, unlike the Newberry one.

The copy in the Metropolitan Museum, New York, also fitted the Benson pattern in regard to these printing points. And so did one in the hands of a leading New York dealer, H. P. Kraus. This completes the survey of the five copies indubitably of the first 1522 edition that the writer has been able to discover in America.

Abroad, the copies in the Kungliga Biblioteket, Stockholm (kindly reported on by Sten G. Lindberg), the Danske Kunstindustrimuseum, Copenhagen (kindly examined by Svend Eriksen), the Biblioteca Nazionale, Florence, and the Biblioteca Nazionale, Rome, also agreed in all these details with the Benson copy. Before the last war, there had been one more 1522 *Operina* recorded in Italy: at the Biblioteca Civica in Verona. But Giovanni Mardersteig, Director of the Officina Bodoni, the leading scholar printer of Italy, believes that this copy was destroyed in a Second World War air raid.[5] This copy had been taken out of its binding and was framed, leaf by leaf. It is not now likely, therefore, that all these frames will suddenly re-appear so many years later. So the copy may, fairly safely, but most unfortunately, be considered 'lost'.

This leaves only two more copies of the 1522 *Operina* that can be traced: one in the British Museum and one belonging to Baptiste Galanti in Paris. These copies turned out to agree with each other, and to differ from the Harvard and the Benson copies (and all the rest), thus complicating the problem by making three varying types instead of two. The London copy was first reported on by A. F. Johnson; later (June 1959) the writer and Mr Johnson examined the copy together in the British Museum, using a strong magnifying glass to be sure that no retouching had been done to this original by the printer of a 1926 facsimile[6] edition of the *Operina* as

Finisce
la
ARTE
di
scriuere littera Corsiua
ouer Cancellares=
cha
Stampata in Roma per inuentione
di Ludouico Vicentino,
scrittore

CVM GRATIA & PRIVILEGIO

Finisce
la
ARTE
di
scriuere littera Corsiua
ouer Cancellares=
cha
Stampata in Roma per inuentione
di Ludouico Vicentino,
scrittore

CVM GRATIA & PRIVILEGIO

Fig. 10. D 4ᵛ of British Museum (left) and
Benson copies of *La Operina*.

certainly had been done to his photographic reproductions.[7] There had been none. The British Museum copy certainly appeared to be in every respect as sound and unsophisticated a copy as either the Harvard or the Benson one, and seemed somehow to lie between the two (Fig. 10). For while it did not have the breaks on A 2^r (here resembling the Harvard copy) it did have the Benson block on C 1^r. Also, while it agreed with the Harvard copy in lacking any breaks in the cartouche on D 4^v, it registered evenly, had slight evidence of wear on its upper border, and had no printing of words underneath (again resembling the Benson copy).

With all these points in the British Museum copy, the copy owned by M. Galanti in Paris concurred, according to his careful report, and the net score can be summarized most succinctly as follows: of type 1, a single copy (Harvard); of type 2, two copies (as just described); and of type 3, eight copies, including the Benson one.

Now, at last, with all the evidence obtainable by personal inspection or by correspondence at hand, it is possible to come to some pretty certain conclusions, providing only that more copies—despite two years' search!—do not appear. There are, as has several times been stated, three pages in respect to which the known 1522 *Operina* copies may vary: A 2^r, C 1^r, and D 4^v. Only one copy of the eleven studied has major, and textual, differences from the others. That is the Harvard copy. For, first of all, it has '& Ugo da Carpi Intagliatore' printed *beneath* the cartouche on D 4^v, which occurs nowhere else. This phrase must have been printed *before* the cartouche in this copy, since it underlies that ornament, and is clearly similar to, and part of, the text printed above. The cartouche itself may have been printed by hand, since it registers badly (Fig. 9). And herein lies a very practical reason for eliminating two printing operations once Arrighi had decided to obliterate the name of his woodcutter (and rival?).

Since there are these *textual* differences, as William H. Bond of the Harvard Library observes, there are *two issues*—not simply variant copies, or states, of a single issue. The British Museum and the Galanti copies, on the other hand, have no textual differences from the Benson and its seven related copies. The differences that do exist have only to do with *the degree of wear* on the wood blocks from which A 2^r and D 4^v are printed. In the first two named, the wear is clearly less than in the last eight. For the British Museum and Galanti copies have no evident wear at all on A 2^r (where actual breaks occur in the Benson copy and its fellows), and only slight wear on the top border of the ornamental cartouche, on D 4^v, where there are decided breaks in the others.

One can, therefore, conclude that there are at least two distinct issues of the first 1522 edition of Arrighi's *Operina*: the first known in only one copy so far; the other in at least two states, of which the British Museum and Galanti copies represent the earlier and the Benson copy and its seven companions the later.

How much time intervened between these two states there is, currently, no way of telling. If they are roughly handled, wood blocks can be quickly broken. But since there are four breaks involved on two pages (A 2ʳ and D 4ᵛ), and some signs of additional wear as well on one of these pages (D 4ᵛ), the chances are that there was an appreciable time lag, and not simply a sudden accident. The next *edition* of the book *printed from these same blocks* that we now know is dated *1532* at Venice (not Rome). In it, these same breaks can be observed—and one or two others. A comparison of the watermarks of all these second issue copies might, however, throw more light on the degree of time lag, depending on whether it is found that these were printed from the same, or from different, batches of paper.

The differing arrangement of C 1ʳ in the Harvard copy from all the other first edition copies studied has a further and inconclusive ramification. On the one hand, the later date of the arrangement in all other copies is supported by the fact that the second edition of the *Operina* (Rome, 1525) follows the arrangement found in these copies. But on the other hand, the third edition (Venice, 1532) returns to the pattern of the Harvard copy, as does also the fourth edition (Venice, 1533). Then, the fifth (Venice, 1539) goes back to that of the group of copies of the first edition (and to the second edition). One is tempted to wonder where the trail might lead in the further editions of 1543, 1545, 1546, and 1557, even though no essential service to the subject of this essay would be rendered thereby.[8]

Much more important are a few words on the conclusive evidence, from the Harvard copy of the first edition, that Ugo da Carpi cut the wood blocks. It has never been possible before to state this categorically, though it has been suggested several times in print.[9] For an inference could be gained from several sources. First, there is the lack of evidence that Arrighi was a woodcutter and, secondly, the admission by Arrighi, in the first edition of his second book, *Il modo* (Venice, 1523), that Eustachio Celebrino was the woodcutter for that booklet. Why then should Arrighi have wanted to cover up the participation of Ugo da Carpi in his first book, the *Operina*?

There is no answer. All that is certain is that the two men had a falling out—the first evidence of which is the suppression of Ugo da Carpi's name in the Harvard copy of the 1522 *Operina*. And another, even more drastic indication, is the fact that in 1525 Pope Clement VII took all rights to the book away from Arrighi and vested them in Ugo da Carpi. For on the recto of the second leaf in this second edition there is a 17-line printed paragraph in Latin that is very comprehensive and decisive. The

Pope sided with Ugo da Carpi—but Arrighi retained the wood blocks! Either he hid them in Rome, or he sent (or took) them to Venice, where they appeared in the third edition of 1532, with Arrighi's name on the title page (and Ugo da Carpi's nowhere to be seen). In any case, Ugo da Carpi was unable to use them for his 1525 edition and had to recut every one of the blocks in the book. Finally, he celebrated his (temporary) triumph over Arrighi by placing in his colophon the words: 'Stampata in Roma per inventione No, di Ludovico Vincentino. RESURREXIT UGO DA CARPI'! He also added a very poor imitation of the earlier cartouche, on which is spelled in large capitals the word 'SEPULCH/RUM'! He did not, however, remove Arrighi's name from the text, on the many pages in which it occurred, but contented himself with his colophon repudiation of the writing master. One might suppose he could easily have omitted Arrighi's name, since he had to recut the wood blocks in any case. Had he not the calligraphic skill to redesign these pages? The poorly proportioned cartouche may be evidence in that direction.

One final copy of the first edition of the *Operina* should be discussed—if indeed a copy in the Newberry Library at Chicago, dated Rome, 1523, represents such, and is not a sophisticated example of a later edition. This copy is in a modern binding, contains the *Il modo* as well as the *Operina*, and has thirty leaves, with continuous pagination,[10] collating A–C, a–d, in fours except c in six. One should note this is two leaves less than a full copy of the two books ought to contain. That fact in itself is suspicious, as is the fact that the first leaf verso and the last leaf recto are blank (which is not true in any other edition, issue, or copy of the book that the writer has seen). If these two leaves were conjugate, and the whole book bound as a single gathering, one might consider that the two leaves in question might be a special wrapper. But they are not conjugate, as witness a thin strip of paper that joins them, and the fact that the watermarks on the two leaves do not fit together. Furthermore, a small stain on the bottom of the second leaf, which communicates itself to further leaves of the book, does not do so to the first leaf, in which there is also a wormhole that does not carry through to the second. Equally troublesome, in the eyes of Dr Bond, and of David Foxon of the British Museum, both of whom examined the Newberry copy with the writer, is the fact that the first and last leaves are much fresher, and somewhat cleaner, than the leaves in between. How could genuine covers of a book remain cleaner than its contents? One is forced to consider that they are much later additions.

This hypothesis is confirmed by an examination of the printing on A 1^r and A 30^v. Both show small differences from the 1522 edition prototypes. For the printing on A 1^r does not have quite the same ornamentation on the stem of the first (capital) L, and that on A 30ᵛ, while it reproduces the lower half of A 12ᵛ, has had the date changed from MDXXII to MDXXIII, without removal of the comma after the last word 'debent,' which at the very end of the book makes no sense. The examiners, therefore, came to the conclusion that the text on these leaves involved printing from blocks made in close facsimile of the original printing in question, but not from blocks of the period. In this opinion, Mr Wells, of the Newberry Library, who kindly supplied the copy for study, concurs.

One other thirty-leaf copy of the two combined books (supposedly 1522 as far as the *Operina* is concerned) is described by Essling,[11] but cannot be presently located. It apparently has a different collation from the Newberry copy (C in six, rather than c).

Is this also a confection? Or a ghost? Only time will tell. And only time will prove whether there are not more editions, issues, and variant states of this book. After all, being a block book, the *Operina* is more easily juggled about so far as single pages are concerned (as opposed to making corrections on them) than a book printed from movable type.

NOTES

1 James Wardrop, 'Arrighi Revived', *Signature*, no. 12 (July 1939), p. 31. Sigismondo Fanti in 1514 and Johann Neudorffer in 1519 wrote earlier treatises, but for professional scribes.

2 Lot 63 in Carl J. Ulmann sale, Parke-Bernet Galleries, New York, 15–16 April 1952.

3 Contained in *Signature*, new series, no. 10 (1950), pp. 22–48.

4 No other recorded copy of the 1522 *Operina* has the small dash near the signature mark.

5 Dr Mardersteig also kindly reported on the copy in Florence.

6 *The Calligraphic Models of Ludovico degli Arrighi Surnamed Vicentino: A Complete Facsimile*, with introduction by Stanley Morison (Paris, privately printed for Frederic Warde, 1926).

7 Mr Lindberg of the Kungliga Biblioteket, Stockholm, has given many instances in a letter to the writer.

8 For a list of editions see A. F. Johnson, 'A Bibliography', *Three Classics of Italian Calligraphy*, ed. Oscar Ogg (New York, 1953), pp. 251–8.

9 E.g. Wardrop, *Signature*, p. 33.

10 Exact description in Johnson, 'A Bibliography', p. 254.

11 Prince d'Essling, *Les livres à figures vénitiens de la fin du XVᵉ siècle et du commencement du XVIᵉ* (Paris, 1907–14), part II, ii, no. 2181.

12 This essay first appeared in *Harvard Library Bulletin*, XIV, 3 (1960): EDITOR.

A. S. OSLEY

The Origins of Italic Type

Many people tend to think of the *italics*, which they see in a printed page, as a slanting type used for emphasis. The first italics, however, were designed for a quite different purpose. They were modelled on the *cancellaresca* style of handwriting. Such slant as they had (and it was only a few degrees to the right) was a function of their cursiveness. Moreover they were employed for the complete text of a book, not scattered like condiments on roman type. Here we shall consider the work of the two pioneers of italic type-design—Francesco Griffo and Ludovico Vicentino, more commonly known as Arrighi.

THE ALDINE ITALIC

The conception of italic type is attended with a certain amount of mystery. The place of birth is known—Venice. And the parents were undoubtedly Aldus Manutius the Elder and Francesco Griffo (or Griffi) of Bologna,[1] an accomplished type-cutter. Aldus was born about 1450 and died in 1515. He was one of the greatest of Italian printers, specialising in the production of sound editions of the Greek classical authors, for whom a great demand then existed. His first books were printed in a clear, serviceable roman type. Around 1500 he seems to have had a brain-wave. He divined that the new reading public of the Renaissance needed the classics in a cheap, portable form. So in 1501 he brought out the first pocket edition of Virgil (Plate 30). Not only was the size of the book small and convenient and its price low, but it was printed throughout in a new italic type. The format was a sensational success and rapidly imitated in other European countries.

At the end of this Virgil, Aldus pays tribute to his type-cutter, praising the type 'cut by the skilled hands of Francis of Bologna'.[2] Elsewhere, he claims that he has 'invented beautiful letters of a *cancellaresca* or cursive style which gave the appearance of having been written by hand'; and again, 'I have caused to be cut a cursive *can-*

cellaresca type of an entirely new design of great beauty'.[3] The inference we are meant to draw is that Aldus conceived the idea and that he deliberately wanted to give his editions the appearance of a book written in the chancery cursive. If we accept Aldus's account, his purpose can only be guessed. It may simply be, as is often stated, that he thought the chancery script would give him more words to a page.[4] Or was he merely doing what he had done for the Greek classics? Or could it be that readers were finding that the printed Roman book, for all its advantages, was monotonous to eyes attuned to the irregularities of manuscript? It is perhaps significant that his type imitates an *informal* cursive, which may, in fact, have lent plausibility to the picturesque myth (still repeated sometimes) that he wanted to imitate the hand of Petrarch.[5]

(a)

Si quiſquam eſt, qui accuſandi caſus in is per es di phthongum miratur excuſos typis noſtris, id à nobis

(b)

ipsa oſtendit & iudicat. Quis eſt n. Tam cupidus in proſpicienda

(c)

Commendo tibi quintiane nros Noſtros ducere suamen libellos

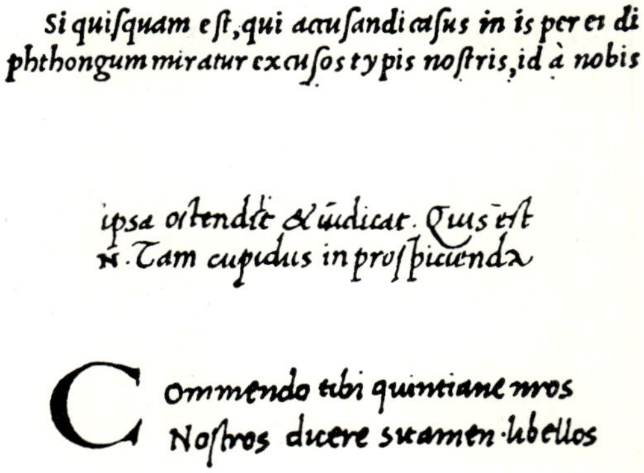

Fig. 11. Comparison of first Aldine type (*a*) with (*b*) hand of San Vito (see also Plate 45), and (*c*) hand of Pomponio Leto.

Could he actually have had any particular model in mind? When, earlier, he produced his editions of the Greek classics, his Greek founts seem to have been modelled on the contemporary Greek handwriting practised by his friends, particularly the Cretan, Marcus Musurus. It may be thought reasonable to examine whether any of his friends could have inspired the Aldine Italic. At present no reliable evidence is known. Mr James Wardrop put forward Bartolomeo San Vito of Padua (1435–?1518) as a possible candidate:[6] and Mr Fairbank confesses that, of all the numerous scripts he has studied, that of Pomponio Leto (1428–97) most resembles the Italic of Aldus[7] (Fig. 11). So far as historical evidence goes, I have not been able to trace any connection between San Vito and Aldus. On the other hand, a certain Candidus Romanus, when writing to Aldus for a job, thought it worth stating that he was a pupil of Leto.[8]

Orso al uostro deſtrier ſi po ben porre
Vn fren; che di ſuo corſo indietro il uolga:
Ma'l cor chi leghera, che non ſi ſciolga;
Se brama honore, e'l ſuo contrario abhorre?
Non ſoſpirate: a lui non ſi po torre
Suo pregio, perch'a uoi l'andar ſi tolga:
Che, come fama publica diuolga,
Egli è gia la: che null'altro il precorre.
Baſti che ſi ritroue in mezzo'l campo
Al deſtinato di ſotto quell'arme;
Che gli da il tempo, amor, uirtute, e'l ſangue;
Gridando, d'un gentil deſire auampo
Col ſignor mio; che non po ſeguitarme,
Et del non eſſer qui ſi ſtrugge et langue.

Orſo al voſtro deſtrier ſi po ben porre
Vn fren; che di ſuo corſo indietro il voga:
Ma'l cor chi leghera, che non ſi ſciolga;
Se brama honor, e'l ſuo contrario abhorre;
Non ſoſpirate: a lui non ſi po torre
Suo preggio, perch'a voi l'andar ſi tolga.
Che, come fama publica diuolga,
Egli è gia la: che null'altro il precorre.
Baſti che ſi ritroue in mezzo'l campo
Al deſtinato di ſotto quell'arme;
Che gli da il tempo, amor, virtute, e'l ſangue;
Gridando, d'vn gentil deſire auampo
Col ſignor mio; che non po ſeguitarme,
Et del non eſſer qui ſi ſtrugge, & langue

Orſo al uoſtro deſtrier ſi puo bē porre
Vn frē che di ſuo corſo idietro il uolga
Ma'l cor chi leghera, ch non ſi ſciolga
Se brama honore, el ſuo cōtrario abhor
Nō ſoſpirate, a lui nō ſi puo torre   re?
Suo pgio, perchauoi l'andar ſi tolga,
Che, come fama publica diuolga,
Egli e gia la, ch nullaltro il precorre.
Baſti che ſi ritroue in mezol campo
Al deſtinato di ſotto quell'arme
Ch gli da il tēpo, amor, uirtute, el ſan
Gridādo, dū gētil deſire auāpo   gue
Col ſignor mio, che nō puo ſeguitarme
Et del nō eſſer qui ſi ſtrugge, et lāgue.

Fig. 12. Francesco Griffo's first, second and third italic types.

109

But perhaps if we turn to Francesco Griffo's side of the story, we may feel that the solution lies elsewhere. Little is known of the life of this distinguished type-cutter. He cut Roman, Greek, Hebrew and italic letters for Aldus. A somewhat choleric man, he quarrelled with Aldus shortly after the publication of the *Virgil* in 1501 and went over to a rival printer, Soncino, for whom he cut his second italic (Fig. 12). After a year or two he left Soncino and tried his fortune with other printers until, finally, he set up his own business as editor, typographer and printer. His third italic can be seen in the four books, which he published about 1516 with the aim of surpassing Aldus in the production of pocket editions (Fig. 12). Nothing more is heard of him after 1518. He is known to have killed the husband of his daughter, Caterina, in a quarrel and was probably executed for this crime.

In the dedication to Cesar Borgia contained in his *Petrarch* of 1503, Soncino says of Griffo: 'Francesco is not only able to cut the standard types but he has invented a new kind of letter, called *cursive* or *cancellaresca*. He—and not Aldus Romanus or others who have cleverly tried to borrow his plumes—is the original inventor and designer. He cut all the type used by this Aldus.' Griffo, in a preface to his *Petrarch* of 1516, states that he has devised a cursive form which will give pleasure to anyone of taste partly because of its novelty and elegance and partly because of its convenience. Again, Doni, writing in 1552, tells of Aldus's 'handsome type like handwriting, which he either discovered or at least claimed to have been the first to introduce'.[9] There can be no doubt that Francesco played a crucial part in the conception of the Aldine Italic, in particular overcoming the technical problems involved in designing a type to look like cursive handwriting.

A. Sorbelli raised the question why it took much longer for the cursive type to be designed compared with Roman and Gothic types, which were themselves imitations of manuscript.[10] His answer is that the difficulty of cutting letters with long ascenders at an angle over a square base required an unusually expert designer such as Francesco. For purely commercial reasons, e.g. keeping the number of characters in the type box to a minimum, not wasting metal, and avoiding unnecessary punching, the designer had to eliminate as far as possible the numerous tied letters characteristic of an informal script. Francesco actually has 65 joins in his first italic, used in the *Virgil* of 1501 and the *Dante* of 1503,[11] but is able to cut them down considerably in his later work. Others hold that the joins were an integral part of the design in order to simulate handwriting (Fig. 13).

In the present state of our knowledge, the riddle of the Aldine Italic remains unsolved. It seems reasonable to suppose that the idea of printing an italic book came first to Aldus Manutius (perhaps even when handling Petrarch's manuscript!), but that the execution was left to Francesco Griffo, in which case he could have modelled his type on his own handwriting. At any rate, it is not necessary to suppose that the original model—if indeed it be not a conflation of a number of hands of the 1490's—must be a friend of Aldus.

Fig. 13. Griffo's ligatures (enlarged).

ARRIGHI AND HIS ITALIC TYPES

In his own day Arrighi was more commonly known as Ludovico Vicentino,[12] i.e. he was 'of Vicenza'. Mr F. A. Thomson of Stockholm, who elsewhere in this volume writes on the significance of Arrighi's *Clitia* manuscript, has argued convincingly that he was a native of the village of Corneto, which, as the crow flies, is about fifteen miles from Vicenza.[13] Our knowledge of Arrighi's life is limited to the years 1510–27 and is derived almost entirely from his own work.

Between 1509 and 1517 war (and its inevitable concomitant, plague) ravaged Vicenza as Venetians, Spaniards and Germans fought over it. Arrighi, perhaps, fled to Rome for safety about 1509. At any rate, it was at Rome that he set up in the book trade and sponsored the publication of a travel book called the *Itinerario de Varthema Bolognese nello Egypto*.[14] Printed by Stephano Guillireti and Hercule di Nani, it tells us nothing of Arrighi, who is not heard of again until about 1515. An obscure tradition exists that he was teaching handwriting in Venice. He certainly seems to have left publishing and taken up calligraphy. For, between 1515 and 1522, he was writing manuscripts in Rome for such patrons as Vittoria Colonna and Cardinal Giulio de' Medici, later Pope Clement VII. He lived in the Parione quarter of the City, the district of scribes, notaries and stationers. His regular job was professional scribe in the Apostolic Chancery, where he and his assistants copied and dispatched papal briefs. The qualities required (and magnificently displayed) were speed, accuracy and legibility. Arrighi's skill became so prominent that he was 'constantly entreated, and even forced, by many friends' to bring out a handwriting manual. *La Operina di Ludovico Vicentino da imparare di scrivere littera Cancellarescha*, dated 1522 (though perhaps published later) achieved immediate popularity. It was quickly followed by his *Il modo de temperare le Penne*, issued in Venice and dated 1523. At this time Arrighi, who, like Griffo, was probably not an easy man to work with, was having trouble with his partner. The original blocks of *La Operina* had been cut by Ugo da Carpi. He wanted to extend the business and issue more books in the chancery script. Arrighi refused. Ugo then complained to Clement VII that he had been tricked and obtained the privilege of reprinting *La Operina* on his own account. It looks as though he had some legitimate claim, which Arrighi refused to admit.[15]

The upshot was that Arrighi dissolved his partnership with Ugo da Carpi, left his employment with the Vatican, and went off to Venice, where he found a new collaborator, Eustachio Celebrino, who illustrated and probably cut blocks for *Il modo*. The association was short-lived; by 1525 Eustachio was working with Tagliente.

Arrighi returned to Rome. His name appears in a census list of about 1526, which reveals that he now lived in the Rione of Ponte, the business quarter of Rome. His main occupation was book publishing, and he had his own press. He entered into yet another brief partnership, this time with Lautizio Perugino, a superb craftsman, who cut his types for him until about 1526. Lautizio is usually identified with the goldsmith and seal-engraver Lautizio de Bartolomeo dei Rotelli.[16]

Arrighi printed both for the Vatican and for men of letters, of whom the most distinguished was Gian Giorgio Trissino (1475–1550), poet, humanist, spelling reformer and author of *La Sophonisba*, the first classical drama in the vernacular. He was evidently pleased with Arrighi's work.[17] Nevertheless, all was not plain sailing. For Trissino, writing from Vicenza on 17 July 1525 to Tommaso da Lonigo in Rome, says: 'I'm sorry that our friend Lodovico is in trouble: however, as I said before, you may advance him on my account 25 or 30 ducats, provided you take every precaution when so doing to see that I do not lose the money.'[18] It seems likely that 'our friend Lodovico' was Arrighi.

The Emperor Charles V was engaged in a long-standing dispute with Clement VII. His armies broke into Rome on 6 May 1527. The Pope just had time to take refuge in Castel St Angelo. For eight days the sack continued, and some 4000 citizens perished. Arrighi was almost certainly one of them. On 5 June the Pope signed an act of capitulation. He conceded an enormous ransom and a promise of absolution to the Imperial troops. The brief announcing this indemnity was published on 8 June. It was, curiously enough, printed in one of Arrighi's types and in his own printing-house. But, although his business survived the sack, this document does not *necessarily* mean that he himself was alive in June.[19] In any event, after 1527 the rest is silence.

The full story of the types used by Arrighi cannot yet be written. The libraries and archives of Europe have still to be fully explored. The main outlines are, however, becoming clearer. Whereas the Aldine Italic was designed to imitate handwriting and to cram as much text as possible into a page, so that substantial classics could be presented in a pocket-size format, Arrighi, although he too imitated handwriting, was far less interested in economy of space. His books, produced in small quantities for wealthy patrons, are of quarto size with wide margins, and the texts are usually short and contemporary. He never printed a classic. His types are designed accordingly. They are about 16 point in size and contain far fewer ligatures than the Aldine Italic. They are always calligraphic, never cramped; their long ascenders and descenders invest his page with a spacious, elegant look.

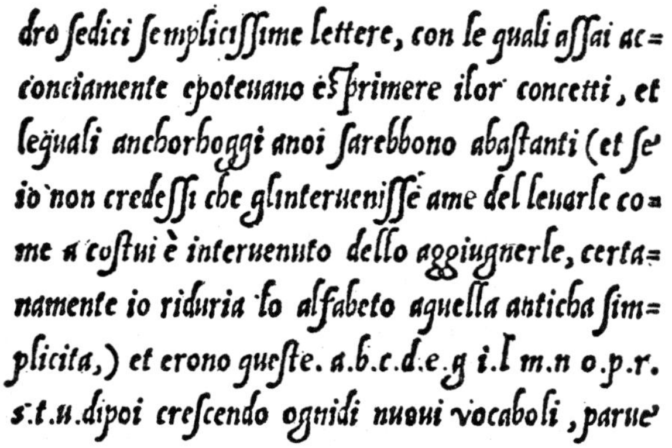
dro ſedici ſempliciſſime lettere, con le quali aſſai ac=
conciamente epoteuano eſprimere ilor concetti, et
lequali anchorhoggi anoi ſarebbono abaſtanti (et ſe
io non credeſſi che glinteruenisſe ame del leuarle co=
me a coſtui è interuenuto dello aggiugnerle, certa=
namente io riduria lo alfabeto aquella anticha ſim=
plicita,) et erono queſte. a.b.c.d.e.g i.l m.n o.p.r.
s.t.u.dipoi creſcendo ognidi nuoui vocaboli, parue

Fig. 14. Arrighi's first italic. From A. Firenzuola, *Discacciamento de le nuove lettere* (1524).

The majority of Arrighi's books were printed between 1524 and 1525. The type used is sometimes referred to as 'Arrighi's first italic' (Figs. 14 and 15). E. Casamassima considers that two distinct types were employed in these books.[20] The truth is rather that one basic type was designed, but that variants of some individual letters were cut and are often used unsystematically. The design also successfully embodies two Greek letters, required by Trissino for his spelling reform. The terminals of the ascenders curve delicately to the right, as in a formal hand. The letters *p* and *q* either have a terminal curving to the left or are straight and serifed. In the combinations *ff* and *sp*, the final *f* and *p* end in a serif. The letter *d* sometimes curves slightly back at the top and sometimes sweeps right back. The letter *g* may go straight down to end in a calligraphic flourish or its spine may be bent. The letter *v* is either symmetrical or has a flourish on the left arm. The capitals are formal Roman, varied with cursive (swash) alternatives. The general effect of this graceful type, which Lautizio Perugino cut, is of lightness and ease.[21]

Another type, which we may designate 'Arrighi's second italic', makes its bow in 1526 (Figs. 16 and 17). It is a larger face than the first italic: heavier, more virile and

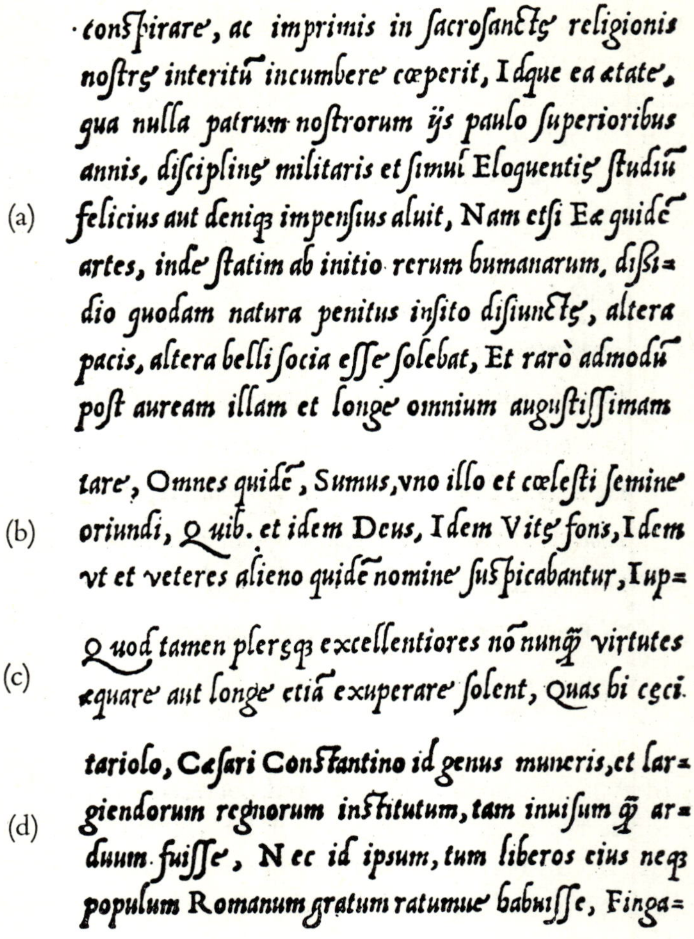

(a) *conſpirare, ac imprimis in ſacroſanctę religionis noſtrę interitū incumbere cœperit, Idque ea ætate, qua nulla patrum noſtrorum ijs paulo ſuperioribus annis, diſciplinę militaris et ſimul Eloquentię ſtudiū felicius aut deniqʒ impenſius aluit, Nam etſi Eæ quidē artes, inde ſtatim ab initio rerum humanarum, diſſi= dio quodam natura penitus inſito diſiunctę, altera pacis, altera belli ſocia eſſe ſolebat, Et rarò admodū poſt auream illam et longe omnium auguſtiſſimam*

(b) *tare, Omnes quidē, Sumus, vno illo et cœleſti ſemine oriundi, Q uib. et idem Deus, Idem Vitę fons, Idem vt et veteres alieno quidē nomine ſuſpicabantur, Iup=*

(c) *Q uod tamen plerςqʒ excellentiores nō nunǣ virtutes æquare aut longe etiā exuperare ſolent, Quas hi cęci.*

(d) *tariolo, Cæſari Conſtantino id genus muneris, et lar= giendorum regnorum inſtitutum, tam inuiſum q̄ ar= duum fuiſſe, Nec id ipsum, tum liberos eius neqʒ populum Romanum gratum ratumue habuiſſe, Finga=*

Fig. 15. Arrighi's first italic, illustrating (*a*) variants of *p, q* and double *s*, (*b*) variants of *v*, (*c*) variant of *Q*, (*d*) variants of *d* and *g*. From G. Sauromanus, *Ad principes Christianos* (1524).

more stylized. Casamassima is on firmer ground here in detecting two separate types. But it seems preferable to think of a single design, of which there were two slightly different versions. The main features of the first are the small sharp eyes of the open letters; the closed loop of the 'antique' *g*; the use of the same character for *v* and *u*; and the wide use of serifed ascenders and descenders, even in *y, f* and long *s*. The letters *f* and long *s* are also found with a calligraphic terminal. The usage of variants is sometimes highly irregular.[22] In the second version of the design, the

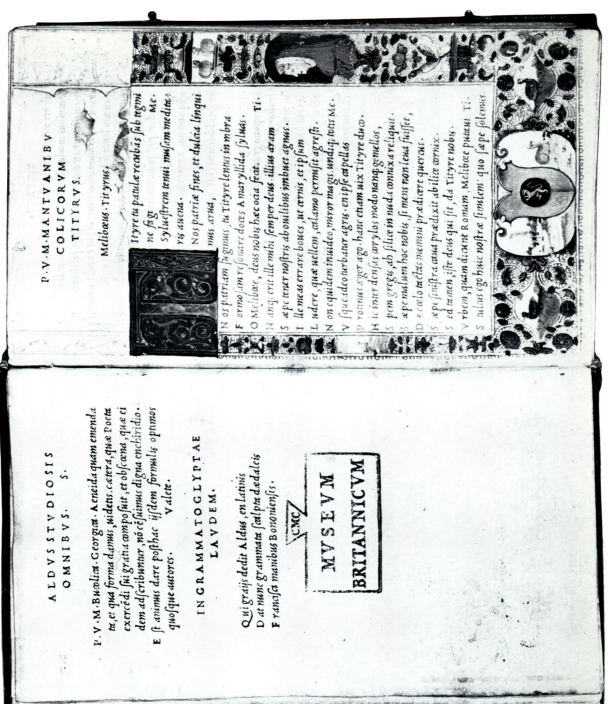

30. The first italic printed book: *Virgil* (1501), published by Aldus Manutius with type designed by Francesco Griffo: see p. 107.

bases of *γ*, *f* and long *s* are curved and subtle modifications in others letters have
the effect of letting in more light (Fig. 17).

persimilem, Verum MOMVS ſtrenue pu-
gnando, inter primos terrorem inferebat, atq3
ingenti clamitans uoce, Ita ne (aiebat) surda
monſtra, fœdiſsimæ ſæculorum peſtes, Sacro-
ſanctū ALITHIAE Numen impetitis?
simulq3 infeſtis cōcurrens armis, captis cæſisq3
plurimis, tela perfringere, abrumpere, detrunca
re, et perſonas, quibus hoſtium uultus tegeren-

Fig. 16. Arrighi's second italic, illustrating alternative forms of *f*
and long *s*. From P. Collenuccio, *Apologi IIII* (1526).

S ub terram ueniente hyeme, ſtant frigore inertes,
D um redeat terris tepidi clementia ueris.
T um demum egreſſi, ad ſolem squalentia terga
C onuoluunt poſita turpi cum pelle ſenecta.
. A nnuus hic illismos, at bombycibus ipsis
T er pigra, dum uiuent, renouabit corpora ſomnus.
I amque age, iam grandes fœtus, iam ducitur ætas,
V ltima, turgenti filum tralucet in aluo
O mnibus, accingunt alacres, operique parant ſe.

Fig. 17. Arrighi's second italic, as used by Arrighi in his last work.
From M. H. Vida, *De Bombyce*, bound with *De Arte Poetica* (1527).

A small italic of about 11 point, related to this design, is occasionally seen for
example in the margins of Collenuccio's *Apologi IIII* and the *Itinerarium Philippi
Bellucii*, and in the colophon of the *Specchio di Esopo*. The *Oratio de pace* of Julius III
has an introductory page in an Aldine Italic.

We complete this survey with the types found in the early editions of *Il modo*. The
story of these early editions is far from straightforward, as the reader will see from

Mr Philip Hofer's treatment of the subject elsewhere in this volume. Complete agreement does not exist about the exact date of *Il modo*. Suffice it to say that the first edition contains four pages printed in a type based on a fine regular hand (Fig. 18).

De le uarie sorti de littere poi, che in questo Tratta-
tello trouerai, se io ti uolessi ad una per una descriuere
tutte le sue ragioni, saria troppo longo processo; Ma
tu hauendo uolunta de imparare, ti terrai inanzi que
sti exempietti, et sforcerati imitarli quanto poterai, che in ogni modo seguendo quelli, senon in tutto,
almeno in gran parte te adiuterano conseguire quella
sorte di littera, che piu in esso ti dilettera. Piglialo
adunque, et con felici auspicii ti exercita, che a chi uno
le conseguire una uirtu niente glie difficile.

Fig. 18. Type used in the first edition of *Il modo*.

It was probably cut by Eustachio Celebrino under Arrighi's supervision and almost certainly represents the first version of Arrighi's italic type, based on his own handwriting. The type found in later contemporary editions of *Il modo* is unlikely to be by Arrighi (Fig. 19).

De le uarie sorti de littere poi, che in questo Tratta-
tello trouerai, se io ti uolessi ad una per una descriuere
tutte le sue ragioni, saria troppo longo processo: Ma
tu hauendo uolunta de imparare, ti terrai inanzi que
sti exempieti, et sforcerati imitarli quanto poterai
che in ogni modo seguendo quelli, se non in tutte,
almeno in gran parte te adiutarano conseguire quella
sorte di littera, che piu in esso ti dilettera. Piglialo
adunque, et con felici auspicii ti exercita, che a chi uo-
le conseguire una uirtu niente glie difficile.

Fig. 19. Type used in another early edition of *Il modo*.

Griffo and Arrighi must have known each other's work, but no contact between them has been traced.[23] It is from the traditions established by these two great contemporaries that all our italic types are derived.

Grateful acknowledgement is made to the Trustees of the British Museum for permission to reproduce illustrations.

APPENDIX
Arrighi's Manuscripts and books as at present known

MANUSCRIPTS

1. Ludovico de Varthema, *Itinerario*. Biblioteca Nazionale Centrale, Florence, Cod. Landau Finaly 9. *c.* 1510 (Attributed by Emanuele Casamassima).
2. Valerius Maximus, *Factorum et dictorum memorabilium libri*. Private ownership (Frank Allan Thomson at Stockholm). 1515–16. (Plate 33.)
3. Aristotle, *Ethica*. Universiteits-Bibliotheek, Amsterdam. 1517. (Plate 32.)
4. G. G. Trissino, *La Sophonisba*. British Museum, Add. MS. 26873 (fragmentary).
5. *Book of Hours*. Fitzwilliam Museum, Cambridge, MS. J. 156.
6. Pandolfo Collenuccio, *Apologi* and Lucian, *Dialogi*, translated into Latin by Livius Guidoloctus. British Museum, Royal MS. 12 C viii. *c.* 1520.
7. *Two briefs*, in *Renaissance Handwriting* (Fairbank and Wolpe), pls. 16 and 17. (Attributed by Alfred Fairbank.) 1520.
8. *Missale Romanum*. Berlin, Kupferstichkabinett 78 D 17.
9. Cicero, *Letter to Quintus*. British Museum, Add. MS. 11930. (Attributed by Alfred Fairbank: see p. 271 below.)
10. *List of benefactors* of the Ospedale di San Giovanni in Laterano, Archivio di Stato, Rome. MS. 1010. (Attributed by Wardrop.)
11. N. Machiavelli, *Clitia*. Colchester and Essex Museum, England. *c.* 1525. (Plates 31, 34, 35 & 36 *a*.)

PRINTED BOOKS, ETC.

1. Clemens VII, *Bulla...contra homicidas*. Vicentino and Lautizio, dated Prid. Idib. Junii 1524.
2. Blossio Palladio ed. *Coryciana* (Latin poems in honour of Johann Goritz, Protonotary Apostolic). Vicentino and Lautizio, July 1524.
3. G. G. Trissino, *La Sophonisba*. Vicentino and Lautizio, July 1524 (another edition September 1524).
4. G. G. Trissino, *Rime del Trissino*. Vicentino, September 1524.
5. G. G. Trissino, *Oratione...al Serenissimo Principe di Venetia*. Vicentino and Lautizio, October 1524.
6. G. G. Trissino, *I ritratti*. Vicentino and Lautizio, October 1524.
7. J. B. Fuscano, *Al illustriss. S. don Loisi di Cordova duca di Sessa*, etc. Vicentino and Lautizio, October 1524.
8. J. B. Fuscano, *Al disertiss. cultor di Muse, M. Jano Vitale*, etc. Vicentino and Lautizio, October 1524.

9. P. Aretino, *Esortatione de la pace tra l'Imperadore e il Re di Francia.* Vicentino and Lautizio, 15 December 1524.

10. A. Firenzuola, *Discacciamento de le nuove lettere,* etc. Vicentino and Lautizio, December 1524.

11. C. Silvanus Germanicus, *In Pontificatum Clementis Septimi pont. max. panegyris.* Vicentino and Lautizio, December 1524.

12. Clemens VII PP., *Monitorium contra clericos...super habitu et tonsura et aliis.* 2 December 1524.

13. G. G. Trissino, *Al Reveren. Mons. Giovan Mattheo Giberti etc.* 1524.

14. G. G. Trissino, *Epistola...de la vita che dee tenere una donna vedova.* Vicentino and Lautizio, 1524.

15. G. G. Trissino, *Canzone...al Santissimo Clemente settimo P.M.* 1524.

16. G. G. Trissino, *Epistola...de le lettere nuovamente aggiunte ne la lingua italiana.* 1524.

17. B. Casalius, *In legem agrarium...oratio.* Vicentino and Lautizio, 1524.

18. G. Sauromanus, *Ad Principes christianos de religione ac communi concordia.* 1524.

19. G. Vitale. *Iani Vitalis Panhormitani...in pacem Hymnus.* 1524–25.

20. P. Aretino, *Canzone in laude del sig. Datario.* Vicentino and Lautizio, 1525.

21. Claudio Tolomei, *De le lettere nuovamente aggiunte, Libro di Adriano Franci da Siena, intitolato il Polito.* Vicentino and Lautizio, 1525.

22. *Aliquot Declamatiunculae et Orationes e Graeco in Latinum versae.* Vicentino and Lautizio. 14 January 1525.

23. Z. Ferrerius, *Hymni novi ecclesiastici.* Vicentino and Lautizio, 1 February 1525.

24. G. Melezio. *Ioannis Meletii...tragica Elegia ad Italiam et Galliam infelices.* 28 February 1525.

25. P. Cursius, *Poema de civitate Castellana Faliscorum.* Vicentino and Lautizio, 29 March 1525.

26. G. Borgia, *Ad Carolum Caesarem Opt. Max. Monarchia.* 1 April 1525.

27. C. Marcellus, *In Psalmum Usque Domine oblivisceris mei.* Vicentino and Lautizio, 12 April 1525.

28. F. Cattani da Diacceto, *Panegirico.* 1526.

29. P. Collenuccio, *Apologi IIII.* Vicentino, 1526.

30. P. Collenuccio, *Specchio di Esopo.* Vicentino, 1526.

31. Julius III P.P., *Joannus Mariae Archiepiscopi Sipontini ad Principes christianos oratio de pace.* Vicentino, 1526.

32. *Itinerarium Philippi Bellucii.* Vicentino, 1526.

33. Clemens VII P.P., *Perpetuatio officiorum etiam Romanae Curiae* and other works. Vicentino (dated 1525).

34. M. F. Calvo, *Antiquae urbis Romae cum regionibus simulachrum.* Vicentino, April 1527.

35. M. H. Vida, *De arte poetica,* etc. Vicentino, May 1527.

36. Clemens VII P.P., *Breve 'Cum nuper exercitus...',* dated 8 June 1527.

37. Ludovico Vicentino, *La Operina,* dated 1522.

38. Ludovico Vicentino, *Il modo de temperare le Penne,* dated 1523 (4 pages of type). Vicentino and Eustachio Celebrino.

N.B. This list owes much to the work of Alfred Fairbank and Emanuele Casamassima.

NOTES

1 Sometimes referred to as Francesco Raibolini (cf. Wardrop, *The Script of Humanism*, p. 35), but most authorities reject this attribution.

2 'scalpta daedaleis Francisci manibus.'

3 P. de Nolhac, *Les Correspondants d'Alde Manuce* (1888).

4 See Aldus's Preface to his *Juvenal*.

5 Cf. A. F. Johnson, *Type Designs* (2nd ed. 1959), p. 95.

6 *The Script of Humanism*, p. 35.

7 *Journal of the Society for Italic Handwriting*, no. 32, p. 9.

8 P. de Nolhac, *op. cit.* p. 28.

9 A. F. Doni, *I Marmi*, ed. Chiörboli, p. 191.

10 A. Sorbelli, 'Francesco Griffi da Bologna, (*Gutenberg Jahrbuch*, 1933), pp. 117 *et seq.*

11 Updike, *Printing Types* (3rd ed. 1962), I, 129.

12 Manzoni (*Studii di Bibliografia Analitica: Studio Secondo*, 1882, p. 30) lists the following variants: Lodovico degli Arrighi Vicentino, Lodovico degli Arrighi, L'Arrighi, Lodovico Vicentino, Il Vicentino, Ludovicus Henricus Vicentinus, and Vicentinus. Wardrop's list ('Arrighi Revived' in *Signature*, 12 July 1939, p. 26) is: Ludovico (Lodovico) Vicentino, Arrighi or degli Arrighi or degli Arrighi Vicentino, Henricis or De Henricis, Ludovicus Vicentinus or Ludovicus Henricus. One could add to both lists—see Note 14 below!

13 *Biblis*, 1959/60, 'Arrighis Ställning i Bokstavskonstens Historia', p. 16. He rejects Wardrop's view (*op. cit.* p. 30) that Corneto was the Etruscan Corneto Tarquinia.

14 'ad instantia de [at the instance of] Maestro Lodovico de Henricis da Corneto Vicentino.'

15 The papal privilege was transferred to Ugo in 1525 in the following terms: 'Si alias per Ludovicum Vicentinum fuit impeditus ut is hos novos characteres in lucem dare ac vendere non posset, Nos tamen communem hominum et utilitatem et, iusticiam attendentes et praecipue quia is (ut constat) ab eodem fuit defraudatus, volumus ac de integro concedimus ut ipse Ugo possit ipsos characteres imprimere, libellosque formare quos et quoties voluerit, eosque dare vaenum.'

16 Mentioned by Cellini, e.g. in his *Life*: attribution first made by Manzoni.

17 'Just as in handwriting he has excelled all our contemporaries, so, with this fine new invention for executing with the printing press almost everything which he used to do with his pen, he has beatan every other printer with his beautiful type.' *Epistola del Trissino de le lettere nuovamente aggiunte ne la lingua italiana* (1524).

18 Bernardo Morsolin: *Giangiorgio Trissino* (1894), p. 416: 'Che M. Lodovico nostro sia tanto inzaccarato mi duole: pur come ho già detto, son contento che per venticinque o trenta ducati sia sovvenuto su li miei argenti. Tuttavia facendo al cosa più cautamente che si può, a ciò ch'io non li perdesse.' This reference seems not to have been noticed hitherto.

19 Cf. Lamberto Donati, *La Bibliofilia*, LI (1949), 158.

20 *Gutenberg Jahrbuch* (1963), pp. 24–36.

21 A rough division of the first italic may be made, as Casamassima does, according to whether the terminals of the letters *p* and *q* are curved or straight. But exceptions occur. In the *Bulla Clementis Papae Septimi*, for example, the word *perpetrabantur* on p. 12 contains both versions. A more arresting instance may be seen in the *Hymni novi ecclesiastici* of Ferrerius. The Introduction has the ascender of the *d* slightly curved; the immediately following Index has the version with the ampler curve; then the book reverts mainly to the first version, but after p. 57 the second version takes precedence.

22 A striking example can be found in Collenuccio's *Apologi IIII*. Most of the book is printed consistently with the straight *f* and long *s*. At signature N (one page) and in the *Argumentum* of the fourth apology the curved versions appear. From Signature O to the end, the two variants are used indiscriminately. What is the explanation of such large inconsistencies as this and that described in the previous note? Is it haste? Or could it simply be that, when he received his material, Arrighi rapidly sketched it out in book form, and his assistants merely copied what they saw, including the anomalies of a swift hand? (On a somewhat similar theme, see F. A. Thomson's article on the significance of Arrighi's *Clitia* MS., p. 121 below.)

23 But Soncino, for whom Griffo worked around 1503, probably employed Arrighi's partner Eustachio Celebrino in 1527 (see Luigi Servolini, *Gutenberg Jahrbuch*, 1944/9, p. 184.

24 The most recent work on Arrighi includes: (*a*) F. A. Thomson, 'Arrighis Ställning i Bokstavskonstens Historia', *Biblis* (1959/60); (*b*) Alfred Fairbank & Berthold Wolpe, *Renaissance Handwriting* (1960); (*c*) B. Corrigan, 'An Unrecorded Manuscript of Machiavelli's La Clizia', *La Bibliofilia*, LXIII (1961); (*d*) E. Casamassima, 'Ludovico degli Arrighi detto Vicentino copista

dell'Itinerario del Varthema', *La Bibliofilia*, LXIV (1962), 'I Disegni di Caratteri di Ludovico degli Arrighi Vicentino', *Gutenberg Jahrbuch* (1963); (*e*) Bent Rohde, 'Lodovico Vicentino som Bogtrykker', *Fund og Forskning*, XI (1964); (*f*) Alfred Fairbank, 'Italic in its own Right', *Alphabet* (1964); (*g*) Emanuele Casamassima, 'Ancora su Ludovico degli Arrighi Vicentino (Notizie 1510–27) risultati di una "Recognitio"', *Gutenberg Jahrbuch* (1965).

25 The material in this article originally appeared in the *Journal of the Society for Italic Handwriting*, Nos. 38 and 40.

fuora si ordineranno le' nuoue' noze': le' q̃ li
fieno femmine': et non maschie': come' quelle'
di Nicomaco.

Finis.

CANZONA.

Ui che' si intente' è quell'
A mime' belle': Exemplo honesto humile
Mastro saggio è gentile'
Di nostra humana vita udito hauete'
Et per lui conoscete'
Qual cosa schifar desi: Et qual seguire'.
Per salir dritti al cielo
Et sotto rado Velo
Piu altre' assai ch'hor fora lungho adir
Di cui preghiam' tal' frutto appo uoi sia
Qual merta tanta uostra Cortesia

Finis.

31. From Machiavelli's *Clitia*: writing attributed to Arrighi: see p. 123.
Colchester and Essex Museum (fol. '51' (49)^v)

To face p. 120]

tant recte' quidem iudicare' non poſſunt : niſi fortu
ito . Magis autem ad ea comprehendenda fortaſſe'
fuerint apti . Cum igitur noſtri maiores ea quæ'
ad facultatem ferendarum legum pertinent ſine'
perſcrutatione' reliquerint : nos ipſos iſta fortaſſe'
præſtat conſiderare' et omnino de' republica per
tractare' oportet : ut quoad fieri poteſt ea philoſo
phia perficiatur quæ' circa res humanas uerſatur.
Primum itaq; ſiquid recte' ſit a maioribus dictu;
id enitamur recenſere'. Deinde' ex congregatis reb⁹
publicis conſiderare' quænam ciuitates et rerum pu
blicarum ſingulas euertunt atq; conſeruant . Et qua'
ob cauſas aliæ' recte' gubernantur : aliæ' contra. his
enim perſpectis magis fortaſſe' perceperimus quæ'
nam ſit R eſpublica optima et quomodo unaqueq;
diſpoſita quibusue' legibus utens ac moribus bene'
fuerit conſtituta . Dicamus igitur hinc initio ſum
pto .

Ludouicus Vicentinus Scribebat R omæ' Anno
     Salutis . M . D . X V I I . Menſe' octob .

32.   From Aristotle's *Ethica*, written by Arrighi (1517): see p. 126. (Reduced)
Universiteits-Bibliotheek, Amsterdam

sa uoce proculcatum . Nihil enim eum
aliud agere . quam . ut conuiuium suum
moraretur . respondit . et huius dicti con
scius securo animo coenare potuit . Ille ue
ro etiam in foro non erubuit . P . Scipione
socerum suum legibus noxium quas ipe
tulerat . in maxima quoq3 reorum . et il
lustrium . ruina muneris loco a iudicibus
deposcere , maritalis lecti blanditij statu
reipu . temperando .

Externa . De Alexandro Rege .
SAtis multa de nris . aliena tunc
adijcientur . Alexandri Regis
uirtus , et felicitas , tribus insolentiæ gra
dibus exultauit euidentißimis . Fastidio
enim Philippi , Iouem Hammonem pa
trem asciuit . tædio morum et cultus mace
doniæ . uestem et instituta persica assu
psit . Spreto mortali habitu . diuinum ca

33.   From Valerius Maximus, written by Arrighi (*c.* 1515): see p. 126.
In possession of Frank Allan Thomson, Stockholm

quella disputa che gia facessi con quelli Phy-
fici, per la quale tanto riso intendo si leuò
nelle schole. ESO. Voglio dirtelo, erano in
Confesa li Philosophi di Grecia, per non se
accordare in trouare li principii le cause de le
cose naturale, Io mi fecinanzi, e scopersi il uol
to alla uerità, la quale hauea menata cõ min tã
ta furia di parole se leuarono cõtra la meschi-
na che scl non fusse stato, ch'io subito lascosi,
l'hariano morta, onde io dissi loro ch'io sapeua
la cõclusione di quello si disputaua, narandoli
che caribde appresso Sicilia, quale prima sorbe
e poi rutta l'acqua, una uolta sorbi li mõti, la se-
conda le isole, a la terza nel rutar butto fora la
terra la quale hora habitamo, alhora odito questo tanto riso si leuò nella turba, che fu cosa
mirabile, parendo a circunstãti ch'el fosse ben
fatto, come che alle gran falsità et errori, mi-
glior rimedio nõ sia, che porui gl'incontro una
espressa e gran busia, come uno amico mio

Greco

soleua essere uno huomo graue resoluto, respet
tiuo dispensaua il tempo suo honoreuolmente.
& si leuaua la mattina di buon'hora. udiua la
sua messa. prouedeua aliutto del giorno: dipoi
s'egli haueua faccenda in piaza, in mercato: o i
magistrati: e le faceua quanto che ne & esi ridu
ceua con qualche Cittadini tra ragionamenti ho
noreuoli o esi ritraua incasa nelle scritteo do
ue ragguagliaua suoi scritture. riordinaua suoi
conti. Dipoi piaceuolmente con la sua brigata de
sinaua & desinato ragionaua con il figliuolo ad
munuialo dauagli ad conoscere gl'huomini. & cõ
qualche exemplo antico & moderno gl'inseguaua
uiuere. Andaua di poi fuora consumaua tutto'l
giorno o in faccende o in diporti graui & hone
sti. Venuta la sera sempre l'Auemaria le troua
ua in casa. Stauasi un poco con essioui al fuoco, se
glieua di Verno: dipoi se nentraua nello scrittoio.
ad riuedere le faccende sue. Alle tre hore si cenaua
allegramente. Questo ordine della sua uita era u

34. Comparison of Colchester *Clitia* MS. fol. '18' (16)ᵛ with *Specchio di Esopo*, printed by Arrighi in 1525: see p. 127. (Both reduced)

[*To face p. 121*

FRANK ALLAN THOMSON

The Significance of the Colchester Clitia MS.

One of the reasons why I cannot remember how long it is since I had the good fortune of first meeting Alfred Fairbank personally (I had known him for a long time through his writings) is that I cannot now imagine my life without his friendship. It can hardly be more than a decade, though, for the occasion was a 'week-end course' arranged by the Society for Italic Handwriting, in one of the first years of its existence, at Jordan's Hostel, near Beaconsfield (since then, alas, destroyed by fire, if I am rightly informed). He was the most inspiring teacher—I have known few men so modest about their gifts, and fewer still with his capacity of imparting the fruits of them to others in the most efficient yet unobtrusive way. We spent much of the time discussing subjects which I had been burning to ventilate for a long time, and as with great reluctance I took my leave he said laconically: 'Write to me.' Those words gave rise to a correspondence which has been going on ever since and in the course of which we have shared and discussed a series of discoveries and problems with the freedom born of complete mutual trust and respect for each other's views. He has always been most generous with advice and helpful suggestions, gifts of photographs, photostats and many other things. Our correspondence has been punctuated by delightful personal reunions, though unfortunately all too infrequent, and my enjoyment of the pleasant hospitality of Alfred and Elsie Fairbank's home.

In the spring of 1960 he told me in a letter about Professor Beatrice Corrigan's discovery in the Colchester and Essex Museum of a MS. of Machiavelli's comedy *Clitia* and its possible attribution to Arrighi. He also sent a small photograph of a page, which caused me to ask whether this attribution was based on the similarity of the script to Arrighi's last italic type. Later on the same year I spent some time in England, and Alfred Fairbank and I motored up from Brighton to Colchester to have a look at the MS. It was getting late, for the traffic was slower than I had expected, and my companion got out at a public call box and rang up the Curator, Mr M. R. Hull, M.A., who very kindly promised to wait for us, and subsequently received us very cordially in spite of our lateness. Soon after that we were sitting side by side poring over the MS. page after page, in the waning light of the summer evening, and I know that we both felt keen gratitude to Professor Corrigan for having brought the MS. to our attention.

Later on Mr Hull very amiably allowed the MS. to be lent for some little time to the British Museum where I had another opportunity of studying it, and with his permission had it microfilmed. From this microfilm I afterwards had a complete, full-size photographic reproduction made, and then discovered that one opening was missing. With great patience Mr Hull, to whom I explained this in a letter in March 1961, took the trouble of arranging a separate negative to be made of this opening, and sent it to me. I think this is the proper place to repeat my deep gratitude to him for all his kindness and helpfulness.

Since then I have 'lived with' *Clitia* and made a few discoveries which I imagine might be of a certain interest. I wish to add, as I now abandon the chronological narrative, that the opinions, conjectures, and conclusions expressed in this study are entirely my own, and that I assume full responsibility for them. I also apologize to Professor Corrigan for not being able wholly to share the views about the Colchester MS. expressed in her extremely interesting essay in *La Bibliofilia*, 1961, Dispensa 1ª, pp. 73 *et seq.*, which is brimming over with fascinating bits of historical information and a pleasing wealth of biographical detail, brought to light by her research. Largely on the strength of the illumination, she advances the theory that the MS. was a presentation copy commissioned as a wedding present for Lorenzo Ridolfi and Maria Strozzi and attempts to transfer the date of their wedding from 1529 to 1525, when she believes the MS. to have been written.

THE APPEARANCE OF THE COLCHESTER MS.

The book is bound in a very fine contemporary binding, for which it was previously exhibited. When you open it, you get a surprise; for the MS. is executed on very coarse paper, which is partly in a worn and dilapidated state and has been rather clumsily mended, obviously in connection with the binding. The sumptuous illumination of fol. 2ʳ, as well as the painted initials make a slightly incongruous impression. The numbering of the leaves has been made by a later hand and shows a curious anomaly. There is a gap between 10 and 13 without any corresponding gap in the text (the break between 10ᵛ and '13'ʳ is in the middle of a Canzona of which the text, identical with one from *Mandragola*, is complete). Later, 25 has been repeated on two consecutive leaves, but corrected to 24 on the first. Thus there are actually only 49 folios, i.e. 98 pages, fol. '22' really being 20; '32', 30; '42', 40; and '51', 49.

Before having seen the MS. itself and on the basis of a photograph, Alfred Fairbank had written to me: 'The shaky quality of the *La Clizia* MS. makes me think he was in poor health.' In point of fact, this impression is wholly due to the poor quality of the paper. The initial part of the MS. up to, and including fol. '21' (19), is lettered with the precision of a printed book in serifed italics, and it has taken an extremely skilled hand to produce this effect in spite of the paper.

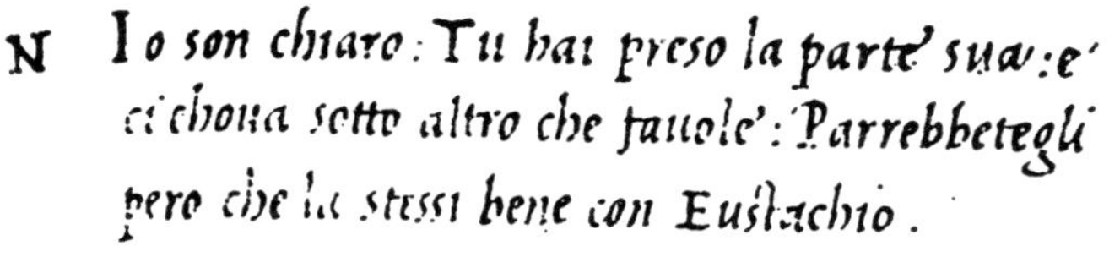

Fig. 20. Colchester *Clitia* MS. fol. '22'ʳ. Note letter *h* in word 'chiaro'.

At the top of fol. '22' (20)ʳ (Fig. 20) a first sign of haste turns up—the first *h* (in *chiaro*) gets a kern instead of a serif. There is no reason to assume any interruption or lapse of time, nor is there any reason to believe that anybody else took over; for the transition to a different, freer hand is very gradual, and the same narrow nib is continuously being used. The writing is done at increasing speed, it seems, until the last *Finis* at the bottom of fol. '51' (49) (Plate 31) which looks like a cry of relief. What happens is that, for some reason, the scribe gives up the cramping type-design lettering and allows traits from his ordinary hand, though modified by the narrow nib and an attempt to maintain certain essentials (such as spacing and arrangement), to creep in and become increasingly dominant. Except for the kern, which becomes the rule from fol. '22' (20)ᵛ onwards, there are frequent joins, letter shapes like *s, g, g,* the ampersands *&, &* and—on the last page—*&*. The slope, too, becomes freer.

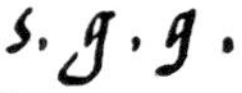

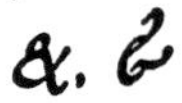

WHO WROTE THE MS.?

The main reason for connecting the MS. with Arrighi is the fact that the lettering of its initial part closely resembles one of his type-designs—for he was not only a calligrapher but a printer and type-designer as well.[1] For the present purpose I think it is sufficient to distinguish between three different type-designs of his and between the two versions of the last of them. The only extant example of the earliest one occurs in a few pages of his second manual (*Il Modo de Temperare le Penne* printed in Venice 1523). Why this beautiful and harmonious type was not used again is difficult to say. It may have been because it was technically too complicated to handle for more than a few pages, for his next type, used during 1524 and 1525 when he was printing in Rome with Lautizio Perugino, also closely resembling his written hand in that it has kerns and mostly *ʒ*, has particularly one flaw, an *f* that has a tendency to tilt over backwards, and the cross-bar of which points upwards. This may have been one of the reasons why he invented a completely new design, used in 1526, which has serifs, *ʒ* and straight descenders of *f* and *ſ* (like the ones of *p* and *q*). These must have been easier to manipulate, but the difficulty seems to have been overcome, for in a new version of this type he goes back to *f* and *ſ*. As far as I know there is only one book, printed with this final (to my mind his most perfect and beautiful) type: Vida's *De Arte Poetica etc.*, in May 1527, just before the Sack of Rome (in which Arrighi is supposed to have perished). The initial script of the Colchester MS. is practically identical with this type.[2] One can almost see, however, how the scribe restrains his hand in order to keep the tails of *f* and *ſ* within the body of the type.

If the Colchester MS. had been in a complete and consistent imitation of the printing type from beginning to end it might have been difficult, though, to affirm that he wrote it himself. Mr Philip Hofer, of the Library of Harvard University, owns a MS. which is an exact facsimile of Giolito's 1546 edition of Aretino's comedy *Il Filosofo* and could hardly be distinguished from the original printed book, if it did not possess a colophon which declares it to be the work of the calligrapher Amadeo Mazzoli of Forli (in 1762).[3] Curiously enough there is in the Marcian Library of Venice a MS. facsimile (ZZ. 4. It. 11. 41/11—Colloc. 7402) of the 1537 *Clitia* edition, printed by Maciochi in Florence. By reproducing the title page and the first Canzona here we kill two birds with one stone for it is practically identical with the printed edition (I should be surprised if it was not penned by Mazzoli as well) (Fig. 21).

Fortunately for us the 'type' part of the MS. has a few extremely Arrighian traits. On a couple of occasions there are breaks in the shape of bold ligatures and flourishes, e.g. on fol. 4ᵛ, where the repeated word 'fantastico' inspires him to three flamboyant *st* ligatures, of which we recognize the style from *La Operina* (and from his MS. books). Sometimes he is also unable to resist flourishes into top and bottom margins. A close scrutiny reveals many typical traits of his personal *ductus*.

In the case of the Colchester MS. there is of course also the alternative to be considered that a pupil might have written it. In that case it would, however, also surely have been a slavish imitation—more or less successful—from beginning to end.

CAN THIS MS. BE A PRESENTATION COPY?

I thus feel convinced that Arrighi wrote the MS. himself—but for what purpose?

124

CLITIA

Comedia facetiſſima di Clitia com-
poſta per lo ingenioſo huomo
Nicolo Macchiauelli
Fiorentino nuoua-
mente ſtampata.

M. D. XXXVII.

CANZONA.

Quanto siè lento il giorno,
che le memorie antiche
fa ch'hor per noi sien monſtre, & celebrate
ſi uede, perche intorno
tutte le genti antiche
ſi ſono in queſta parte raunate,
noi che la noſtra etate
ne'boſchi, & nelle ſelue conſumiamo
uenuti anchor qui ſiamo,
io Nimpha, & noi paſtori
ogn'un cantando e noſtri antichi amori.
Chiari giorni, & quieti,
felice, & bel paeſe,
doue del noſtro canto il ſuon ſudia,
per tanto allegri, & lieti
a queſte noſtre impreſe
farem co'l cantar noſtro compagnia,
con ſi dolce armonia,
& partirenci poi
io nimpha, & noi paſtori
& tornirenci à noſtri antichi amori.

INTERLOCVTORI.

Cleandro	Palamede
Nicomacho	Pirro ſeruo.
Euſtachio fattore	Sofronia.
Doria Ancilla	Damone
Soſtrata	Ramondo Napolitano.

Fig. 21. Title page and first Canzona of *Clitia* (MS. Marc. ZZ.4. It. 11. 41/11-Colloc. 7402),
a facsimile of Maciochi's printed edition of 1537.

Frank Allan Thomson

A lot of importance in this respect has been attributed to the illumination. It is easy to forget that illumination is extremely deceptive, is always added afterwards, and is not necessarily connected with the production of the text at all. Anyone familiar with Arrighi and his work on seeing this MS. must say to himself *a priori*: 'If this is Arrighi—and I am convinced that it is—it cannot possibly be a commissioned presentation MS.' We know fairly well what Arrighi's products in that field look like. In this connection I think the following are worth mentioning: the *Aristotle* (Plate 32) which seems to have belonged to Vittoria Colonna, signed with his name in the colophon in October 1517 (now in the Amsterdam University Library); the *Missale Romanum* (now in Berlin) also signed in the colophon and executed in 1520 for Cardinal Giulio de' Medici, later Pope Clement VII; the *Collenuccio*, according to its preface given to Henry VIII by Geoffrey Chamber (British Museum Royal MSS. 12 C viii); the *Valerius Maximus* executed, probably in 1515 and at all events before January 1516, for Altobello Averoldi, Bishop of Pola (in the present writer's possession (Plate 33)).[4] The most striking feature of all these, written on exquisite vellum, is the unswerving consistency of the hand, and the never-wavering skill: page upon page of untiringly uniform and beautiful writing. The *Aristotle* contains 376 written pages, the *Collenuccio* has 173, the *Valerius Maximus* 232; and the example from the latter is chosen from the last few pages. The *Missale Romanum* is a special case, for it does not contain one word of cursive. All the remaining MSS. are in various, but extremely similar, versions of the 'cancellaresca', of which script he gives account in his two manuals *La Operina* (1522) and *Il modo de temperare le Penne* (1523), and, in the latter, he says: 'Hauendoti io descritto, Studioso Lettor mio, l'anno passato uno libretto da imparar scriuere *littera Cancellaresca, la quale, a mio iudicio, tiene il primo loco*....' Whatever hand he uses, it would be no exaggeration to say, though, that his MS. books are among the most consistent ones ever produced. They have the kind of uniformity born of enormous skill in conjunction with speed. One thing seems certain. Particularly if he had been pressed for time, he would not have chosen for a gift book the strait-jacket of the type-design, but a version of the 'cancellaresca', which he could write in his sleep, with ease and speed and a faultless result (a mere 98 pages after all).

That Arrighi with his devotion to calligraphy could under any circumstances have executed a commissioned MS. book on coarse paper and in the kind of inconsistent writing we have seen in the Colchester MS. is, to my mind, completely out of the question. Geoffrey Chamber wrote in the dedication to Henry VIII of the *Collenuccio* in praise of the calligrapher: 'Qui, quantum fieri potuit, curaui ut politissimis characteribus conscriberetur, Vt hoc ceu inuitamento quodā addito ad legendum

126

CANZONA

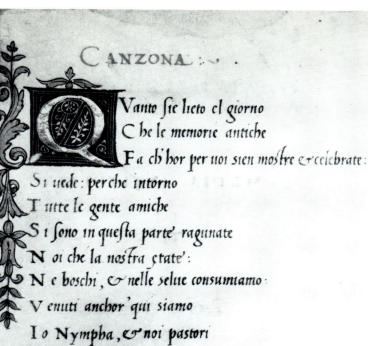

Vanto sie lieto el giorno
Che le memorie antiche
Fa ch'hor per uoi sien mostre & celebrate:
Si uede: perche intorno
Tutte le gente amiche
Si sono in questa parte' ragunate
Noi che la nostra etate':
Ne boschi, & nelle selue consumiamo:
Venuti anchor' qui siamo
Io Nympha, & noi pastori
& gyam' cantando insieme e nostri amori.
Chiari giorni & quieti
Felice & bel' paese
Doue del nostro canto el suon' s'udia
Per tanto allegri & lieti
Ad queste nostre imprese
Faren' col' cantar' nostro compagnia
Con si dolce armonia
Qual' mai sentita piu non fu da noi

35.   Colchester *Clitia* MS. fol. 1ʳ: see p. 129.

36a.   Illuminated initial from Colchester *Clitia* MS. fol. 2ʳ: see p. 132.

36b.   Illuminated initial from *Pamphilia*: see p. 132.
National Library of Scotland, Edinburgh (Acc. No. 1554: Z. 30. 4. 4)

[To face p

librum allicerere.' That could hardly have been said in the present case. And no one who has seen and handled the *Aristotle*, *Collenuccio* or *Valerius Maximus* would call the Colchester *Clitia* a 'beautiful and expensive' MS.

THE REAL PURPOSE OF THE MS.

To form an opinion of this, the first thing we have to do is to eliminate the illumination, which did not exist when the writing was produced. It then becomes obvious that here we are dealing not with Arrighi the *calligrapher*, but with Arrighi the *printer*. What we have is the MS. for the compositor, of which the first part is also a detailed printer's layout. Even if the paper is inferior to any used in his printed books (where it is very carefully chosen, of high quality, and its thickness varying according to the number of leaves), *this* purpose warrants the extremely careful treatment of the initial part of the book and explains why it was not necessary to go on in the same way to the end. It also explains why he could permit himself a few flourishes: they would not influence his printer's type. On the other hand their existence shows that had he been free to choose he would have used his 'cancellaresca'. If we compare a page (Plate 34) from the *Specchio di Esopo*, printed by Arrighi in 1526, with a page from the first part of the Colchester MS., we shall find that the layout is practically identical, 20 lines; margins about 1:1:2:3; proportion of text block (about 75 + :140 mm) just a little more elongated than 1:√3; proportions of the page almost exactly the Golden Section (*Clitia* 140:230 mm, *Specchio di Esopo* 130:210 mm—of course slightly cut by binder). These and 1:√2 are proportions Arrighi often applies. In his MS. books Arrighi often uses signatures and regularly catchwords, intended for the binder. These catchwords are very neatly written *vertically* in the lower margin (along the ruled line next to the centre margin). In his *printed* books the catchwords are *horizontal*, and this is the case in the present MS. as well. The *first* catchword is on fol. '22' (20)^v, after the increasing speed has become manifest, so it seems likely that the compositor, clamouring for copy, has received the first 40 pages with their final connecting catchword. The next one—still more hastily written—is already on fol. '32' (30), i.e. only after another 20 pages. And then the third and last one is on fol. '42' (40) marking 20 more pages. Each time presumably the compositor has got the new batch that was ready, and finally the remaining nine leaves. It is perhaps the handling in the printing shop that is responsible for the dilapidated and mended state the bound sheets are now partly in.

That a printed book—and consequently also its layout—provides spaces for initials (and borders) is quite in order and was normally the case in Arrighi's printed books. In *De le Lettere...* three line spaces are left, in *Specchio di Esopo* two, in *Vida* four in some places, two in others. (Out of a total of forty-two spaces for initials in the Colchester *Clitia*, two—at the bottom of pages where no more was available—have the height of two lines; thirty-five of three lines—in five cases one of these wholly empty; and five of four lines, regularly having the corresponding indention to form a square.) A copy of *Vida* in the British Museum (C. 4. h. 5) is on vellum and has decorated initials as well as a border with a coat of arms on the first page. (It is obviously completely incongruous that he should have produced anything like the *Clitia* MS. as a gift book at the same time!)

For Arrighi it was a natural procedure to write out a book the way it was going to look when printed: for one thing that was what he had done with his writing manuals. It seems quite possible, too, that the epigram by Marcantonio Casanova, shown in *Il modo* (1523), might be from a written layout for the printed version (in his second type) of Palladius' *Coryciana* published by Arrighi in 1524 (see figs. 1 and 2 in James Wardrop's 'Arrighi Revived', *Signature*, O.S. no. 12).

Careful and detailed layout is not unknown among present-day printers either. Jan Tschichold (in *Schriftkunde Schreibübungen und Skizzieren*, Basle, 1942, p. 61) describes a detailed layout or 'mise en page' in these words: 'Die Wirkung einer tadellosen Skizze *darf sich kaum von jener der fertigen Arbeit unterscheiden*.' It is typical of our age that he recommends the *pencil* as the best medium for imitating the printed type, but for Arrighi it was quite natural to use the pen, for to him his type was simply a translation of his pen-written letter. We may be quite certain that his high ambition to achieve the best possible 'mise en page' made him prepare detailed layouts for his printed texts. Another proof of his ambition has been pointed out to me by Mr A. L. van Gendt (of Amsterdam) who tells me that two different 'issues' of Arrighi's printed *Sophonisba* (see A. F. Johnson, *Type Designs their History and Development*, 2nd ed., 1959, p. 130) are actually entirely different editions, the text of the later one having been *reset* with another length of line, etc. He was consequently not quite satisfied with his first attempt. (There is a MS., unfortunately badly damaged by fire, of *Sophonisba* in the British Museum, which with great likelihood is attributable to Arrighi (illustrated in *Arrighi Revived*). Arrighi's printed version is in his second type, which still is very close to his written hand.)

It should perhaps be remembered that the laudatory words about him by Trissino, partly quoted by Professor Corrigan, were actually in praise of the *printer* Arrighi. He says: '...il quale, si come nel scrivere ha superato tutti gli altri de l'età nostra, così, havendo nuovamente trovato *questo bellissimo modo di fare con la stampa quasi tutto quello, che prima con la penna faceva*, ha di belli characteri ogni altri, che stampi, avanzato'.

THE SIXTEENTH-CENTURY PRINTING HISTORY OF 'CLITIA'

I am fully conscious of having spoken above as if there existed a printed Arrighi edition of the comedy, but I must admit that I have never seen one, though I still hope to do so.

According to Adolf Gerber's remarkable bibliographical work on Machiavelli (*Die Handschriften, Ausgaben und Uebersetzungen seiner Werke*, Part 2, 1912, p. 77) there are only three extant separate editions of *Clizia*, the earliest one the 1537 printing of Maciochi in Florence (with the curious colophon in Greek characters), of which the source has hitherto been unknown. Gerber says, however, prophetically: 'vorausgesetzt dass es nicht noch eine ältere, bisher noch nicht wieder zum Vorschein gekommene gibt'. As may be seen from the facsimile of the title page, identical with the original but for a missing colon (Fig. 21), it says, 'nuovamente stampata' which normally means that there has been a previous edition. Now there is a curious characteristic of all the extant early editions that they lack a line, the fourth one from the end, of the introductory Canzona, which should consist of two eleven-line stanzas but, in all these cases, has only ten lines in the second one. In modern editions this line has been supplied from the only previously known complete MS. (Gerber, part 1, 1912, pp. 101–2), which, however, is not an autograph one of Machiavelli's. If we compare the beginning of the Canzona in the Colchester MS. (Plate 35) with the facsimile of Maciochi's 1537 edition (Fig. 21) we shall find that this line 'Qual mai sentita più non fu da voi' is present in Colchester as the bottom line of the page but absent in Maciochi, though, apart from this, the arrangement is very similar, the title being CANZON*A* (at the end the facsimile has CANZON*E*) and the beginning of the second, incomplete, stanza marked by the C in the margin. If we look more closely at Arrighi's MS. page we shall find that whereas his layout throughout the book is 20 lines a page, through an oversight this page occupies the space of *21* lines. Obviously it has become necessary to move this line, but the layout of the following page already fills it completely—and so, somehow or other, the line gets lost. (Curiously enough, thanks to another slip, of the pen in that case, it has become evident that the *Valerius Maximus* MS. is copied from Aldus's 1502 or 1503 edition.) It is my belief, then, that the printing was actually carried out and that a copy of this edition was Maciochi's exemplar. Though he abandons the learned forms, *Sophronia*, etc., so consistent with Arrighi, the associate of Sadoleto and Trissino, who quoted Latin in his manuals, he retains CLITIA, which in later editions became CLIZIA. It is difficult to say whether the previously known MS. (Florence, Bibl. Riccard, 28) was Arrighi's source. They have traits in common (e.g. Canzon*a*, the use of the article *el*), but it is perhaps most likely that they have a common source. It seems improbable that the Bibl. Riccard. MS. could have been copied from Arrighi's layout, for after this had served its purpose a printed edition existed and such a copy would have been rather pointless. On the other hand Professor Corrigan affirms, as a result of her careful collation of the texts, that variations in the Colchester MS. '*in several cases afford the only manuscript authority for readings in the first edition*'. This 'first edition' is the Maciochi 1537 one, and since it lacks the Canzona line, which exists in our MS., it seems obvious that these readings can only have been transmitted through a *printed* Arrighi copy. Since a few MSS. exist, which are actually sixteenth century handmade imitations of contemporaneous printed editions (sometimes no doubt because they were already out of print or so expensive that copying was in fact cheaper), it is only fair, to ask the question: could the Colchester *Clitia* be an attempted imitation of a *printed copy*? That, however, would necessitate firstly the assumption of *the existence of a now lost edition in Arrighi's type containing the subsequently-dropped Canzona line*; secondly some sort of explanation of the disappearance of this line in all the other sixteenth-century editions.[5] Obviously a meaningless labyrinth. Apart from that, of course, the flourishes in the first part of the MS. and the final free hand show that no attempt at such imitation was made.

WHEN WAS ARRIGHI'S 'CLITIA' PRINTED?

In 1526, when Arrighi was still using the earlier version of his third type, he was fairly active, and at least four or five works have survived (from 1524 and 1525 at least nineteen works, printed in his second type, are extant). The only work in the type of the *Clitia* design is *Vida* printed in May 1527, which leaves a lacuna of at least the first four months of that year. That would perhaps be the most likely period.

The man who ordered the printing was probably Machiavelli himself. Earlier on it was believed that *Clitia* was first performed in 1526, but Professor Roberto Ridolfi has shown that it must have been in 1525, and on 13 January that year. When Machiavelli visited Rome in May–June in the same year (for the last time before he died, exactly two years later) in order to present his *Istorie Fiorentine* to Pope Clement VII, he may have spoken to Arrighi about it and given him a copy. There are many links between the two men. Sadoleto's mother was a Machiavelli for one thing; but there is also reason to believe that Machiavelli had had some dealings with Arrighi's 'scriptorium' on an earlier occasion.

Delay is not unknown in the printing trade, and Arrighi was very busy just then with possibly more remunerative projects. Machiavelli was not a rich man (even if he had received 120 gold ducats from the Pope's private purse), and there are some indications that Arrighi often had financial difficulties.[6] That in all probability the printing was not carried out until 1527 consequently does not seem too unnatural.

Certain linguistic features maybe point to an original Machiavelli MS. as Arrighi's exemplar. I have got the impression that the use of the article *el*, which crops up now and then, is a Florentine characteristic. It occurs, for example, in the Mandragola edition by an unknown printer (1518) shown by Professor Roberto Ridolfi in *Biblio-filia*, 1964, Dispensa 1ª, p. 51, and in a letter from Cardinal Niccolò Ridolfi of May 1524, quoted in *Bibliofilia*, 1964, Dispensa 2ª, p. 176, by Brian Lawn. I imagine that a detailed philological analysis of the Colchester MS. might be fruitful.

A WEDDING GIFT? THE ILLUMINATION

As we have seen the *manuscript* cannot have been commissioned as a gift for the Ridolfi–Strozzi wedding, since it originally had another completely independent function. The very facts that the bundle of papers was torn and dilapidated before being bound and that the book entirely lacks any dedication alluding to the recipients and the occasion, are in themselves sufficient to refute that theory. It is also highly unlikely—and rather a discourteous idea—that a wedding gift should have been ordered so late that it could not be properly executed.[7] And how could there be time for the painting of the laborious illumination which was, of course, done *after* the writing?

The question of the wedding date and its relation to the time of production of the MS. becomes less important but not uninteresting. From what has been said previously, it is obvious that the MS., directly connected with, and surely almost simultaneous with the printing, cannot have been produced earlier than the end of 1526 or rather one of the first few months of 1527. As to the marriage, I do not think that Machiavelli's undated letter (of 1525) necessarily means that the *wedding* had taken place. He probably simply refers to the marriage contract of August 1524, which may perhaps have been followed by a betrothal. As far as I can see, there is no real reason to doubt that the actual wedding took place in 1529.

Consequently the MS., which can have been produced no later than the first four months of 1527, existed at the time of the wedding. It might then have been in the hands of someone, who had it adorned with the illumination and gave it to the young couple. Somehow I doubt this, too. Would a rather crude comedy about an old man, planning by ruse to jump into a sixteen-year-old bride's bed and replacing her bridegroom, primed with aphrodisiacs 'strong enough to rejuvenate a ninety-year-old' (*Clitia*, Act IV. 2) really be a suitable wedding present for a young couple of the greatest refinement?

Mr Alfred Fairbank's keen eye for calligraphy and illumination does not seem to have deceived him when he considered that the same hand illuminated the Colchester *Clitia* and the Edinburgh *Pamphilia* (NLS MS. Acc. No. 1554—Z. 30. 4. 4), for the initial S fols. 2ʳ (Plate 36 *a*), of the former seems almost identical with the S of fol. 6ᵛ (Plate 36 *b*) of the latter. Apart from that there are very great similarities down to small details. Since several MSS. seem to exist, illuminated by the same artist, further research might help us to establish when he was active. So far the Ridolfi arms (alone) in *Pamphilia* point to Lorenzo's having commissioned the illumination himself (if it had been Niccolò's, who was also a great book-collector, there would have been a Cardinal's hat) for his reputedly fine library, and personally I imagine that this was the case with the *Clitia* illumination as well. (It would seem possible then that the illuminator was a Florentine one.) The joined coats of arms may thus have been added to the no longer (Machiavelli died in 1527) acutely scandalous comedy much later, when Maria was not a blushing bride any more—perhaps had turned out to be made of sterner stuff than ever expected; for her sister Luisa seems to have died of poisoning at her home, if I remember rightly in 1534.

To my mind the likeliest solution of the riddle is that the Arrighi layout was acquired by (or given to) Lorenzo Ridolfi as a collector's piece and that he had the book illuminated and bound. I think the calligrapher-printer's fame must have warranted that, especially if some time had elapsed since his death. The fact that a fairish number of his books, though they seem to have been printed in small and exclusive editions, have survived (there are three in my own modest collection) shows how highly appreciated they were—even if the *Clitia* edition is still hiding.

WHERE WAS THE MS. HIDDEN ALL THE TIME?

Having reached this point, I cannot finish without speculating a little about the whereabouts of the MS. during the earlier years of its existence. After the presumed 1527 (or late 1526) Rome edition of Arrighi's, *Clitia* seems to have been reprinted in *Florence* more or less once every ten years: 1537, 1548 and 1556. We have seen that considerable care was taken to correct particularly the 1548 Giunti edition, which on the title page calls itself 'nuovamente corretta e ristampata'. How can it be, if the MS. actually existed in the Ridolfis' possession, and Lorenzo was a man of literary interests and presumably with a soft spot for *Clitia*, that this text was never consulted or offered for collation? For if it had been, the missed-out Canzona line would without a doubt have crept back into place. (That no autograph MS. of

Machiavelli's seems to have existed for consultation might be because it had been taken to Rome and given to Arrighi for copying and subsequently got lost, though his own layout MS. happened to survive.) It is possible that everybody assumed that Arrighi's printed edition must be identical with his layout, but it could also be that his MS. was in fact rediscovered much later than we have ever thought. Knowledge of the time when the illuminator flourished would be a help, and the date when either of the Ridolfi–Strozzi spouses was widowed would be a *terminus ante quem*. Ridolfi was still active in 1560, i.e. even after the last separate edition was published (1556).

NOTES

1 Apart from Tagliente's weak imitation (1524 and later), which could never be mistaken for Arrighi's type, this was, in its various manifestations, unique at the time. Its unique character may be judged by comparison with the italic of Maciochi's 1537 edition, which belongs to the Aldine tradition with roots in the (Venetian) book-hands of the 1490's. An easy criterion is the letter *a*, which in Arrighi's designs has the *cancellaresca* flat top.

2 Compare Fig. 20 with the illustration from Vida's *De Arte Poetica*, shown elsewhere in this book, Fig. 17.

3 This MS. is mentioned in Curt F. Bühler, *The Fifteenth Century Book* (University of Pennsylvania Press, 1960), p. 36, plate 11b.

4 Dr Emanuele Casamassima (of the Biblioteca Nazionale Centrale of Rome) has published (*La Bibliofilia*, 1962, Dispensa 2ª, pp. 117 *et seq.*) an extremely interesting study of an Arrighian MS. book (Cod. Landau Finaly 9. c. 1, Florence, Biblioteca Nazionale Centrale) of the *Itinerario* of Varthema, subsequently printed by Arrighi and his associates on 6 December 1510. This is a gift copy written with great consistency in an early, somewhat looser version—two variants in fact—of Arrighi's *cancellaresca*, and presented to Vittoria Colonna in an introductory letter followed by a dedication to her mother, Agnesina di Montefeltro, Duchess of Tagliacozzo. As Vittoria is addressed as the wife of Fernando d'Avales, Marquess of Pescara, the book must have been executed *after* her wedding on 27 December 1509, in all probability in 1510. It has 11 + 59 leaves.

Other examples of Arrighi's book-hand will be found in Fairbank and Wolpe, *Renaissance Handwriting* (Faber and Faber, 1960), plates 60 and 61, and *Journal of the Society for Italic Handwriting*,

no. 35 (summer 1963), pp. 16 and 17. The *Collenuccio* shown in *Alphabet 1964*, ed. R. S. Hutchings, p. 90.

5 The line is, of course, absent also in the Testina editions of *Tutte le Opere* of Machiavelli.

6 See elsewhere in this volume A. S. Osley, 'Origins of Italic Types', p. 119, note 18.

7 To form an opinion of Arrighi's speed of production, I may refer to the MS. of Aristotle (Plate 32). A number of leaves are now missing, but it still contains 376 pages of 23 lines of $4\frac{3}{4}$ in. (120 mm). According to the colophon (*Ludouicus Vicentinus scribebat Romae anno salutatis M.D. XVII. mense octob.*), this seemingly gigantic feat was performed within one month, which means, even if he worked every single day, more than a dozen pages a day, perhaps actually 14 or 15 since there must have been breaks for various purposes. (Trials have shown it to be possible to produce the writing of one such page in 20 minutes, and *his* hand was particularly skilled. There were of course a number of other, subsidiary, tasks though, so perhaps one would have to allow half an hour a page.) He could consequently produce 98 of *these* pages in the space of a week.

Of the 98 pages of the *Clitia* MS., each of 20 lines of 3″ (75 mm), 40 are carefully but 58 very hastily written. Trials have given 10 minutes for a packed page in an imitation of the latter hand, so *he* probably wrote them faster; and, if we then allow *him* 20 minutes a page for the careful lettering, it is probably ample. This would mean a maximum of 23 hours or about three 8-hour days. His enormous skill and the obviously increasing hurry perhaps make it likely that he completed this MS. in even less time. Such short notice for a wedding present would seem to be out of the question.

SOME WRITING MASTERS

BEN ENGELHART &
CHRIS BRAND

Gerard Mercator—Cartographer
and Writing Master

THE MAN

He was a great man, his life nourished by a richly-stocked mind. An *uomo universale*, ambitious in the scope of his scientific work, he depicted the entire surface of the earth in his maps and published a universal history. He disliked, however, being a celebrity and played no part in the political and religious struggles, in which that age was so rich. He received orders from princes such as Charles V, Granvelle and William IV of Kleef, but only accepted modest payment for his services, never using these connections to his own advantage.

He studied at the gymnasium in 's-Hertogenbosch at the expense of his great-uncle, pastor Gijsbert, and later attended the college at Leuven as a 'poor student'. But, in the sphere in which he was to attain fame, he was completely self-taught. He was a humble man who never complained even when he was imprisoned for three months on a false charge of heresy in his native city. Although born and bred in the Southern Provinces of Holland (Rupelmonde), he spent more than half of his working life in Duisberg, which granted him citizenship when he was being attacked for his religious beliefs in Leuven. Here he died, still writing his last book...on 'creation'.

THE WRITING MASTER

Why Mercator, who was not a calligrapher by profession, composed a treatise on handwriting is hard to guess. In 1537, he had finished his map of Palestine and in 1538 his map of both hemispheres. He felt in need of a good legible style of lettering for the text of these maps. The industrious 28-year-old cartographer was not content to adopt the italic script which he employed in his own handwriting, but he made a study of this style in all its particulars. When he had analysed it clearly in his mind, the teacher in him led him to publish a treatise of his own. In 1540, he made wood-cuts of his examples and, in the same year in which his great map of Flanders was finished, his manual, *Literarum Latinarum* was printed.

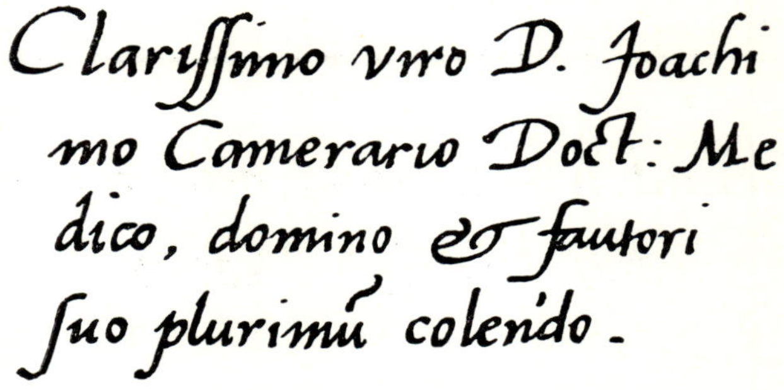

Fig. 22. Mercator's handwriting.

It was the third manual on Italic to be published, but it was far from being a mere copy of its two Italian predecessors, viz. that of Ludovico degli Arrighi, a calligrapher in the Papal Chancery (1522), and that of Giovantonio Tagliente (1524). Although both the Italians produced better woodcuts, especially Arrighi, whose graceful pages are composed in a light, decorative script, we prefer the clear, masculine and ex-tremely legible version of Mercator.

His book contains 54 pages, divided into six sections as follows:

      I Ruling and Cutting the Pen;

     II Hand Position and Penhold—The Technique of Writing;

   III Basic Elements of Small Letters;

   IV Formation of Capitals;

    V Joins; and

   VI Variants of Capitals.

The following reproductions (slightly reduced)
give an idea of the first Dutch handwriting manual.

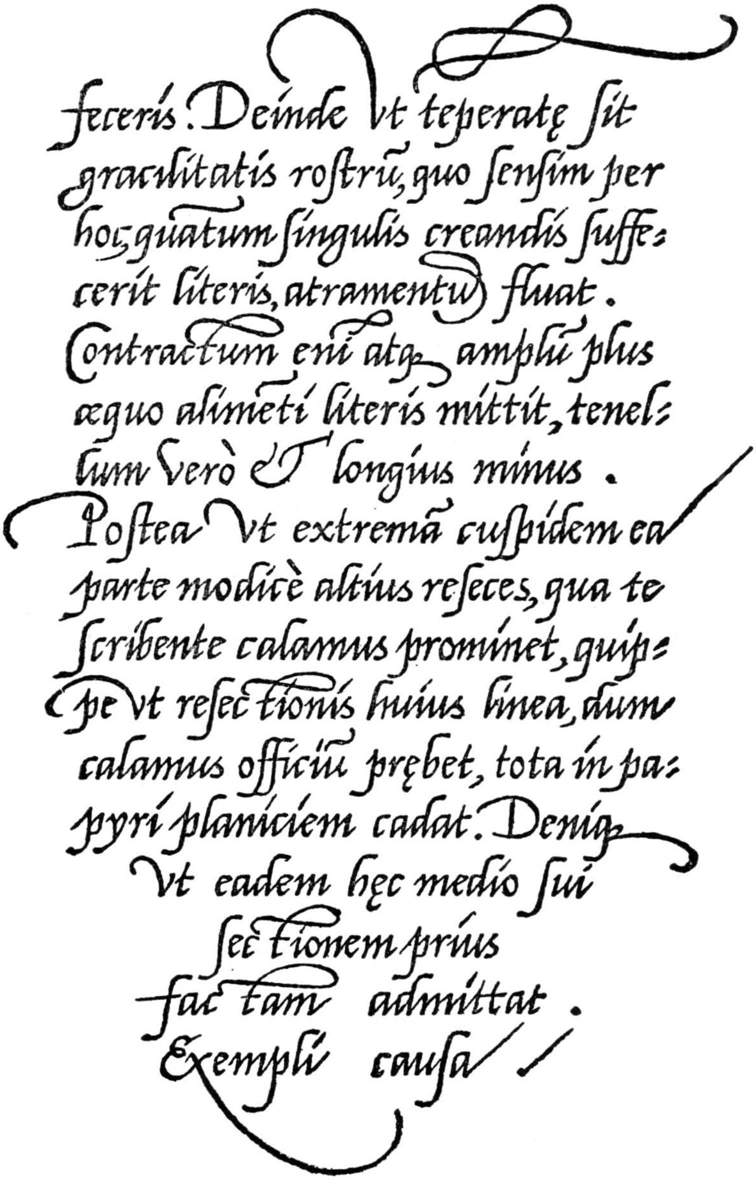

feceris. Deinde vt teperate sit
gracilitatis rostru, quo sensim per
hoc, quatum singulis creandis suffe-
cerit literis, atramentu fluat.
Contractum eni atqz amplu plus
æquo alimeti literis mittit, tenel-
lum verò & longius minus.
Postea vt extrema cuspidem ea
parte modicè altius reseces, qua te
scribente calamus prominet, quip-
pe vt resectionis huius linea, dum
calamus officiu prębet, tota in pa-
pyri planiciem cadat. Deniqz
vt eadem hęc medio sui
sectionem prius
fac tam admittat.
Exempli causa

Fig. 23. Cutting the quill. The Latin text states: 'Then take care to see that the point is of moderate width so that enough ink will run gently down to make each letter. If the point is too short and broad, too much ink will be released to make the letters: but if too narrow and long, insufficient ink will be released. Then you must cut the tip a little longer at the point where the pen pushes forward in the act of writing, so that, as the pen writes, the line of the cut will be in contact with the paper along its full length. Then see that the slit, which was previously made, falls in the centre of this line.'

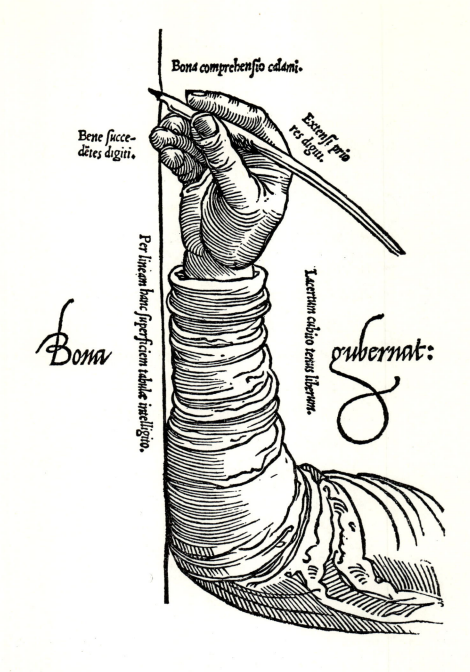

Bona comprehensio calami.

Extensi prio res digiti.

Bene succe- dētes digiti.

Per lineam hanc superficiem tabulæ intelligito.

Lacertum cubito tenus liberum.

Bona gubernat:

Fig. 24. Correct hand position.

140

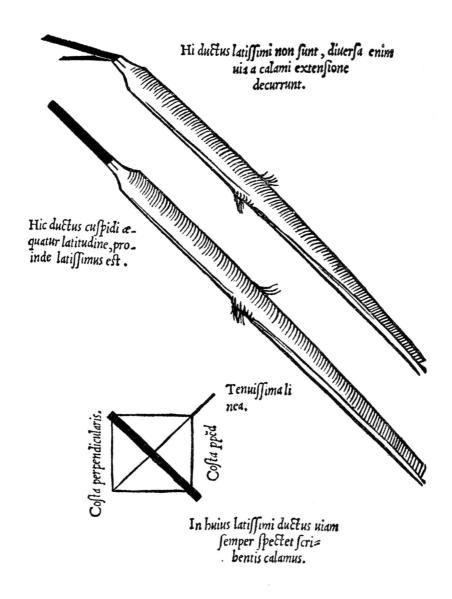

Hi duƈtus latiſſimi non ſunt , diuerſa enim
uia a calami extenſione
decurrunt.

Hic duƈtus cuſpidi æ_
quatur latitudine, pro_
inde latiſſimus eſt .

Coſta perpendicularis.

Coſta ꝑꝑ͞ed

Tenuiſſima li
nea,

In huius latiſſimi duƈtus uiam
ſemper ſpeƈtet ſcri=
. bentis calamus.

Fig. 25. Technique of writing.

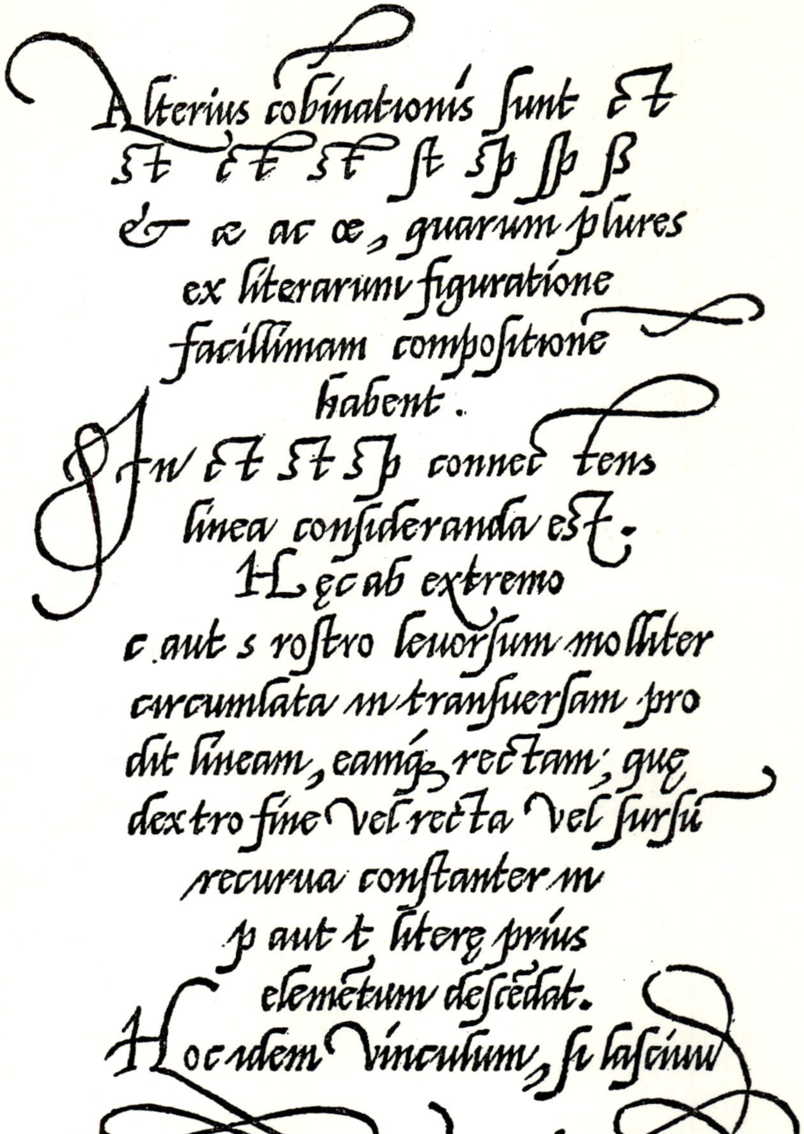
Alterius cobinationis sunt ct
st ct st st sp ssp ß
& æ ac œ, quarum plures
ex literarum figuratione
facillimam compositione
habent.
In ct st sp connectens
linea consideranda est.
Hęc ab extremo
c aut s rostro leuorsum molliter
circumlata in transuersam pro
dit lineam, eamq; rectam; quę
dextro fine vel recta vel sursũ
recurua constanter in
p aut t literę prius
elemẽtum descẽdat.
Hoc idem vinculum, si lasciuu

Fig. 26. Joins: *st*, *ct*, etc. 'The following belong to another family—*ct*, *st*, *sp*, *ss*, *ae*, *ac*, *oe*, most of which readily combine in accordance with the formation of the letters. In joining *ct*, *st*, *sp*, we must attend to the ligature. This is carried smoothly across from the top of *c* or *s* in a direct line which, at its right extremity, joins the downstroke of *p* or *t*, either bending slightly upwards or coming in at right angles.'

Sextum Caput.

Capitales literæ minoribus singulæ singulis commensura
tione respõdent, ut qui minores idem & maiores propor
tionatas reddere norit, eadem quoq; propensio in dextrũ
est, uel (si lubet) status perpendicularis. M tamen suæ co
gnominum in latitudine baud quaquam accedit, sed qua
drato minor paulo reliquis panditur latius,
Parantur autem singulæ hoc
ordine.

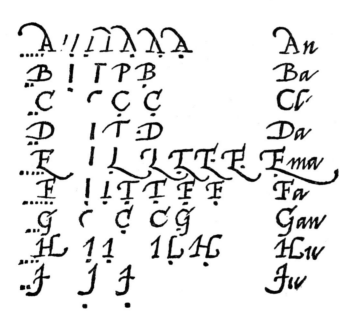

Fig. 27. Construction of capitals.

143

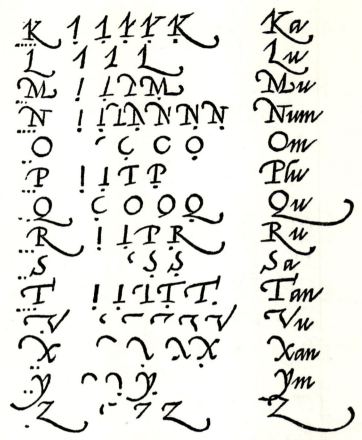

Harum autem figurarum , quæ extra corporis molem se
proteruius effundunt ultra cæteras uaria subinde affe=
ctant prodire forma, quod idem & minores aliquot lite=
ras facere diximus,qua in re suffecerit tum libellum totū
tum alphabeta sequentia loco exemplaris proponere.

Fig. 28. Construction of capitals.

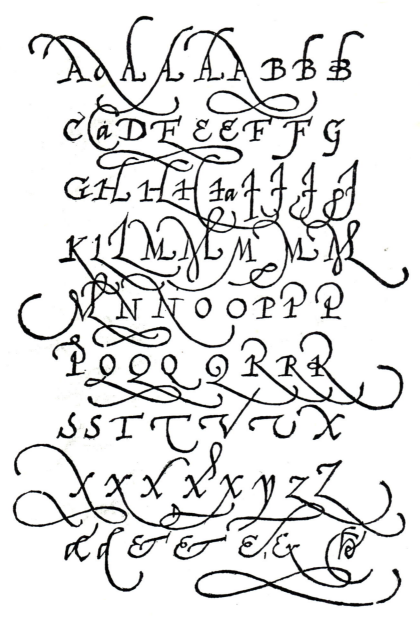

Fig. 29. Variants of capital letters.

Fig. 30. Variants of small letters.

CARTOGRAPHER AND CALLIGRAPHER

The many maps and globes which Mercator made and his well-known Mercator's Projection, which made it easy for sailors to set their course, stamp him as one of the greatest of cartographers. To his cartographic work belonged another service, which has hitherto had insufficient recognition. While he was not the first man to use Italic

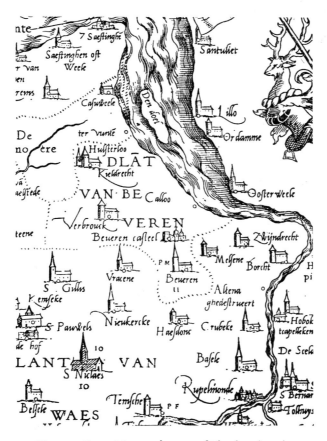

Fig. 31. From Mercator's map of Flanders (1540).

for map-lettering, he demonstrated that Italic was without question ideally suited to this purpose. Compare, for example, van Deventer's map of Zeeland (1545) with Mercator's map of Flanders (1540) in Figs. 31 and 32.

The tradition established by Mercator was carried on by the calligrapher and cartographer, Jodocus Hondius of Amsterdam, who bought the complete collection of engraved copper-plates from Mercator's children and made use of them when producing his atlas in 1606. In cartographic literature the period from 1550 to 1700 is rightly called the Dutch Period. Would it be too much to claim that this is in some measure due to Mercator...the Writing Master?

NOTE

This essay is derived from an English translation printed with the Dutch original. With the permission of Werner Renckhoff, Duisberg, West Germany, to whom grateful acknowledgements are made, I have made a number of changes for greater accuracy and readability and put into English some Latin of Mercator. The blocks from Mercator's manual have been specially made for this volume. In the original *Gerard Mercator* (Oudenbosch, 1959) they were slightly reduced: EDITOR.

Fig. 32. From van Deventer's map of Zeeland (1545).

STANLEY GODMAN

John Hodgkin: Writing-Master and Calligrapher (1766-1845)

John Hodgkin's ancestors were farmers or wool staplers leading quiet industrious lives at Shipston-on-Stour and members of the Society of Friends from its foundation. He himself was born in a cottage in Sheep Street, Shipston-on-Stour that still survives, as does the rather grander home of his uncle Thomas Hodgkin (1744–1810), who was the first member of the family to turn to a teaching career and became a writing master at Ackworth. John was educated partly by his uncle and partly at a Friends' school at Worcester. At the age of 21, in 1787, he was appointed private tutor, at Youngsbury in Hertfordshire, to Hudson Gurney and to Thomas Young (1773–1829) who later attained fame as physician and Egyptologist.[1] Though only in his teens, Thomas Young appears to have been co-tutor to Hudson Gurney as well as fellow-pupil.

It was during these four years at Youngsbury that Hodgkin conceived the idea of a book on the Greek script and enlisted the help of Thomas Young. The *Calligraphia Graeca*, which appeared in 1807 and is Hodgkin's most distinguished contribution to calligraphy, was dedicated to Thomas Young who, as Hodgkin acknowledged in his Preface, 'at a time when my affairs prevented me from pursuing this subject as I had intended, provided all the necessary materials for the book.' Hodgkin continued: 'I consider his friendship as one of the most delightful things which fortune has granted to me, for he combines amazing industry with great talent. And besides his outstanding knowledge of other branches of learning, he has achieved such skill in the Greek language as few others have done and such elegance in forming Greek characters as scarcely any other man up till now. I would not willingly alter even a punctuation mark in the writings of such a man: therefore receive in his own words the preface which he has so kindly sent me for use in this book.'

Calligraphically, the most valuable parts of Young's Latin Preface are his 'Directions for Writing the Greek Characters', which Hodgkin, 'in conformity to the recommendation of Dr Charles Burney', translated 'for the use of boys in the lower forms' in the shorter edition of *Calligraphia Graeca*, which he published under the title *Specimens of Greek Penmanship*.

Of Young's script, dating with his 'Directions' from 1793 when he was only 20, Hodgkin wrote: 'It may be said of Dr Young's mode of forming the Greek characters that it does not rest its claim to the notice of the public upon any innovation in the shape of the letters; but upon the facility with which it enables the learner to produce, with the pen, that form of them which is most generally approved in the British universities.'

Young's 'Directions', set in Bulmer's type, for achieving this script were as follows:

DIRECTIONS
FOR WRITING THE GREEK CHARACTERS.

THE pen to be used in forming these characters must not have a very long split; it should be nibbed a little obliquely, and that part which is usually next the thumb should be the shorter; it should be held so that the hollow part be turned towards the middle finger: by these means the ascending strokes, and those, which are made in a direction towards the right hand, will be thick. The letters may be divided into ten classes, according to the place where the pen begins in forming them: the first contains $\alpha\ \varsigma$ $\delta\ \theta\ o\ \rho\ \sigma\ \varsigma\ \phi\ \omega$, the beginning of the first part of each of these is near the bottom, and its greatest thickness near the top: the remaining part is begun from the same place as the first, and made, according to the shape of the letter, at one stroke; except $\theta\ \rho$ and ω, which require three, and ς four strokes: the second class contains $\beta\ \int$, the first part of the former ends a little above the middle of the lower arch; the latter is made at one stroke: the next is ε, made at twice, each stroke beginning at the middle: γ is made at one stroke, and χ with two; they begin at the upper part on the left, with a stronger line than the fifth class, viz. $\eta\ \iota\ \varkappa$ $\nu\ \upsilon\ \psi$, which are all made at one stroke, except ψ. It is unnecessary to explain the method of forming ζ and ξ: the stroke of the ϑ is at first fine and curved, then increases in thickness, afterwards becomes fine, and lastly thick. The λ is begun with a thick ascending stroke, and finished with a fine descending one: beginning with a fine stroke μ is finished with two turns similar to the last part of the α: lastly, π ϖ τ 7 are begun with thick transverse strokes, and finished with fine strokes, except ϖ, which is nearly like ω. These directions will be more easily understood by referring to the two last lines in the page of alphabets, where the beginning of each letter is marked by a point placed opposite to it, and the latter strokes of the pen are distinguished from the first by a difference in the line; the first stroke being black, the second left open, the third crossed, and the fourth dotted.

To illustrate the script thus expounded by Thomas Young, the *Calligraphia Graeca* contains nineteen plates. Of those illustrated here, the first is a translation by Thomas Young himself of some lines of King Lear (Act I, scene 4 beginning 'Heare, Nature...' and concluding 'To have a thankless childe'). The second is a series of iambic hexameters selected, as Young explained in his Preface, 'from Menander, Euripides, Philemon, Phocylides, Theognis, Hesiod and others'. The lines are arranged in the order of the Greek alphabet (Plates 37 & 38).

The work ends with a chart displaying seventeen forms of the Greek alphabet ('Variae alphabeti Graeci per aetatis ordinem formae') ranging from an early Pelasgian to a codex of A.D. 1400. Three main sources of these comparative alphabets were Bernard de Montfaucon's *Palaeographia Graeca* of 1708 (Montfaucon was 'virtually the creator of the science of Greek palaeography'); Thomas Astle's *On the Radical Letters of the Pelasgians and their Derivatives* of 1785 which also appeared as an Appendix to the second edition of his *The Origin and Progress of Writing as well hieroglyphic as elementary* of 1803 (first edition 1784). A third source was Edmund Chishull's *Inscriptio Sigea antiquissima* of 1721.

The *Calligraphia Graeca* had very influential supporters: the subscribers included Edmund Burke, Charles Burney, and Richard Porson. Porson (Professor of Greek at Cambridge from 1792) is said to have considered that in some respects his own exquisite Greek script was surpassed by that of Thomas Young. Young himself referred to this in his article on Porson in the Supplement to the 4th edition, 1824, of the *Encyclopedia Britannica*: 'Mr Weston in speaking of his "matchless penmanship" has observed not very intelligibly that "here indeed he thought himself surpassed by another person, not in the stroke but the sweep of his letters"; what Porson really said was that with respect to "command of hand" that person had the advantage but he preferred the model on which his own hand was formed. His writing was in fact more like that of a scholar, while the method explained in Mr Hodgkin's *Calligraphia* exhibits more the appearance of the work of a writing-master.'

Hodgkin's work was conceived primarily with a view to raising the standard of Greek writing at schools and universities, and a critic in the *Eclectic Review* of April 1810 wrote: 'Whoever has noticed the clumsy and inelegant forms of Greek writing which prevail in our public schools and universities must be sensible of the utility of such a work. Some excellent Grecians have produced such disgraceful manuscripts, executed as might authorize the suspicion of their adopting the vulgar notion that execrable handwriting is a mark of gentility and taste. If this elegant work of Mr Hodgkin were introduced into schools as a copy book it would contribute much to prevent the evil of which we complain.'

Hodgkin published three further works, all of which were designed to raise standards of handwriting. The first of these, published in 1804, was entitled *Definitions of Some of the Terms Made Use of in Geography and Astronomy Intended for Learners to Impress on their Memories by Transcribing*. In the Preface he appealed especially for the 'approbation of the respectable characters who preside over our grammar schools.... In those schools much time cannot, with propriety, be devoted to penmanship but when we consider the convenience resulting to the scholar from the acquisition of an expeditious, legible hand, it seems desirable that the young student should be taught to regard it as an object worthy of his attention.' For confirmation of his plea for greater attention to penmanship Hodgkin referred to chapter 10 of *An Essay on Education* by the Rev. William Barrow, late Master of the Academy, Soho Square (2nd ed., 1804).[2] Barrow wrote (p. 277): 'Quintilian has told us that the nobility in his time despised the mechanical dexterity of writing a fine hand; and not many years ago the same affectation had an extensive influence on people of fashion in England. A letter was often considered as the more genteel the less conveniently it could be read. Elegant penmanship, however, seems at present to possess its due estimation among us. It has risen in value with every other object of taste and decoration.' And, in a passage which Hodgkin quoted verbatim, Barrow wrote of 'the celebrated Roger Ascham': 'It may perhaps gratify curiosity to observe that the celebrated Roger Ascham about the middle of the 16th century was one of the first who cultivated amongst us those arts of ornamental writing in which we now so greatly excel all nations around us that he was indebted for his appoint-

ΛΕΑΡΟΥ ΑΡΑΙ.

Ἀλλ' ὦ νέμουσα τῶν βροτῶν κράτη Φύσις,
Ἄκουε δὴ νῦν τάσδε πατρῴας ἀράς·
Ὦ δαῖμον, εἴθε προυλίθου βλάστας πολὲ
Ἐκ τοῦδε τέρατος ἐξαναστήσειν τόκου,
Γνώμην μελαγχρῶθ' ἐπεσάτους ἀπαιδίαν·
Αὔαινε κῶλα τεκνοποιὰ νηδύος,
Ἔχοι δὲ μήποτ' ἐξ ἀπευκτοῦ σώματος
Τέκνον πεφυκὸς γηροβοσκὸν εἰσιδεῖν·
Εἰ δ' ἔστ' ἀνάγκη τήνδε τεκνοῦσθαι βρέφος,
Ἄστοργον αἰεὶ καὶ πικρᾶς χολῆς γέμον,
Ῥυτίδας ἀώρους ἐγχαραττέτω ταχὺ
Μητρὸς μετώπῳ, πανταχοῦ λύπην φέρον·
Δάκρυα δὲ θερμὰ ἀπ' ὀμμάτων στάζοντ' ἀεὶ
Ἄλοκας βαθείας ἐνλάβοι παρῇσι·
Κηδῶν δ' ἁπάντων, τῶν τε μητρῴων πόνων
Καταφρονείτω καὶ καταγελάτω τέκος·
Ὅπως ἐπαύρῃ τῆσδε τῆς ἁμαρτίας,
Παθοῦσά τι, ὀψέ περ, σαφῶς ποτ' ἐκμάθῃ
Ὅσῳ πάθημ' ὀξύτερόν ἐστι δήγματος
Φονίου δράκοντος, ἡ τέκνων ἀχαριστία.

ΜΕΤΕΦΡΑΣΕ
ΘΩΜΑΣ ΙΟΓΓΙΟΣ

αψϟα.

37.   Greek version by Thomas Young of a passage from *King Lear*: in John Hodgkin's
Calligraphia Graeca: see p. 151. (Reduced)

Ἅπαντα δοῦλα τῷ φρονεῖν καθίσται.

Βροτοῖς τὰ μείζω τῶν μέσων τίκτει νόσους.

Γυναικὶ δ᾿ ὄλβος ἂν πόσιν στέργοντ᾿ ἔχῃ.

Δένδρον παλαιὸν μεταφυτεύειν δύσκολον.

Ἐχθροὺς ποιοῦσι τοὺς φίλους αἱ συγκρίσεις.

Ζήσεις βίον κράτιστον, ἂν θυμοῦ κρατῇς.

Ἢ λέγε τι σιγῆς κρεῖττον, ἢ σιγὴν ἔχε.

Θάρσει· λέγων τἀληθὲς οὐ σφαλῇ ποτέ.

Ἴστω δὲ μηδεὶς ταῦθ᾿ ἃ σιγᾶσθαι χρεών.

Κρίσει δικαίᾳ καὶ δίδου καὶ λάμβανε.

Λόγος γὰρ ἐσθλὸς φάρμακον φόβου βροτοῖς.

Μὴ λέγε τι δώσεις· μὴ δίδωσι γὰρ λέγων.

J. Hodgkin scripsit.   *H. Ashby sculpsit.*

Published as the Act directs Oct.r 1.st 1794, by J.Hodgkin, and sold by H.Ashby, King Street, Cheapside, London.

38. Alphabetic list of apophthegms from classical authors: in John Hodgkin's
Calligraphia Graeca: see p. 151. (Reduced)

[*To face p. 15*

ment of correspondent and secretary to the University of Cambridge hardly less to the elegance of his penmanship than to the excellence of his Latinity.' In 1811 Hodgkin published *An Introduction to Writing Exhibiting Clear and Concise Rules for the Formation and Combination of the Letters* and finally, in 1812, with a dedication to Dr Charles Burney, *A Sketch of the Greek Accidence Arranged in a Manner Convenient for Transcription by Means of which Learners may be Assisted in Committing it to Memory.* As a supreme example of the profit to be gained from repeated transcription Hodgkin referred to Professor Porson: 'When a boy he not only read his lessons over as often as other boys but he repeatedly transcribed them. . .for this extraordinary trouble he considered himself amply repaid.'

As a private tutor with a busy and lucrative practice, Hodgkin taught a great variety of subjects but he always 'attached much value to beautiful penmanship'.[3] His pupils were mainly 'the daughters of wealthy merchants and bankers'.

In 1793 Hodgkin married Elizabeth Rickman of Lewes in Sussex,[4] by whom he had two distinguished sons: Dr Thomas Hodgkin (1798–1866), who in 1832 discovered Hodgkin's disease (enlargement of the lymphatic glands and spleen), and John Hodgkin (1800–75), barrister, law reformer and Quaker preacher, from whose marriage with Elizabeth, daughter of Luke Howard, the 'father of meteorology', there stemmed on the one hand Alfred Waterhouse, the architect, whose daughter Mary Monica married Robert Bridges, Poet Laureate; and, on the other, Mariabella and Edward Fry, whose children included Roger Fry, the art critic, and Margery Fry, penal reformer and Principal of Somerville, who was the friend and mentor of Dorothy Crowfoot Hodgkin, wife of Thomas Hodgkin (also descended from John Hodgkin and Elizabeth Howard), who won a Nobel Prize for Chemistry in 1964.[5] Two of John Hodgkin's direct descendants have played a distinguished part in the more recent history of British handwriting. Mary Monica Bridges, wife of the Poet Laureate, published in 1898 a *New Handwriting for Teachers*,[6] and her cousin Roger Fry contributed an 'Artistic comment' on the handwriting in the thirty-four facsimile plates, which Robert Bridges published in *English Handwriting* (S.P.E. Tract, no. XXIII, Oxford, 1926, pp. 85–92).

Finally, the author of the Foreword to this *festschrift*, Lord Bridges is a great-great-grandson of John Hodgkin.

NOTES

1 See Alexander Wood and Frank Oldham, *Thomas Young: Natural Philosopher 1773–1829* (Cambridge University Press, 1954), pp. 272 *et seq.*

2 On Barrow, see E. B. Castle, *Moral Education in Christian Times* (1958), pp. 178–80.

3 See the account of John Hodgkin by his grandson Thomas Hodgkin in Louise Creighton

Stanley Godman

Life and Letters of Thomas Hodgkin (1917), pp. 1 *et seq.*

4 On Elizabeth Rickman, see 'The Verrall Family of Lewes', by P. Lucas in *Sussex Arch. Coll.* LVIII, 107 *et seq.*

5 Cf. Walter Schwarz, 'The Amazing Mrs Hodgkin' (with a family tree showing descent from Luke Howard and John Hodgkin) in the *Observer Magazine*, 13 December 1964.

6 See Alfred Fairbank, *A Book of Scripts* (King Penguin Books, 1949), p. 22 and plate 55. The 'very warm friendship of Edward Johnston with the Bridges', which began in the summer of 1899, is recorded by Priscilla Johnston in *Edward Johnston* (Faber and Faber, 1959), p. 95.

7 Grateful acknowledgements are made to the British Museum for permission to reproduce plates from *Calligraphia Graeca*.

154

RAY NASH

Benjamin Franklin Foster

American penmanship in the first half of the nineteenth century can count more than a hundred writing masters teaching and publishing their 'systems'. All the systems were based on the analytical method published by John Jenkins in his *Art of Writing* (Boston, 1791). The English master Charles Snell had earlier pointed out that *i, o, u, h,* and *y* are 'leading letters', to one or two of which all others are related; and John Clark, in turn, that the English round hand is composed of an oval and a straight line and 'the Fundamental Letters are *l, o, n, j*'. The Jenkins 'plain and easy system' reduced both the minuscules and capitals to just six elementary strokes each—though *s* and *k*, among others, gave him trouble, and he conveniently forgot the unnecessary *z* altogether. Said Jenkins, 'two things are absolutely necessary to be attended to, that any one may soon become master of this art. The first is, to get a perfect idea of each principal stroke well impressed on the mind. The second is, to acquire the right motion of the fingers, or pressure of the pen, in order to draw those strokes upon the paper.'

Those who came after Jenkins cheerfully took over his analytical system, adding curlicues and alternates to his principal strokes as they deemed expedient. But the new generation placed more emphasis on motion. A rapid running hand, that is, one that would keep the nib sliding forward at a good rate and provide for arm, hand and fingers to drive it, was the proper recommendation for a man of business. The host of writing masters who could, or persuasively promised to, inculcate such a facile mercantile script in a few easy lessons reaped a rich reward. Among them the subject of this paper stands alone as the American writing master who devoted his life to education and authorship in the commercial subjects and thereby achieved an international following. As teacher and writer he single-handedly invaded the Old World; in mid-career he was able to boast that upward of two million of his copy-books had been sold, in England and France as well as at home. Moreover, he won the good opinion of educational critics and held their respect. In brief, Benjamin Franklin Foster deserves better of posterity than he has thus far received. The purpose of this article is to gather data already known and to record some new findings about him with particular reference to his contributions in the field of penmanship.

Foster's life story ends on a more positive note than its beginning. Even so, the notice of his death as published in the New York *Times* for 18 November 1859 on p. 5, is disappointingly inconclusive:

FOSTER — BENJAMIN FRANKLIN FOSTER
    At Providence, R.I. on Friday, Nov. 11, in the 57th year of his age.
    Mr Foster was well and favorably known in this country and in England as a teacher of and writer on Penmanship and Book-keeping, to which specialties he devoted a long life with great assiduity and eminent success. He leaves a wife and child and numerous relatives and friends to lament his loss.
    Maine and New Brunswick papers will please copy.

From this the inference is drawn that Foster was born in 1803 and that he was perhaps native to the frontier country on the northern boundary of Maine with New Brunswick. His reference to 'the log cabin, where I was initiated into the mysteries of "pot-hooks and hangers"' falls in with the theory. If it has substance, the schoolboy Foster would doubtless have been furnished with the Jenkins second edition, 1813, which was distributed by the Massachusetts legislature throughout that commonwealth, including the District of Maine. Whoever wishes to stand on firmer ground than such conjecture regarding Foster's personal history has to follow the thread of it in and round about his bibliography. For the purpose, a descriptive chronological listing of his American publications on penmanship has been attempted and will be found at the end of this article.
    Foster first appears at the age of 25 teaching writing 'at his establishment no. 84 Broadway, New-York' (see bibliography, no. 1). The document in evidence is a twenty-four page pamphlet of testimonials in favour of the Carstairian system. A much more substantial document, issued two years later, was *Practical Penmanship*, a 'developement' of the Carstairian system (Albany, 1830). How, after introducing the popular London-based system into the United States, Foster came to carry it up the Hudson River to the state capital, is to be traced in the minute book of the old Albany Female Academy. The first relevant entry is dated 2 July 1829:
    'Mr Crosswell, from the committee to report upon the subject of a teacher of

writing, stated that the committee had received proposals from Mr Benjamin F. Foster and from Mr Noyes. That Mr Foster would teach six hours a day for four hundred dollars a year, and that Mr Noyes could be procured for six hundred dollars per annum.'

'Whereupon, Resolved, That Mr Benjamin Franklin Foster be and he hereby is elected teacher of writing for one year; and that he be allowed four hundred dollars for his services.'

The high bidder, Enoch Noyes, was better established in the profession than Foster. He had published at Boston in 1821 *An Analytical Guide to the Art of Penmanship*, systematizing and simplifying the correct principles of the round and running hands, as he said, which was well known through New England. In this very year he was bringing out, at New York, *Noyes' System of Practical Penmanship*. The two hundred dollars difference though was decisive.

In Albany during that winter of 1829–30 Foster applied himself to the job with good results, as attested by newspaper clippings about the school programme. For example, 'The Carstairian system of writing has been introduced under Mr Foster— a system which deserves to be spoken of in the highest terms and which it is hoped will receive the particular attention of our superintendent of common schools'. Or again, in a report of several gentlemen appointed to select the best performances in writing by the young ladies, 'Considered as a whole, they reflect the greatest credit upon the institution, and upon the gentleman who superintends this branch of instruction,...' Would Foster be advanced?

An entry of 22 April 1830 in the minute book states that 'A treatis on penmanship by the teacher of writing, B. F. Foster, was submitted to the Board for the purpose of receiving their opinion of its merits', and referred to Messrs Crosswell and Hawley. They reported back two days later: 'Mr Crosswell from the committee to whom was referred Mr Foster's Treatis on Penmanship made the following report which was read and accepted: On motion Resolved—That Mr Smith and the Principal be a Committee to enquire whether a qualified female to teach writing can be procured and report to this Board.' The search for a qualified female to replace an ambitious young man with highfalutin notions need not have been prolonged. The thrifty, hard-headed Dutchmen back in February had already provided for the contingency by employing as assistant to Foster, at no stated remuneration, a Miss Henrietta Van Benthuisen. She could probably teach the Carstairian system acceptably for a mere two hundred dollars or so.

Foster dated the Preface to his *Practical Penmanship* from the Albany Female Academy on 10 April 1830. On the expanded title of the second issue (bibliography, no. 3) he was still in Albany but had become accountant and teacher of writing in a different school, the Albany Academy. The situation is confirmed a year later when, in being named by the American Institute of Instruction as winner of its Prize Essay on Teaching Penmanship, he was identified as teacher of writing in the Albany Academy and author of *Practical Penmanship*. The essay was first published in *Annals of Education*, Boston, in the April 1833 number (vol. III, pp. 145–59).

On the strength of that success, Foster moved to Boston. He is listed for the first time in the city directory for 1834 as an instructor, with a house at 30 School Street. The next year his vocation is changed to accountant and his residence to 126 Cambridge Street, and so through 1837. On 22 April 1835 Foster married Catharine Kuhn, daughter of John and Sarah Lapham Kuhn of Boston. After five years she died, in England; they had no children. The date of his second marriage has not been learned. Before Independence Day of 1835 he was principal of Foster's Commercial School at 116 Washington Street, Boston, offering courses in penmanship, book-keeping, business arithmetic and accountancy. As qualification for teaching the last branch he cites 'seven years' experience as a book-keeper in an extensive mercantile house'. At the same time he is bringing out *Foster's System of Penmanship*, on the title page of which the name of Carstairs is reduced to diamond type, though further on the author handsomely pays his respects to 'the celebrated Carstairs'—especially in the French edition of his work edited by M. Julien. Foster was now within ten years of seeing his own *Cahiers crayonnés d'écriture* published at Paris.

The Boston publishers continued through the ensuing years to turn out Foster's copy-books and writing books combined (see bibliography, nos. 7–11). During 1836 two reviews in *Annals of Education* favourably called attention to the Foster's Elementary Copy-books series, of which eight books had been completed by October. The author himself meanwhile was circulating a prospectus for a commercial academy he was opening at 183 Broadway, in New York City. The *Annals* in the September 1837 number carried a review of *Exercises in Current Hand Writing, for the Use of Foster's Commercial School, Broadway, New York*. And Foster addressed himself to the wider educational community in *Education Reform: a Review of Wyse* (New York, 1837), which has secured him a spot in the *Cambridge Bibliography of English Literature*. Finally, on the subject of penmanship, the friendly *Annals* edited by William C. Woodbridge, who had actually benefited from a course of 'twelve lessons from an able assistant of Carstairs' in London, reported in the September 1838 number: 'We have seen a neat little pamphlet just issued from the press of Perkins & Marvin of this city, entitled, "Remarks on Teaching Penmanship", by Mr B. F. Foster, whose reputation as a teacher and author on Writing and Book-keeping are well known. It is designed as an introduction to a set of large and small hand copies, which we understand Mr F. is preparing to publish.' This was undoubtedly *The Penman's Guide* (Boston, 1838), with engraved plates by Foster's associate in New York, George Jones.

Foster's own interest turned increasingly to book-keeping and accountancy. With characteristic zeal he delved into the history of merchants' accounts and was determined to review everything ever written in English on the subject. His *Clerk's Guide* and *Commercial Book-keeping* had both been noticed in the 1837 volume of *Annals* (Boston). *The Merchant's Manual* and *The Theory and Practice of Book-keeping Simplified* are featured on the title page of *Penmanship, Theoretical and Practical* (Boston, 1843). The English edition of this book, published the same year, announces the *Theory and Practice of Book-keeping* text as recently issued and, below, offers the following note of biographical interest: 'Mr Foster continues to receive classes and private pupils in Book-keeping, Penmanship, Commercial Calculations, &c. Young gentlemen are qualified by Mr F. for the Counting-house or Government situations in an expeditious and superior manner. Schools and Families attended. Address, 131, Fleet Street, (care of Messrs. Souter & Law).' The publication of *The Theory and Practice of Book-keeping Illustrated and Simplified*, Foster's first London appearance, which he dates 1840, possibly indicates the beginning of a sojourn abroad. So far as the Boston city directory goes, Foster was not in those parts from 1837 till the mid-'forties, nor does there seem to be any affirmative evidence of his being in New York during the period. His *Double Entry Elucidated; An Improved Method of Teaching Book-keeping* came out in 1845 at London. The Boston directory for the year 1846–7 has Benjamin F. Foster listed for a house near Tyler Street, and the following year at 24 Marion Street. After that, straight along till 1857, a Benjamin Foster is entered for a house at 30 Marion Street. It seems impossible that the latter could be our man, unless perhaps he was named as a non-resident owner of property. The clear fact that Foster's books collected in England were shipped to Boston in the spring of 1852 lends some colour to this interpretation. He evidently was in Boston that September. And Mrs Benjamin F. Foster is listed at 43 Marion Street in the 1853 directory, as though she may have stayed in Boston while he proceeded on to New York or made another trip to England.

The books, more than 150 of them, were those he had gathered in compiling *The Origin and Progress of Book-keeping; Comprising an Account of all the Works on this Subject, Published in the English Language, from 1543 to 1852, with Remarks, Critical and Historical*, of which the Preface is dated 23 March 1852, published at London. In the author's presentation copy of this bibliographically valuable work in the Boston

Athenaeum is the following pencilled note: 'The Books in this Cat: were shipped to Boston "pr Deucallion" which ship was lost in April last & nothing saved. B. F. Foster. Sept. 25 '52.' The author has meticulously corrected a date in the same copy and made several more marginal notes. At the back of the book are twelve pages devoted to descriptions of Foster's works, including his Pencilled Copy-books in three series with an exposition of the system, and an account of the successful defence of his copyright in the British courts. The copyright for the Pencilled Copy-books in America was taken out at Boston in 1852, and they were being actively promoted in the years following.

Were it not for Foster's mordant literary talents displayed in the appendix to his *System of Penmanship* (Boston, 1835), the splenetic outburst of the last publication in his bibliography might be explained by the bitter loss of the *Deucallion*'s cargo.

As proved by the following advertisement: 'Writing, Arithmetic, Book-keeping, &c. are taught upon sound elementary principles by B. F. Foster, at his residence, 387 Broadway, N.Y., where young gentlemen are qualified to discharge the duties of a Book-keeper with facility, accuracy, and dispatch,' he had returned to New York, and here in 1854 he published *Writing and Writing Masters: The Principles of the Former Developed, and the Fallacies of the Latter Exposed*, which chastises all the mountebanks and their magic methods, and even with Carstairs does not spare the rod: '. . . The inventor of this marvellous system claims great credit for originality; but these claims, as I shall show, rest on a very sandy foundation,' and so forth. However, there had been a measure of critical detachment in his 'developement' twenty-four years earlier, when he had been the chief Carstairian apostle in America, with regard to this matter of originality: '. . . Carstairs, as I am informed, is the first of the English teachers of Writing who has simplified the art by reducing all the letters to a few elementary strokes. In this country, however, what he has done in this respect, has been anticipated by Jenkins and others....' Again, in the *Report* (Albany, 1830), speaking through the committee, he bows to Jenkins:

'Carstairs, whose system is now to be considered, published his Lectures on the Art of Writing, a new system in 1814....'

'Jenkins appears entitled to preference, at least for seniority. He published his system in 1791. He does not go into the principles of combination in words and sentences, except in large hand. He is entitled to the merit of having given a very correct analysis of letters, useful rules for their formation, and directions for the position of the body....'

In reconsidering, as a veteran, the claims of Carstairs—even as a new disciple of Carstairs—Foster sounds as though he would not think those who called Carstairian the Système Americain so far amiss. He might smile at M. Chandelet's introduction of Carstairs to the French as 'des Etats-Unis' in 1828, but the analytical part was basically Jenkins, was it not? He apparently did not question the source; certainly he refused to credit Carstairs with the invention.

Mr Alfred Fairbank in *A Book of Scripts* (in speaking of Carstairs's arch-rival J. H. Lewis) threw out a suggestion that the English systematists 'possibly influenced by an American penman, John Jenkins, unified the alphabet and simplified teaching (too much, perhaps, for letters are entities) by building up letters with a few elements'. Foster is in agreement.

We are grateful to Mr Fairbank, and to Mr John Carter who helped point the way, for laying out this course in pursuit of Benjamin Franklin Foster.

FOSTER'S AMERICAN WORKS ON PENMANSHIP

1. Testimonials, in favour of the Carstairian system of writing, as taught by Mr Foster, at his establishment no. 84 Broadway, New-York. New-York: Printed by Elliott and Palmer, 1828.

> 24 pp. 170 × 110 mm. Original tan printed wrappers.   NN

2. Practical penmanship being a developement of the Carstairian system. By B. F. Foster. Illustrated by 24 engravings. Little and Cummings, Albany; Carey and Lea, Philadelphia; G. and C. and H. Carvill, New-York; Hilliard, Gray, Little and Wilkins, Boston. B. D. Packard and co., printers, Albany. 1830.

> Engraved frontispiece; 112 pp.; 8 unnumbered leaves of advertisements; 22 engraved plates numbered 2, 4–23 with an extra plate numbered 20A following number 20. 220 × 130 mm. Light green cloth over boards.   ICN   Franklin Inst.   MH   NNC

3. Practical penmanship, being a development of the Carstairian system: comprehending an elucidation of the movements of the fingers, hand and arm, necessary in writing; their combinations and application, with remarks on the impediments which retard the progress of learners, and the errors resulting from the common methods of teaching. Illustrated by 24 engravings; shewing the position of the fingers in holding the pen,—the process of penmaking,—and a series of peculiarly novel and ingenious exercises, calculated to improve, speedily, the imperfect writing of adults, and to lead beginners, on rational and philosophical principles, from the simplest elements of penmanship, to the attainment of a free, rapid, and elegant current hand. By B. F. Foster, accountant, and teacher of writing in the Albany Academy. Albany: published by O. Steele. For sale by Carey and Lea, Philadelphia;

Pl. 23 *1ᵉ Combination*

multum multum multum mult

them them them them them them

a b c d e f g h i j k l m n o p q r t u v w x y z

M m M m M m M m m

Fig. 33. From Foster's *Practical Penmanship* (1832).

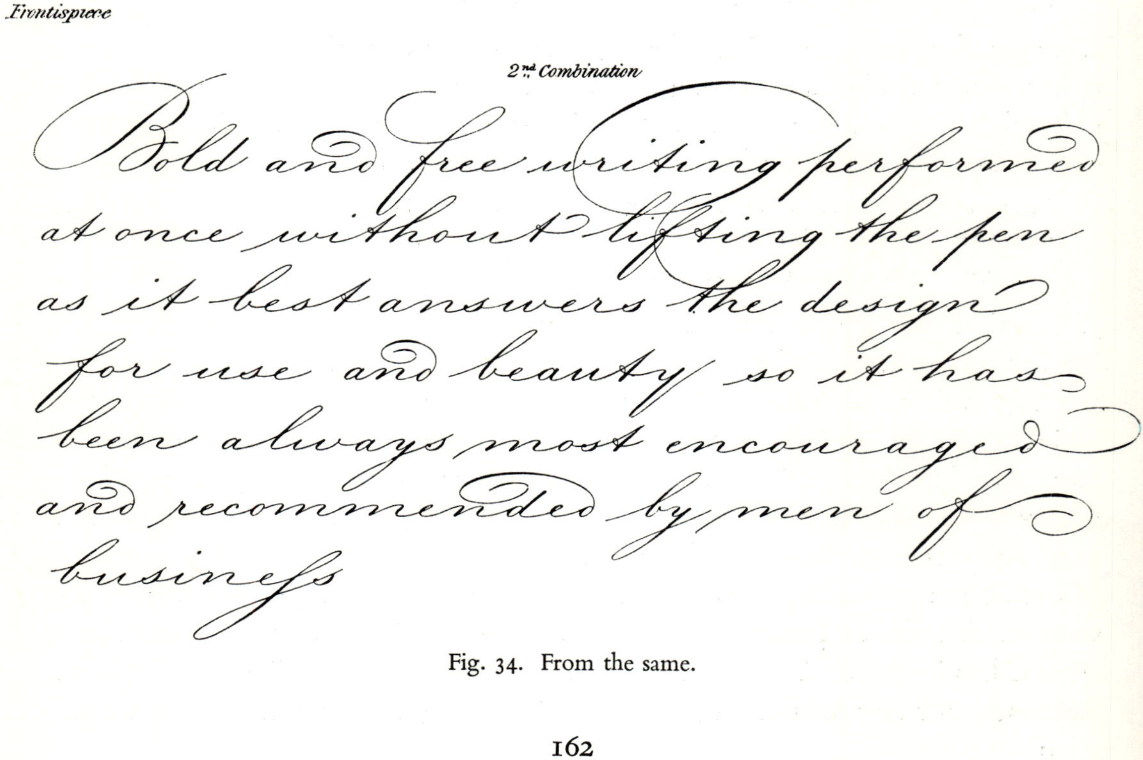

Frontispiece

2ⁿᵈ Combination

Bold and free writing performed
at once without lifting the pen
as it best answers the design
for use and beauty so it has
been always most encouraged
and recommended by men of
business

Fig. 34. From the same.

162

Hilliard, Gray and co. and Carter, Hendee and co. Boston; Collins and Hannay, and N. and J. White, New-York. 1832 (see Figs. 33 & 34).

> This is a reissue of the preceding title. The collation is the same except, in addition to the frontispiece, there are plates numbered 2–23 and 20 A, making the total of 24. The advertisements are not present though there is a two-page 'Notice of this Work' before the frontispiece. Original cloth over boards with yellow printed label.
>
> NhD   ICN   MWA   NNC   NN   RPB

4. Report of the committee appointed by the Albany Institute to examine the system of writing invented by Carstairs.

> In the preceding work pages [vii]–xx are devoted to this report dated February 1830 and, according to the prefatory note, prepared by S. DeWitt Bloodgood in behalf of the committee, whose other members were Dr Lewis C. Beck and Dr Philip Ten Eyck. Foster's substantial authorship of the piece cannot be doubted.

5. Prize essay on the best method of teaching penmanship. By B. F. Foster, teacher of writing, stenography, and book-keeping; author of 'Practical penmanship,' &c. New edition, revised and improved. Boston: Clapp and Broaders. 1834.

> 60 pp. 182 × 113 mm.   MWA   DLC   ICN   MB   NN   NNC

6 (a) Foster's system of penmanship: or, the art of rapid writing illustrated and explained. To which is added the angular and anti-angular systems. Exemplified with plates. By B. F. Foster, teacher of writing and book-keeping—author of a Development of Carstairs' system; Prize essay on the best method of teaching penmanship, &c. Boston: published by Perkins, Marvin, & co. Philadelphia: Henry Perkins. 1835.

> 4 pp.; engraved frontispiece; 104 pp.; 15 engraved plates marked A–HH, I, 1–3, K–L. Illustrations in text. 228 × 140 mm.   NhD   ICN   MB   NNC   RPB

6 (b) ......Philadelphia: Henry Perkins. Boston: Perkins, Marvin, & co. 1835.

> Variant imprint; only 12 engraved plates A–HH, I, K–L. The Pennsylvania University copy lacks the four pages at beginning and plates F–G and L.   CSmH   PU

7. An alphabetical set of small hand copies, adapted to Foster's system of penmanship. Boston: Perkins & Marvin.—Philadelphia: Henry Perkins.

> Printed wrapper with title; 8 unnumbered engraved plates. The eighth is signed W. B. Annin, sc. 78 × 197 mm. The copyright date is 1836.   MWA   NNC

8 (a) Foster's elementary copy-books designed to lead the learner, upon simple principles, from the first rudiments of penmanship, to a perfect knowledge of the art:—being a new and improved plan of teaching; by which the trouble and loss of time in ruling horizontal and diagonal lines, and setting copies, are avoided, and the attainment of penmanship is greatly facilitated. Adapted to schools and private

instruction. By B. F. Foster, teacher of writing and book-keeping—author of a 'Development of Carstairs' system,' 'Prize essay on the best method of teaching writing,' 'Foster's system of penmanship,' &c. Boston: published by Perkins & Marvin. Henry Perkins, Philadelphia. 1836.

> Printed wrapper with title, including wood-engraving, Correct Position of the Hand and Pen, and copyright notice; 16 leaves of ruled writing paper headed by copies white on black, printed from wood-engravings. 202 × 167 mm.
> The book described is designated above the title as No. 1.
> ICN MWA, no. 6, (1837) NN, nos. 2, 3, 6 NNC, nos. 1, 2, 3, 6

8 (*b*) ......No. 5...Boston: published by Perkins & Marvin. Collins, Keese, & co., New York,—Bennett & Bright, Utica.—Hoyt & Porter, Rochester. Henry Perkins, Philadelphia. 1840.

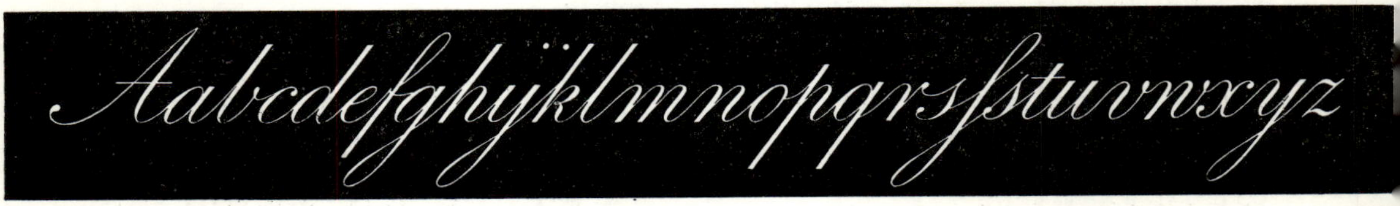

Fig. 35. From Foster's *Elementary Copy-books*, no. 5 (1840). Retouched.

9. The penman's guide: a series of large text, small hand, and current-hand copies; with remarks on teaching penmanship. By B. F. Foster, author of 'The art of rapid writing explained'; 'Elementary copy-books'; 'Commercial book-keeping'; 'Counting-house assistant'; 'Merchant's manual'; 'Hints to young tradesmen,' &c. Boston: Perkins & Marvin.—Philadelphia: Henry Perkins. Entered...1838....

> Printed wrapper with title; 8 pp.; 26 unnumbered engraved plates. 75 × 197 mm. The first plate is signed Engraved by Geo. Jones and Co., 183 Broadway, New York.   MWA NNC

10. (New series) Elementary copy-books: an improved plan of teaching penmanship; whereby the learner's progress is secured, and the labor of the teacher greatly facilitated. By B. F. Foster, author of 'Theory and practice of book-keeping simplified,' 'Art of rapid writing illustrated,' 'Prize essay on the best method of teaching writing,' 'Penman's guide,' &c Boston: published by Benjamin Perkins. New York: Collins, Brother & co., and Roe Lockwood. Philadelphia: Perkins & Purves. Entered...1842, by Benjamin Perkins....

> Printed wrapper with title, including a wood-engraving of Correct Position of the Hand and Pen, and a three-line quotation from Locke; 16 leaves of ruled paper each with two wood-engraved lines of copy, unnumbered. 201 × 157 mm.
> The book described is designated at the top of the title-page 'Current Hand No. X.'
> NhD NN

11. Foster's exercises in current-hand writing; designed to facilitate the labor of the teacher, and to enable young learners to acquire an elegant, rapid, and masterly use of the pen;—being an improved process of teaching mercantile penmanship, founded upon rational and philosophical principles. Adapted to schools and families. By B. F. Foster, teacher of writing and book-keeping—author of a 'Development of Carstairs' system,' 'Prize essay on the best method of teaching writing,' 'Foster's system of penmanship,' 'Elementary copy-books,' &c. Boston: published by Perkins & Marvin. Collins, Keese, & co., New York.—Bennett & Bright, Utica,—Hoyt & Porter, Rochester.—Henry Perkins, Philadelphia. 1840.

Printed wrapper with title; 16 leaves of ruled writing paper with wood-engraved headline copies, white on dark ground. 203 × 166 mm.

NNC, nos. 7 and 8   NN, no. 8 (1837), another issue (1840)

Fig. 36. 'Wrong postures: right posture'.
From Foster's *Elementary Copy-books* (1842), etc.

Fig. 37. Position of the paper.
From the same.

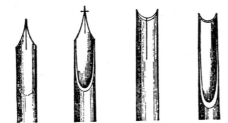

Fig. 38. Penmaking. From Foster's *Penmanship, Theoretical and Practical* (1843).

Fig. 39. From the same.

165

12. Penmanship, theoretical and practical, illustrated and explained. By B. F. Foster, author of 'Elementary copy-books;' Prize essay on the best method of teaching penmanship;' 'The merchant's manual;' 'The theory and practice of book-keeping simplified,' &c. &c. Boston: published by Benjamin Perkins. 1843.

> Wood-engraved frontispiece, 52 pp. with wood-engraved illustrations; full-page plates numbered 1–36 printed from wood-engravings in red ink. 195 × 123 mm. Brown embossed cloth over boards stamped in gilt 'Foster's Penmanship Illustrated'.
>
> NhD ICN MWA NNC TxU WU

13 (*a*) Improved system of writing. For the use of schools and families.—Just published, in twelve numbers, Foster's pencilled copy-books: being a new process of instruction....By B. F. Foster....Boston: W. J. Reynolds & co. and S. K. Whipple & co.....

> Printed wrapper with title, 8 pp., 6 leaves inserted at center with wood-engraved copies printed on both sides. 155 × 185 mm.
> 'The specimen pages in this Prospectus are intended merely to exhibit the general features and plan of the books....'
>
> MH

13 (*b*) Foster's pencilled copy-books, complete in twelve numbers. Being a new process of instruction....

> Published by W. J. Reynolds and Co. and S. K. Whipple and Co., Boston. Copyright 1852.
>
> NN (nos. 5, 8, 9)

14. Writing and writing masters: the principles of the former developed, and the fallacies of the latter exposed. By Benjamin Franklin Foster. Consulting accountant and commercial teacher; author of 'Prize essay on the best method of teaching penmanship,' 'Double entry elucidated,' 'The counting-house assistant,' and other scholastic works. Truth, whether in or out of fashion, is the measure of knowledge, and the business of the understanding; whatsoever is besides that, however authorized by consent, is nothing but ignorance, or something worse. Locke. New York: Mason Brothers, 23 Park Row. 1854.

> 32 pp. with wood-engraved illustrations in the text. 227 × 146 mm. Blue printed wrapper.
>
> NhD

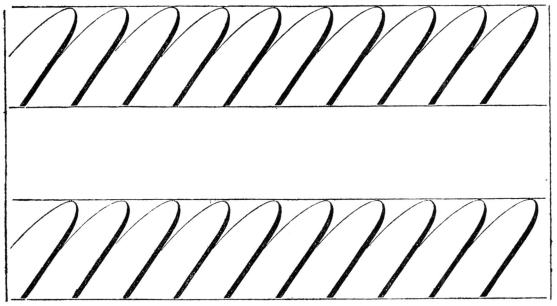

Fig. 40. 'Initiatory Exercises'. From the same.

Fig. 41. 'Text Hand'. From the same.

167

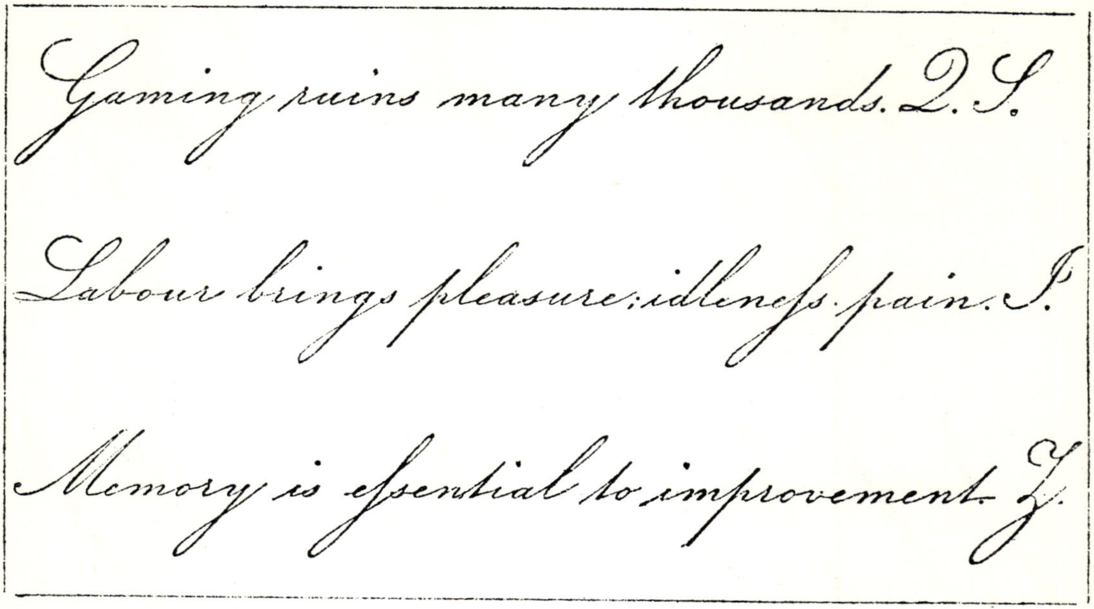

Fig. 42. 'Current Hand'. From the same.

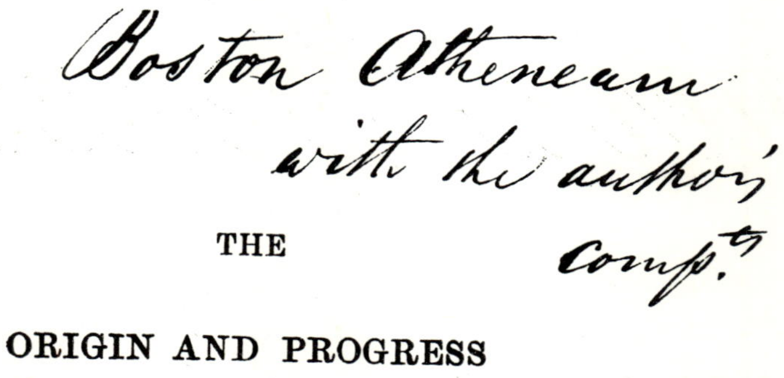

THE

ORIGIN AND PROGRESS

Fig. 43. Foster's autograph: Boston (1852).

SIR FRANCIS MEYNELL

According to Cocker

I begin with a quotation from *Tom Brown at Oxford*, the Tom Brown whose schooldays are well known (perhaps too well known).

This is how it runs: 'So you ought to be, according to Cocker, spending all your time in sickrooms.' 'According to who?' 'According to Cocker.' 'Who is Cocker?' 'Oh, I don't know. Some old fellow who wrote the rules of arithmetic, I believe.'

But by a delightful irony, Edward Cocker was only in the scantiest way an arithmetician, and his fame, thus immortalized in a false phrase, is nevertheless deserved, not by writing the rules of arithmetic, but, in a word, by writing. Though it is not as familiar today as it used to be (a Victorian Chancellor of the Exchequer used it to defend his figures), the phrase 'according to Cocker' meaning exact and unquestionable, is accepted by the *Oxford English Dictionary*. Who, then, was Cocker?

Edward Cocker was born in 1631 and died in 1676. Pepys employed him to engrave on the diarist's 'new sliding rule with silver plates'. He records: 'I find the fellow by his discourse very ingenious [a word of praise] and among other things a great admirer and well-read in our English poets, and undertakes to judge them all, and that not impertinently.' He was writer, writing master, engraver and producer of no fewer than twenty-five books of his own writing and engraving—in several of which the simpler elements of arithmetic appear in second place. What, then, has given him his false, as distinct from his real, fame?

Cocker was a superlative master of writing and of 'striking'—the name given to freehand flourishes and calligraphic figures written literally in freehand, that is, with the hand not resting on the paper. He was distinguished by both the quality and the quantity of his work. Rival writing masters—and how extreme were these rivalries I shall later show—had more than envy to inspire them; copy-books were an alternative to lessons. So one of them writes that 'the rolling-press groaned under a superfoetation of such books as had almost rendered the art contemptible'; and another calls Cocker 'a voluminous Author who, led on by Lucre, let in an inundation of Copy-books'. I give in Cocker's own elegant terms the wording of his first title page:

THE PEN'S TRANSCENDENCIE
OR
FAIR WRITING'S LABYRINTH

Wherein Faire Writing to the Life's exprest
In sundry copies, cloth'd with Art's rich Vest.
By which with Practice thou mayst gain Perfection,
As th'Heaven-taught Author did without direction.
Invented, Written, and Engraved, by

EDWARD COCKER

Such as would learne to write
All or any of the most curious Hands practised in England
Or Hands used by other Nations, and the Art of
Arithmetick in Whole Numbers, Fractions, or Decimalls, or
Logarithms, may be commendably taught, with Expedition.

BY EDWARD COCKER

Dwelling in Paul's Church Yard betwix the Signes of the
Sugar Loafe and the Naked Boy, right over against Paul's Chaine,
Where you may have choice of Copy bookes made by the same Author.
Such as desire to learne privately, may be attended at their Lodgings.
Also you may have anything fairely written, by the said E.C.

1657

But now for Edward Cocker the arithmetician. Ambrose Heal has himself counted 65 editions within 100 years of the book called *Cocker's Arithmetic*. The *Dictionary of National Biography* estimated that there were at least 112. The hub of the matter is that it was published by one John Hawkins in 1678—and this was two years after Cocker's death. There are, it is true, such things as posthumous publications. And why should we assume that the book was fudged off on Cocker? There is a rich answer to that question. There had already been published a book called *The Young Clerk's Tutor*,

Whereby ingenious youths may soon be made
For clerkship fit, or Management of Trade.

170

On the title page of this book appeared, prominently but ambiguously, Cocker's name. 'A close investigation,' says Sir Ambrose Heal, 'leads one to suspect that the preface modestly signed J.H., betrays the hand of John Hawkins as that of the real author of the book, and that he had used Cocker's name to conjure with. It seems therefore that the same questionable method may have been repeated by Hawkins with regard to the *Arithmetic*.'

A name to conjure with. Yes, indeed. A forged name to conjure with. Cocker's success as writing-master caused the forgery of his name on the *Young Tutor*. The success—it ran into fifteen editions—of the *Young Tutor* made even more attractive a false ascription of the *Arithmetic*. It did more. In 1685, nine years after Cocker's death, Hawkins was at it again with *Cocker's Decimal Arithmetic*. Nineteen years later came *Cocker's English Dictionary*, bearing Hawkins's name as editor, twenty-eight years after Cocker's death. And H. B. Wheatley makes the delightful suggestion that if Hawkins had only lived longer Hawkins would have found *Cocker's Compleat Dancing-Master* and *Cocker's Compleat Cookery-Book* among the papers of the deceased. But the fun doesn't stop there. Hawkins himself had died twelve years before the Dictionary was published, so that its ascription to Cocker and to Hawkins was a double fraud. As a publisher, I do not wish to denigrate my brethren even of another epoch, but one is compelled to note that all these books were published by one little group of London Bridge booksellers. They had a good name for their series, and by Cocker they would stick to them.

What is the chief characteristic of Cocker the penman? It is gaiety. In Sir Ambrose Heal's words, 'he refused to take the job seriously and delighted to embroider his copy-books with fantastic creatures, exotic birds, dragons, dancing bears, angels, fauns, sea monsters, grotesque masks, warriors and delightful ships, all woven into an absurd medley of ornament round his pages. For sheer command of hand his knots and flourishes are wonderful pieces of exuberant penmanship.' In this Cocker was reverting, against all the tendencies of the time, to an earlier flamboyant fashion.

And it was not only in his penmanship that Cocker showed his gaiety. His instructions are full of endearing couplets, endearing and also exact; as this on the italic hand

> On oval wheels should fair Italian run
> Smooth as the whirling Chariot of the Sun.

Where did Cocker stand as a penman? He belonged to an age when writing was still a matter of many different hands—hands commended by the politeness of the varied occasion even more than suited to varying taste. (Martin Billingsley lists in 1618 five hands for differing degrees of formality. He, by the way, is early in the discourtesies between penmen. He refers to his competitors as 'lame penmen', and 'botchers'.) But in the thirty years between Cocker's first and his last copy-books there was one occasion which came to predominate over all others—the occasion of commerce. And Cocker was the transitionalist penman; he gradually conformed to this paramount demand for wide simple clarity in his letters, if not in his framework decorations. Indeed, I suppose that it was the necessary curtailment of fun in the hand of commerce that prompted him to retain and develop his extraliteral exuberance; a needed compensation.

The other influence on the style of writing—other to the occasions of commerce—was the new use of the 'rolling-press', that is, of intaglio engraving. The first copy-book to be reproduced by this method was published in Bologna in 1571. The first in England was Billingsley's in 1605. The tool of the copper-engraver produced an extraordinarily brilliant line, and masters (and their pupils) were led to employ a correspondingly fine pen. Many penmen were their own engravers; and it was inevitable that they should seek to write a hand with the pen that could fully exploit the wonderful finesse of their brains. The method of reproduction predominated over the thing to be reproduced. Copperplate engraving largely made what came to be regarded as the copperplate hand, just as the quill pen largely made, and the broad-nibbed steel pen still largely makes—at least makes possible—the italic hand.

Before the rolling-press, before engraving, the copy-books were printed letter-press, with an actual coarsening of the original. Fine lines were impossible.

But to go back to the commercial reason. In 1648 Oliver Cromwell determined to reduce the marine power of the Dutch and increase the mercantile power of the English. His means was the Mercantile Act, which provided that every cargo carried to England must be carried in an English ship. As our commerce expanded, the English style of writing also spread, at home and abroad. Commercial clerkship became an important career. Mr Stanley Morison says, 'It would be an exaggeration to claim that the English national script, still termed copy-book or copperplate, possesses an attractive personality. It is colourless, thoroughly unromantic and dull. These, however, were precisely the qualities which commended it to those who wrote our invoices, and to those abroad who received them.'

By the middle of the eighteenth century the copy-book or copperplate style was paramount, without 'sprigges', without 'striking', and with the exaggerated slant that made for speed. George Bickham in 1754, referring back to Cocker's day, has this to say: 'Our forefathers practised a small running secretary hand; they practised many others as well. And it was as great a rarity to meet with a person who had not been so taught as it is now to meet one that is. To talk then of round hand, and persuade the practice of it, was the same thing, as it would be now to introduce a new character unknown to the generality of mankind. But at length the excellency and usefulness of the round hand prevailing with many eminent penmen, to show the delicacy of it, and its natural tendency to facilitate and despatch business being considered, it is universally received and practised by all degrees of men, in all employments, the law only excepted.'

All degrees of men. The italic hand, more elegant, more courtly, easier, the 'oval wheels' of Cocker, survived for a long time, chiefly as a hand for ladies—not then engaged in commerce. Bickham himself published in 1739 *A Compleat Set of Italian Copies for the use of the Ladies of Great Britain.* In this he followed the precept of Billingsley, a hundred years before him; for Billingsley, who taught Charles I his beautiful italic hand, says of what he calls Roman (we, Italic) 'a hand of great account and of much use in this Realme. . .it is conceived to be the easiest hand that is written with the pen. . . . Therefore it is usually taught to women, forasmuch as they, having not the patience to take any great pains, besides phantasticall and humoursome, must be taught that which they instantly learn.' But with the new copperplate hands dominating the country and Europe, towards the end of the eighteenth century, even the ladies were catered for, as if they indeed had become possessed of the 'patience to take great pains'.

I must now develop that second part of my theme which concerns the dramatic rivalries among the penmen. For this I must leave Cocker; it was not his wont, it was not 'according to Cocker' to lambast his brother writers. (I wish I could use the term 'brother and sister' writers; but I find that there were only four professional women writing masters among the 450 penmen in Sir Ambrose Heal's list.)

In those ampler days, the teachers did not have one common enemy. By no means. They had each other. Partly the battle was between styles, between the severe and those with the *esprit gai.* But even more it was between personalities, and for glory, and for the lucre that glory brought.

Isaac D'Israeli, born in 1761, the father of Benjamin, has a chapter in his *Curiosities of Literature* on the history of writing masters. He pokes enormous fun at the pretentions of the masters, and that fun-poking is in itself a sad sign of the changed times. Listen to him on the man he calls 'the late Tomkins': 'a recent instance of one of these egregious calligraphers may be told of the late Tomkins. This vainest of writing masters dreamed through life that penmanship was one of the fine arts, and that a writing master should be seated with his peers in the Academy! He bequeathed to the British Museum his *opus magnum,* a copy of Macklin's Bible profusely embellished with the most beautiful and varied decorations of his pen; and as he conceived that both the workman and the work would alike be darling objects with posterity, he left something immortal with the legacy, his fine bust by Chantrey, unaccompanied by which they were not to accept the immortal gift! When Tomkins applied to have his bust, our great sculptor abated the usual price, and, courteously kind to the feelings of the man, said that he considered Tomkins as an artist! It was the proudest day in the life of our writing-master,

'But an eminent artist and wit now living, once looking on this fine bust, declared that this man died for want of a dinner. Our penman had long felt that he stood degraded in the scale of genius by not being received at the Academy, at least among the class of engravers. The next approach to academic honour he conceived would be appearing as a guest at their annual dinner. These invitations are as limited as they are select, and all the Academy persisted in regarding Tomkins as a writing-master! Many a year passed. Every intrigue was practised, every remonstrance was urged, every stratagem of courtesy was tried; but never ceasing to deplore the failure of his hopes, it preyed on his spirits, and the luckless calligrapher went down to his grave— without dining at the Academy.' But I must turn again to the rivalries. . . .

There are two formal and famous jousts of the pen, and D'Israeli records them both. The first was between Bales and Johnson, in 1595. Johnson, young and arrogant, had persistently provoked Bales by libels on his skill. And Bales, therefore, issued a challenge 'to all Englishmen and strangers to write for a gold pen of £20 value. . . best, straightest and fastest. . . in a slow set hand, a mean facile hand and a fast running hand, and to write truest and speediest, most secretary and clerk-like, from a man's mouth, reading or pronouncing either English or Latin.' Johnson, by way of accepting the challenge, posted all the city with contumelious phrases against Bales, taunting him particularly with the poverty that had allegedly made him suggest a pen worth £20 instead of the £1000 Johnson says he was willing to wager. Imagine, £1000 in those days! On Michaelmas Day the trial opened before five judges 'before a multitude like a stage play, and shouts and tumults'. At first it was level pegging. Bales won the test for the manner of teaching scholars, the test for writing from dictation in English and Latin. Johnson won the roman hand, Bales the bastard secretary and set text, Johnson the court hand. So in pure writing it was two all. But Bales had a card up his sleeve; he produced suddenly his 'masterpiece, secretary and roman hand four ways varied'. The challenger was out-written and Bales was awarded the pen. Did that silence Johnson? Certainly not. Again Johnson placarded the city. Bales, he said, had got the pen from the judges by pretending that his sick wife longed for a sight of it. The judges, he declared, having thus lost the pen to Bales in any case, had therefore felt obliged to give a verdict that suited the occasion, to follow the pen with the verdict rather than the verdict with the pen. Bales disproved the libel and adopted the pen as his shop sign.

We shall glance now at one more contest, one as late as the reign of Queen Anne. It was set between Mr German and Mr More. But there were no printed libels, no shouts, no tumults. Decorum was so far honoured that Mr German insisted that Mr More should set the copy. This he did, neatly enough, with a pun on his own name:

> As more, and More, our understanding clears,
> So more and More our ignorance appears.

Copies of this text in various hands were submitted for judgement: the umpires found themselves wholly unable to choose between the merits of the parties. At length one of them discovered that Mr German had omitted in one copy the dot of an *i*. That won the pen for Mr More.

More, in his *Essay on the Invention of Writing* has the following passage, which is quoted for ridicule by Isaac D'Israeli, but I confess to finding it fine in thought and statement: 'Art with me is of no party. A noble emulation I would cherish, while it proceeded neither from nor to malevolence. Bales had his Johnson, Norman his Mason, Ayres his Matlock and his Shelley; yet Art the while was no sufferer. The busybody who officiously employs himself in creating misunderstandings between artists, may be compared to a turnstile, which stands in every man's way, yet hinders nobody; and he is the slanderer who gives ear to the slander.'

Bales had his Johnson. We have heard that history. 'Ayres his Matlock and his Shelley.' I can say no more of this contest—not a formal competition, but a bout of criticism—than that it concerned Mr Shelley's partiality for 'sprigged' letters when the fashion was against them. But Matlock was also against Cocker. He writes of the 'misleading labyrinth of the confused examples of Mr Cocker'. Snell, another master, declaims against 'our late Authors who have made Owls, Apes, Monsters and sprig'd Letters...in the hopes, by amusing the ignorant, to gain the Reputation of Masters'.

I conclude with a discovery, at any rate an assertion—and he was a singularly accurate man—of Isaac D'Israeli's. 'There is a strange phrase', he says, 'connected with the art of the calligrapher, which I think may be found in most if not in all modern languages, "To write like an angel". Ladies have frequently been compared with angels; they are beautiful as angels, and sing and dance like angels; but however intelligible these comparisons are, we do not so easily connect penmanship with the other celestial accomplishments. This fanciful phrase "to write like an angel" has a very human origin. Among those very learned Greeks who emigrated to Italy and afterwards into France, in the reign of Francis I, was one Angelo Vergecio, whose beautiful calligraphy excited the admiration of the learned. His name, Angelo, became synonymous for beautiful writing and gave birth to the vulgar proverb, to write like an angel: to write like Angelo.'

Fig. 44. From Sir Ambrose Heal's *English Writing Masters*.

This essay is based on a lecture delivered by Sir Francis Meynell to the Society for Italic Handwriting.
EDITOR.

PRECEPT AND PRACTICE

JAN TSCHICHOLD

Non-Arbitrary Proportions of Page and Type Area

Two constants determine the proportions of a well-made book: hand and eye. The healthy eye is always two hand spans from the book page, and everyone holds books in the same way.

Book sizes are determined by their function. They are related to the hand and body size of adults. Even books for children must not be produced in folio size, as this format is difficult to handle for a child. A high, or at least adequate, degree of handling comfort is expected: a book as large as a table is a monstrosity, books the size of postage stamps are playthings. Very heavy books are equally unwelcome; older people might not be able to move them without help. Giants would need much larger book formats and newspapers: dwarfs would find our books much too large.

There are two main groups of books: those which we place on the table in order to study them and the others, which we read leaning back in a chair or armchair, or sitting in a train. Books for studying should be propped up in front of us at an angle. But reading posture has nothing to do with the size and volume of educational books. Their formats range from large octavo to large quarto; larger formats are exceptions. Books for study or 'table books' lie on the table and cannot be held during reading. Books which we prefer to hold during reading come in a wide range of octavo formats.

There are many proportions of page sizes, that is the ratio between width and height. Everyone knows the Golden Rule, at least from hearsay: exactly $1:1.618$. The proportion $5:8$ is nothing else than an approximation to the Golden Rule. It is difficult to make this claim for the proportion $2:3$. Apart from the proportions $1:1.618$, $5:8$, and $2:3$, the proportions $1:1.732$ $(1:\sqrt{3})$ and $1:1.414$ $(1:\sqrt{2})$ are predominantly used for books.

The geometrically definable 'irrational' page proportions $1:1.618$ (Golden Rule), $1:\sqrt{2}$, $1:\sqrt{3}$, $1:1 \cdot \sqrt{5}$, $1:1.538$ (rectangle from the pentagon) and the simple 'rational' proportions 1:2, 2:3, 3:4, 5:8, 5:9 I call clear, intended and well-defined, all others being unclear and arbitrary. The difference between a clear and an unclear proportion though often very small, is noticeable.

Many books, however, show none of these clear proportions, but an arbitrary proportion. It cannot be explained, but it is a fact that areas of geometrically well-defined intentional proportions are more pleasing or more beautiful to man than those of arbitrary proportions. An ugly format inevitably produces an ugly book. Since the usefulness and beauty of a printed product, whether book or leaflet, depend on the proportions of the final paper size, he who wants to make a beautiful and pleasing book must therefore first determine a format of well-defined proportions.

A uniform proportion, whether it be 2:3 or 1:1·414 or 3:4 or any other well-defined proportion, is not adequate for every kind of book. Once again it is the function, which determines not only the size of books but also their page proportions. Thus the wide proportion 3:4 is excellently suited to quarto books, because these lie on the table. Whereas a pocket book in the proportion 3:4 is both difficult to handle and ugly. Even if it is not actually heavy, we can hold it in the free hand only for a short time, and moreover both halves of the book constantly fall back: the book is too wide. This also applies to books in the A 5 format (14·8 × 21 cm, 1:$\sqrt{2}$). A small book which is to be held must be narrow, since we cannot control the pages otherwise. The proportion 3:4 is unsuitable in this case; one of the proportions 1:1·732 (very narrow), 3:5, 1:1·618, or 2:3 is suitable.

During the Middle Ages, at a time when many books were written in two columns, book formats with the proportion 1:1·414 were frequent. Gutenberg, however, preferred the proportion 2:3. During the Renaissance period, the book proportion 1:1·414 is scarcely encountered. On the other hand, numerous narrow, small folio books of great elegance were produced, which should serve us as models.

How ugly books had become during the nineteenth century was apparent around the turn of the century. The type area was placed exactly in the centre of the page, and all four margins were of the same width. The pair of side margins lost their connection and therefore fell apart. The ratio of the four margins to one another was rightly recognized as a problem, and efforts were made to determine it on a numerical basis.

But these efforts were misapplied. Only under special conditions can the margins represent a rational progression (that is, one which can be expressed in simple figures, inner margin to top margin, outside and lower margins) as for example 2:3:4:6. The margin progression 2:3:4:6 is only possible when the paper format has the proportion 2:3 and this is also followed by the type area. Should the paper have a

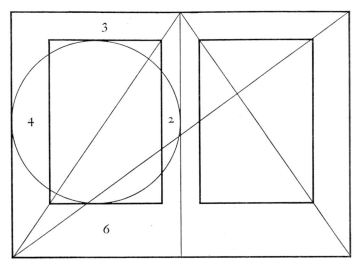

Fig. 45. The secret canon which underlies many late medieval manuscripts and incunabula. Discovered by Jan Tschichold, 1953. Page proportion 2:3. Text and page area of the same proportions. Height of the text area equal to width of the page. Margin relationships: 2:3:4:6.

different proportion, for instance $1:\sqrt{2}$, a margin progression of 2:3:4:6 produces a type area differing in proportion from the page size and this results in disharmony. The secret of a beautiful book page therefore cannot necessarily be found in a relationship of marginal widths that can be expressed in simple numerical terms.

Harmony between page size and composition results when both have the same proportions. If the position of the type area and the page format are successfully interrelated, then the margin widths become functions of the page format and construction and cannot be divorced from the two. The margin widths thus do not govern the book page but result from the page format and law of composition, the 'canon'.

Before printing was invented, books were written by hand. Gutenberg and the early printers used the written book as their model. The book printers took over the laws of book form which the scribes had followed for a long time. That there were some guiding lines is certain: countless medieval manuscripts after all show great conformity in the proportions of their formats and in the placing of the written area on the page. But these laws have not been handed down to us. They were workshop secrets. Only by making measurements of medieval manuscripts can we attempt to ferret them out.

Gutenberg moreover did not invent any new laws. He followed the workshop secrets of the initiated. Probably Peter Schoeffer, who, as an outstanding calligrapher, was certainly familiar with these gothic workshop secrets was involved.

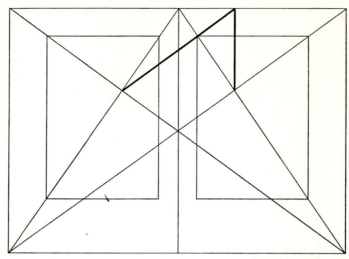

Fig. 46. Division into nine according to van de Graaf, illustrated on the page proportion 2:3. The simplest road to the canon of Fig. 45. Geometry replaces calculation.

I have measured up many medieval manuscripts. By no means all of them follow any law exactly; even at that time there were books made in poor taste. Only those manuscripts which were evidently laid out with deliberation and artistry are significant.

In 1953 I at last succeeded, after much effort, in reconstructing the Golden Canon of late Gothic book page layout, as it was used by the best scribes. It is illustrated in Fig. 45 Here the height of the written area is the same as the width of the paper: with the page proportion 2:3, which is a condition of this canon, one-ninth of the paper width constitutes the inner, and two-ninths the outer, margin; one-ninth of the paper height represents the top, and two-ninths the lower, margin. The written area and the leaf have the same proportions. Other empirically developed schemes had occasionally demanded identical proportions of written area and leaf, but *without the interlinking in the diagonal of the double page*, which is here present for the first time as a fundamental part of the construction.

The key to this layout is the division into nine of the width and height of the page. The simplest method is that discovered by Joh. A. van de Graaf, illustrated in Fig. 46.

The last and most satisfying confirmation of the correctness of my result illustrated in Fig. 45, has been given to me by the Villard diagram illustrated in Fig. 47. This little known and exciting gothic canon produces harmonic divisions and can be constructed in any rectangle. It can be used to divide any distance exactly into any desired number of equal parts, without use of another measure (Fig. 48).

We must not believe, however, that the format proportions 2:3, which are part

182

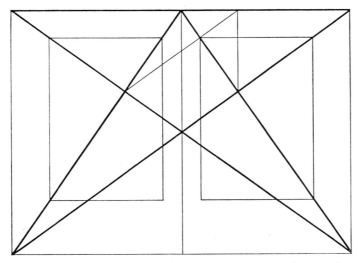

Fig. 47. The Villard diagram. In our diagram of the page construction there is also a variation of the harmonical proportion canon of Villard de Honnecourt. Villard was an architect from Picardy who lived in the first half of the thirteenth century. His *Sketchbook*, a manuscript, is kept in the Paris National Library. With the aid of this canon, which is shown in the thicker lines, any distance can be divided exactly into any desired number of parts without other measurements.

of this scribes' canon, can meet every requirement. The late Middle Ages demanded neither special handling ease nor even elegance from a book. Only during the Renaissance period did printers start to produce graceful, easily handled books of light weight. Gradually small format books in the proportions still in use today: 5:8, 21:34, $1:\sqrt{3}$, and the quarto format 3:4 were introduced. Beautiful though the proportion 2:3 may be, it is far from being suitable for all books. The function and character of a book frequently demand another good proportion.

However, the canon of Figs. 45 or 46 can also be applied to these other format proportions. With every book format, it leads to a non-arbitrary and entirely harmonious position of the type area. Even the relative size of the type area can be altered without destroying the harmony of the book page. We first consider the book formats of the Golden Rule, the proportions $1:\sqrt{3}$, $1:\sqrt{2}$ and quarto (3:4), at the same time applying the division into nine, as developed in Villard's canon in Fig. 48; for this also can be constructed in any rectangle (Figs. 51 and 52).

Figs. 53 and 54, square and oblong format, show that in the same way harmonious and non-arbitrary type areas can be composed even in unusual formats. Oblong formats are suitable for music and books with oblong illustrations; here the page proportion 4:3 will usually be better than the proportion 3:2, which is too squat. Even the division into nine is not the only correct one, although it is the most

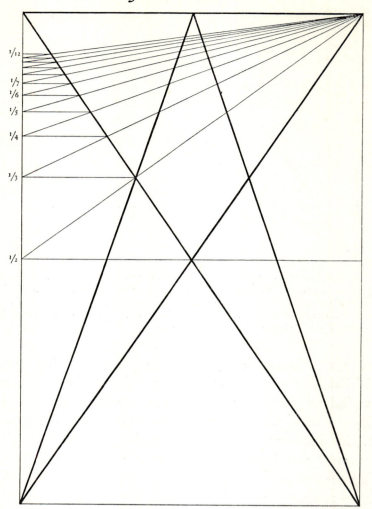

Fig. 48. The Villardcanon applied to a rectangle of the proportions 2:3. The depth of the page
is divided down to a twelfth.

beautiful. By dividing the page in twelve we obtain, as shown in Fig. 55, a larger
type area than that in Fig. 45. Fig. 56 illustrates the division into six of the height and
width for the page proportion 2:3, after the small handwritten prayer-book of Marcus
Vincentinus in the late fifteenth century, which is reproduced in table XX of Edward
Johnston's well-known text-book. It gave me deep satisfaction when in my canon I
discovered the key to the magnificent page layout of this masterpiece of calligraphy,
which I have not ceased to admire for over forty years. The written area is half as high
as the vellum; the page is 13·9 ×9·3 cm in size, and contains 12 lines of 24 letters.

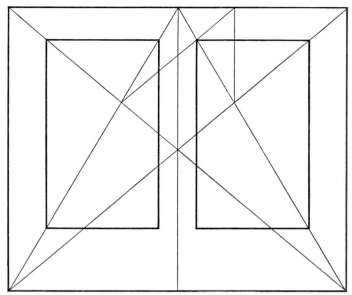

Fig. 49. Page proportion 1:√3 (1:1·732). Paper height and depth divided into nine.

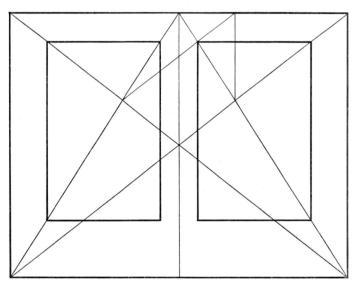

Fig. 50. Page proportion of the Golden Rule (21:34). Paper height and width divided into nine.
(For the page proportion 2:3 see Figs. 45 and 46).

The paper height can, if necessary, be divided at random. Even narrower margins than those shown in Fig. 55 are possible. Only the interlinking of the type area with the diagonals of the single and double page must be preserved, because this alone ensures a harmonious proportion and position of the type area.

The typographical system, which is based on the 12 points of the pica em, has neither in origin nor of necessity any connection with the canon expounded here, nor even with the book page of the proportion 2:3 used by Gutenberg and Schoeffer. During the early period of bookprinting, neither the typographical point nor the pica em were known. There were no generally valid measurements. Even the measurements based on the human body, such as pace, ell, foot, thumb width (inch) were not exactly defined. Given areas were probably divided by means of the Villard canon, and every man calculated with his own units, which were by no means rigidly or universally applicable.

Naturally the width of the line should preferably be to even pica ems, at least full pica ems, or, in the worst case, half ems, and the inner margins should be to full or half pica ems. The width of the trimmed head and the trimmed format, however, must be given in inch parts, even if it has all been thought out in pica ems. For the bookbinder is only conversant with inches. All these directions must be contained in the specimen sheets which precede production.

Reality, however, rarely allows the mathematically correct size and position of the type area. We often have to be content with an approximation to the ideal. Neither can we always make the typographical type area of exactly the desired height, nor, as a rule, will the mathematically correct gutter be satisfactory. This will only apply so long as the book consists of only one sheet or can be opened to lie completely flat. It is the appearance of the open book which must correspond to the canon. The inner margins must *appear* to be of the same width as the outer margins; the shadow as well as the paper area disappearing in the centre reduce the apparent width of the gutter.

There is no infallible rule how much must be allowed for the inner margins. A great deal depends on the way the book is bound. Thick books generally need a bigger allowance than thin ones. The weight of paper also plays a role. The only way to obtain certainty is by gluing a pair of specimen pages of the right paper into a dummy copy. The width of this dummy must exceed the exact proportions required, by the estimated inner margin allowance: otherwise the outer margin will not be right. Perhaps the dummy copy may have to be correspondingly adjusted afterwards, that is, made wider or narrower. A trimmed page which is wider by a few millimetres hardly affects the proportion of the case, as the case at the fore-edge is about $2\frac{1}{2}$ mm wider, at the head and tail 2 mm each, that is 4 mm higher together, than the trimmed book block. Incidentally it is only the open book and visible paper which count; the size of the case, which depends on the book block, does not count.

The choice of the type size and leading greatly contributes to the beauty of the book. The lines should contain eight to twelve words; anything exceeding that

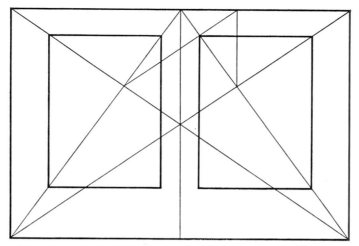

Fig. 51. Page proportion 1:√2 (A size). Paper height and width divided into nine.

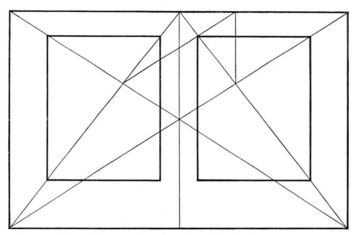

Fig. 52. Page proportion 3:4 (quarto). Paper height and width divided into nine. Here also the type area must repeat the proportion of the page.

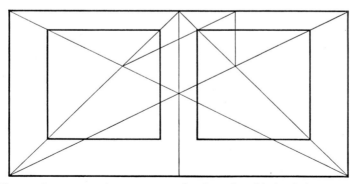

Fig. 53. Page proportion 1:1. Paper height and width divided into nine.

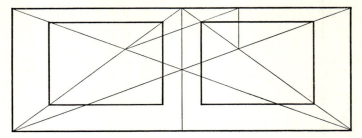

Fig. 54. Page proportion 4:3. Paper height and width divided into nine.

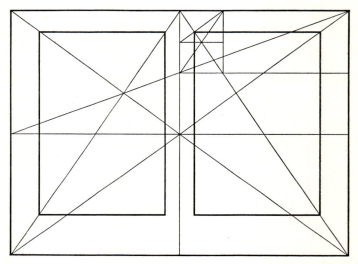

Fig. 55. Page proportion 2:3. Paper height and width divided into twelve by means of Villard's dividing canon, as illustrated in Fig. 48. This geometrical division into twelve is simpler and better than calculation.

number is to be deplored. The wide margins of the division into nine allow some-what larger type sizes than the division into twelve. Lines with more than twelve words demand additional leading. Unleaded type often is a torture for the reader.

When typography was at a hopelessly low ebb towards the end of the nineteenth century, many different styles were naïvely copied but only in their striking external features, such as initials and vignettes. No one thought of the importance of page proportions. Therefore no one made a point of using book formats of exact rational or irrational proportions; nor was the least attention given to a non-arbitrary design of the type area. If, none the less, a beautiful book was produced occasionally, then it was by someone who had often looked at exemplary books of the past and had absorbed some of their measurements, and also a feeling for good page proportions and the position of the type area. But this vague 'feeling' does not provide a reliable

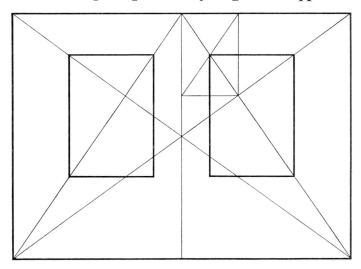

Fig. 56. Page proportion 2:3. Page height and width divided into six. Both applied in a small written prayer-book of Marcus Vincentinus (Marcus de Cribellariis) from the late fifteenth century.

measurement and cannot be taught. Only the scientific study of the perfect works of the past can lead us forward. Just as we owe the most important typefaces of the present to the meticulous study of old printed books, so research into the secrets of the old book formats will also bring us a good deal nearer to the art of book production.

Anyone who produces books or other printed matter must first of all look for the most suitable paper size. Even the most beautiful typeface is of no avail if the format, in itself, is displeasing. In the same way an unharmonious type area in a clumsy position destroys any possible beauty.

Countless type areas, even in narrow formats, are too high. Dissonant or un-harmonious book pages must result when the requirement for a type area in the exact or approximate proportions of the Golden Rule comes into conflict with the page format of the proportions $1:\sqrt{2}$ or $3:4$. If a harmonious page layout is to be produced, then the proportions of the page must either be altered or the type area must be given the proportions of the page.

No one will argue about good book proportions, so long as one is not singled out as correct. The right type area, second condition for a beautiful book, up to now has only been rarely investigated, and, even more rarely, methodically investigated. This aspect also was neglected to such an extent during the nineteenth century that almost any variation seemed permissible. During more recent years, the history of the type area has shown that new efforts are constantly being made to push out un-satisfactory old methods by unusual new ones.

Jan Tschichold

All these efforts have in common the fact that they are arbitrary. The canon had been lost long ago, and with 'feeling' alone it was impossible to track it down. It was only my measurements of countless medieval manuscripts which succeeded in this task. The canon expounded here is free from chance and puts an end to laborious trials. In all its variations it produces book forms where page format and type area are in unfailing agreement with each other; that is to say, they are in harmony.

Fig. 57. Comparison of proportions.
A 1:2·236 (1:√5); B 1:2 (1:√4); C 5:9; D 1:1·732 (1:√3); E 3:5;
F 1:1·618 (21:34) (*Golden Rule*); G 1:1·538; H 2:3; I 1:1·414 (1:√2); K 3:4.

SHORT BIBLIOGRAPHY
(*chronological*)

Gustav Milchsack, 'Kunst-Typographie' ('Art Typography'), *Archiv für Buchgewerbe* (Archive for the Book Trade), no. 8, 291–5; no. 10, 365–72, (Leipzig, 1901). Attempt by an expert librarian to track down the laws governing production of beautiful books. He believes that margin relationships can be rationally expressed in figures.

Edward Johnston, *Manuscript and Inscription Letters* (2nd ed., London: John Hogg, 1911), plate 1. Empirically discovered margin relationships expressed in figures; unassailable in the only example shown.

Edward Johnston, *Writing & Illuminating & Lettering* (7th ed., London: John Hogg, 1915), pp. 103–7. Proportion theories based on practical experience expressed only in numerical proportions.

Friedrich Bauer, *Das Buch als Werk des Buchdruckers* (*The Book as the Work of the Printer*) (Leipzig: Deutscher Buchgewerbeverein, 1920).

Jan Tschichold, 'Die Massverhältnisse der Buchseite, des Schriftfeldes und der Ränder' ('The Proportions of the Book Page, the Type Area and the Margins'), *Schweizer Graphische Mitteilungen*, LXV (St Gall: August 1946), 294–305. Early attempt by the author. Contains more statements than theories. Many illustrations.

Joh. A. van de Graaf, 'Nieuwe berekening voor de vormgeving' ('New Proportions for Design'), *Tété* (Amsterdam, November 1946), pp. 95–100. Demonstrates the simplest way of applying the new proportion of height to width of paper.

Hans Kayser, *Ein harmonikaler Teilungskanon* (A Harmonical Proportion Canon) (Zürich: Occident-Verlag, 1946). Intelligent and learned, like all books by this author. Contains the reference to the proportion canon hidden in the *Sketchbook* of Villard de Honnecourt.

Jan Tschichold, 'Die Proportionen des Buches' (The Proportions of the Book'), *Druckspiegel*, x (Stuttgart, January, February, March 1955), 8–18, 87–96, 145–150. Written in 1953. First publication of the author giving his findings of the medieval scribe's canon. Numerous diagrams and illustrations. In part superseded by the present publication.

Jan Tschichold, *Bokens Proportioner* (the previous title in book form in Swedish). (Gothenburg: Wezäta, 1955.) Finely printed edition, two-colour printing. One of the best Swedish books of that year.

NOTE

This essay is a revised, more concise version of material which has already appeared in *Print in Britain* (special design supplement), XI, No. 5. EDITOR.

NICOLETE GRAY

Expressionist Lettering

In May 1949 I was very surprised, and very pleased, to receive a letter in Alfred Fairbank's handwriting. I had never met him, and this letter came to me out of the blue. It was, of course, about lettering, in particular about 'the expression of the meaning of words by the form of the writing'. In a later letter in the same correspondence, he wrote that he hoped that I would 'keep this interesting side of handwriting in mind', and this is my excuse for offering to him now a word on a piece of expressionist lettering which I have tried to do myself.

It is, however, not about expressionism in handwriting that I am writing; as far as I know, that still remains to be studied. I wish indeed that I could have written about this idea in relation to the very beautiful, free, and varied penmanship of the late Roman cursive scribes of the fifth and sixth centuries, where one feels that even in chancery documents, there is expression in the sweeping curves. In the meantime, I write about expressionism in lettering on a larger, less subtle scale.

In 1962 I was invited by the Shakespeare Birthday Trust to design (and, if I wished, to execute) a panel of lettering to occupy the entire length—about 22 ft—of one wall of the Reading Room of the Nuffield Library at the new Shakespeare Centre, which was being built as part of the centenary celebrations of 1964. The panel was to be decorated with the name of Shakespeare and his contemporary poets and dramatists. As I saw it, this was an essay in expressionism. The problem was to convey, by means of letters, their shape and disposition on the panel, the relationship between the poet and his contemporaries, the difference in their work and character and stature, and their places in the shifting world of Elizabethan and Jacobean life.

In recent years there has been a remarkable extension of lettering on a grand scale. We have not only had a great improvement in shop signs and advertisements, but serious experiments, of which the largest and most interesting was Edward Wright's grand mural for the U.I.A. Congress of Architects of 1961, painted on the temporary exhibition buildings of London's South Bank, and reproduced in *Lettering Today* (1965), edited by John Brinkley. This is primarily an essay in the use of letter-forms as variable two-dimensional shapes, starting points for a build-up of abstract patterns. The designer limited himself to letters thought of as flat, inorganic surface forms, having colour and movement—in the sense of being able to move in front of one another and overlap—and he achieved a very exciting and new mural creation, which included letters of a monumental presence equal to their gigantic size (10 ft or so). Along these lines a lot of interesting experiment is being done in the graphic departments of art schools, and a development into the third dimension is encouraged by the use of expanded polystyrene for making letters. With the use of this very light, white material, it has been possible to experiment in the juxtaposition of letters of great difference in return; the depth of the letter being sometimes as great, or greater than its height.[1] (Plate 39 *a*).

All this, however, I felt largely irrelevant to my problem at Stratford. My letters had, of course, to be welded into a unified design. I also found myself thinking from the beginning in three-dimensional terms. Some names loomed up too from the beginning much larger; but there the common ground ended. My world was classical. All these poets moved within a consciousness of the omnipresent classical tradition; their names must be carved within the humanist idea, that is, with a sense of the organic identity of each character. The letters were not shapes which could be made use of, cut about, swollen or diminished to create some new pattern; they had to stride about on the wood in their own character. And then the wood too was something positive; it was the world in which they lived—a sort of stage—not a space to be filled, but the air in which the letters moved and found their place. In the centre I set a circle and, moving away from it at the sides, two squares, that on the left broken in two, revealing layer upon layer of changing woods, while from behind that on the right, the lower layers of this shifting Jacobean world move out to menace the Elizabethan symmetry.

My link was rather with the other, quite different, experiment in monumental lettering of recent years, that of Ralph Beyer at Coventry. This too is humanist and, unlike the other, it is expressive. The lettered panels at Coventry explicitly recall the early Christian tradition, in accordance with the words which they inscribe; they also owe something to the religious lettering of Rudolf Koch. These letters have an entity, they are each different, and they move individually to form a free pattern. But they all belong to the same family.

I wanted my letters to work at different depths and, as it were, to wear different clothes. The world of Spenser I feel, is like a fascinating tapestry; the letters here should move together into a coherent, rather flowery recessed pattern; whereas Webster is cruel and incisive, with sharp serifs, and a deep section, cutting right through down to the red camwood. As I read the poets and tried to understand their place in their time, their names took on shapes and the letters in them characteristics; Christopher Marlowe with his great R's striding across the wood, like Tamburlaine over the map of the world (Plate 39*b*); Dekker coarse and jolly; and Fletcher courtly and superficial, inlaid in grey sycamore, etc. And Shakespeare himself? One thinks not of him, but of the people he created. He is Protean, impossible to grasp; I found that I was trying, as I carved each letter to express something of his immense revelation of all the depths and delights known to human consciousness. So some of the letters are in boisterous relief; some gay; some, like the last A and R, cut as harsh, ruthless forms through the surface cherry wood down to layers of dark rosewood and ebony. (Plate 39*c*).

The work is interesting, I hope, as an experiment in the sort of expressionism particularly suited to lettering. Not in the use of lettering to convey the feelings of the artist (though the German expressionists of *Die Brücke* did this) but in the treatment of letters in many dimensions (in the widest sense of the word) so that they give formal expression to the meaning of the words transcribed. This is indeed part of the creed of constructivist typography, but I wanted to adapt it to a humanist content.

NOTE

1 A very successful example was shown in the Ministry of Works Exhibition in New Burlington Gardens, designed by H. O. Bryant of the Central Office of Information. (Plate 39*a* reproduced with the permission of H.M. Stationery Office.)

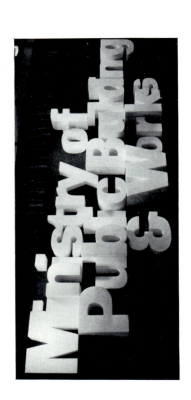

39a. Exhibition lettering in expanded polystyrene, designed by H. O. Bryant (1963). Letters are in very strongly contrasted, very high relief: see p. 194. (Reduced)

39b. Detail from 39c below.

39c. Panel in cherrywood, carved through into layers of grey sycamore, camwood, rosewood and ebony: by Nicolete Gray (1964). 22 ft × 5 ft: see p. 195.
Stratford-on-Avon.

Demonstration sheet of English tudor and italic scripts written by Lloyd J. Reynolds (1964): see p. 198.

[To face p.

LLOYD J. REYNOLDS

Notes on Movement involving Touch

An attractive example of personal handwriting or calligraphy is often praised for its character and style. On examining the script, one usually finds that vitality and freedom of movement are the qualities denoted by 'character'. If the writing lacks these qualities and is without rhythmical movement, it is considered cramped and uninteresting, even though legible.

An infinite variety of pen-movements is possible and, when these involve subtle rhythm and varieties of sensitive touch, the forms they make are pleasing to the eye, even when the movements have not produced letters and words.

Since the Second World War we have seen exhibitions of 'Calligraphy without Words' (New York), 'Lyrical Calligraphy' (Paris) and Japanese 'Modern Calligraphy' by members of the Kaisei-kai, the Society of Artist-Calligraphers. This emphasis on wordless vital movement and delicate touch has quickened into life new movements in drawing and painting in East and West. The traditional calligraphers, those who would not sacrifice the words of a text, may feel that these artists misuse the word 'calligraphy'; but it cannot be ignored that the work has made vivid to an appreciative public the fascination of subtle graphic movement. Its success testifies to the comprehensive and profound nature of Mr Alfred Fairbank's statement that 'Writing is a system of movements involving touch'. I would maintain that it is this non-verbal, tactual-kinetic, aspect of calligraphy, exploited by the unconventional 'writers', which accounts in most part for the importance of traditional calligraphy. The presence of alphabets in *our* writing is inseparable, however, from the graphic qualities.

In my experience, students feel that Mr Fairbank's statement is obvious. It is—on the first, the literal, level of meaning. In these notes I shall attempt to bring out the less obvious levels of meaning involved in the statement.

The distinction between the so-called calligraphy displayed by the art galleries and

Lloyd J. Reynolds

the traditional calligraphy is indicated by that word *system*. Alphabets provide the systems, and each alphabet has its own distinctive system. Compare, for example, the demonstration sheet of English Tudor script (called Secretary, or Cursive black-letter) with the Italic in Plate 40. Few systems of movement show greater contrast. Would it be an exaggeration to say that Macbeth seems to be more in control when his address to the witches appears in the cool rhythms of Italic? The dark swirling movement of the more irrational-appearing black-letter cursive seems quite appropriate to the weird sisters, making their speeches seem even more foreboding of disaster. We shall be concerned with these implicit, associated, meanings.

But first, let us examine the nature of alphabets.

The system of movements required by any particular alphabet involves such variables as pen-angle, pen-scale, proportion, letter-slope, sequence and direction of strokes, design of serifs, and frequency of pen-lifts. Even if more familiar forms of *e, f, h, s* and *y* were used in the Tudor script, the visual impact of this writing is quite unlike that of any other system. These variations of 'systems of movement' give the traditional penman a large repertory of alphabets, from which he can choose one that seems most appropriate to the commission at hand. Furthermore, he has an advantage over the gallery-experimenter; he has the explicit meaning of the words as well as the implicit meaning, or expressive power, of vital movement and sensitive touch. He has also the responsibility of preventing the alphabet from becoming lifeless formula, and, at the other extreme, he must avoid letting the spontaneous and free movements destroy the legibility of his writing.

The concept of the implicit meaning, or suggestive power, of graphic movement and touch is mentioned in the preceding paragraph. How can mere movement and touch have meaning if they produce no words or recognizable pictures of things?

We begin with the rectangle of paper. It is empty, a no-thing awaiting the pen. It is not even empty space, but only potential. But the moment the pen touches the paper and leaves even a slight trace of ink, the paper does become space, and the boundaries of the area are awakened and respond across the space to the tache of ink. It is as if a magnetic field were suddenly activated. Each subsequent **stroke** pours added energy into the field, modifying all previous relationships within its edges. Since this activation of tensions and directional movements occurs if only spatters of ink are dropped on the page, how vital is the effect if the pen sweeps across the paper in an ordered sequence of rhythmical, dance-like movements, whether free or forming letters and words! The casual reader may make an effort to suppress his visual experience of these graphic movements if he is interested in only the explicit,

198

or semantic, meaning of the words. There are others who may perceive the graphic qualities of the writing.

The logic of the system of movements characterizing any particular alphabet is a dialectic relation of inked movement and designed letter counters and interspaces. (There are no letters to be seen in the ink-bottle; the movement simultaneously designs areas of white paper inside and outside the disciplined pen-strokes.) But the logic of this related inked stroke and white paper is not that of conceptual, rational thought. It is rather an organic interrelating of physical sensations (involving visual, kinetic, and tactual imagery, but also imagery of balance, lightness or weight, speed of movement, and sensations even of pain and pleasure). In addition there are psychic impulses, complex associations of feeling-states, and but partially formed suggestions of significance, most of which hover near the threshold of consciousness, all endowing the designs with near-symbolic meanings, and throwing over the forms a mysterious aura of glamour and fascination. Because of these irrational, non-verbal qualities, individuals may differ sharply in their preferences for alphabets, and agree to assign the differences to mere dissimilarities in personal taste. Such a conclusion is the last resort of a confused, if not intolerant, mind. To the perceptive eye, an alphabet is quite as complex as any individual's personality, but an alphabet is less changeable. (However, notice the many kinds of Italic.)

Letter design, then, fuses an implicit meaning of its own with the explicit, or semantic, meaning of the text which is inscribed. The two become identical, as a great actor's interpretation of the character of Macbeth would be identical with that character as we watch the play. When we are caught up in the experience of the play, we should not be conscious of *this* Macbeth as compared with another, nor should we be aware of so-and-so as an *actor* we are watching. An incompetent actor gets between us and Macbeth, as bad letter-design stands between the reader and the text. The implicit and explicit meanings clash.

At first glance, any calligraphy will call attention to itself by the mere fact of its not being dull and hence transparent. In the Renaissance, beautiful writing would not have produced the visual shock which it imparts today. None the less, as one becomes acquainted with a page of calligraphy, its implicit and explicit meanings should fuse, the awareness of significance becoming immediate and incandescent.

The beginning student would probably have no comprehension of the meaning of these observations. He is totally absorbed in the joys and difficulties of mastering such technicalities as pen-hold, scale, letter-slope, letter-width, pen-angle, and the sequence and direction of pen-strokes. But at the beginning he should heed the advice to acquire a feather touch, and hints can be given of its extreme importance to his advanced work.

I should like in the following pages to note some of the teaching techniques and lecture material used to advance the student's awareness of the tactual-kinetic aspects of writing.

For the beginning writer, however, the movements absorb his attention, and he usually ignores the problem of touch by writing with a uniform and excessive degree of pressure. He tends to hold the pen with a clutch that is almost desperate and bears down on the paper in the illusion that force will give him more control over the pen. There are exercises possible that will counteract this disregard of the proper touch, but the problem is still a serious one for beginning writers. If the heel of the hand presses too hard upon the table, the hand will not move freely to the right; hence *f*'s will be turned into tapered strokes and the letters will be too closely spaced. Repeated demonstration and discussion are necessary.

After the student has gained some skill in the careful formation of each letter—and has learned to make diagonal joins—he finds himself upon a plateau; he seems unable to acquire greater speed or any degree of fluency.

At this stage in his learning he lacks confidence in his ability, for his eye is so sharply critical of each pen-stroke that his hand remains nervously tight. The teacher asks the student to write an alphabet-sentence with his eyes closed. The lines will slant crazily and two-stroke letters will have wide gaps between the parts, but the letters will usually have better form. Most important, however, is the unexpected improvement in rhythmical flow of stroke. Finding that he can trust the kinetic imagery within his hand, he is less likely to cramp. Further exercises in 'blind' writing and in writing with peripheral vision only to guide his hand, will increase his self-confidence. He can even learn to write the word 'deed' with eyes closed and with no gaps within the letters. Only by perfecting the kinetic image in hand and wrist can he write with ease or with any degree of grace.

Before introducing the class to free rhythmical writing, it seems necessary to increase the student's awareness of his tactual sensations. Without a delicate and sensitive touch there is little likelihood that the student will be able to write with vital rhythmical movements.

It is necessary that most students spend some time learning to write with a regular, almost metronomic, rhythm before attempting freer rhythmical movements. It may be a necessary step if one is to make certain that the necessary, sensitive tactual sensations will be experienced. Without them, no free rhythm is possible.

However complex or simple the rhythm, it is necessary that contrasting elements be repeated with a degree of regularity. The contrast between the thick stems of down-strokes and the thin hairlines provide four pairs of contrasting elements to experience rhythmically: (1) they contrast visually; (2) they contrast in the amount of friction felt in the fingers; (3) in the slight degrees of pressure involved (little in the thicks and almost none in the hairlines); and (4) they contrast in slower movement in the thicker strokes and swift movement in the hairlines. In writing the word *minimum* the student can experience virtually a perfectly metronomic beat. The introduction of words, which include letters having ascenders and descenders, will vary the rhythm considerably. The gradations of width, pressure, and friction involved in writing entrances and exits, elliptical shoulders, the crossings of *f* and *t*, and dotting of *i* and *j*, etc., are not difficult to incorporate into rhythmical movement, although it probably needs to be demonstrated. If this rhythm is kept going from line to line down the page, a certain momentum will be developed, which will produce a greater ease in writing.

This metronomic writing I regard as only an exercise and do not recommend that it be made habitual, although I have observed a few rare amateurs and professionals who write an informal, personal script in this monotonously regular beat. I use this exercise only as a preparation for freer rhythmical writing, and value it especially for its emphasis on the student's acquiring an increased awareness of the tactual sensation of writing. We are concerned here with formal writing, not with personal rapid handwriting, which usually proceeds in fits and starts, according to the flow of ideas.

A wide variety of exercises can be presented to intensify the student's awareness of vital movement involving touch. I recommend drawing exercises on 'gesture' from Kimon Nicolaides' *The Natural Way to Draw*. Films on modern dance and time-lapse films on plant growth are of value if the student, without glancing at his pad of paper, attempts to capture abstractly, the flow of movement.

Before mentioning any of the other exercises useful in developing skill in rhythmical writing, I should mention the lecture material which precedes this work. Intelligent students enjoy knowing something about the implications of the work they are doing. Ideas and attitudes drawn from the history of the arts may or may not have any immediate effect on the manual skills; but if they inspire ideas and enthusiasms, the work will ultimately benefit. This is not for students who want only quick how-to-do-it information on handwriting, with 'no nonsense' taking up their valuable time. Anyhow, the extreme pragmatists will probably prefer scrawl and typewriters.

The meaning of the concept of movement in the visual arts is so purely non-verbal that it is most difficult to define. Hsieh Ho, in about A.D. 500, attributes the movement to the activity of spirit. St Thomas Aquinas says that the artist imitates nature in its *mode of operation*. Nothing is said here of imitating superficial appearances. Dr Coomaraswamy in his *Transformation of Nature into Art* quotes a lyrical passage from a tenth-century Chinese critic, who wrote that the oriental painter prefers wild animals as subjects and would attempt to capture 'the gallant splendour of their stride. This he would do and no more.' Medieval and oriental painting tend to be calligraphic, eschewing descriptive detail for vital linear movement.

In spite of Bernard Berenson's preference for painting of the Italian Renaissance, he 'equated movement with quality' in a work of art. The value he placed on movement was based, not on a closely reasoned argument leading from basic aesthetic principles, but on a sudden experience of direct visual awareness. He relates in his *Aesthetics and History* that after years of familiarity with art—he had already written two books—he was approaching the façade of San Pietro outside Spoleto one morning and, as he gazed at the leafy scrolls carved on the door jamb, 'suddenly stem, tendril, and foliage became alive, and, in becoming alive, made me feel as if I had emerged into the light after long groping in the darkness of an initiation. I felt as one illumined, and beheld a world where every outline, every edge, and every surface was in a living relation to me, and not, as hitherto, in a merely cognitive one. Since that morning, nothing visible has been indifferent or even dull. Everywhere I feel the ideated pulsation of vitality, I mean energy and radiance....' Berenson sees this quality of movement as constituting the difference between *forms*, which are vital, and mere *shapes*, which are lifeless and diagrammatic. One might see here a criterion for distinguishing between truly calligraphic writing and the coldly perfect yet sterile copies of the model.

Apparently Berenson never attempted to discover if there was a literature devoted to this phenomenon of movement. In fact he wrote: 'I am not competent to deal with the problem, and, having read little philosophy, I do not know whether it has been dealt with.' One can understand the reluctance of an art critic to wander into unfamiliar fields in search of explanations or theories in metaphysics, aesthetics, or depth psychology. Nevertheless, among art students today, Hsieh Ho's six canons are well known. Living during the Southern Ch'i dynasty (A.D. 479–502), this painter and critic is considered 'the first systematic writer on art'. Dr Chiang Yee, Vernon Blake, Laurence Binyon, Mai-mai Sze, Sheldon Cheney, Ananda K. Coomaraswamy, Kuo Hsi and Arthur Waley are among the many who have written in our time about Hsieh Ho's penetrating first canon of painting. It is variously referred to as the principle of 'spirit resonance', 'rhythmical vitality', 'spiritual rhythm', 'life movement', etc. See Fig. 58, where the Chinese characters are reproduced. They

Fig. 58. Chinese characters:
'Chi'i yun sheng tung', written
by Professor Chen Bong Wai.

were written especially for this essay by my friend Professor Chen Bong Wai. The four Chinese characters read 'Ch'i yun sheng tung'. *Ch'i*, 'Heavenly Breath', is composed of a vertical cross with one grain of rice or of other cereals in each of the four quarters. Above the 'wrapping up' stroke are three strokes which are the vapour, spirit, or breath of these symbols of Heaven's bounty when they are sacrificed. This Heavenly Breath can be equated with the Hebrew *Ruach*, the spirit of God which *moved*, *brooded* or *hovered* over the face of the waters in the beginning of creation. In Sanskrit this *Breath* is *Prana*; in Greek, *Pneuma*; in Latin, *Spiritus*. It is usually regarded as imminent throughout the cosmos, as well as transcendent.

The second Chinese character is based on a representation of cowrie shells on the right and, beside it, a mouth with sounds issuing above it. Together, they are read *yun*, and can be translated as 'resonance', 'vibrations' or 'rhythm'.

The third character is recognizable as a young plant growing up out of the ground, which is represented by the long horizontal brush stroke at the base. It is called *sheng*, and is translated as 'life'.

The bottom character presents a sinew or muscle (at the right) signifying 'force'. At the left is the sign for 'early', 'dawn', or 'east'—the sun part-way up a tree. Here the *dawn* character signifies that the force is of great significance, and the two are read as *tung*, which can be translated as 'movement'.

The four characters can be read: 'Heaven's Breath, moving rhythmically, produces life-movement.' Other translations are 'operation of the spirit of life-movement'; 'rhythmic vitality, or spiritual rhythm expressed in the movement of life'; 'life movement through the rhythm of things'. A more literal translation could be: 'Heavenly Breath's rhythm vitalizes movement.'

One may object that this sounds rather mystical, but then Berenson felt that his revelation at Spoleto was rather close to a mystical experience.

Blasé as we may be, we still speak of calligraphy in the traditional way as being *spirited*, *vital*, and *lively*—words which refer to the profoundly mysterious quality of movement.

Jacques Maritain (*Creative Intuition in Art and Poetry*) quotes Hsieh Ho and, in commenting on the first principles, says that, if the Chinese artist makes painting a branch of calligraphy, 'it is because the very vigour and alertness of these *touches* of the brush express the *movement* of life perceived in things' (the italics are mine). He could be writing of our Occidental calligraphy.

'Movement involving touch' can take us far afield. But no matter how far one pursues the subject, the explanation of what it is and the understanding of how it operates is always just beyond our grasp, as if we were racing toward a rainbow.

Notes on Movement involving Touch

We shall never find formulae or recipes for producing truly calligraphic movement involving touch. But the study has its value, even if it only makes us more perceptive of excellent work when we see it. If, as we study it, we can learn to 'make the pen begin moving all over again', as the Chinese advise, we may learn something that will improve our own pen-movements. But the most important result these studies could have would be to make us more intensely aware at all times of every aspect of our act of writing. Sometime the *right* relation of movements involving the touch of the pen may open our eyes to the inner meaning of the word 'calligraphy'.

JOHN DREYFUS

Emery Walker: A Victorian Champion of Chancery Italic

Appreciation of sixteenth-century humanistic scripts 'began many years ago', as Alfred Fairbank reminded us in his introduction to *Renaissance Handwriting* (1960). His paragraphs on 'The Contemporary Revival of Italic Handwriting' mention a volume owned in the 'seventies of the last century by William Morris and sold after his death by Sotheby's, who catalogued it as containing Arrighi's *Operina* (Rome, 1525) and *Il modo de temperare le Penne* (Rome, 1523); G. A. Tagliente's *Lo presente libro insegna la vera arte delo excellente scrivere* (Venice, 1525); and Sigismundo Fanti's *Thesauro de Scrittori* (Rome, 1525), all four works bound together in old red morocco. Fairbank also reported that manuscript books written by Morris in Italic were displayed at the first exhibition of the Arts and Crafts Exhibition Society in 1888. But we must be grateful to Oscar Wilde for reporting a little-known incident at the same exhibition, which may surprise and delight Fairbank—as well as other enthusiasts for the italic hand.

Writing in *The Pall Mall Gazette* for 16 November 1888, Wilde gave a lively account of a lecture on 'Letterpress Printing and Illustration' delivered the previous evening at the New Gallery in London. He described how a photographic projection of a page from Arrighi's writing book 'was greeted with a spontaneous round of applause' from the large and attentive audience. Wilde added that 'the lecturer made some excellent suggestions about modern copy-books and avoiding slanting hand-writing', and he singled out the lecturer himself for special praise. 'Mr Walker's explanations were as clear and simple as his suggestions were admirable...[He] has the keen artistic instinct that comes of actually working in the art of which he spoke. His remarks about the pictorial character of modern illustration were well-timed, and we hope some of the publishers in the audience will take them to heart.'

John Dreyfus

After the lecture, the New Gallery stayed open until 11 p.m. to give the audience an opportunity to go round the exhibition. Never before had the crafts of metal-work, plaster-work, dyeing and weaving, calligraphy, printing and bookbinding been displayed on equal terms with the fine arts of painting, sculpture and architecture. One exhibit of book illustration must have given special satisfaction to Oscar Wilde, a headpiece for 'The Remarkable Rocket', one of the fairy stories in his recently published book, *The Happy Prince*. Wilde had suggested the exact composition of this headpiece to G. P. Jacomb Hood, whose design had then been reproduced by the Typographic Etching Company. This firm provides a link between Wilde and the lecturer, for Walker had gained his first knowledge of the printing trade while working at the Typographic Etching Company under the guidance of its founder, Alfred Dawson.

Walker's experience of presswork and process engraving were both derived from Dawson, who also taught him to draw. As a boy, Walker had read most of the books in his father's house. He soon began to rummage through the penny and twopenny boxes outside booksellers' shops, and acquired the habit of buying anything which drew his attention, and for which he had the necessary pence. About the age of 13, he came across an elementary book on bibliography, from which he learned for the first time something about the invention of printing and the names of eminent printers. With this knowledge, he bought as many examples of their work as he could afford. He also made extensive use of the British Museum, where he studied both printed books and manuscripts. In 1883, he left the Typographic Etching Company to establish the firm of Walker and Boutall, where he undertook letter design, map printing, engraving and the photographing of works of art.

When the Art Workers Guild, led by Walter Crane, formed a committee to organize an exhibition of works of art under conditions similar to those which had hitherto existed only for the fine arts, Walker was invited to join the committee. The exhibition programme included a series of five lectures, in which members were to demonstrate the possibilities and limitations of their crafts. Names of most of the lecturers were easily agreed, but when it came to printing, Walker was found to be the only committee member with some knowledge of the craft. He was, however, unused to speaking in public, and only agreed to deliver the lecture at the insistence of his friend, T. J. Cobden-Sanderson, who was to give a lecture in the same series on 'The Beauties of Bookbinding'.

With little confidence in his powers as a speaker, Walker decided to illustrate his lecture with photographic lantern slides, which were still quite a novelty at that period. The expense of making nearly thirty slides did not deter him, for he had at his disposal the photographic resources of his own firm. Yet he can scarcely have anticipated the effect which the sight of his enlarged projections were to have on his distinguished audience. Arrighi's Italic drew the applause, but Morris was so inspired by the huge enlargements of early printing types that he later obtained large photographic prints from Walker (a duplicate set is still preserved in the St Bride Foundation Institute). These prints were closely examined when Morris designed his own types for the Kelmscott Press. Not only was Walker the inspiration of this venture— he remained until Morris's death his devoted friend and adviser. The two men were neighbours in Hammersmith and had been friends for four or five years before the 1888 lecture. The story of their collaboration has been told in several printed accounts of the Kelmscott Press, but Walker's part in creating the first chancery italic type of the twentieth century has so far escaped more than a passing mention, and it is to this achievement that I will now turn.

Walker's Italic, like the Kelmscott types, had its origin in his 1888 lecture. He repeated that lecture many times with additions and improvements. A version entitled 'The Art of Printing' delivered on 30 January 1890 was reported at length in *The British and Colonial Printer and Stationer*. Walker laid emphasis on the dependence of type design upon calligraphy. When he showed a slide of Livy's *History of Rome*, printed in 1469 by Sweynheym and Pannartz, he commented upon a large initial letter added to it by an illuminator. Italian writing of this period, he declared, was so beautiful and its connection with contemporary type so intimate that he hoped to emphasize the point by showing other slides. These included one page set in Italic from an Aldine edition of Cicero's Letters, and two pages from Arrighi's writing book of 1523 in which, said Walker, was seen in perfection the living standard of beautiful letters of which he spoke. 'With letters like these before him, it was almost impossible for a punchcutter to produce types without grace,' he declared. Some ten or fifteen years later, this assertion was put to the test, when Walker provided the eminent punchcutter, Edward Prince, with drawings based on a sixteenth-century chancery italic for use as a model in cutting a new italic for the Cranach Press, Graf Harry Kessler's private press in Weimar.

Kessler was a man of great fortune, intelligence, taste and charm. Born in Paris of a German-Swiss father and an Irish mother, he had been sent to Clifton College before completing his education at Bonn and Leipzig. He visited England in 1904 for the express purpose of obtaining Walker's advice on the design of books to be published by the Insel Verlag. Through Walker he met many leaders of the Arts and Crafts Movement, including Edward Johnston and Eric Gill, both of whom drew title pages for several Insel Verlag books. By 1904, Walker enjoyed a reputation in

Germany as well as in England, for he had supervised the design and manufacture of all the types used by England's leading private presses—Kelmscott, Doves and Ashendene. Punches for these types had been cut under Walker's guidance by Prince, who had worked as a freelance since 1883, after an apprenticeship in the 1860's to another great punchcutter, Fred Tarrant.

At Kessler's request, Walker undertook to produce a roman and an italic type for use at the Cranach Press; once again Walker engaged Prince to cut the punches. The Roman was to be based on the type used by Jenson at Venice in 1470 (which has also been the model for the Doves Press type, drawn in Walker's studio). The accompanying Italic was to be based on a type used in Tagliente's writing book of 1525—one of the four writing books, bound together in the old red morocco volume owned by William Morris, which Walker purchased for presentation to May Morris after the sale at Sotheby's. Walker photographed the cleanest page of Tagliente's italic in that volume, and then provided his draughtsman with enlarged bleach-out prints, upon which the letters were redrawn in ink. The success of this method depended upon the clarity of the original and on the understanding of the draughtsman, coupled with the expertise of the punchcutter. Because the Italic was intended for use as a secondary type with the Jenson-based Roman, Tagliente's proportions had to be severely modified by cropping the ascenders and descenders.

Kessler also required a Greek and a black-letter type, for which he persuaded Johnston to provide drawings. In the course of their frequent meetings, Kessler developed a great affection for the calligrapher, and a deep respect for his judgement. He therefore decided to seek Johnston's opinion on the smoke proofs of the italic lower case which Prince had almost completed by the summer of 1912. Kessler was sensitive enough to realize that several of the letters seemed 'to be much wanting in *character*', and after hearing his suspicions confirmed, he persuaded Johnston to explain to Prince the anatomy of the faulty letters. Kessler did not anticipate any difficulties with Prince, who had confessed to him that he had no pretensions to being a *designer* of types, but simply considered himself as 'a craftsman *carrying out* other men's designs'. Johnston gave his explanations in the form of large chalk drawings, some of them sketched out 5 in. high on a roughly textured paper: the outlines were then drawn in by hand, and notes added by Johnston on points of particular importance (see Plate 41).

Despite this outside intervention Walker continued to be responsible for producing the type. He cannot have objected in principle to a calligrapher giving explanations to his punchcutter, for according to a letter written by T. J. Cobden-Sanderson, Walker had himself admitted that 'though it may not be desirable for the calli-

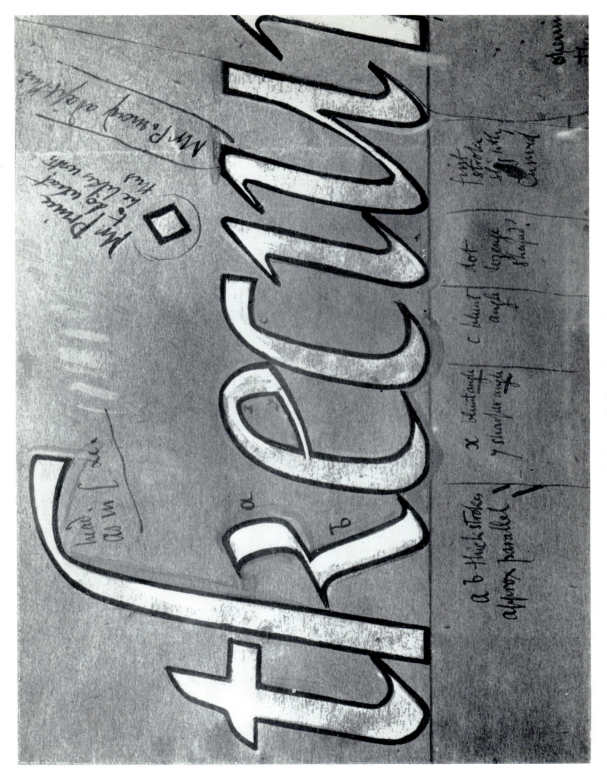

41. Sketch by Edward Johnston for the guidance of Edward Prince: see p. 210.

see p. 210.

4. Dec. 1912. Note: I am working on these proof[s].

co∫ta del temperatore &

della canna da la ban‑

del tuo occhio dali ra∫o

della temperatura della

42 *a*. Portion of the drawing for the Cranach Press Italic prepared under Emery Walker's direction. Reproduced from a photograph formerly in the possession of Edward Johnston, and annotated in his own hand. Note the inconsistent shapes, especially of the four *o*'s in line three.

della temperatura della,

42 *b*. Photographic enlargement made from William Morris's copy of Tagliente's *Lo presente libro insegna la vera arte delo excellente scrivere* (Venice, 1525), shown for comparison with the last line of Walker's redrawing of this passage, reproduced above. Note the more generous ascenders and descenders.

radila con la∫co∫ta del temperptore
ione ∫a mita della canna da la ban‑
on lo fauore del tuo occhio dali ra∫o
o alla penna della temperptura della
Mr Johnston's letters underlined

42 *c*.

A reduced print of the photograph shown as (*a*) above, on which the underscored letters are smoke proofs of punches, cut by Edward Prince in accordance with Edward Johnston's designs and instructions. Reproduced from a photograph formerly in Johnston's possession, and reduced to correspond with the actual size of the Cranach Press Italic.

[To face p. 211]

graphist to be a student or *practitioner* in punchcutting, it *is* desirable that the punch-cutter should be a student of calligraphy'. Unfortunately Prince had passed the age of 65 when Johnston began to teach him the finer points of calligraphy. Moreover his patience, and that of Walker, were both sorely tried by the never-ending criticisms made by both Kessler and Johnston. An agonizingly protracted correspondence developed between Kessler, Johnston, Prince and Walker. Although Kessler was confident that Walker's design could be basically retained by Johnston 'while thoroughly correcting and sharpening (vivifying, brisking up) all the details', Johnston was not the man for such a compromise solution. By the summer of 1913, a new set of drawings for the lower case had been completed by Johnston, and the Walker model was finally abandoned. Prince began to engrave a new set of punches, but work was interrupted by the outbreak of war; the set was unfinished when he died in 1923. The punches were finally completed in 1931 by G. T. Friend, who also cut a new set of capitals in accordance with Johnston's designs.

It must be admitted that Walker and his draughtsman failed to capture with pen and ink the vigour of the original types used by Tagliente (Plate 42). Their task was not made easy by the quality of the photographic enlargement on which they worked: the original pages had not been crisply printed, so outlines became fuzzy in enlargement. Prince inevitably failed to distil from these redrawn letters the essential character of Tagliente's design, while Kessler's insistence upon the Italic aligning with Jenson's Roman robbed it of its rightful proportions by cropping the ascenders and descenders. Nevertheless, credit must be given to Walker for his pioneer contribution in reviving chancery Italic in the twentieth century. I offer this paper as an appropriate tribute to Alfred Fairbank who has also enriched twentieth-century typography by a handsome chancery Italic of his own design.

The illustrations show photographs now preserved with the Kessler–Johnston correspondence at the University Printing House in Cambridge (also the repository for the Cranach Press punches). I am indebted to the University Printer, Brooke Crutchley, C.B.E., for permission to reproduce these photographs.

ALEC HAY

Handwriting in Schools

Some years ago a report on handwriting in British schools was published by a well-known pen manufacturing company. This report went further than its title would indicate: for the survey, on which the conclusions were based, was carried out not only in schools but among authors who, the report naïvely adds, 'are naturally interested in handwriting', and personnel directors. As for authors, one remembers with delight the beautifully clear and orderly MSS. of John Galsworthy, who founded a trust to award prizes for handwriting in London schools, a trust maintained for some years by his widow but now, unhappily, exhausted. But I recall also a postcard from Cambridge, sent by a distinguished novelist after a day spent with me in London, intimating, as far as I could decipher it, that he had lost his wits as we crossed Westminster Bridge. Fortunately, it turned out to be only his hat, and even that he did not lose in my company.

Of personnel directors I know very little and, indeed, very few. They are, I take it, those whose signatures appear at the foot of their letters over their names in typescript without which, so frequently, the recipient would not recognise his correspondent.

The replies to the questionnaire from which the report was drawn up made it clear that there had been a serious decline in standards of handwriting. Regrettably, it gave no indication of the earlier standards, and thus one is left wondering about a decline from what. The survey was conducted among 1402 schools, classified as:

255 Convent Boarding Schools   192 Boys' Public Schools
761 Grammar Schools   194 Girls' Public Schools

representing some 17,000 teachers all over the country, which is approximately the number of teachers in London, and 750,000 pupils, rather larger than the number in London primary and secondary schools.

213

One could have wished for a more exact classification of these schools. The number listed as Public Schools seems to suggest an extent of fee-paying establishments over-generous, even in this age when one is assured forcefully but ungrammatically that 'you never had it so good'. However, there it is, a report which tells you that, in the opinion of some, the decline started well before the beginning of the outbreak of war in 1939; but there is also a strong body of opinion that the real rot set in rather more than a decade ago, since the dawn of our material prosperity. No inquiry from the authors reached me in my capacity as the then Chief Inspector of Schools in London nor, as far as I know, was the head of any London school consulted. Thus it was, understandably, that I read later with a slightly startled glow of satisfaction that 'the L.C.C. seems to be far more active in this field than any other Local Education Authority and has arranged for handwriting lessons to be given in a number of secondary schools'. This appears to be a reference, not closely inquired into, to classes for teachers conducted in school time by Mr Fairbank following his retirement from the Admiralty. Already these classes have given proof of their inestimable value to the cause of handwriting in schools. From them there flows back into schools a stream of teachers, keen, convinced and equipped to bring about a much-needed reformation. By this time, Mr Fairbank must have had at least 400 teachers as his pupils.

For some years it was my unfortunate lot to examine in detail applications from teachers in London for a place on what is called the Council's Promotion List, a list of aspirants approved as suitable for Headships of Primary Schools within the London County Council area. As the years went by I noticed an increasing number of forms filled up in italic handwriting and, whilst I was in duty bound to be as impartial and balanced in judgement as such wisdom as God has given me permits, I confess that a neat, legible, even beautifully filled up form disposed me to the thought that here was someone with what the Society of Friends calls a 'concern' for handwriting, a concern which will doubtless extend to their teaching of it to young children. 'O si sic omnes!' If only this concern were universal, those of us who worry about handwriting in schools would find our worries rapidly vanishing.

A valuable and stimulating encouragement has come of late years from the inclusion in the Ministry's publication *Primary Education* (H.M.S.O. 1959) of a chapter all to itself on Handwriting, deriving, one hopes, from the courses conducted by Mr Fairbank for the ministry whilst he was still a civil servant. The chapter explains the ministry's deep concern to give handwriting once more its proper dignity as the most universal of all crafts.

If teachers would adopt and apply the principles so clearly stated in this chapter, the problem of teaching handwriting in primary schools would be solved. The first need is for the right start. Mr Fairbank in his *Handwriting Manual* provides a lower-case alphabet, by the use of which children learn ligatures from the beginning. All teachers will agree that this is what is wanted at this early stage. The writing of single letters, isolated, without joins, gives the young child the idea that the individual letter is the most important shape he is required to make, whereas the whole purpose of this elementary training (parallel with the teaching of reading) is to bring the pupils to an understanding and correct transcription of whole words and, as rapidly as possible, to progress to phrases and complete sentences. Mr Fairbank's various publications are designed to ensure this progress.

For many years a series called *Beacon Reading* has been in almost universal use in infants' schools. Mr Fairbank has supplied its counterpart in the series *Beacon Writing*. It is to be hoped that *Beacon Writing* will be adopted by teachers of young children as widely as *Beacon Reading* was in its day. Such happy adoption would ensure the reformation and marked improvement in the handwriting of British children within a very few years.

Some of those who have studied the pedagogy of handwriting would advocate the need for teaching it twice during school life; once in childhood and again in adolescence. For schools admitting older children, many of them probably brought up on a bewildering variety of writing styles, Mr Fairbank's *Italic Handwriting Cards* provide the opportunity for teaching a hand at once simple, easy to acquire and lovely, one of which children would be proud and from which their school would gain an enviable reputation. Italic certainly makes a strong appeal to the older pupil who often desires a new stimulus in the adolescent period. There is evidence, too, of Italic as a form of therapy for older pupils otherwise regarded as backward. Boys and girls once having acquired enough skill to set down a page of fair script, pleasing to them and their teachers, have developed a sense of attainment and been known to show unexpected progress in other studies.

These Handwriting Cards now published by Dryad, were first known as the *Barking Handwriting Cards*. They were compiled at the request of the late Joseph Compton, at the time Education Officer for the Borough of Barking. Subsequently, he held a similar appointment in the Borough of Ealing and for some years was Chairman of the Executive Committee of the Society for Italic Handwriting. Himself an accomplished scribe, his interest in Italic was maintained over many years, and his encouragement of the use of the style in the schools of Ealing enabled at least one primary school there to reach a standard of clarity, beauty and speed attained only elsewhere by the young writers attending Lord Cholmondeley's school in Cheshire. Joseph Compton occupies an honoured place on the roll of those who have sought, and still seek, to improve the quality of handwriting in schools everywhere.

Unhappily, in countless schools for infants (ages 5–7) the style, if it can be called that, known as 'print-script' is in widespread use. Some teachers defend print-script on the ground that it enables children to recognize more readily the symbols on the printed page. Rather do I think that if children are revealing themselves as seriously slow readers, the causes lie much deeper than in the difference between round, up-right letter-shapes and their narrower, slightly sloping counterparts, and an educational psychologist should be consulted. There is no confusion here: young children regard them as variations of the same alphabet. Infants have been known to dis-tinguish between 'writing' and 'printing', and no one would say they are very far wrong in doing so. Be that as it may, any fears a teacher may have that children's ability to read the printed word may be hindered because they do not print, but write, are groundless. From my own observations in the few, the very few, infants' schools where children write and do not print from the start, it would certainly seem that their power to recognize, within the range of accepted variations of the Roman alphabet, is far greater than most teachers of infants admit. An inspection of the handwriting of children attending the Cholmondeley School at Malpas in Cheshire, where they are taught to write from the start, demonstrates the fallacy of the print-script argument.

I wish the colleges training students for service in infants' and junior schools would follow the lead given by the Brighton College of Arts and Crafts, where Mr Fairbank has conducted courses in Italic with the result that young teachers from this college start with both knowledge and convictions about handwriting, the teaching of which becomes one of their major tasks when they begin duty in schools. The Brighton students acquire a hand not only legible but a delight to look at: they can also write on the blackboard, that first of all visual aids. And it cannot be said that this latter accomplishment is universal among Training College students starting their first teaching job.

There are instances of children learning to write in the infants' school who, on passing to the junior department, are taught a fresh style or who, even in different classes of the junior school, are compelled to follow different styles with successive teachers. What may be generally accepted as a good model of handwriting may be discouraged in the upper part of the primary school or in the secondary school by teachers whose own preference is for another style. The bewilderment of the child who cannot reconcile these different approaches is readily understandable.

Handwriting in Schools

The position would be very different if more uniformity and consistency prevailed throughout the schools; for handwriting must be the responsibility of a team not only within one school but, because of inter-school transfers, within a whole area.

The schools must select the best models upon which to base their work together with the tools, materials and exercises best calculated to assist children to develop the most satisfactory hand. They must ensure that the child can ultimately write a legible, fluent hand and one in which clarity and beauty are not lost when rapidly written.

From William Morris onwards, many have given care and thought to the study of handwriting, and there are now many reliable books of reference available. Of particular value are the records and research of such masters as Edward Johnston, Graily Hewitt and Alfred Fairbank. Each examined the subject from the historical, the aesthetic and the technical points of view, and the influence of their teaching is seen, if somewhat sporadically, in many widely differing schools.

The first task is for the teachers to select a model, for which the choice is wide, from the earlier Roman and Carolingian books, the missals which came from the *scriptoria* scattered across Europe in the Middle Ages, to the formal and informal hands of the Renaissance and later so-called commercial hands used in the eighteenth and nineteenth centuries.

The tradition of the copperplate, civil service hands dies hard. Many teachers were taught these hands, and it is obviously easier to teach what one has practised from childhood than to adopt a new method of writing in later years.

There is a general feeling that commerce is attached to this tradition, but it is improbable that Wilfrid Blunt's pupils at Eton, Robin Treffgarne's at Harrow and Dom Patrick Barry's at Ampleforth, who write so well in the style they have been taught, will find their writing unacceptable in industry or the professions.

A few schools are fortunate in having for competition among them an annual prize for writing given by Lord Cholmondeley. His advocacy and powerful support have, for many years, been the chief means of keeping active the cause of reform, and the Society for Italic Handwriting, that small but by no means still voice, is privileged and honoured to have Lord Cholmondeley as its President.

It has been objected that the reformed hands produce a dead uniformity. That is not true: just as in learning to write from the older copy-books, uniformity was aimed at in the earlier stages, but in course of time the individual developed mannerisms which were personal to him, so a similar development of individual characteristics follows with the reformed hands. This reservation, however, ought to be made; that deterioration cannot be so chronic with the reformed hands as it is, with such exasperating consequences, with the old. Further, a teacher engaged to instruct the whole of the lower half of a large secondary mixed school in London in writing Italic has something to say about this supposed danger of monotonous and drab uniformity in handwriting. He reports that, after three months of lessons, he can very readily pick out any six samples of his pupils' writing and say who the writer is. So much for these groundless charges.

Many Principals of Teacher Training Colleges would like to include Handwriting in the course but lack of time is pleaded, as it is in most secondary schools. Too many subjects are pursuing too few hours. Yet the drop in standards of legibility has produced a situation so serious that in 1959 the Joint Matriculation Board of the Northern Universities took the unusual course of issuing a letter with the publication of the results, in which reference was made to the negligent and slipshod way in which many candidates wrote. The letter went on: 'A large number, possibly an increasing proportion, do not appear to think it worth while considering the effect on an examiner of handwriting which is frequently illegible. Examiners comment on this and so do those who later come in contact with the candidates after they leave school in universities and colleges, in industry and the professions. The Board is, therefore, drawing the attention of its Panels of examiners to the need for them to use the powers they already have to penalise candidates for bad presentation and to ask them to consider whether their powers could be increased.' More specific is Regulation 14 of the Southern Universities Board, which ordains that candidates must present scripts in which the writing is clear and legible. Badly written scripts will be referred to a panel, which has power to fail a candidate. The situation raises issues, which cannot be baulked by parent or teacher. If a child is not given proper instruction in handwriting, there is the possibility of his failing a vital examination in his career because of this neglect. One step towards awareness of the importance of handwriting in schools has been taken in the London area. There, Her Majesty's Inspectors now include in their reports a reference to the handwriting as observed in the school generally, and the Inspectorate of the London County Council has undertaken to do the same in its reports.

The current situation is not rosy, but the neglect of past years is being recognized. There is probably more genuine interest in handwriting in schools today than at any time during the past twenty-five years, thanks, very largely, to the advocacy and effort of Alfred Fairbank, to whom we owe a large debt, not only for giving practical direction, but for his scholarly and fascinating historical research and study.

Strenuous efforts are needed to guide this new interest into productive channels. The rewards to the nation culturally will be large: in financial terms they will be inestimable, and the Post Office will no longer need to spend money on notices in newspapers appealing for the clear addressing of mail. Signs of a revival of interest in handwriting can be discerned in the scripts, based on italic forms, now seen in many advertisements.

Whether we like it or not the pressure of life today does tell heavily against good handwriting. Most of us are called upon to write too much and too quickly: we thus corrupt the shape of our writing and become accustomed to low standards. But it remains as true now, as it was nearly 2000 years ago, when Quintilian wrote that 'men of quality are in the wrong to undervalue, as they so often do, the practice of a fair and quick hand, for it is no immaterial accomplishment'.

THE SPREAD OF MODERN ITALIC

GEOFFREY TILLOTSON

Italic Revival: Early Days

The excuse for publishing my recollections is that they concern the early days of the Italic renaissance, which now lie far in the past, and also that they bring in well-known names, including that of Alfred Fairbank himself.

I often wonder what it must feel like to be Fairbank who knows, and has known for the last forty or fifty years, that whenever he takes a pen in hand he will achieve one further example of perfect lettering. With him there is no categorical difference between the formal and the informal because both are characterized by regularity. It may be that I use the word 'perfection' too glibly, being myself a person who can so seldom achieve any of it. Perhaps Fairbank sees his work as imperfect with a perfection lying beyond it, but if so, then Bach did ! For me, Fairbank is the perfect craftsman. Since 1933 I have received many letters and postcards from him, all of which are masterpieces of penmanship. They are so beautiful that one scarcely cares to read what they are saying—in any event one knows it will be pleasant, coming from him. The plain fact is that they are works of art and so have no message. What we should all like to see are the million minutes he wrote during his career as a civil servant. They must look very beautiful on the smooth duck-egg blue paper[1] amid the surrounding scribble or typescript. For me, beauty of lettering gets in the way of the intellect, and I imagine Fairbank's fellow civil servants unable to attend properly to his animadversions because they could not stop gazing at them. Did he himself, I wonder, modify at least the expression of his meaning so as to use words that gave him most pleasure to shape—as I myself in my young days would prefer 'inquire' to 'ask' so as to try once more to rise to the opportunity to make a worthy *a*, a *a* as lively as a tadpole.

It was quite by accident that I met the italic writing in 1926, but it was the sort of accident that had more chance of happening the longer it was delayed. Even by the late 'twenties, there were perhaps a few score people—many, I suspect, teachers of art—who had been fascinated by the specimen of Italic in Edward Johnston's famous book, and had begun to imitate it. I myself had learned the copperplate alphabet at my village school. Copperplate and all the many kinds of hands that were debased from it, were the only samples of handwriting that could be met with in those days. Nor was there more than a beginning of the reformed alphabet in new founts of type. During the 'twenties there was very little to encourage one to see that copperplate itself was a debasement of a style introduced into England in the sixteenth century and already debased by the seventeenth. Italic script was a means of doing away with the decadence of three centuries.

After learning copperplate I had tossed about from style to style when, having become a grammar school boy, I had left writing lessons behind me. I copied in turn the hands of those schoolmasters who wrote well. I remember how delighted I was when I found that the mistress who taught me Latin made the final minim of the *n*'s and *m*'s descend below the line in a long curve. Having no standards, I applauded this practice, mainly because I had never met it before, and introduced the extravagance into my own chaotic practice.

My introduction to Italic I well recall. It was in the Michaelmas term of 1926. I dropped into the lodgings of a college friend in St John's Street, Oxford, and, waiting for him to appear, I looked, as I was intended to, at the cards and envelopes displayed on his mantelshelf. Among them was an envelope written in Italic. Its elegance was exquisite. To get me firmly on the hook, the opportunity had been taken to link the two letters in the abbreviation for 'saint'—*st.* I gazed and gazed, and knew very well what wealth to me the show had brought.

My friend, Eric Walter White, cannot have given me the envelope or it would be included in my collection, but he did better still—he introduced me to the writer in person, who was Walter Shewring of Corpus Christi College, one of the best classicists among the undergraduates of his day. If I lack the envelope that introduced me to his hand, I have the following, which I received from him a few days later when our meetings and correspondence began:

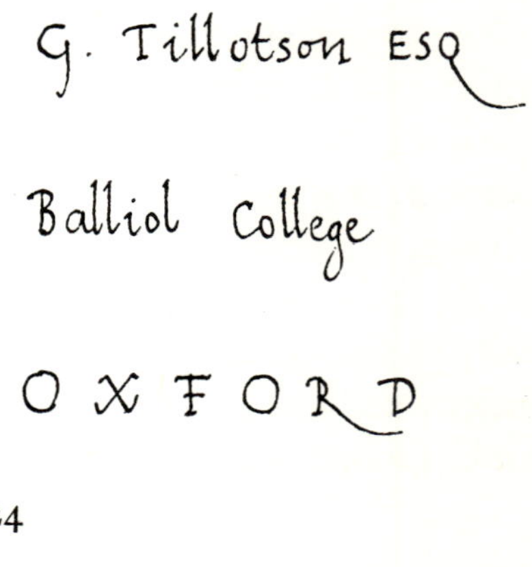

Fig. 59.

A little later came an envelope with the following delightful flounce:

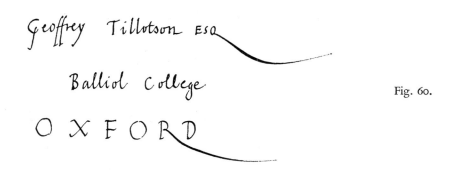

Fig. 60.

I need not try to set out in detail what followed so quickly. I found Shewring not only a writer of Italic himself but the means of my being introduced to the Italic of one or two other people. He was a friend in particular of Stanley Morison. When Morison had lectured on printing at Bristol Grammar School, Shewring, then a schoolboy, had asked him an 'intelligent question', and so had started a correspondence about new type-faces, some of which Shewring, I think, helped Eric Gill, another friend of his, to design. It was about this time that Bridges edited an S.P.E. (Society for Pure English) tract on handwriting, which, as his postcard to me stated, sold out prior to publication, and though reprinted never got into the shops. I borrowed a copy from a library and saw there the hand of Mrs Bridges, whose writing cards of 1896 were still in print, and another fine example of Morison's. (There was also a hand I did not then properly value, that of Mrs Bridges' daughter, Elizabeth Daryush, which showed how good italic writing could be when written fast and free.) Meanwhile I was diligently practising Italic on my own account. The last word on my efforts is that of Morison, whom I had begged to treat my collection as his wastepaper basket, and from whom I got the following kindly snub: 'I like your hand, but I suppose it is just a trifle "studied" at present isn't it?'[2] A further S.P.E. tract appeared on the same topic and reproduced those marvellous five pages of Fairbank's hand, introducing the new italic style in a practical way. He opened my eyes to the way handwriting can be analysed, especially in his demonstration of what might be called 'units of continuity'—those strokes of the pen which, in writing a word, compass a few letters and parts of letters at a stretch. Why I did not write to Fairbank I do not know, but even a voracious novice might well feel that to beg for more than the five pages in the tract would be an impertinence. Accordingly it was he who wrote to me:

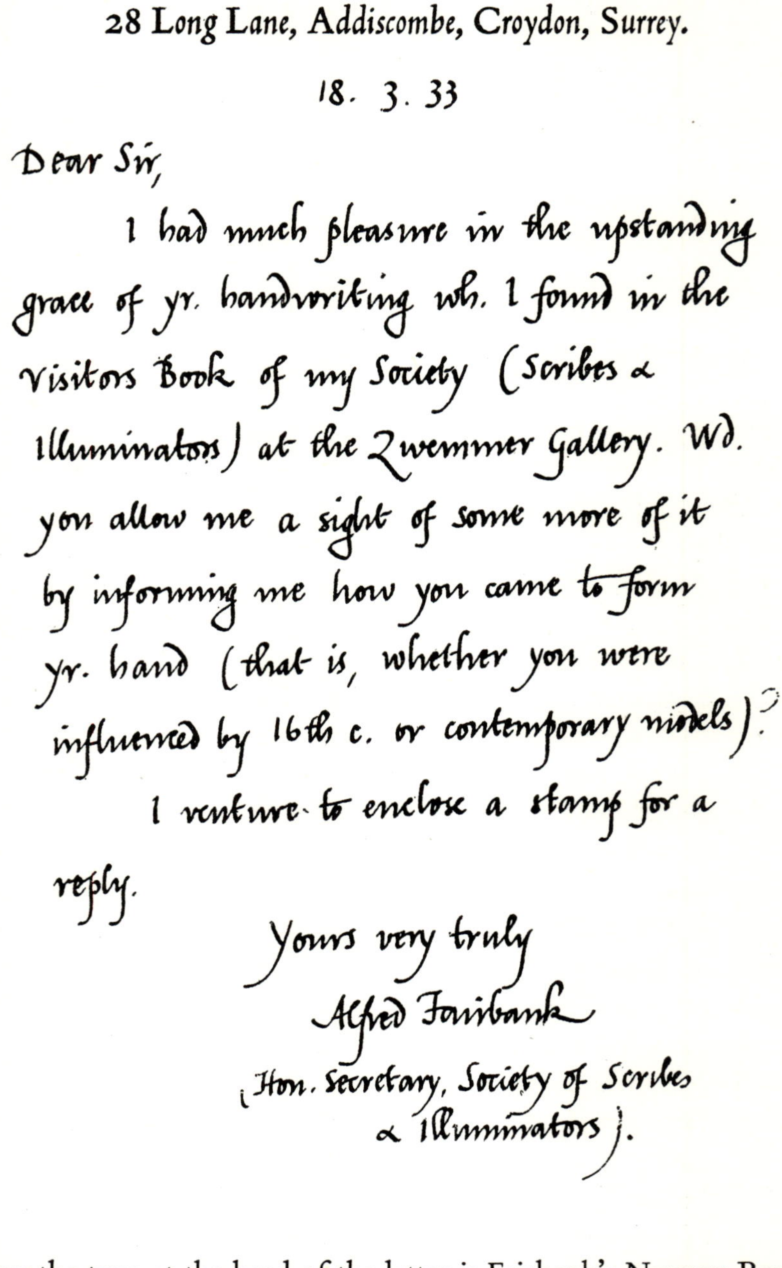

28 Long Lane, Addiscombe, Croydon, Surrey.

18. 3. 33

Dear Sir,

I had much pleasure in the upstanding grace of yr. handwriting wh. I found in the Visitors Book of my Society (Scribes & Illuminators) at the Zwemmer Gallery. Wd.

Fig. 61.

you allow me a sight of some more of it by informing me how you came to form yr. hand (that is, whether you were influenced by 16th c. or contemporary models)?

I venture to enclose a stamp for a reply.

Yours very truly
Alfred Fairbank
(Hon. Secretary, Society of Scribes & Illuminators).

(By the way the type at the head of the letter is Fairbank's Narrow Bembo Italic.)

226

My reply brought the following:

28 Long Lane, Addiscombe, Croydon, Surrey.

21. 3. 33

Dear Mr. Tillotson,

Thank you indeed for yr. letter. I am glad to hear you are doing something to stop the decay of handwriting. There are very few of us interested and the poor taste of the average teacher is a bulwark to defend the impossible copperplate hand. But we may be successful. Already the Education officer of the L.C.C. has taken some action, as you will see in the accompanying copy of an R.S.A Journal (wh. will you please accept?)

I have not seen Mr. Shewring's hand. I wonder how many other italic writers you know who I have not heard of. I shd. like to see yr collection, & I will

Fig. 62.

227

15-2

see what I can find to add to it.

Do you remember R.B. in the S.P.E. tract complained of my "cramping or unkind pen."? Last year Watermans gave me a pen wh. has caused me to put aside all the unkind nibs I had put up with since R.B. reproduced my letter. The pens I recommend in the manual are too broad for me.

I wish I had been able to include yr. hand in the Zwemmer show : when television becomes an educational possibility perhaps we can combine to show how the upstroke shd. be sidled in the making of italic letters. In the meantime I hope we may meet.

Yours sincerely
Alfred Fairbank

His next letter exhibits me in a comic light. But it also marks the entry into our circle of the splendid James Wardrop, whose untimely death twenty years later robbed Renaissance studies of a keen participant:

228

28 Long Lane, Addiscombe, Croydon, Surrey.

17. v. 33

Dear Tillotson,

I hope I may often have the pleasure of exchanging ideas about handwriting with you: you have such sound views: It was very good of you to suggest we shd. do something to awaken America. I was feeling at the time so overwhelmed with work that the very idea seemed threatening & I fear I must have seemed less appreciative of yr. kindness than I was.

Fig. 63.

Enclosed is a list of MSS at the B.M. some of wh. I think wd. give you keen pleasure & all of wh. wd. interest you for one reason or another.

I have written to James Wardrop (at the V. & A. Museum) this evening telling him that I have suggested you shd. get in touch with him.

Yours

Alfred Fairbank

I had already introduced Fairbank to my friend and colleague John Butt, whom I had converted to the practice of Italic. This explains the reference in the first sentence of this next letter:

28 Long Lane, Addiscombe, Croydon, Surrey.

13. X. 33

My dear Tillotson,

It wd. give me great pleasure to meet you both again in the near future. I have no engagements other than Tues. 17th Oct. & Wed. 25th Oct. & I am free each evening from 5 onwards.

Fig. 64.

Will you allow me to suggest this: that I bring James Wardrop with me – on the understanding that we each pay for our own food. This is not 'independence', but a desire to simplify future meetings. Wardrop leaves the V. & A. Museum at 5. If you agree I will find out his vacant dates. I have already suggested to him that we 4 shd. meet – he had agreed.

This wd. constitute the first meeting of the Ascham Society. I suggest the following rules:

(1) That there shall be no rules.

(2) That there shall be no subscription

It wd. be a pretty thing to discuss the bearing of rule (1) or rule (2) in the interstices of time. But perhaps any hiatus in conversation wd. be filled by debating the pronunciation of the Society's title. All mtgs. shd. begin by toasting Q. Elizabeth's glorious memory & influence, & end by deploring the pen-manufacturer's vile goods. Motto: 'All right' in italics.

I have been thinking that very soon we shall have to start a journal, but I can't think of anybody who wd. be fool enough to stand the expense.

Yours

Alfred Fairbank

How long ago it all seems. As Shewring put it in his postcard of the other day: 'My years [in Oxford] seem closer to Jude's Christminster than to the Oxford of to-day', with its evidence before the Franks Commission. Even America has been awakened! Italic is everywhere, and Alfred Fairbank's name a household word.

Reverting to 1926, I can see that the advantage of the italic alphabet was that it gave me a standard by which lettering of all sorts could be analysed. Copperplate also provided a standard, but when I practised copperplate I was too young to see the use of a standard. Italic had another use—it was so beautiful that all other lettering seemed inferior to it. And in 1926 it chimed in with my maturing interests in general. Those were the days when people were turning again to the music of Bach and Scarlatti, which was beginning to be performed on clavichords and harpsichords.

I was as passionate about these instruments as about Italic—but the harpsichords in 1926 were of the true kind, plucked by a quill not by a jack of brutal steel. I think Italic also had the advantage for me of helping me to cut myself off—as some of us tried to do in those days—from the world of commerce and vulgarity!

What was soon borne in upon me was that Italic existed in a wide variety. There were as many sorts of Italic as there were hands to write it. And, in those days, all the hands that wrote it were gifted to write well. Handwriting may well show character and certainly shows personality. It also shows physiology. The power to write well is as much a physical power as anything else. Many people who are painstaking by nature—as their clothes, say, proclaim—are yet quite unable to achieve, with all the will in the world, good handwriting. They cannot form the letters, try as they will. In those days only writers who could write well took up Italic. Nowadays when so many write it, many write it badly. I am more tolerant now of non-italic hands than I was in 1926. There has been such a lot of incompetent italic writing that I prefer the writing of those gifted to use a pen, even though their style is based on the copperplate alphabet, to the writing of those who, with every advantage of the italic style, fail to write it well.

I am grateful to Mr Stanley Morison and Mr Walter Shewring for their allowing me to quote from their letters to me.

NOTES

1 BY EDITOR: *They do. But, alas, most were written on a dismal buff paper. Fairbank's minutes excited the attention of many temporary civil servants who joined the Admiralty during the war and had referred to them the files of the Director of Dockyards, in whose Department he was serving. Among the temporaries were Nigel Abercrombie (now Secretary General of the Arts Council of Great Britain) and myself. A hazard which, in those days, a man interested in reforming his handwriting was obliged to accept, was the inevitable comment that his minutes* were written 'just like that chap Fairbank's'. *Such is the human inability to distinguish between one Chinese and another.*

2 When Mr Morison wrote to me agreeing that I could quote from his letter of 1926, he added the following to his permission: 'It is a fact, too, that I myself began the practice of a "studied" Italic. In my experience a cursive, reasonably current but kept under implicit control, takes time for development.'

PAUL STANDARD

How the Italic Hand came to New York

Alfred Fairbank's name and interests swam into my ken in the mid-'twenties through comments in the London *Mercury* by the late B. H. Newdigate, whose book-production notes must have taught many a reader a new respect for the shapes and uses of letters in both written and printed form. In 1926 and 1927 this respect was deepened by *English Handwriting*, two tracts of the Society for Pure English edited by Robert Bridges. They contained a statement about quality in handwriting as written out by Mr Fairbank, and some specimens of current practice in English. I was thus prepared for the notice in the *Times Literary Supplement* of *A Handwriting Manual* upon its publication in 1932. I ordered a copy from the publishers; and as soon as I had read it, I wrote my thanks in a typewritten letter to the publishers (The Dryad Press, Leicester) and ordered half-a-dozen copies to give away. My dictated letter could now comment upon the manual itself—and, somewhat extraneously, upon the author's new Monotype face, Narrow Bembo Italic. I fervidly deplored this type's lack of popularity, while duly praising the Gregynog Press for its pioneer use of this slim and elegant type. Only when my secretary brought me the typescript did I realize how strongly my enthusiasm had been expressed. Chastened, I added a suggestion to ignore my sermon and just send the books. These arrived promptly and were presented to delighted friends, all of us vowing to acquire the italic hand.

I set to work at once. My special difficulty lay less in managing the shapes with my edged pen than in checking my propensity to speed. This speed factor, inherited from a boyhood exposure to the Palmer Method of Business Writing, was in the end to become an asset; but in the beginning it was a deterrent, inducing distortion and irregularity. I had in my high-school days, of course, lost most of my Palmer script;

what little was left disappeared at Columbia in the scramble to keep up with class-room note-taking. But I kept on with my practice, spurred alike by the Fairbank exercises and the Renaissance facsimiles in his pages.

Some two months rolled by. Then, one Wednesday morning, as I was preparing to set out for the weekly Amherst Club luncheon of the Typophiles, the postman arrived with a small batch of mail, which one of my staff accepted for sorting. In a few moments I saw the lad starting for my office with a smallish square white envelope, his eyes firmly upon it as he proceeded—a degree of concentration un-common for him. I wondered, but said nothing. He too was silent, still studying the envelope before him, and at last, embarrassed, he offered it with the words: 'I've never seen anything like it.'

Neither had I. Addressed to me, it bore British stamps and a Croydon postmark. But my name looked, or perhaps sounded, as if spoken in some distant Renaissance roll-call. I felt as if transported to that age. Carefully I slit open the flap and saw, or heard, a full consort of viols and recorders through lines harmonious in form and placement, and memorably affecting in the friendly message they bore. The author of *A Handwriting Manual* had signed the letter, explaining that my own had lately been forwarded him by the publishers, and he was simply writing to thank a distant correspondent for having brought him rather more appreciation from abroad than he had found at home. I remember wondering, as I kept running the text over and over, whether such a script, had it to convey some deep curse, would not by its gracious shapes extract the sting and hint a remedy. I took the letter out to show to my staff. All fell silent, including the letter's bringer. All were struck by an ex-perience unique in their lives. All watched in silence as, letter open in hand, I left the office for the appointed lunch.

During my ten-minute walk southward down Madison Avenue from 44th to 36th Street and eastward to Lexington Avenue, I kept re-reading the letter. Stopped by a traffic light, I would watch my distracted fellow-pedestrians and wonder if I could not cure their evident anxieties by a sight of the healing medicine I held in my hand: sense, quickly returning, told me I could not. Arrived at the club, some thirty fellow-Typophiles were quickly told of my treasure, and I watched it make the full circuit of the long table, and then confided to them the existence of the Fairbank manual, of which some 25 copies were at once ordered. Further orders continued through the months that followed. Soon the entire membership, largely recruited from the printing and publishing world, possessed copies, and so gained a fresh sense of the edged pen's contribution to the making of letter-forms.

Thereafter the book began its longer journey into the homes and hands of laymen.

How the Italic Hand came to New York

At the same time the art schools, in which lettering was taught, all saw in the Fairbank *Manual* a useful teaching aid. George Salter's classes in the Cooper Union were perhaps the first in the United States thus to use it. Later on, when I began to teach there and at the Parsons School of Design and at New York University, I added the handy Penguin *Book of Scripts* to increase the student's awareness of the historic development of certain scripts, its use continuing to this day.

The Fairbank letter described above had, of course, to be answered; but, as it had to be done in longhand, I preferred to wait some weeks longer until my developing Italic should seem less defacing to the original. But I did answer, and so began a correspondence now strengthened by three personal visits on as many trips to England.

As to the *Manual* itself, it must, in the history of the italic hand's revival in this century, be the only instructional volume written out of a full mastery of the hand it professes to teach. This requirement may sound like a truism but is now become a paradox, and the time gives it proof. When the Fairbank *Manual* appeared, its author had already been writing the italic hand formally and informally for almost a quarter century. No author of a rival manual in our century can approach this extent and depth of dedicated study—as indeed a glance at the rash of other volumes will readily confirm. What is now most needed—surely in the United States and perhaps in Britain—is more and more teacher-training in Italic. In each of the dozen eastern private schools I have converted to Italic, I have been fortunate in finding one or more of the teaching staff possessed of uncommon aptitude for this seductive script; and there is reason to hope that the need and the value of supreme italic performance will be recognized. Once so recognized, the cause of italic writing will be properly launched for a long period of years to come.

BENT ROHDE

'... for there is so much to do!'

This heading is a quotation from a letter written to me by Alfred Fairbank two years ago. It ends: 'My handwriting now suffers from my age: 68. I could wish I was 58 again, for there is so much to do!'

This letter is shown in the Danish manual for italic handwriting *Bredpen-kursiv* (Bent Rohde and Ejnar Philip, Den grafiske Højskoles Skrifter, Copenhagen, 1964) as an example of a fluent, personal and graceful hand. It is placed on the very first page, because without the work of Alfred Fairbank we in Denmark would have been unable to start a significant reform of Danish handwriting, hitherto limited to a small group of specially interested people, such as graphic designers, typographers and a few architects, who taught themselves Italic from the *Dryad Writing Cards* or *Beacon Writing Books*.

Writing in itself is traditional, but in Denmark we had no historic tradition of fine writing. However, during the period when the *cancellaresca corsiva* spread over Europe, we find a small group of Danish scholars for whom, as nowadays, it was just as natural and vital to write a fair hand as to speak clearly and with grace.

Although the intellectual forces symbolized by the Renaissance and the ideas of humanism were developing in Italy as early as the fourteenth century, Denmark and the northern countries had to wait for the revival of science and religious life. But when later the Renaissance reached our shores, this influence in Denmark too gave rise to an interest in the Latin script among scholars.

Only when humanism had been generally accepted in Germany, the Netherlands and France, the countries with which Denmark during the late Middle Ages had close cultural relations, did it exercise an influence on our country during the first decades of the sixteenth century. And from that time we too date the introduction of Latin writing into Denmark.

The majority of university students of the sixteenth century in Denmark had to go to North German universities to improve and to finish their education after their studies in Copenhagen.

Those who adopted the ideas of humanism in Denmark had studied for shorter or longer periods in Paris and Louvain—the two universities where Erasmus had influenced teaching. Undoubtedly Danish humanists learned the new style of hand-writing during their stay at foreign universities.

By the middle of the sixteenth and the beginning of the seventeenth century, a handful of educated men in Denmark were writing the italic hand with skill, not only for documents and formal writing but also for everyday purposes.

The greatest name in Danish humanism, *Christiern Pedersen*, was the first to use Latin script in Denmark, namely in a letter to the Danish King Christian II, written in 1522, which is now in the Record Office ('Rigsarkivet') of Copenhagen.

A fluent humanistic cursive was written by one of the leading men of the reformation, *Povl Helgesen*, lecturer of Theology in the University of Copenhagen. His clear, legible hand appears in the famous chronicle *Skibbykrøniken* written by him in 1533–4 (Arnemagnaeanske Håndskriftsamling 858, 4to).

The Danish Royal House used the Latin script for foreign correspondence during the sixteenth century. Latin was employed for correspondence with England, Scotland and France; with other countries it was usually German.

Letter-books with Latin correspondence are preserved in Rigsarkivet from about 1560. Up to the end of the sixteenth century, fine examples of fully developed *cancellaresca corsiva* appear periodically. Big lacunae in chronology are filled in by well-preserved drafts. One of these we now bring to light (Fig 65). The draft, dated 7 June 1556, was written by an unknown scribe in the King's Chancery. It reveals an incipient interest in the new script which was to be used in the chancery. The contents of this document reflect the insecurity of those days on the seas. It is a letter of protection, issued by the King of Denmark, Christian III, for Carolus Scotus, captain of *Vacca* as he was leaving the country to fight against the pirates. The object is to prevent the brave captain from being regarded as a pirate himself in the course of his duty.

The sixteenth-century models of the chancery hand originated in Italy. But it is natural to assume that our unknown scribe so enjoyed the beautiful and clear script, which he was able to study in the letters received by His Majesty from the English Royal House, that he wished to copy it. In Rigsarkivet we have an opportunity to see a very extensive collection of attractive letters from this correspondence between the English and the Danish Royal Houses during the years 1435–1602.

Alfred Fairbank's seventieth birthday is the occasion for my publishing these first,

238

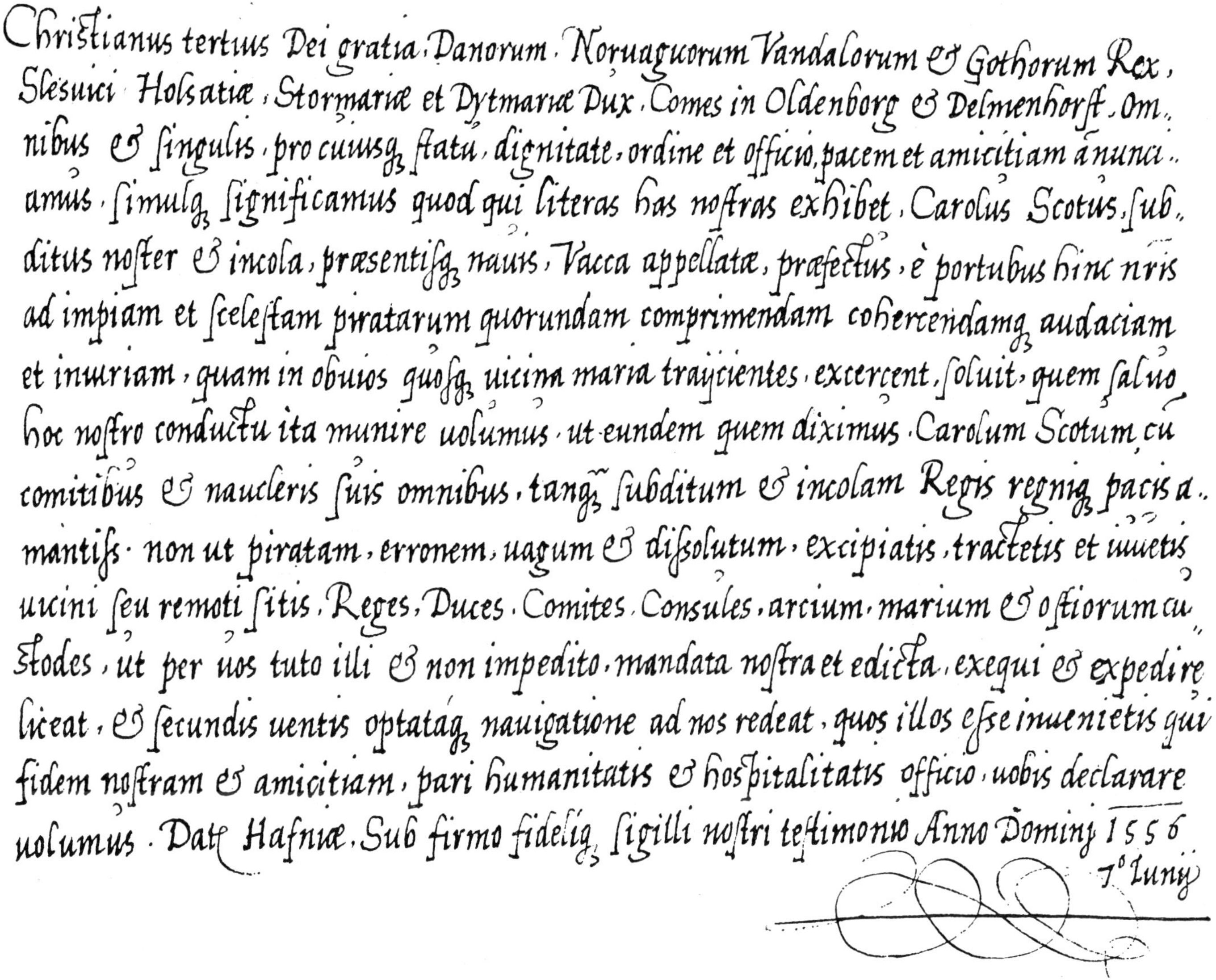

Christianus tertius Dei gratia . Danorum . Noruagiorum Vandalorum et Gothorum Rex , Slesuici , Holsatiæ , Stormariæ et Dytmarciæ Dux . Comes in Oldenborg et Delmenhorst . Om-nibus et singulis , pro cuiusq3 statu , dignitate , ordine et officio , pacem et amicitiam a nimci amus , simulq3 significamus quod qui literas has nostras exhibet , Carolus Scotus , sub-ditus noster et incola , præsentiisq3 nauis , Vacca appellatæ , profectus , é portubus hinc nris ad impiam et scelestam piratarum quorundam comprimendam coercendamq3 audaciam et iniuriam , quam in obuios quosq3 uicina maria traiicientes , exercent , soluit , quem saluo hoc nostro conductu ita munire uolumus , ut eundem quem diximus , Carolum Scotum , cu comitibus et nauclerìs suis omnibus , tanq3 subditum et incolam Regis regniq3 pacis a-mantif3 , non ut piratam , erronem , uagum et dissolutum , excipiatis , tractetis et iuuetis uicini seu remoti sitis , Reges , Duces , Comites , Consules , arcium , marium et ostiorum cu-stodes , ut per nos tuto illi et non impedito , mandata nostra et edicta , exequi et expedire liceat , et secundis uentis optataq3 nauigatione ad nos redeat , quos illos esse inuenietis qui fidem nostram et amicitiam , pari humanitatis et hospitalitatis officio nobis declarare uolumus . Dat Hafniæ . Sub firmo fideiq3 sigilli nostri testimonio Anno Domini 1556 .

7⁰ Iunij

Fig. 65. Letter of Protection issued by King Christian III (1556).

incomplete notes on the introduction of *cancellaresca corsiva* in Denmark. It was only possible for us in Denmark to carry out such an investigation by reason of his stimulating and valuable researches, which have become known (among others) to the students of The Graphic College of Denmark through his articles and books. It was, in fact, a former student of this college, Miss Birgit Sylvander, who provided the historical notes for this article.

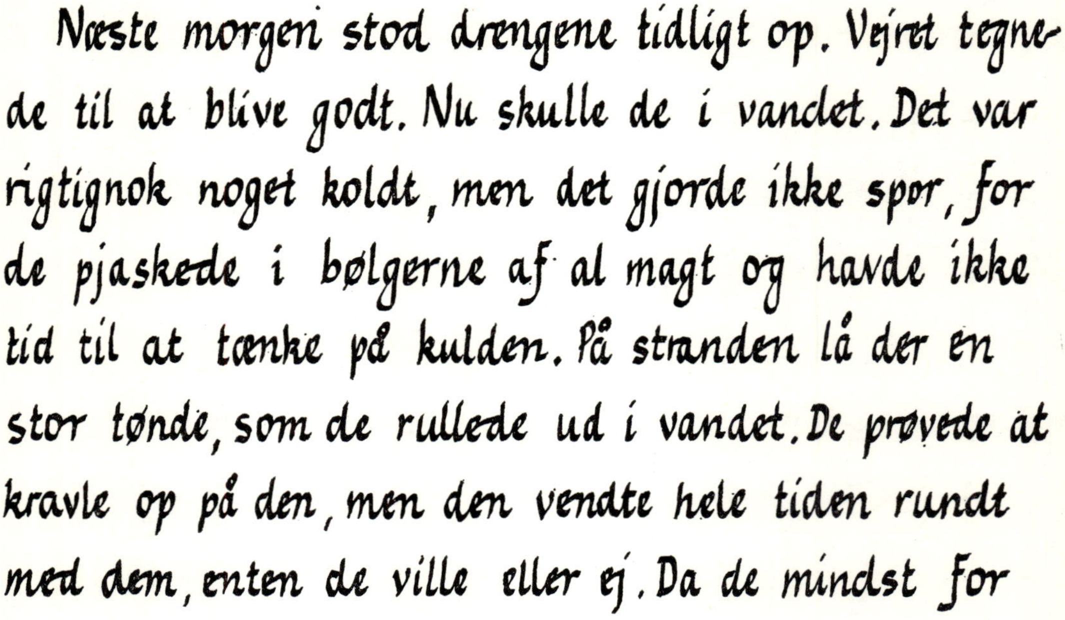

Næste morgen stod drengene tidligt op. Vejret tegne-de til at blive godt. Nu skulle de i vandet. Det var rigtignok noget koldt, men det gjorde ikke spor, for de pjaskede i bølgerne af al magt og havde ikke tid til at tænke på kulden. På stranden lå der en stor tønde, som de rullede ud i vandet. De prøvede at kravle op på den, men den vendte hele tiden rundt med dem, enten de ville eller ej. Da de mindst for

Fig. 66. One of the first results of italic teaching in Denmark. The writer, 12-year-old Henrik, was taught by his father uninfluenced by any other writing system.

The Graphic College occupies a central position in Denmark in regard to italic handwriting today. In particular, two lecturers, the printer Ejnar Philip and the book designer Erik Ellegaard Frederiksen have inspired hundreds of students by their own fine hands and by their reference to the *Dryad Writing Cards*.

I myself was one of these students and, when later I became a teacher myself, I was able to run evening-classes in Italic, for which I have used Mr Fairbank's methods and models with great success for the last seven years. It is only certain linguistic differences between English and Danish that makes it necessary to publish a Danish manual.

If italic handwriting is to gain further attention in Denmark, a code of instruction for children must be prepared. From an educational point of view the difficulty is that a style of writing, which in some ways resembles the English print-script, was introduced about ten years ago. This writing system has been widely adopted and created a much-needed improvement in the writing lessons of the schools. But because it is based on the rigid principles of the perpendicular and the circular, it lacks the qualities required for rapid, everyday cursive handwriting.

Each school in Denmark has the right to decide what teaching methods it wishes to use. For that reason, a child who changes his school will probably have to change his writing model because, in addition to the 'Formskrift', a lot of schools are still using a hand reminiscent of the English Round Hand.

★ ★ ★ ★ ★

The quotation from Shakespeare's *King Henry V* 'We few, we happy few, we band of brothers' is an apt description of the practitioners of italic handwriting in Denmark. Without Alfred Fairbank's inspiring contribution we should have been unable to take the first steps. He has made it easy for us to continue the work; for we feel, just as he does, that 'there is so much to do!'

PEN TO PAPER

16·2

One of Alfred Fairbank's keenest interests in the last decade has been the Society for Italic Handwriting, which he was largely instrumental in founding. As has been related elsewhere, this Society, born naturally from the Society of Scribes and Illuminators, quickly took root and acquired a life of its own. In the following section, the Rev. C. M. Lamb contributes an essay on the parent Society, while Miss Anna Hornby gives an account of the Society for Italic Handwriting, of which she was secretary for many years. Then follows a short anthology, which I have compiled from the Society's quarterly periodical, originally called the *Bulletin* and now the *Journal*. The anthology is arranged in chronological order.

Grateful acknowledgement is made to the contributors.

EDITOR

C. M. LAMB

Notes on the History of the Society of Scribes and Illuminators

The emergence of a prophet or a teacher of marked originality arouses a ferment in the minds of those who come within the orbit of his influence, and inspires with enthusiasm those who are ready to accept the revelation communicated to them. But, in succeeding generations, such enthusiasm fades unless steps are taken to preserve it, though such a process of preservation only too often leads to a loss of spontaneity in the elements of the teaching conserved. Such 'canalization' appears to be necessary for the maintenance of that which is in danger of being lost; but it is effective only at a price, at times heavy indeed.

So it is not surprising that attempts have been made to ensure the preservation of the teaching of Edward Johnston, which formed the subject matter of the revival of the craft of the calligrapher during the first half of this century. And these attempts aimed at supplementing the treasures of his book, *Writing & Illuminating & Lettering*, that unrivalled text-book of the craft, by preserving the skills of the craftsman and demonstrating their application and practice.

Miss Priscilla Johnston, in her life of her father, has described the foundation of the 'Calligraphers' Society' about the year 1910, and quotes his description of the object of the society, of which he was President, as the advance of lettering, and to claim for such objects as manuscript books 'a place among real things—in the simplest, yet in the best sense—as works of art'. One of the more valuable achievements of this Society was the arranging of an exhibition of calligraphy in Germany, in which Anna Simons, a member of the Society, gave much help. This exhibition did much to kindle the enthusiasm with which Johnston's teaching was received in Germany, and from which has sprung that appreciation of the craft, to be seen in the work of the present-day calligraphers on the continent. But, alas, after a few years of what

Johnston described as its 'stormy history', the Society came to an end, and its place was not filled until the founding of the Society of Scribes and Illuminators in 1921.

In the June of that year, at the suggestion of Lawrence Christie and Graily Hewitt, both early pupils of Edward Johnston, who were then teaching the writing classes at the London County Council Central School of Arts and Crafts in Southampton Row, a society was formed of those 'interested in writing and illuminating for the purpose of periodic discussion and occasional shows'. The Society was attempted informally, the only 'officer' being a secretary; expenses were to be met by a small subscription, and it was envisaged that committees would be appointed only for special purposes, and the conduct of the Society would be generally directed by the members. On such lines, expressed in a letter signed by Louisa Puller, the secretary *pro tem.*, circulated in May 1921 to those likely to be interested in the project, a beginning was made. A meeting was called for 30 June, when a body of rules was drawn up, which expressed the ideals shared by many concerned with the establishment of the crafts in those days. For instance, it was declared that the object of the Society was the advancement of the crafts of writing and illuminating by the practice of them for themselves alone, without any necessary consideration of reproduction or commercial advantage. And that the aim of the Society be zealously directed towards the production of books and documents wholly handmade, regarding other application of the work as preliminary or subordinate, but not excluding it from its scope. A laudable rule was that the Society be conducted with as little formality as possible, and another that the spirit and attitude of a candidate for membership towards the craft be deemed of great importance, it being the aim of the Society to foster a body of sincere and vital endeavour rather than of mere technical ability or mechanical accomplishment.

On such a basis the Society started its career, and on 30 September the first meeting of the Society was held at the Art Workers' Guild, when an address on heraldry was given by Mr Oswald Barron, the distinguished herald, and the writer of a daily column in the *London Evening News* over the signature of 'The Londoner'. The notice calling the meeting was signed by Louisa Puller, as honorary secretary, and Dorothy Hutton, as honorary financial secretary. Miss Puller, who continued as Secretary for some years, and did much for the fledgling society by her enthusiasm and versatility, died a few years ago; Miss Hutton is still a member of the Society, and in her distinguished work has admirably fulfilled the objects assigned to it 45 years ago. In July of the following year, the first exhibition of the Society was held in the Brook Street Art Gallery, off Bond Street, when 106 items were contributed by 31 members. The exhibition was well received and resulted in the sale of a number of works.

This was the beginning of a series of exhibitions arranged by the Society which has done much to spread the knowledge of the present state of the craft, and has brought to a wide public a reminder of the high degree of skill attained by members. A great deal of pleasure has been enjoyed by many of all classes who appreciate the beauty of the work displayed. Exhibitions have been held in a number of London galleries, and at the Victoria and Albert Museum, the First Edition Club, the Architectural Association, and the Crafts Centre of Great Britain. An exhibition was sent to New York in 1938, which resulted in much interest being aroused, and led to the establishment of a group which has spread appreciation of the craft from coast to coast of the United States. More recently, the Society has arranged exhibitions in the provinces, one in Maidstone in 1964 attracting almost 8000 visitors; another is to be held in Manchester during this year (1965).

The Society's exhibitions have attracted the attention of British Royalty, who have visited the exhibitions and displayed great interest in them. It is said that on one occasion a well-loved royal personage was so interested in the tools and methods employed in the craft that a fountain pen belonging to a member supervising the exhibition at the time went home with the royal visitor, to be acknowledged soon after by an autographed portrait sent to the member concerned.

The Society has from the first sought to maintain the highest standards of craftsmanship, and has therefore admitted as members only the really skilled candidates for membership. This has often resulted in disappointment for rejected candidates. To mitigate such disappointment, and also to keep in touch with those who showed promise of attaining the required standards but clearly still had need of further instruction and experience, an associate membership was introduced in 1945. But less than a dozen applicants were offered this class of membership, and it was found that very few of those who accepted it proceeded to full craft membership. So, after some years, it was discontinued, and no elections to the associateship are now being made.

The Society has with great diligence maintained its rule of quarterly meetings, at which qualified speakers address the members about some aspect of the craft on which they can speak with authority; such as the manufacture of gold leaf, or the laying and burnishing of gold leaf in the decoration of manuscripts; the binding of modern manuscripts, or the rebinding of those which have survived from distant centuries; the manufacture of vellum and parchment; or the nature of the pigments employed in ancient manuscripts. Such technical discussions are of value to all members of the Society, particularly to those of shorter experience. Of recent years, the custom has grown up of having an open meeting in March, usually at the Art Workers' Guild Hall in Queen Square, at which a speaker of distinction addresses an invited audience of members and friends, on a subject related to the objects of the Society. The list of lecturers who have thus addressed the Society includes such distinguished names as Edward Johnston, Eric Gill, Emery Walker, Sir Sydney Cockerell, Dr Eric Millar, Dr E. A. Lowe, James Wardrop, Dr Hilary Jenkinson, Berthold Wolpe, Dr Penrerleith, Dr Oakeshott, Dr Julian Brown and D. H. Turner, to mention only a few of them. One of the major occasions, which some members recall with relish, was when John Farleigh addressed the Society, and Bernard Shaw was a member of the audience and joined in the discussion which followed the lecture. Meetings are invariably well attended, and the speakers have the pleasant task of lecturing in a hall crowded to capacity.

Another enjoyable event arranged annually for members has been a summer visit to a place likely to be of interest. During the years visits have been arranged to the British Museum, the Victoria and Albert Museum, Westminster Abbey, Lambeth Palace, the Society of Antiquaries, to colleges of the older universities, to Eton College, and the libraries of Canterbury and Winchester Cathedrals, where fine manuscripts are to be found. Such visits are seldom without their lighter aspects; and, as these notes are a contribution to a *festschrift*, it may be relevant to record that on a visit to one of the more august of the institutions mentioned, where (a limit having been set to the size of the party and inadvertently exceeded by two additional members) the venerable librarian introduced the leader of the party to the Provost—a connoisseur of manuscripts of world-wide eminence—saying, 'This is Mr Fairbank. He has gone beyond the limit!' However, in the event all was well, and the members enjoyed the sight of some superb manuscripts.

In 1952 it was decided to extend the range of membership of the Society by the admission of lay members who were interested in the craft and willing to add their support to the Society. This has proved a useful innovation and has resulted in the addition of over 200 names to the roll of the Society. Such members are invited to all meetings of the Society, can make use of its library and, if they practice the craft, can submit works for the exhibitions. But they have no share in the management of the Society. Such membership has been accorded to many interested individuals in the British Isles, the U.S.A., and other parts of the world.

In 1954 a generous benefaction from the widow of Col. J. C. H. Crosland made possible the compilation of a series of essays embodying the experience of senior members of the Society in calligraphic subjects. These were published by Messrs

Faber and Faber under the title of *The Calligrapher's Handbook*, and have proved of value to students of the craft.

In 1924 and 1925 several small groups of members were set up to study particular problems in need of investigation; and fruitful results accrued from these. A heraldry group explored the use of heraldic decoration of manuscripts, and compiled a useful portfolio of illustrations and designs: other groups dealt with skins as writing surfaces; the pigments to be employed in decoration; the preparation of inks; and, probably the most productive of them all, cursive handwriting. For behind all the glory of a richly adorned manuscript, the Society has always had an interest in the promotion of a hand for use in the humdrum concerns of daily life, which shall be legible, beautiful and not beyond the capacity of the majority of people. These studies led to the development of that interest in the humanistic hands of the Renaissance which Mr Fairbank has made so much his own. And from that the transition to all the problems of a standard of handwriting and of the teaching of children in schools has naturally followed. Indeed, here is to be seen one of the most important and far reaching results of the 45 years work of the Society; for however much it may be decried as too traditionalist for these days, it has certainly shown the way in which questions relating to a cursive hand suitable for ordinary use today can be solved. From all this work of the Cursive Group of 1935 has flowed the impetus which led to the founding of the Society for Italic Handwriting, a sturdy offspring, of which the Scribes and Illuminators can be justly proud.

When Mr Fairbank was appointed a Commander of the Order of the British Empire the Society of Scribes and Illuminators asked him to become their President, which he consented to do; and for twelve years he fulfilled all the duties connected with this office with approbation. When he felt the time had come for a change, and that the Society needed an annually elected Chairman, he relinquished the post of the first (and, probably, the only) President of the Society.

ANNA HORNBY

The Society for Italic Handwriting

I talic handwriting, which is gaining recognition today as a fine practical hand for everyday use, is derived from the beautiful humanistic cursive scripts of the Renaissance. Since the turn of the century a discerning few have appreciated both the beauty and the utility of the humanistic cursive and have adopted it as a basis for their own handwriting. But it is only within the last fifteen years that the renascence of these scripts has reached a wider public.

The Society for Italic Handwriting in its adoption and adaptation of an earlier script could almost be said to be repeating an event in the history of western handwriting by its return to earlier standards. Of the periods in this history, the one that has contributed most to the traditions of today by its scripts and types is that of the Italian Renaissance. The interest of the Florentine leaders of the Renaissance in the classical works of the ancient Roman authors caused searches to be made for manuscripts. Many of these freshly discovered manuscripts had been written out in the Carolingian scripts of the ninth to the twelfth centuries. The beauty and clarity of these scripts appealed to the Florentines, were preferred to the scripts then in current use and led to the evolution of the humanistic hands. The scholar Poggio, for example, is thought to have written in 1402–3, with skill and assurance, a humanistic (roman) script. The development of the related cursive (italic) hand is less easy to follow. The introduction of the medieval join and the reduction of pen-lifts is to be noted in the writing of Niccolò Niccoli and in the scripts of many other fifteenth-century manuscript books and documents. By the beginning of the sixteenth century there were fine italic hands and the first italic type; while in 1522 appeared the much-admired printed manual *La Operina* by Ludovico Vicentino degli Arrighi, giving instruction and models of the *cancellaresca* or Chancery hand. In his Preface, Arrighi said he was writing ' . . . not only for this age but also for posterity . . . ': even so, he might have been surprised to know that, almost four and a half centuries later,

251

facsimiles and translations of *La Operina* have helped to spread the present interest in the chancery hand in England, the U.S.A. and on the continent. The humanistic cursive hand, which was also used in England and many European countries, shows cursive handwriting at its best; from the end of the sixteenth century, through a variety of causes, handwriting has gradually deteriorated to the sorry state with which we are so familiar today.

The present impulse towards an improvement in the quality of handwriting springs initially from the same source as the revival of formal calligraphy. William Morris is known to have studied Arrighi's models in about 1873, and Edward Johnston illustrated a semi-formal hand in his *Writing & Illuminating & Lettering*, which was an inspiration to Fairbank and others. In 1898 Mrs M. M. Bridges, the wife of the Poet Laureate, made a positive move with her book *A New Handwriting for Teachers*, which gave a model based on 'italianised gothic': Robert Bridges himself later published two *Tracts on English Handwriting* (1926–7). Graily Hewitt, in 1916, published in his *Oxford Copybooks* an italic hand derived from his study of the Manuals of G. B. Palatino and Francisco Lucas. Although a fine script, it lacked joins and was therefore unsuitable as a speedy workaday hand. Alfred Fairbank, a pupil of Hewitt, was the first to produce a model, closely adapted from the humanistic cursive, which was practical, beautiful and simple enough for children; in fact, both adults and children have learned from his models with equal success. Fairbank's model owed more to G. A. Tagliente and Lucas than to Arrighi, although his admiration of the latter is well known. His first exemplar, in 1932, entitled *Woodside Writing Cards* was followed in 1935 by the *Barking Writing Cards* later known as the *Dryad Writing Cards*. He also interested George Hughes in the production of an edged dip-pen suitable for italic writing in schools. Fairbank's instructional book *A Handwriting Manual*, first published in 1932, was the forerunner of numerous books on the subject, but remains the most outstanding. His latest models for schools, *Beacon Writing Books*, bear out a very important fact: that italic writing can be simplified suitably for infants, thus making it possible to begin the teaching of writing on the same basis as that on which it may continue to develop, without interruption, into a mature hand. Unfortunately, as things are at present, it is only too likely that a child will be taught a different form of writing with each change of school; none the less italic handwriting does provide the means to a logical progression in the teaching of handwriting.

The use of contemporary italic handwriting remained very limited until after the Second World War when, suddenly, there arose a surprising surge of public interest in a reform of handwriting through the adoption of an italic hand. Enquiries were addressed to the Society of Scribes and Illuminators in such numbers as to be embarrassing and the President, Alfred Fairbank, assessing the situation, urged that the time was ripe for the creation of a new organization devoted to italic handwriting. The Society of Scribes and Illuminators sponsored a meeting in London on 25 November 1952, and the Society for Italic Handwriting was founded. Joseph Compton, C.B.E., was elected Chairman. In January 1954 the Marquess of Cholmondeley, the Lord Great Chamberlain, whose interest in italic handwriting is well known, accepted the office of President. Air Chief Marshal Sir Theodore McEvoy, K.C.B., C.B.E., succeeded Mr Compton as Chairman in June 1962. From an initial 63, membership had risen by the end of the first year to 500 and continued to rise rapidly during the next few years. An early analysis of the membership showed twice as many men as women; that about one-third were from those connected with education, the remainder being people from all walks of life, including some junior members. The one qualification for membership is an interest in the subject. From the beginning, the Society has attracted members from overseas and is represented in over thirty countries. In the U.S.A. and Holland, interest has been sufficient to generate independent organizations.

The aims of the Society are to promote the use of italic handwriting; to increase the pleasure and skill of its members in their writing; to provide a forum for discussions and lectures and to offer assistance to teachers of handwriting, always with the purpose of improving standards.

The Society's work has been roughly in three fields: the teaching of Italic; propaganda; and research into original manuscripts. Handwriting courses for members have been held, and instructors have been recommended for classes run by local authorities. Arnold Bank, Wilfrid Blunt, Professor Julian Brown, Will Carter, Alfred Fairbank, Dr Alec Hay, Dr R. W. Hunt, Sir Hilary Jenkinson, Sir Francis Meynell, Reynolds Stone, Beatrice Warde and Berthold Wolpe are among those who have given lectures at the Society's regular meetings.

The first issue of the Society's quarterly *Bulletin* appeared in December 1954 (it is now sought for as a 'rare book' by members); type-written and produced by photo-litho, its format was amateur. By October 1962, however, with the thirty-second issue, the Society was in a position to produce a high-quality quarterly, renamed the *Journal*. Authoritative articles on all aspects of the Society's work appear in the *Journal*, which forms the main link with the widely scattered membership; its distinguished contributors hail from many countries besides Great Britain. Important discoveries of Renaissance manuscripts have been first reported in its pages.

With limited funds the Society's publicity has depended to a great extent on the ambassadorial activities of its members and on the circulation of exhibitions of hand-writing. Such exhibitions have been shown not only in many parts of Great Britain, but in South Africa, Australia, Canada, Denmark, Holland, New Zealand, Puerto Rico, Northern Rhodesia, Sweden, Uruguay and in the United States, where an exhibition has been on tour constantly since 1955.

The Society has much work still to do if it is to achieve its aims. Italic is slowly finding its way into the schools, and, where it is well taught, results have fully justified all that is claimed for it. There is, however, a real danger from misguided teaching, where the essentials have not been understood; the over-compressed, angular, sometimes ornate, sometimes unjoined, often illegible results erroneously called Italic are damaging to the cause of genuine italic writing. Few people, it seems, can remain impartial about contemporary Italic. The Society has attracted many keen supporters; it has also met with fierce opposition and provoked much discussion. It can truly claim the greatest measure of responsibility for the awakening 'handwriting consciousness' apparent today.

ANTHOLOGY

H. E. R. ALEFOUNDER
Italic and a Septuagenarian

As a schoolboy, the only subject for which I always had good marks was handwriting—civil service style. When I started work, handwriting fascinated me and I developed a facility for copying the hands and the signatures of my colleagues and chiefs. Some said I should probably find myself sooner or later in prison for forgery. Happily they were wrong. But I suppose that always having had a free hand—although no good at drawing—was an advantage when I came to entertain myself with Italic in my retirement. On the other hand, it was a disadvantage that, throughout a long lifetime in which I had to do a lot of writing, I had formed a very rapid but unbridled style. When I began Italic I found that all my descenders curled the wrong way, my *m*'s and *n*'s spread out and kicked up their legs at the end of the words, and my *t*'s objected strongly to diminished stature.

I had known Alfred Fairbank (hereinafter referred to as F.) for many years. From him I first learned to know a serif when I met one. I recall daily train journeys with him, thirty or more years ago, when he talked to me of uncials, minuscules and majuscules, while the other occupants of the carriage listened and probably wondered whether we were a pair of conspirators. He was little more than a youth then (I was much older) but he already had that absorption in his subject which so impresses all those who come to know him at the present day.

Of course, I read his books with pleasure, but it was not until I found myself with time on my hands in retirement, and the S.I.H. [Society for Italic Handwriting] was formed, that I began to try Italic. I would have spells at it of several days. By painfully slow application I could copy F.'s script, but it looked a laboured, unlovely job, and I would decide that I should never be able to make it my normal hand, and would pack it up for months at a time. Then I would have another spell at it, and another, and reach the same decision. I had joined the S.I.H., but only as an onlooker. Then it was decided to form a branch in Sussex, where I now live, and I heard that F. was coming to live in Sussex and join the branch, so I made another start.

And now, here is an interesting thing. I suppose my many abandoned spells must have contributed, but in this latest one I found that Italic was beginning to come naturally. When dashing off a letter in my old unbridled hand, I began to find that Italic, like cheerfulness, was always breaking in. A day came when I told myself that I could now use the italic hand for all purposes, quickly enough for letter-writing, and that I never need return to my old hand. It is not yet all that I desire. Those *t*'s still dodge me at times, and the *m*'s and the *n*'s are still unruly, but I feel that it is at last good enough to encourage me to keep on. The high-ups in the S.I.H. would probably regard it as a poor specimen, but I have reached the stage when friends and relatives, who are not judges, ask me to do things for them 'in your nice writing'.

Sitting down to start was always a business. I had in mind that boy seated at a desk in F.'s *Manual*, the paragraph on hygiene, and the many other directions. I asked myself whether my posture was symmetrical and balanced, whether my feet were placed firmly in front of me, whether my elbow was held lightly and naturally away from the body, and whether I was holding my pen lightly, as Edward Johnston always did, so that a teacher could easily pluck it from my fingers. Having settled myself in these respects, I was ready to begin. There was one point, however, that F.'s *Manual* did not cover, and about which I was always at a loss—whether my tongue should be out or in.

Of course, I have tried many pens. I must have a fountain pen. I cannot go back to dip pens. I have never been able to allow myself to buy one of the expensive makes, but have tried many of the cheaper ones. The one I am using now suits me best so far—it is one of those advertised in the *Bulletin*—but I feel that it is not the perfect one for my hand. I find that a medium is too broad, and a fine too fine. I wish they made something in between.

Anyhow, Italic is providing me with another pleasant hobby, for which I am grateful, and my experience as a beginner at the age of 73 may encourage others much younger.

1956

Anthology

SIR SYDNEY COCKERELL
Good Handwriting

Robert Bridges, Poet Laureate, printed in 1926 and 1927 two tracts on English Handwriting containing facsimiles of examples that he thought worthy of commendation. In the Preface to the first of these tracts he declared that illegibility in writing to a stranger was an unpardonable breach of good manners. There is no doubt that in too many of our schools this dictum has not been taken to heart. Writing is tolerated that, besides being ill-formed, is slovenly, slipshod and clumsy, and the pupil has no idea that he is forming a habit that will tell against him all his life.

What, then, should be aimed at by both teacher and taught? Legibility is, of course, the first thing. Every letter should be distinctly formed in such a way that it cannot be mistaken for any other letter. It ought not, for instance, to be possible to mistake a *u* for an *n*, or vice versa. If all such confusions are avoided, and words and lines are well spaced, the primary object of handwriting is accomplished, and the reader can have no cause for complaint.

Nevertheless, such a piece of legible writing would not have attracted the attention of Robert Bridges if it had not one or more other qualities. These are beauty, character and style. To write beautifully as well as legibly requires much practice, some study of fine examples, and a good deal of zeal. At one famous public school there has been great emulation in the last few years to excel in this respect, with the result that many boys have acquired beautiful handwriting that no one could fail to admire and that will be a great asset to them as long as they live. For a beautiful script may easily make all the difference when two applicants of otherwise equal qualifications are seeking the same appointment; I have heard of its determining a choice between fifty competitors.

Style and character, the other factors I have mentioned, must come largely of themselves as part of the individual make-up. We all know what style is in cricket, in tennis, in dancing, in skating and even in ordinary gestures—a subtle perfection of which the possessor is hardly conscious. This is a quality of the best handwriting. So is character, which is the personal stamp that makes one piece of good penmanship differ from another that may lack it, and that enables one to recognize and name the writer as often as one sees an example of his script.

But in seeking these qualities there are some pitfalls. One feels that some scripts on which much effort has been spent are a little affected, too self-conscious. An air of spontaneity must be aimed at. Above all, there must be a total absence of swagger.

Pretentious signatures are apt to give a bad impression. And illegible signatures, or illegible initials, which baffle the reader, are (to return to Robert Bridges) sheer bad manners. There is no excuse for them, unless the writer suffers from some physical disability that prevents his writing clearly.   1956

ALFRED FAIRBANK
Bartholomew Dodington

Bartholomew Dodington was born in Middlesex in 1536 and died in 1595. He was buried in the North Transept of Westminster Abbey but it is not known just where. At Cambridge he became a Fellow of St John's College in 1552 and a Fellow of Trinity College about 1560. In 1562 he was made Regius Professor of Greek. For some years he was Auditor of the Imprest. Not much is known of him except what can be learned from his letters and the note in the *Dictionary of National Biography*.

When I came upon his writing in 1931 he seemed to have been forgotten as a penman, although to me he is outstanding among the many fine writers who were Fellows of Cambridge University.

The earliest example of his writing I know was written in 1558 for the University to Cecil asking him to become its Chancellor (Plate 43a). The writing is in the 'Cheke hand' (i.e. a current italic hand introduced by Sir John Cheke which has some strange characters). The next two letters, in date, which I have noticed are of 1561: one is in a set pointed Italic (Plate 43b) whilst the other is in the Cheke hand. Later, his set Italic became rather more angular. He retained the use of his Cheke hand until at least 1581. As one can see, he wrote exquisitely in Greek, and it seems probable that he also wrote the Secretary hand (set and free) and a set text hand. His script of the 1590 letter (Plate 44) is precise and austere but is lightened by the delightful swash capitals and flourished ampersands. The patterning is superb: the excellent spacing of letters and of lines and the play of ascenders and descenders between the strips of pattern are all 'just right'. The hand is not a model for our time as regards shapes of letters and potential fluency, but yet it is an inspiration.

The influence of Ascham on Dodington as well as of Cheke may be assumed. When 30 he was on such terms with Ascham that the latter gave him a book (now in the library of St John's College, Cambridge). Several of his letters were addressed to Lord Burghley and two of them (1567 and 1568) concern Cecil's nephew, Henry Cheke, to whom Dodington was a companion. I am inclined to think he taught the italic hand to the Second Baron Burghley.   1959

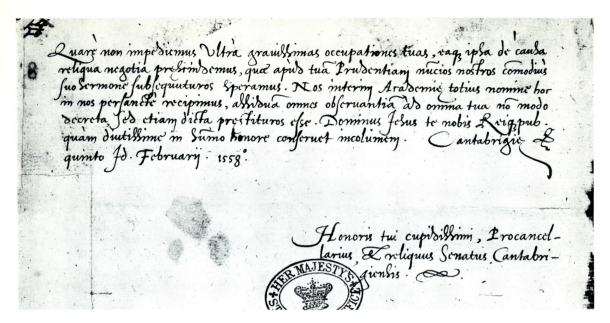

43 *a*. From a letter from Cambridge University to Cecil, asking him to become Chancellor (1558):
see p. 258. Writing attributed to Bartholomew Dodington. (Reduced)
Public Record Office, London (SP 12/2, fol. 83ᵛ)

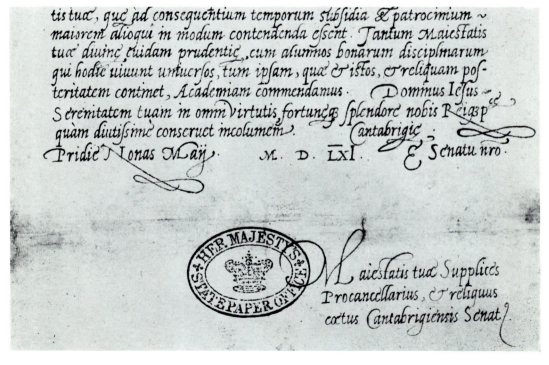

43 *b*. From a letter written by Bartholomew Dodington on behalf of Cambridge University, thanking
the Queen for confirming and increasing its privileges (1561): see p. 258. (Reduced)
Public Record Office, London (SP 12/17, fol. 10)

Cum benignitatis tuæ erga me ex quo me primum in patrocinium tuum recepisti
tanta magnitudo sit, Honoratissime Domine, ut eidem nullis officijs meis, nedum
exili hoc scribendi genere queam satisfacere: non committerem hoc tempore, ut tam leui
munere defungens, auribus tuis potius, quæ grauissimis reip. causis patere solent, conarer
obstrepere, quam tacita recordatione beneficiorum tuorum memoriam celebrarem;
nisi talis oblata esset occasio, qualem prætermittere sine scelere uix posse uiderer. /
Detulit enim ad me iampridem scilicet patre, nuper autem benignissimo patrono orbatus,
filius fratris mei, se cum supplex tecum ageret de Locatione illarum etiam renouanda,
quas ei pater suus Westmonasterij reliquit, à te responsum quidem perliberale abstulisse,
sed tale duntaxat, ut cum me habitare in eisdem intelligeres, fontem beneficentiæ tuæ
mihi magis, quam illi aperueris. Reliquam etiam significationem summæ erga me
beneuolentiæ tuæ sermone subsequebatur: quam ego nullis meis meritis uel præteritis,
uel expectatis euocatam, grata animi memoria, & omni obseruantia, quoad uixero,
colam. Sepenumero etenim in aurem insusurrans uox illa Theognidis ualde hanc
labem uitandam esse monet: Δειλους ϵὖ ἕρδοντι ματαιοτάτη χάρις ϵστιν ἴσον καὶ
σπείρϵιν πόντου ἅλος πολιῆς. Sed quæ esse omnino gratia poterit, quæ à me profecta
tantam assequi Dominationis tuæ bonitatem queat? aut quid denique gratuita bene=
ficentia tua præter se spectat? quæ in summo splendore quasi maioribus theatris pro=
posita, non usque eò se sustinet, quoad precibus (quod uero plerisque usuuenit) exorari possit:
sed ipsa se mihi offert ultrò, et quodammodo ad petendum allicit. Quid igitur? oblatamne
conditionem tam benignè solus ipse uerecunda quadam recusatione amittam? At
dixerit aliquis fortasse: Μισω σοφιστὴν, ὅστις οὐχ αὑτῷ σοφός. Ego uerò cum in hoc
ipso facile Prudentiæ tuæ probauero, mihi pietatis potius erga cognatum fratris filium,
quam proprij commodi ducendam esse rationem, tum illi uel soli delatum hoc quicquid
erit beneficij ut utrique commune à tua beneficentia profectum, non agnoscam solum,
sed profitebor etiam libenter. Quo nomine gratulor sanè utrique nostrum: esse scilicet
et summa facultate qui possit, & egregie propenso animo qui uelit, nostræ
seorsim solitudini ac inopiæ suis temporibus subuenire. Sed illa scilicet & fuit
iampridem, & deinceps erit semper gratulatio mea maior, quòd communis patriæ hijs
difficillimis temporibus quasi in uigilia quadam consulari manes, eandemque in tanta
orbitate spe magna sustentas. Quæ ut quam diuturna sit magnopere omnibus est
expetendum, mihiq; iuxta cum alijs uota indies facienda pro tua longa incolumitate, &
honoris amplificatione, proposui, ut pergas porro communi saluti sic operam nauare, ut
præteritorum prosperis progressibus, felices etiam futurorum exitus respondeant. /
Westmonasterij XII. Calend. Maij.   1590.

                                        Honori tuo deditissimus,
                                          Bartholomæus Dodingtonus

44.   Letter with Greek script: Dodington to Cecil regarding his nephew's house at
Westminster (1590): see p. 258. (Reduced)
British Museum, London (Lansdowne MSS. Vol. 63, Art. 84)

[To face p. 259

Anthology

NOTE BY EDITOR. The following is a letter which the late James Wardrop wrote to Mr Fairbank on Dodington in his own accomplished hand. A more extended article about Dodington by Mr Fairbank was printed in *Motif* 9, p. 80 (Shenval Press Ltd., 1962).

30, Trebovir Road, London, s.w. 5

17th July. 1953

Dear Alfred,

It's long since anything pleased me as much as has your gift — gauge of your sure instinct for fine things. I am quite lost in admiration for the new 'Dodingtons', and grateful for your willingness to share them with me. No Englishman, surely, ever wrote half so well; and you are entitled to the utmost credit for your discovery. I hope you will extend that credit in an illustrated article, which you are so eminently qualified to write.

B.D. must have had a consuming interest in penmanship per se; since he took such pains to perfect his style, and changed it more than once: there is, I remember, an intermediate stage between the round and the pointed. I am in no doubt as to which I prefer: the 1561 letter embodies all the qualities I prize in a hand, and which I have myself vainly attempted to compass. It is quite unlike any English hand known to me. He must have been familiar with xvth cent. Italian scripts before, as I presume, he became attracted by models, engraved or otherwise, of the Palatino type. In adopting the pointed style, D. became more of an artist, perhaps; but lost some grace and individuality by the way. At least half a dozen contemporary Italians could have matched the latter; but none of them could possibly have produced that writing of 1561, so personal, so eloquent of the whole man. How English he remains, despite the Italian and Greek influences! The 'secretary' _e_ in the word 'Jesus' betrays the inalienable Elizabethan.

The Greek piece is a thing of beauty which has won Mary's approval, and excites my envy. Both the photostats I shall greatly prize. By way of reciprocity, I hope to send an offprint from a little contribution I recently made to the Harvard Library Bulletin: the illustrations will, I think, interest you. If the thing turns up before I leave for the U.S., you shall have it.

Thank you for your good wishes. I have taken on an enterprise of some magnitude; and I sometimes find it hard to believe that, all being well, I shall gaze on the Pacific in about three months' time; and (an equally attractive prospect) dodge a good part of the winter. This summer calls for a bit of dodging, too: I'm sorry it has been so unkind to you. Get well soon, and accept my best thanks

Yours

James W.

Fig. 67.

Anthology

MARGARET HORTON
Chinese Italic

Lee Kwok Wing first walked into my classroom in the autumn of 1959; from the first he seemed a rare bird. It was not only that, unlike the usual art student, he had come very early and had brought all the tools required of him; it was not only that he appeared quite silently on his bast sandals and stood suddenly before me in his dark-blue padded jacket, reminding me of the ninth-century Chinese poet. ('*The first leaf already flies from the tree. In the first cold I have donned my quilted coat.*') In his quiet figure there was an earnestness not often seen in a lifetime. With difficulty he said 'Good morning', for he spoke no English yet and, seating himself in the front row, he carefully placed pen, ink and paper symmetrically on the desk. He could not understand the teacher's words and this hurt him, but he looked closely at books and wall-displays; watching every movement and seizing at once on the meaning of photographs and engravings he understood the italic penhold without any trouble; holding his pen delicately like a Chinese brush he went to work. No sooner did a line or shape appear on the blackboard than it reappeared with terrifying accuracy on his paper. That this was much more than imitation was soon apparent; collecting all the books and photostats available he would spend a long time quietly turning the pages, pointing now and then to things of particular excellence. Though by the end of the year he spoke very good English, he was as yet still unable to speak or understand more than a few words, but week after week his work was chosen by the class as the best in the room. ('What do you expect?' the students said good-humouredly, 'He's Chinese!') And we remembered the Chinese proverb, '*Those who speak know nothing; those who know are silent*'.

Lee had brought with him from Hong Kong two exquisite rolls of traditional painting; these he unrolled the length of the room (an endless landscape of hills, trees, temples, waterways; an endless procession of court beauties in palace galleries), explaining through an interpreter that they belonged to his family collection. This was the first glimpse we had of his unique background. For more information I have to thank Mr Michael Griffith, a former student, now Art Adviser in Hong Kong: 'Lee Kwok Wing was born in Hong Kong in 1929. His father is Mr Lee Chung Chai, himself an artist, as are three of his four sons. The sons describe their father's life as hermit-like, devoted to the arts of calligraphy, poetry and painting. He has that rare quality of broadmindedness and impeccable good taste. His sons therefore received a truly liberal education in the arts.... The background of real criticism and truthful vision has been a most happy one for Lee Kwok Wing. He is like an artist of China's greatest Dynasty, the T'ang, whose artists received influences from all quarters and used them all.... Fortunately, Lee Kwok Wing is a teacher. He was trained in Hong Kong for this, but needed it little, except that the world reads certificates. He taught in a Hong Kong government school for fishermen's children and there, from 1950 to 1956, he created Hong Kong's first Children's Art. He was transferred to the government vernacular Teachers' Training College, where he, with his brothers in turn to help him, has been enormously successful.'

When Lee showed me a painting he had done in the traditional manner of water, cliffs and trees, I asked him to make a rhyme-sheet of a poem on the Chinese Utopia; he listened, was silent and went away. Next class he brought us the first of his long pages incorporating (perhaps for the first time?) Chinese scenery and italic writing. Again like 'an artist of China's greatest Dynasty, the T'ang', he drew the 'vision of space', of hill and river, landscape and distance. Late, in the literature group, we were to discover his passion for the T'ang poets and to hear his unforgettable readings of their verse. (The group made a recording of these poems, with translations, and presented it with slides and music.) For his special study he wrote a history-by-examples of Chinese calligraphy; to our joy, his examples were taken from the poems the group had so much appreciated, and he included a series of paintings illustrating them. One of the pages incorporating italic writing and Chinese appears here. (Fig. 68).

In his last letter Lee wrote: 'After we endeavour much in Hong Kong people start to pay attention and try to learn italic handwriting: be assured that when I receive the *Renaissance Hands* [the recent book by Fairbank and Wolpe] I'll be very happy and sure I'll spend much time to study it up.' A picture of industry and high standards characteristic of Lee Kwok Wing. 1960

The Fisherman

Liu Tsung-yüan

The fisherman at night sleeps near the Western Precipice.
At dawn he draws clear water from the Hsiang and
   burns the bamboos of Ch'u.
Mists disperse and the sun rises but no man comes,
Only (is heard) the squeaking of his oars among
   the green hills and waters.
Turning round I see the horizon as if it merged with the flood.
Over the precipice the aimless clouds chase each other
   across the sky.

           Translated by Soame Jenyns

漁　翁

柳　宗　元

漁翁夜傍西巖宿，　曉汲清湘然楚竹。
烟銷日出不見人，　欸乃一聲山水綠。
迴看天際下中流，　巖上無心雲相逐。

Fig. 68. Chinese Italic by Lee Kwok Wing.

Anthology

ALFRED FAIRBANK
Bartolomeo San Vito

Mr Richard King, whose work for italic handwriting in the U.S.A. is well known to members, kindly sent me two photographs of pages of manuscripts in the Spencer Collection of the New York Public Library. The Curator of the Collection has been good enough to permit the reproduction of the one now shown (Plate 45), a page of a Horace (*Epist*. Lib. I. xviii). The other was a page of a famous copy of Valerius Maximus. It was a pleasure not only to send thanks for an international courtesy but to suggest that the *Horace* was written by Canon Bartolomeo San Vito of Padua and the *Valerius Maximus* was probably written by Antonio Sinibaldi, a fine Florentine calligrapher. One thing leads on to another, and it now appears that this Fifth Avenue Library has three San Vito manuscripts: the *Horace*, a *Lectionary* and, surprisingly, the *Valerius Maximus*; for whilst it seems that Sinibaldi wrote the text, yet San Vito wrote the titling roman capitals and inserted a line in the text in his inimitable minuscular writing.

The late James Wardrop introduced me to San Vito's *Eusebius* in the British Museum in 1931 but only since the Second World War has the identity of the scribe been established; and this was by the researches of James Wardrop and Dr Augusto Campana, lately of the Vatican Library. San Vito, I understand, was born in 1435. I would guess that the Horace was written in the 1470's. He not only wrote manuscripts but he must have had an organization for producing them, or have been involved in one; for several manuscripts are known to me where he has used fine roman capitals in gold and colours in writing titles, chapter headings, etc., whilst some other scribe has written the text. His output must have been large; for I have notes of nine of his manuscripts in the British Museum and many elsewhere.

The Plate shows a number of features to be found in San Vito's scripts and the commonest is possibly the large *t* at the end of the first line of the text. The marks in the margin are significant and so is the ligatured *ct*. The script is lively and so much the more because of his failure to keep his letters to a consistent size: e.g. *m* and *n* are generally larger than other letters. Later in life he developed a shake (James Wardrop told me that San Vito suffered from arthritis) but this uncertainty, oddly enough, is much less noticeable in his minuscles than in his capitals. It is possible that he was famous for his written roman capitals in his day and that he particularly enjoyed making them. A number of his books are very finely illustrated.   1961

Anthology

GEO. W. HUGHES
The First Italic Pen

One morning in the early 'thirties I found on my desk a letter from an address at Croydon with an S.O.S. from a Mr Alfred Fairbank. Now it happened that, during the First World War, I had a colleague whose handwriting I greatly admired; he told me it was half-uncials and was a medieval form. I had not then even so much as looked at old scripts and in my ignorance jumped to the conclusion that something to do with half-uncials was in the wind, so that I felt quite enthusiastic about the letter. Moreover, although old scripts were outside my ken, I found it quite a fascinating thing to construct or select pens for varied forms of writing—once, when in Calcutta, I even ran across a visiting Tibetan and seized the opportunity to design a pen for him. As a boy, at the time when the science of metallurgy was still very young, one of the first books I put on my shelf had been *Mixed Metals* by Hiorns; it was followed by others; and later on I bought two heavy French treatises, one about surface tension and capillarity, the other really applicable to the behaviour of metals in structures, but which I had to reapply as best I could from the large and regular forms of structures to the small and irregular formation of pens.

It was clear that the writing (of which I had doubts) was directional writing, that is to say, as subsequently defined in the very first issue of the *Bulletin*, writing in which the variation in thickness of the strokes is made by the direction in which the pen is drawn and not by pressure. So far so good; but it was also clear from the examples of 'cancellaresca' I had been shown that it was *purely* directional and that application of any pressure at the wrong point vitiated the hand.

Now Saudek was just a name to me, but I had read various articles by those who deduced character from handwriting which stressed the individual rhythm of writing pressures, and it seemed to me to be one thing for a calligrapher such as Mr Fairbank himself to suppress his natural inclinations and quite another to get the general public to do so. If it could not be suppressed the resultant of pressure must be minimized, and that demanded a fairly stiff nib and one in which the slit opened as little as possible when pressure was in fact applied.

That, in its turn, posed another problem; for it is the slit of a pen which regulates the flow of ink to the point and the problem was not made any easier of solution by the additional requirement that the point was required to be quite flat across, which deprives it of the reserve of ink given by the capillarity of a curved surface. Moreover, such flatness could not be attained by a similar device to that used in our

'Ajusto' and 'Football' series of pens, namely a flat channel, for the thin strokes would not be thin enough to suit 'cancellaresca', and it must be borne in mind that the incurved interior of such a channel provides in itself a tiny ink-reservoir.

All in all, it was quite a problem, but it was one that had to be solved, and in this I have since been confirmed by looking into the rise and decline of 'cancellaresca' itself; when it was in the hands of experts it flourished; as it came into the hands of all and sundry, it succumbed to these unwanted pressures; it deteriorated and faded out of use. Even the uninhibited writing of some of the old experts as revealed by the articles of the late Mr James Wardrop in *Signature* shows a similar deterioration.

To return to the making, steel would be unsuitable both as having *too* high a tensile strength, and because for reasons, which it will be more convenient to explain later, the straightness of the edge would be impossible of control; ordinary metal with a flat point subject to pressure would dub up. It needed something in between. Fortunately, I had recently made an alloy of (for metal) high tensile strength which, by dint of rolling down to an extreme reduction in some rolls I had, I made stiffer still, while retaining good resiliency.

So I instructed the toolmakers to make the requisite tools. The precise positioning of the flat was, and is, most critical and more than one set of tools had to be rejected; the curvature of the rest of the pen, the length of the slit and the optimum thickness of the metal had to be found by experiment and first one pen and then another and another submitted to Mr Fairbank and tested out by him in writing.

So much for the first Flight Commander, which was the broad point. But when he had approved that one, Mr Fairbank wanted in addition finer-pointed varieties. I agreed fully with him: for tastes in the size of writing differ very widely, but I could see that there was another headache in store, which I will proceed to explain.

When you cut or shear anything, the resultant edge has always a certain amount of roughness and, in the case of pen nibs, this is rectified by a process of mass polishing which smooths over the extreme edge, and, even more important, the spot where the slit meets the edge. But one cannot in this process, which we call 'shaking', smooth one place without smoothing another and inevitably the corners are rounded off as well; indeed, if the 'shaking' process be continued long enough, one is left with a round edge all the way along instead of the straight one that this writing demands; that is precisely one of the reasons why steel could not be used; for, in the case of steel, the 'shaking' process has to be further extended to remove the scale that develops in the hardening. It will be readily understood that, with a given pen, the extent of this rounding of the corners is constant, irrespective of the width of the point, and thus the percentage taken up by the rounded portion becomes greater as the point-width is lessened.

After trial and error I overcame this by incorporating minute lugs at each corner; these lugs or projections, culminating as they do at an acute angle, both attract the polishing preferentially and, as they round off, do so on a curve inclining tangentially to the rearward instead of to the front edge of the pen. Finding them beneficial, I incorporated them in the broad point also. It was unpopular with the toolmakers and had to be forced through, as blanking tools with these projections are difficult to make and need constant maintenance; also, if the lugs do go wrong, it causes subsequent trouble in other processes.

That, in outline, is how the first italic pen came into being.   1962

P. WALLIS MYERS
Teaching Handwriting
(I) THE CHILD OF 5 YEARS

This is the age when children's eyes are discovering shapes and recognizing letters. Their total concentration—like that of an artist—is on shape because their minds have not yet developed sufficiently to comprehend the abstract meaning of words. This is the time for one artist, the teacher, to speak to the other artist, the child, with sensitivity and appreciation because they can both share the beauty of letter shapes.

Some of these 5 year olds have discovered the mechanism of reading; they can distinguish words with their eyes, and perhaps with their ears, and pronounce them with their tongues and they can make magic—in fact, they can read ! It is a big effort of the mind and of the will. They perform it rather than understand the words they read. What they do understand, however, is the world of 'make believe', and the medium of the imagination is the most powerful way of reaching the interest of these first-year pupils. I tell them stories round the letter shapes and then we draw them.

The act of imitation is so strong in infant children that they will pretend that they are writing at great length. Their *u*-shaped scribbles can be watched and analysed by the teacher, who is aware that writing is based on movement and the patterns that it makes. Today, if you are watching us at school, we are all making up our own stories and filling pages with flowing pattern. Observe with me their movements as they write. Their little round hands clutch the pencils or crayons and their wrists manipulate its movements rather than their fingers, which have not yet gained sufficient control. Already the personality of the child shows in the variation of this one repetitive *u*, in its individual vitality and in its arrangement on the page. Each child will find her own size and spacing. Some are writing very small and compressed on a large page of unlined paper. Others have a natural sense of alignment and a springing rhythm. Some are writing very big and running into the margin space. Here is a child who is concentrating on equal word spacing in certain places so that her writing becomes blocks of pattern with vertical spaces of white as well as horizontal ones. This last example shows how strong the primitive sense of pattern is in all of us. Surely this should be kept alive in later stages of writing. You will see some children moving their mouths as they write. One of the most fascinating things is to watch a child completely absorbed in her actions—the total concentration is amazing. When all this 'doing' is finished, I say 'Who would like to read out the story you have written?'—a show of hands—and then the chosen child proceeds. She looks very hard at her pattern of *u*-shapes and she pretends to read her story, even stopping here and there to try to read a word that is difficult to see, when in actual fact her imagination needs a chance to catch up with her tongue. Here again, then, the teacher learns that it is the story that makes the movement of writing come alive.

When a letter shape is discovered by the child, it is then practised over and over again and woven into rhythms such as the zigzag or the *u*- or *n*-curve, etc., until its construction is thoroughly learnt. Colour enhances pattern. The brush is a sensitive tool and encourages free arm movements which are good for the more inhibited child. I suggest plenty of writing patterns with different tools. The coloured crayon slides almost too easily over the paper without sufficient contact with the surface and it is not therefore a tool to be habitually using. The blackboard chalk is better for touch and works well on sugar paper. It is sometimes useful to stick large pieces of paper to the tables with Sellotape; otherwise the paper slides as the child writes because her control is occupied entirely with the act of writing and she cannot keep the paper steady as well. The pencil is rather spidery unless it has a soft, black lead, but it always remains a sensitive tool. Purposeful pattern writing during the infant stage is an essential part of learning to write and the only way of linking shape to movement. It is generally possible, at a later stage, to pick out those whose writing has been built up on this pattern-making practice. Their writing shows a more confident rhythm than that of those who have learnt to write merely through drawing shapes and copying examples.

It would not be fair to suggest that the first year of learning to write is made up of a glorious set of progressive stages. There are many setbacks and difficulties along the way. For instance, parents so often teach children to draw the capital letters before they come to school, and these are confused with minuscules as the child proceeds to write and the rhythm of movement is lost thereby. Perhaps the main difficulty is that, by the time the child is nearing 6, he or she may be developing a desire to communicate in that difficult language—English—with its extraordinary spelling. Their rhythm of movement is then constantly interrupted by queries about spelling. They become concerned with a series of symbols strung together in unrelated sizes; ascenders and descenders for example, lose their proportions in the child's great effort to express his thoughts in writing. I think that by the time the child reaches this stage (and it is a most exciting stage in his development) he should have learnt his letter symbols and their relative grouping sufficiently for them to have become a habit of movement. Woe betide the child then, who is still making his *d*'s or *p*'s from the bottom up or the wrong way round, or the child who sprawls his *e* or makes his *t* tower above other letters, because he is now using writing as an expression of his ideas—it has become a tool of his mind—and his interest is not entirely focused on the joy of making a letter shape!

(2) THE CHILD FROM 6–8 YEARS

My experience of teaching children of this age-range comes from a pre-junior school of the Girls' Public Day School Trust, which caters for selected children in three age-groups. The kindergarten enter at 5 years. They move up the next year to become those restless, energetic creatures called the Transition. The latter live their experience at school with an appetite that is, at times, almost overwhelming. They are used to school ways and they are able to be themselves more easily and to enter into all the school activities that await them. They are learning to express themselves and to control themselves in a society in which they take the middle place. So often, in the middle school, in any age-range, we find a boisterous set, which at the same time gives spirit to the community.

When discussing the capabilities of this age group in the art of handwriting, it is important to bear in mind their stage of development. Their energies are most easily directed towards creative activities in which the imagination can find expression. So we will expect to find them writing their own stories—even if we cannot interpret their symbols—creating their own patterns to cover their books and making copious pictures to communicate their ideas. They have neither the patience nor the manipulative control to perfect the letter shapes at this stage; but they have discovered a medium of handwriting—difficult as it is with its spelling and spacing—through which they can create and express.

269

The third group are the 7 year olds, who reign at the top of the school. They are terribly anxious to do it the 'grown-up' way, as they find themselves in the position of seniority. They are ready to apply themselves far more carefully to learn the exact shapes of the letters and they will settle to copy-book practice with a patience that delights in progressive repetition towards the perfect model. They will take trouble over presentation and they will be prepared to re-do a piece of work until it is worthy of the 'grown-up' look. This is the age to introduce penmanship and to establish a real appreciation for fine writing.

May I describe to you a lesson with the 6 year olds and one with the 7 year olds, so that you can see the difference between these two age-groups.

We are all set in the Transition classroom to do a piece of original writing on un-lined paper, mainly to give the teacher and me a chance to observe. First, we check positions, placing of paper, placing of hands, arms and pencil. Then we think about the arrangement of the writing on the page. We feel the space all round the edge of the paper which will become the margins. We put the pencil where we mean to start and see if it looks comfortable for margin space. We might even do one or two lines of pretend (magic) writing, to see where we go for the next line and to get the feel of writing. Then we are off, with a total concentration on the composition. We wriggle and shuffle and twist and turn, but even our next-door neighbour is no disturbance because we are caught up in the activity of creative writing. Listen to one child's description that morning:

Fary Tiptoes was a very prity fary
Once she sat on a butercup
and her dres was made of pettels
as the flower had dew
her dres glisend with dew.

And there was more besides. They were hard at it for half an hour with extra drawings at the end. They did not ask about spelling so that they could keep the continuity between mind and hand. Results were varied. Some had written themselves into a splendid rhythm of firm downstrokes interspersed with curves. Several had pushed p's and g's into the air and made their descenders come on level with the bottom of an a. Others had confused the d with the b in their excitement, and so on. The arrangement, on the whole, was good, though size of writing varied a great deal. As I watched them at work, I realized how hard it was for them to control that pencil and to make it say just what they had in mind. In some efforts the spelling was so weird that it was impossible to interpret their great ideas, although the spacing of their writing was orderly. Then we switched over to drawings, and all was well.

270

Consentire suis studijs qui crediderit Te
F autor. utroq; tuum laudabit pollice ludum.
P rotinus ut moneam. si quid monitoris eges tu.
Q uid de quoq; uiro : & cui dicas sæpe uideto.
P ercontatorem fugito : nam garrulus idem est.
N ec retinent patulæ commissa fideliter aures.
E t semel emissum uolat irreuocabile uerbum.
N on ancilla tuum iecur ulceret ulla : puer ue
I ntra marmoreum uenerandi limen amici.
N e pueri dominus pulchri, care ue puellæ,
M unere Te paruo beet : aut incommodus angat.
Q ualem commendes etiam atq; etiam aspice : ne mox
I ncutiant aliena tibi peccata pudorem.
F allimur : & quondam non dignum tradimus. ergo
Q uem sua culpa premit deceptus omitte tueri :
V t penitus notum si tentent crimina serues :
T uterisq; tuo fidentem præsidio : qui
D ente Theonino cum circum roditur. ecquid
A d te post paulo uentura pericula sentis.
N am tua res agitur paries cum proximus ardet.
E t neglecta solent incendia sumere uires.
D ulcis in expertis cultura potentis amici.
E xpertus metuit. tu dum tua nauis in alto est :
H oc age : ne mutata retrorsum te ferat aura.
O derunt hilarem tristes : tristemq; iocosi.
S edatum celeres : agilem nauumq; remissi.
P otores bibuli media de noc te falerni
O derunt porrecta negantem pocula : quis

45. From Horace, *Epistles*, written by Bartolomeo San Vito: see p. 264.
Spencer Collection, New York Public Library (reproduced with acknowledgements to the Curator)

[To face p. 270]

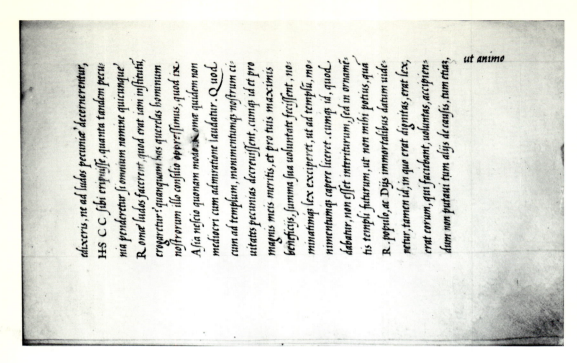

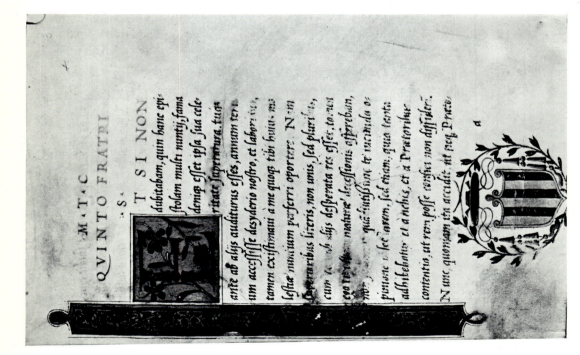

46a and b. From Cicero, *Epist. ad Quintum Fratrem*, written by Arrighi: see p. 271. (Both reduced)
British Museum, London (Add. MS. No. 11930)

The 7 year olds were ready to be taught and they watched the writing on the board with a critical eye. Together we discovered the letter *a*. We compared its directional shape with a journey that took us straight to the window, on our left, then down a ladder to the ground floor level, and finally in through the front door and up the staircase back to 1 G classroom again. In this way we really analysed the shape and movement of the letter. Then a great deal of practising went on until we distinguished the good from the bad ones. We ticked the best and studied those on the board, and then each one came up to make a white chalk *a*. A great deal of comment on the shape of the *a* was aroused. We all became *a*-conscious as we looked at writing examples on the walls. And this comes from a class only just turned 7 years, who are looking forward eagerly to beginning with the pen.

Finally, something must be said about the place of writing in the curriculum at this age. The teacher is concerned with the growth and development of the 'Whole Man'. Writing must be a part of the living experience of the child. There can be few rules about direct teaching at this stage because so much depends upon the teacher's own feeling for the subject. If he or she enjoys shapes and patterns and the layout of writing, then the children will be influenced by the well-written notices that they see at school and this will be the best training in good design. The children will unconsciously absorb good spacing of letters and lines and good arrangements.

We live in a country with a great literary background and there is no doubt that we take to words with more joyful understanding than we take to shapes or sounds. We love the composition of words, but do we bother very much about the 'good looks' of words? The teacher who cares about 'good looks' in all her display work will be the one who greatly influences the children's standards.   1962–3

ALFRED FAIRBANK
The Arrighi Style of Book-hand

Illustrations of pages of two manuscript books I had noticed in the British Museum were shown in the *Journal* for autumn, 1962; now it is my privilege to give some particulars of another fascinating manuscript I have come upon—a letter from Cicero to his brother Quintus, which may have been transcribed by Ludovico degli Arrighi (Vicentino). This manuscript, shown in Plates 46*a* and 46*b*, is Add. MS. No. 11930, a small octavo book of 18 leaves, with pages 6¾″ × 4¼″. There are various features of the script to be seen in the Arrighi *Collenuccio* (Royal MS. 12. C. viii, British Museum: *cf. Renaissance Handwriting*, plates 60 and 61, and the Society's

Bulletin No. 15). Also, the initial letter shown in Plate 46*a* is in the style of initials in the Arrighi *Missale Romanum* at Berlin, written in 1519.

According to notes in pencil made by Sir Frederic Madden (1801–73), the arms are of Cardinal Antonio Trivulzi, a member of a famous Milanese family, who was created by Pope Alexander VI in 1500 and who died in 1508; but Madden also stated that a second cardinal of that name, nephew of the first, was created in 1557 by Paul IV and died in 1559. On the assumption that the book was made for the earlier Cardinal Trivulzi, it seemed to me that the book, though small, became important as a singularly early work of Arrighi's. However, the note below by the Editor [not printed], throws more light on the significance of the heraldry and probably disposes of any claim that the book was made before 1509.

Any member who has seen the *Book of Hours* at the Bodleian, illustrated in plate 13 of the Bodleian picture book *Humanistic Script of the Fifteenth and Sixteenth Centuries* (Douce 29), will have been impressed by the closeness of the styles of both writing and illuminating to those of the Arrighi MS. books. I have assumed that that book was written by F. Ruano, a Spanish scribe appointed to the Vatican Library in 1541 as 'scriptor latinus'. Moreover, an earlier Spanish scribe working in Rome, Genesius de la Barrera, made in 1519 a manuscript book in a script closely resembling that of Arrighi (Paris, Bibl. Nat. lat. 244). In these confusing circumstances, a definite attribution of the Cicero to Arrighi cannot be made at this juncture, but I think it can be accepted as the work of the master.

Another manuscript book, namely Cod. Landau Finaly 9.c 1, Biblioteca Nazionale Centrale, Florence, has been claimed for Arrighi by Dr Emanuele Casamassima in *La Bibliofilia* (LXIV, 1962, Dispensa 2ª, pp. 117 *et seq.*). 1963

R. W. HUNT
Humanistic Script in Florence in the Early Fifteenth Century

The early history of humanistic script in Florence is now much better known thanks to the work of Professor B. L. Ullman, *The origin and development of humanistic script* (Rome, 1960), and it is possible to distinguish the styles of various scribes. Ullman has shown that the inventor of the new script was Poggio Bracciolini. The earliest manuscript written in it, so far known, is a copy made by Poggio of the *De verecundia* by his patron, Coluccio Salutati. It is not signed or dated, but there is evidence to show that it was copied shortly before Poggio left Florence for Rome in 1403. His first signed and dated manuscript is the copy of Cicero's *Letters to Atticus* written in

1408 (Plate 47 *a*). In the winter of 1408–9 when he was in Florence he copied in twelve days Eusebius-Jerome, *Chronicle* (Florence, Laur. 67, 15). From 1414 to 1422 he was out of Italy. Thus in the vital early period Poggio was away from Florence, except for fleeting visits, but he was in close touch with Niccolò Niccoli, who was, in Ullman's view, the sponsor of the new script. Poggio's absence does not, of course, rule out the possibility of his influence. Ullman has found two unsigned manuscripts at Florence in Poggian style, which are dated 1405 and 1406, and a signed manuscript by Guglielmo Tanaglia, one of the executors of Niccoli's will, which is dated Florence 1410 (St Gall, Stadtbibliothek 298).[1] It contains Eusebius-Jerome, *Chronicle*, and is, I believe, a direct copy of the manuscript written by Poggio the year before.[2]

Poggio can hardly be called a professional scribe, nor can the writers of the manuscripts we have just enumerated. The first professional writer of the new script in Florence who signed and dated some of his manuscripts is Giovanni Aretino. He is followed by Giacomo Curlo and Antonio di Mario. Nothing is known of Giovanni Aretino apart from the books he copied. Ullman has identified thirteen, seven of which are dated between 1410 and 1417. I can add a fourteenth in the Bodleian Library (MS. D'Orville 78). It is not signed or dated, but both Professor Ullman and Mr Fairbank have examined it and agree to the attribution. It has an erased note of ownership of Cosimo de' Medici,[3] and so presumably was written for him, as were several other books copied by Giovanni. It contains the eight speeches of Cicero discovered by Poggio on his explorations in 1417, and so must have been written after this date. Ullman speaks of the 'uniform excellence' of his script, and says that, compared with Poggio's, it is 'thinner and slopes slightly'. The accompanying plate (Plate 47 *b*) will best show the difference in style. Giacomo Curlo is first found as a scribe copying two manuscripts for Cosimo de' Medici in 1423 (at Florence) and in 1425 (at Rome).[4] They contain the *Brutus* and other rhetorical works of Cicero which had been discovered in 1421. If Giovanni Aretino had been available, we should have expected him to receive the important commission of copying this new classical text. After Giacomo Curlo left Florence he engaged in a political and diplomatic career, but he was later retained as a copyist by Alphonso V of Aragon, King of Naples (1446–58). It is from this later period that Plate 48 *a* is taken, but his script seems to have remained unchanged throughout his life. Ullman says of him that his script shows clearly that he was 'a disciple of Giovanni Aretino'.

The third scribe, Antonio di Mario, was far more prolific than the other two. Ullman has listed forty-one manuscripts written by him stretching from 1417 to 1456. He also wrote books for Cosimo de' Medici. The earliest is dated 1426.

Ullman says of Antonio that his 'earlier work resembles Poggio's script more than his later products, though even this lacks the graceful firmness of the master.... Fairly long serifs at the end of the descenders distinguish his script from Poggio's.' It appears that, to begin with, Antonio followed the model of Poggio but that later he came to be more and more influenced by Giovanni Aretino. The accompanying plate (Plate 48 *b*) is taken from a manuscript belonging to the Englishman, Andrew Holes, who is known to have bought books in Florence about 1440.[5] The resemblance between Antonio and Giovanni is found not only in general aspect, but in certain tricks. Giovanni occasionally divides the '*ct*' ligature between the end of one line and the beginning of the next. This 'freakish absurdity' (Ullman, p. 107) was followed both by Antonio and by Giacomo Curlo.[6] Again in one of his manuscripts Giovanni inserts addresses to a patron, such as 'Lege feliciter mi Nicolae dulcissime'. Similar addresses are inserted by Antonio; for example in a book written for an English patron, William Gray, afterwards Bishop of Ely, 'Lege feliciter, mi suavissime Ghuiglielme'.

It is not my intention to elevate Giovanni Aretino at the expense of Poggio. Poggio was incomparably more important. But the style of humanistic script in Florence was, it seems to me, set by Giovanni Aretino, who was chosen as copyist by Cosimo de' Medici not later than 1411/12. It was only natural that his successors in Florence, also working for the Medici, should follow the model he created. Its influence persisted into the next generation in the work of Piero Strozzi and Antonio Sinibaldi.

1963

NOTES

1 Microfilms are in London University Library and in the Bodleian Library. Another manuscript written by him is Modena, Bibl. Estense VI. F. 21, *Quintilian*. It is dated 1420.

2 It would be worth while following up the progeny of this family of Eusebius-Jerome. Two copies, which appear to follow it page by page are those written by Antonio di Mario in 1426 (Edinburgh, National Library of Scotland, MS. Adv. I. I. 5), and by an unknown scribe in Florence in the same year (Cambridge, Fitzwilliam Museum MS. 285).

3 'Liber Cosme Iohannis de Medicis.' Thanks to the skill of the photographer, the inscription is more legible here than in the original. Miss A. C. de la Mare, to whose help I am much indebted, tells me that there are other instances of Cosimo's note of ownership in the middle of a book; see, for example, Ullman, *The Humanism of Coluccio Salutati* (Padua, 1963), p. 162, n. 40. The manuscript was cited as 'o' by A. C. Clark in his edition of Cicero's Speeches (Oxford Classical Texts, vol. IV, and *Anecdota Oxoniensia*, classical ser. part XI, 1909, p. 10), but the recent discovery of Poggio's own copy (MS. Vat. lat. 11458) has taken away its textual importance.

4 P. O. Kristeller in *Manuscripta*, V (1961), 38 adds to Ullman's list Toledo, Bibl. provincial 222, *Lactantius*, which is dated 1428.

5 Not in Ullman's list, but referred to on p. 105, n. 14. Only fols. 1–91 are in his hand. It was identified by Miss A. C. de la Mare. The monogram 'A.M.' is on fol. 66a.

6 Ullman, plate 51. Examples in MS. New Coll. 249 are on fols. 17ᵛ, 28. Mr N. R. Ker has pointed out to me that, though this may be a 'freakish absurdity', it was a practice regularly employed by the scribes of the eleventh and twelfth centuries; see his *English Manuscripts in the Century after the Norman Conquest* (Oxford, 1960), plate 2, line 13. It was no doubt in such earlier 'models' that Giovanni found it.

47a. From Cicero, *Epist. ad Atticum*, written by Poggio (1408): see p. 273.
Deutsche Staatsbibliotek, East Berlin (Hamilton 108)

47b. From Cicero, *Orationes*, written by Giovanni Aretino: see p. 273.
Bodleian Library, Oxford (MS. D'Orville 78, fol. 26)

[To face p. 274]

INCIPIT . LIBER . QVINTVS . CONTINENS .
PRAECEPTA . NAVALIS . BELLI . LEGE . FE .
RAECEPTO . MAIESTATIS .

tuae umperator inuicte . ter
restris proelii rationibus abso
lutis . naualis belli residua ut
opinor superest portio . de cuius artibus ideo
pauciora dicenda sunt . quia iam dudum pa
cato mari cum barbaris nationibus agitur
terrestre certamen . Romanus autem popul°

48a. From Vegetius, *Epitome Rei Militaris*, written by Giacomo Curlo : see p. 273.
Bodleian Library, Oxford (MS. Canon. Class. Lat. 274, fol. 105ᵛ)

VOVSQ: TANDEM ABVTERE CATILINA
patientia nostra ? q diu nos etiam furor iste tuus eludet ?
Quem ad finem sese effrenata iactabit audacia ? Nihil
ne te nocturnu presidium palatii : nihil ne urbis uigilie .
nihil timor . pp . nihil concursus bonorum omnium . nihil hic muniti
ssimus habendi senatus locus : nihil horum ora uultusq: mouerūt ? Pa
tere tua consilia non sentis ? constrictam iam horu omnium conscientia
teneri coniurationem tuam non uides ? quid proxima . qd superiore
nocte egeris . ubi fueris . quos uocaueris . quid consilii ceperis . que nostru
ignorare arbitraris ? O tempora ó mores : Senatus hoc intelligit : consul

48b. From Cicero, *Orationes*, written by Antonio di Mario : see p. 274.
New College, Oxford (MS. 249, fol. 20ᵛ)

[To face p. 275]

ALFRED FAIRBANK
What makes a Good Style?

At the outset one must say that handwriting is a system of movements involving touch. The movements make the shapes of letters. Accordingly a good handwriting style must provide for small movements which can be made quickly and produce clear shapes. Conversely, the shapes of letters in exemplars must teach the movements, although themselves static. The deliberate and precise movements of the writing-master's pen must lead on to the rapid movements of free writing.

Handwriting of quality implies penmanship. The pen's point is moved about on paper to lay a trail of ink, and the trail is the writing.

We expect writing to be fluent and rapid. The pen must therefore be efficient, its point moving with little friction over the surface of the paper. Ink must come down the pen's slit with regular flow. Happily, the pen-manufacturers' attempts to make a fine writing instrument at a low cost are meeting with increased success.

The pen makes strokes which are likely to vary in thickness. The variations may be caused by pressure of the pen's point on the paper, or by the pen's edged point. The sharply pointed pen, used with regulated pressures, was the pen of the copper-plate writers. The pen with an edged point, the pen of the Middle Ages and the Renaissance, does not require the skill of regulated pressures; for the pen makes its own thicknesses and gradations and is therefore economical and unifying. The incidence of thickness of stroke is consistent, and this also makes for regularity. Another virtue is that this kind of pen can be held with light grasp and with the pen-shaft pointing rather to the elbow than the shoulder: a better position.

Most of the scripts of the western world may be divided into two categories: those with a circular 'o' or an elliptical 'o'. This division was as marked in the eighth century in England as it is today. The historic circular 'o' is in formal scripts and it is made with two separate strokes. The 'o' of cursive scripts, written with more freedom, is oval and has no pen-lift.

Obviously, economical actions are necessary when writing rapidly. Time does not allow for every letter to be separated. A method of joining letters easily must be included in the handwriting system. Joins are principally those that rise sideways and up (diagonal joins). Others are horizontal.

Another matter of importance is how to reconcile contrary movements so that, for example, *n* does not become *u* and *u* does not become *n*.

Legibility depends largely upon what one is used to reading. What we mostly read is printed in roman and italic types. Roman types are very clear, but a roman hand, because of the pen-lifts, cannot be written quickly enough. Print-script is founded on roman letters and it does not naturally develop into a running hand. Therefore we cannot look to the roman script for a model of cursive handwriting.

To write quickly and clearly calls for a reconciliation of discipline and freedom.

Spacing and placing are features of the art of lettering, which includes handwriting. The adjustments of letter to letter, word to word, and line to line, and the whole column to the sheet of paper by suitable margins, make for good appearance.

A handwriting system will be principally for right-handers but it must serve left-handers too.

The persons who write well do so because they want to write well. An aim in teaching handwriting to children must be to make the activity interesting and attractive. The script should therefore be pleasant to write and read, and the teacher sympathetic and understanding.

If the above specification is accepted, what script embodies the requirements? We have no doubt that Italic is the answer. Italic need not be too narrow, nor angular; it pleases; children like to write it and have done so with distinction; most letters join up conveniently; and it makes fine penmanship. In teaching children handwriting there is, however, a real difficulty, whatever the system: the teacher too often has not been taught the principles of handwriting. How can this obstacle be overcome? When writing manuals and copy-books fail, recourse must be had to films and loop-films, which do not yet exist but are needed to show the movements that make the shapes.

1965

ENVOI

The Image Maker

Hard is the stone, but harder still
The delicate performing will
That guided by a dream alone,
Subdues and moulds the hardest stone,
Making the stubborn jade release
The emblem of eternal peace.

If but the will be firmly bent,
No stuff resists the mind's intent:
The adamant abets his skill
And sternly aids the artist's will,
To clothe in perdurable pride
Beauty his transient eyes descried.

OLIVER ST JOHN GOGARTY

Winter Grasses
Woodcut by MARGARET DARRELL

INDEX

Index

Index

Index

Index

MEDICI, Piero de', 51, 55, 57, 62, 65
MEERMAN, Gerard, 76
MEON, Dominique Martin, 71
MERCATOR, Gerard, **137–48**
MERLIN, Alfred, 35
MEYNELL, Sir Francis, 11, 176, 253
MILLAR, Dr Eric, 248
MISSAL OF ST ELOI, 45
Modo (i.e. *Il modo de temperare le Penne*), by Arrighi, 101, 104, 105, 112, 115, 116, 118, 123, 126, 128, 207
MONTE DI GIOVANNI, 65–8 *passim*
MONTFAUCON, Bernard de, 151
MORISON, Stanley, 17, 19, 106 n., 172, 225, 232
MORRIS, May (daughter of William), 8, 210
MORRIS, William, 4, 5, 7, 8, 17, 24, 96, 207, 209, 210, 217, 252
MUNBY, Dr A. L. N., 79 n., 89, 91 n.
MUSURUS, Marcus, 108

NATIONAL REGISTER OF ARCHIVES, 89
Natural Way to Draw, 201
NEWDIGATE, B. H., 233
New Handwriting for Teachers, 17, 153, 252
NICCOLÒ, Niccoli, 47, 49, 56, 251, 273
NICHOLAS V, Pope, 57
NICOLAIDES, Kimon, 201
NOYES, Enoch, 157

OAKESHOTT, Dr, 248
OGREMONT, Guillaume d', 70
Operina, La, handwriting manual of Arrighi, **95–106**, 111, 118, 124, 126, 207, 209, 251
Origin and development of humanistic script, 53 n., 60 n., 61 n., 272–4
OSIMO (ancient Auximum), 35, Pl. 7*b*
Oxford Copybooks, 252

PALATINO, Giovanbattista, 24, 252, 259
PALLADIUS, Blossius, 117, 128
PALMER METHOD of business writing, 233
PANIGALLIUS, 69
PANORMITA, Antonio, 49, 50, 53 n., 77
PARSLOE, Guy, 82–6 *passim*
PATTERNS IN WRITING, 200–1, 267–8
PAUL IV, Pope, 272
PEACH, H. H., 10, 20
PEDERSEN, Christiern, 238
PENGUIN BOOKS, 25, Pl. 4
PENRERLEITH, Dr, 248

PENS, 9, 10, 138, 139, 141, 165, 174, 246, 252, **265–7**, 275
PEPYS, Samuel, 169
PESENTI, G., 51
PHILARGURUS, slave of Aconius, 39
PHILIP, Ejnar, 237, 240
PHILLIPPS, Sir Thomas, 76, 85, 88, 89, 91 n.
PILSBURY, Joan, 31
PITMAN, Sir James, 9
POGGIO, Bracciolini, **47, 48,** 49, 251, **272–4**, Pl. 47*a*
POLITIAN, 78
POLLARD, Dr A. F., 86
POLYSTYRENE LETTERS, 194, Pl. 39*a*
POMPEIUS, Gnaeus, 37, 38, 39
PORSON, Prof. Richard, 151, 153
POWELL, Alfred, 6, 8
POWELL, Louise, *née* Lessore, 7, 8, 20, 28
POWER, A. D., 8
Practical Penmanship (by Foster), 156, 157, 158, 161, 162
Primary Education (H.M.S.O. 1959), 214
PRIMMER, William C. K., 4, 5
PRINCE, Edward, 209, 210, 211
PRINTSCRIPT, *see* SCRIPTS
PUBLIC RECORD OFFICE, London, 12, 87, Pls. 43*a* and 43*b*
PULLER, Louisa, 6, 246

Q, 'as lively as a tadpole', 223

RATCLIFFE, Rosemary, 31
REDMAN, H. R., 3
Regularis Concordia, 45
Renaissance Handwriting, 13, 23, 119 n., 133 n., 207, 262
RICCI, Seymour Montefiore Roberto Rosso de, *see* DE RICCI
RICKMAN, Elizabeth, *see* HODGKIN, Elizabeth
RIDOLFI, Lorenzo, 122, 131–3
RIDOLFI, Niccolò, Cardinal, 131, 132
RIDOLFI, Prof. Roberto, 130, 131
ROHDE, Bent, 120 n.
Roman Script for Schools, 18, 23
ROOKE, Noel, 8
ROOSEVELT, Eleanor, 11, 20
ROOSEVELT, Franklin D., 11, 20
ROSS, D. J. A., 50, 53 n.
ROYAL AIR FORCE BOOKS OF REMEMBRANCE, 12, 26, **29–32**, Pl. 6

285